SPIES
IN THE SKY

Also by Taylor Downing

Churchill's War Lab
Cold War (with Jeremy Isaacs)
Battle Stations (with Andrew Johnston)
Olympia
Civil War (with Maggie Millman)
The Troubles (as Editor)

SPIES
IN THE SKY

THE SECRET BATTLE FOR
AERIAL INTELLIGENCE DURING
WORLD WAR II

Taylor Downing

Little, Brown

LITTLE, BROWN

First published in Great Britain in 2011 by Little, Brown

A CIP catalogue record for this book
is available from the British Library.

ISBN HB 978 1 4087 0280 2
ISBN CF 978 1 4087 0362 5

Typeset in Palatino by M Rules
Printed and bound in Great Britain by
Clays Ltd, St Ives plc

Papers used by Little, Brown are from well-managed forests
and other responsible sources.

MIX
Paper from
responsible sources
FSC
www.fsc.org   FSC® C104740

Little, Brown
An imprint of
Little, Brown Book Group
100 Victoria Embankment
London EC4Y 0DY

An Hachette UK Company
www.hachette.co.uk

www.littlebrown.co.uk

To the Keepers of the Flame

Contents

Prologue   1

Introduction   9

1 Secret Missions   25

2 Sid Cotton's Air Force   39

3 Crisis   59

4 Medmenham   82

5 The Mad Men of Ham   98

6 Boffins at War   112

7 A Rare Form of Bravery   131

8 The 'Warby' Legend   159

9 Finding the Targets   174

10 Assessing the Damage   194

11 To the Mediterranean and India   208

12 Arguments with Allies   224

13 Planning for Overlord   236

14 Special Operations   256

15	Hunting the Vengeance Weapons	276
16	Towards Victory	311
17	'80 per cent of All Intelligence'?	326
	Epilogue	343
	Author's Note	353
	Acknowledgements	356
	Glossary	359
	Notes	363
	Bibliography	384
	Index	391
	About the Author	407

Prologue

The pilot banked steeply, first to the right and then to the left. Only at this angle could he clearly see the ground he was flying directly over, twenty-nine thousand feet below. The sky above was a deep, dark, azure blue. The sun was a fiery ball, still low on the distant horizon as the morning was not far advanced. At this height, out of range of the anti-aircraft batteries scattered over the countryside below, the landscape looked almost like a map. But it was difficult to detect detail. Flying without any guns and with the armour plating in his Spitfire removed to give extra speed, the pilot had to rely on his high altitude and on being fast and stealthy, invisible to everything on the ground and to anything that might be up in the stratosphere looking for him. He had to be careful not to create a vapour trail, a 'contrail', a line of cloud in the sky formed when the water vapour from an aircraft's exhaust condenses and freezes. If a line of white cirrus-type cloud formed behind him it would act like a giant pointer in the sky to the tiny speck of his aircraft. He would be visible for miles around. So he had to check the weather conditions, the clouds, the temperature, the wind direction, and make sure he was flying just below the height at which vapour trails were formed. This would have the added advantage that if an enemy fighter was preparing to attack and had climbed higher to dive down on him, the interceptor would immediately send out its own vapour trail signifying its approach. There would be a few seconds of critical warning time. Once an interceptor had been spotted, the pilot would 'open all the taps' – that is push on full throttle – and dive slightly to get away from the enemy fighter. This usually worked.

The unheated cockpit was cold, agonisingly cold. There was always the possibility that gauges or measures would freeze up. Frozen crystals could even form around the perspex canopy itself, a sign of the need to reduce height a little. In the unpressurised cabin, the pilot was breathing oxygen through a mask. If the oxygen failed at altitude a pilot would soon begin to feel even colder and start to ache. He would begin to feel a sense of detachment from what he was doing, then would become delirious. Finally, after only about sixty seconds, he would black out. This nearly always resulted in a fatal crash. The pilot had to keep alert and be able to recognise the first signs of an oxygen failure or blockage.

The reconnaissance pilot had just in front of him, in the pouch on his knee, a map. After several hours flying across enemy territory, he needed pinpoint navigation skills to know his precise location. He would calculate his course and his time of arrival over the target area to the second. But a higher wind speed than anticipated up in the altitudes where the trade winds blew, or too much evasive action earlier in the flight, could throw out all his calculations. So, to identify where he should be, he needed to look below.

When he was sure he was over his target – a factory, an airfield, a shipyard – the reconnaissance pilot had no bombs to drop, just cameras to engage. There were two or sometimes three cameras on the Spitfire either in the fuselage, just behind where the pilot sat, or in the wings. One looked vertically downwards, the others were at an oblique angle, allowing the pilot to photograph a broader area in a single pass. The cameras were controlled from a box in front of the pilot, where the gun-sight would otherwise have been. First the pilot would set the interval between exposures. This was calculated so that, by winding the film on automatically after every exposure, each camera could photograph a continuous strip of terrain. Every negative exposed was a huge 7in by 8½in. Flying at thirty thousand feet using a standard 36in lens, each photo covered an area of roughly one square mile. But the detail recorded was such that on a clear, bright day you could easily see vehicles in the photograph moving about on the ground.

If there was no cloud cover, when the reconnaissance pilot had taken his photographs he would then head for home. The same critical level of navigation was necessary to return to his home base. There was no excuse for heroics and under no circumstances was a recon pilot to be tempted into action with the enemy. He had no guns anyway, so he could not fire back. This went against the grain of the bravado necessary to make a good fighter pilot. Reconnaissance pilots had just to find the target, take their photographs, and get home with the photos intact. Sometimes, after miles of flying across the featureless sea, there might still be no sign of the British coast even after a pilot was due to cross it. So he had to check his bearing and speed constantly. A Spitfire uses about a gallon of fuel every minute. Some pilots would return with only a few gallons left in their tanks. That was cutting it very fine.

It takes a special form of bravery to fly for hours on end

across enemy territory or across the sea to photograph a target and then back again with no weapons of any sort. Pilots were accustomed to flying in formations of one sort or another, but recon pilots always flew by themselves. Some of the targets, like Peenemünde on the Baltic, or the Norwegian fjords, involved five- or six-hour flights, superb navigation, and were at the very limits of the aircraft's operational ability. But it was vital to get back – with the photos – rather than to show off or become distracted.[1]

On landing back at his base, the pilot usually felt a combination of exhaustion from so many hours of intense concentration and elation at having got back with his precious images. Mission accomplished. From the moment he landed, the second half of the process would begin. The groundcrew would be waiting. First they would take out the film from the cameras. A car, probably a standard-issue blue RAF Humber Snipe, would rush the camera magazines to the developing and processing unit on the airfield. Within sixty minutes a photo interpreter would be examining the photos. Was that ship still in harbour? Had that squadron of aircraft now deployed to the airfield? Was the factory damaged by yesterday's air raid? Had the enemy tank formation moved forward? Urgent questions with an immediate tactical purpose would be answered there and then and reported by phone or telex to the various intelligence commands that needed instant answers.

The photographs were then taken to the Central Interpretation Unit for further interpretation and analysis. This was located in a big country house overlooking the river Thames, about forty miles from London. The house itself was an unusual late-Victorian structure lined with chalk and topped with mock-Tudor chimneys. Wisteria grew across the outside of the west wing and in the spring perfumed the air with its sweet smell. The site was a top secret establishment, a vital part of the intelligence war, run by the RAF. Its name was RAF Medmenham.

The site teemed with people. Men in their smart blue RAF uniforms rushed hither and thither. A smattering of naval officers with braid on their arms could always be seen, as could army officers in khaki. Later in the war, there were also many Americans in their neat brown uniforms. And, unlike most other military bases, a casual observer here would have instantly noticed the presence of a large number of women, mostly officers from the Women's Auxiliary Air Force. These WAAF officers had an unusual confidence about them as they strode around the grounds, busy with a host of duties. Uniquely in the Second World War, many of these women were not only doing equal work to that of their male colleagues, but in many cases they were in command of sections, in charge of the male officers in their own teams.

Looking more closely, the casual observer would see that this place, RAF Medmenham, was far from a typical RAF base. And it was not just the presence of the many women that was so unusual. Many of the photo interpreters were older than RAF personnel on other bases. Wisps of grey hair sometimes flowed out from under RAF caps. Among these people were some of the best academic brains in Britain. There were archaeologists, geologists, physicists and mathematicians. Archaeologists and geologists were expert at deducing the whole story from a few fragments of information, like seeing the complete picture of a jigsaw with only a few pieces to hand. Mathematicians and physicists were used to reasoning how to perform complex calculations with only limited data. But also at Medmenham there were many from the world of arts and culture – sculptors and artists, musicians and dancers, writers, and briefly a young man who would go on to become a movie idol after the war was over. Even the Prime Minister's daughter was here. It was an elite of sorts. And, along with the Americans who from 1943 seemed to be as numerous as the British, from the beginning there had been Norwegian, Dutch and Polish officers. Their smart outfits added glamour to the multinational look and feel of the place.

The photo interpreters working at Medmenham from April 1941 to the end of the war invented nothing less than an entirely new science. In this war it was vital to understand what was going on across the whole of occupied Europe, a vast area from the north of Norway to the French-Spanish border, from the Atlantic coast in the west, all the way to the Baltic in the east and even across distant Poland. The photo interpreters were putting together an intelligence map of everything of strategic importance that was happening in Nazi-occupied Europe. They looked carefully at the type of ships being built in the shipyards, at the development of new aircraft and their deployment to airfields in northern France or Germany, at the movement of ships, trains, barges, and at the arrival of new masts, scanners or transmitters. Questions could be asked of every new building going up. Was this a new gun emplacement, a new war production factory, or a secret missile launch site? Aerial photographs of the same location a few weeks later might help to provide an answer. And then there was damage assessment photography after a bombing raid. Was the factory that had just been bombed now out of action? If it were being repaired, how long would that take? When would be the optimum moment, with repairs nearing completion, to bomb it again? The amount of information gathered at Medmenham would have astonished anyone outside the secret world of photo intelligence. Nothing much of any wartime significance moved in occupied Europe without being picked up by the photo interpreters. It was said that '80 per cent of all intelligence in World War Two came from aerial photography'.[2] Nothing escaped the spies in the sky.

Introduction

The story of Danesfield House, known as RAF Medmenham, has much in common with that of Bletchley Park, home of the code breakers who succeeded in listening in to the enemy's most intimate communications. Both intelligence operations were based at country houses just outside London, not far from main railway lines into the capital. At Bletchley Park, as at Medmenham, the fine grounds of a once grand stately pile slowly filled with Nissen huts and with concrete and brick outbuildings as more and more people were packed in to the limited space available. At both places an unlikely mix of eccentric scientists and wacky boffins[1] worked long, hard hours. In both Bletchley Park and Medmenham these 'back room boys' (and girls) created an entirely new science in order to solve the immense challenges they faced.

Both centres operated in total secrecy. Not only were outsiders entirely ignorant of what was going on, but at both establishments people in one section had no knowledge of what those in another section just down the corridor were up to. And overall, very few people in either place, except perhaps those in charge, had any broad understanding of how important their work was to the war effort. But the code breaking at Bletchley Park and the photo intelligence that came out of the careful and detailed analysis of aerial photographs certainly *were* important. They helped to save thousands of lives and without doubt shortened the war by months, possibly even by years. The work of the code breakers at Bletchley Park is now well known and has been the subject of movies, novels and television series, as well as countless histories, over the past few years.[2] But that of the photo interpreters at Medmenham is still relatively little known and the characters who walked the grounds of this splendid house overlooking the Thames have been mostly forgotten.[3]

In telling the secret history of the photo interpreters at Medmenham, it will be necessary to pursue certain themes and to follow these themes as they unfold across the years of the Second World War. Broadly speaking this book is chronological, starting with the early days of the war and ending with the final victory in Europe. But within that broad chronology, the book explores the many themes that make up the story of photo intelligence. Some chapters do not pick up at the point when the previous chapter ends but go back in time to tell their own particular story. Whether it is the explanation of how the photo interpreters worked, of finding the targets and assessing the damage of a bombing offensive, or the specific use of photo interpretation for Army operations, each chapter in this book has its own theme that forms an element of the broader story of fighting the Second World War. But photo interpretation is only the second half of the story of the intelligence that came from aerial photography. The first half is the story of the taking of the photographs themselves. There could be no photo intelligence without the brave pilots who daily risked their lives to fly over occupied Europe to record the images for the interpreters to analyse. Their work fits into the long history of reconnaissance in war. And to begin this story, it's necessary to go back a few centuries to trace some of the key developments.

In the beginning it was simply a question of climbing the nearest hill and looking down to spy on the enemy's backyard. From the earliest days of warfare, soldiers have tried to gain the upper hand by discovering the strength of their enemy and how he has deployed his troops, in order to anticipate what he might do next. This is the most basic requirement of reconnaissance. Accompanying the desire to see the 'other side of the hill' is the necessity to communicate this information speedily back to base, where good use can be made of it. From the earliest days, this has been the role of soldiers on horseback, light cavalry, the fastest thing on the battlefield. For several hundred years it seemed to suffice.

Reconnaissance began to change with the advent of balloons in France in the late eighteenth century. Men had always dreamed of flying and of looking down on the world below like a bird, and the balloonists began a period of crazed public interest in aerial flight known as 'ballomania'. Literally hundreds of thousands of Parisians turned out to see these early flights. Soon the military uses of balloons were recognised and in the Revolutionary Wars of the 1790s, the French made considerable progress in the use of gas balloons for reconnaissance. Two companies of so-called 'Aérostiers' were formed. Their balloons were tethered to the ground by two ropes. The balloonists sent their reports by despatching mails in a leather pouch down the ropes to the ground. In Britain, very few people had grasped the scientific or military value of ballooning and the whole business of ascending into the air in a wicker basket suspended below a large, bulbous and highly inflammable balloon was seen as something fit only for madmen or poets.[4]

With the advent of photography in the late 1830s the possibilities for recording aerial observations entered a new era. However, there were severe difficulties in using the first cameras in the air. They were large, cumbersome devices with glass plates that had to be coated with light-sensitive emulsions before exposure. So it was not until 1858 that the Parisian portrait photographer Gaspard Félix Tournachon, who operated under the pseudonym Nadar, took the first photograph from a balloon.

The British Army was pathetically slow to demonstrate any interest in the military applications of ballooning. But by the late nineteenth century enormous advances in artillery extended the range that guns could fire. The gunners needed a way of finding out if they were hitting their targets or just wasting their shells. Balloons provided an aerial observation post from which observers could sometimes see far enough behind enemy lines to report on the accuracy of artillery fire. So, finally, in the 1880s balloons were first used in the annual army manoeuvres at Aldershot and in the last years of the nineteenth century ballooning at last became an acceptable part of British Army life. Balloonists were taught the principles of aerial reconnaissance, including photography and signalling. The standard camera for use in a balloon had a lens with a focal length of 16in and made exposures on glass plate negatives measuring 8½in by 6½in, although the movement of the balloon in the wind was often found to blur the image. A *Manual of Military Ballooning* published in 1896 concluded that 'no modern army would be considered complete without balloon equipment'.[5]

The Boer War was the first major conflict in which aerial reconnaissance played a significant role in the British war effort. Aerial reconnaissance, if only in a primitive form, had established itself, but there were still formidable obstacles to overcome. Not the least of these seems to have been the prevailing view among many British officers that the use of balloons to look into the enemy's backyard was not fair, that it was not really 'playing the game'. This sort of strange prejudice would not survive long in the next major conflagration.[6]

Everything changed when, on 17 December 1903, at Kitty Hawk on the North Carolina coast, Orville and Wilbur Wright succeeded in getting airborne in a biplane with an 8 hp petrol engine. The era of powered flight had arrived. Britain was, once again, slow to get in on the act. The first flight in Britain was not until October 1908 and it was an American showman who led the way.[7] Samuel F. Cody had come to England to organise Wild West stunt shows, which proved very popular and made him rich. He became fascinated with man-lifting kites and spent many years trying to persuade the military authorities of their potential. The Navy was interested; the Army was initially sceptical. Nevertheless he set up shop at Aldershot and was constantly coming up with new ideas. The Army soon grew tired of its irrepressible showman-inventor. Cody won several prizes in early air shows and became something of a celebrity. He did much to make flying popular in Britain, with the public if not with the Army.

The event that really galvanised the public imagination took place in July 1909 when Louis Blériot set off in a small aeroplane from northern France near Calais and forty minutes later touched down by Dover Castle. The press were up in arms at this Frenchman's ability to breach Britain's historic insularity. And they were doubly outraged by official British lethargy with regard to flying, in contrast to the progress that was being made by 'wily continentals'.[8] H.G. Wells blamed the education system in Britain for the national failure in the development of flying machines, summing up the mood of the nation when he wrote prophetically that Britain 'is no longer, from a military point of view, an inaccessible island'.[9]

At this point the British Army possessed only a single aircraft, a Wright biplane. It was difficult to imagine what the future held for powered flight but there was a growing sense that the old-style reconnaissance balloon had had its day. The Germans were investing in larger and more rigid airships, known as Zeppelins. The French were moving ahead with the development of aeroplanes, with improvements in aerial photography and with the training of pilots and observers. Britain, again, was falling far behind.

In 1912 the Royal Flying Corps (RFC) was created with the intention of bringing all military flying under one command, with a Central Flying School at Upavon in Wiltshire to teach flying skills, including aerial photography. Winston Churchill, then aged thirty-seven, was First Lord of the Admiralty, the politician in charge of the Royal Navy. Churchill was an enthusiast for flight and was the first senior political figure to encourage military flying. He gave a great boost to the development of the Royal Naval Air Service with its own school of flying at Eastchurch in Kent. Churchill even started to take flying lessons himself, until he was finally persuaded to give up, after surviving a near fatal accident, by his friends and by his wife, who was pregnant with their third child.[10]

It was becoming clear to some people that the principal task of military flying must be for reconnaissance and the first aircraft exclusively intended for this purpose, the Reconnaissance Experimental 1 (RE-1), was built in 1913. It was equally logical that the first clash of armies would no longer be between cavalry or advanced patrols on land but between aviation scouts flying out ahead of the ground forces looking for the approaching enemy. With considerable vision and foresight, General Sir James Grierson said after manoeuvres in 1912, 'Personally, I think there is no doubt that, before land fighting takes place, we shall have to fight and destroy the enemy's aircraft ... warfare will be impossible until we have mastery of the air.'[11] In the Army war games held that summer, Grierson decisively beat his opponent largely thanks to his use of aerial reconnaissance. His opponent was General Sir Douglas Haig.

With the outbreak of war in August 1914, Britain sent a small expeditionary force to continental Europe that deployed to the left of the French Army. Accompanying the British Expeditionary Force were four squadrons of the RFC with sixty-three aircraft. From the start of the war the reconnaissance role of the RFC was paramount. The aircraft in use were still remarkably primitive, consisting of pieces of canvas held together with wire and powered by tiny engines. Aircraft could be thrown around by a gust of wind or tossed about by thermals. Flying against a strong wind, they sometimes slowed almost to an embarrassing halt. They were fragile and far from stable platforms for the use of binoculars or telescopes. Navigation was immensely difficult and sometimes the pilots had to land and ask where they were. It was very basic, seat-of-the-pants-type stuff. But the brave young pilots and their observers were slowly learning lessons and would lay the foundation for extraordinary advances in aerial reconnaissance over the next few years.

In the stalemate of trench warfare that dominated the Western Front for most of the war, the military used aerial photographs to construct maps of the enemy lines, to identify where their artillery was positioned and to watch for reinforcements of men and materiel being brought up to the front. The first cameras, known as the 'A-type', were fragile handheld devices that the pilot or observer had to point over the side of the plane. The A-types used 5in by 4in glass plate negatives and the operator had to separately load and unload each plate. It was a cumbersome process that required real skill and much patience, but the quality of the photographs was excellent. It became standard practice throughout the war for trench maps showing the German dispositions, based on aerial photos, to be distributed to the infantry before every assault.

Some aerial photographs were taken vertically downwards, but pilots soon learned the value of taking photos at an oblique angle which allowed the 'eyes in the air', as the reconnaissance aircraft were called, to see further behind German lines.[12] New techniques emerged to improve the role of aerial observers in spotting for the artillery. Lightweight telegraphic radios were fitted to aircraft and they enabled far more efficient Morse code communication with ground controllers. New cameras fixed to the aircraft fuselage, the 'C-type', replaced the awkward hand-held cameras. The pilot activated these as he flew across enemy lines, further improving the quality of aerial photography.

The Germans of course were also rapidly developing their own aerial observation techniques, and as the RFC and the French aviators tried to prevent German observation flights from crossing Allied trenches, so an air war developed with each side trying to protect its own airspace. The first aerial combats consisted of pilots leaning out the side of their cockpits and firing at enemy planes with revolvers or rifles. From the spring of 1915 the observer in the standard British observation aircraft, the BE2c biplane, was issued with a portable Lewis machine gun. But in firing it he had to avoid hitting his own propeller, wings or rigging, which was no easy task when trying to shoot at a fast-moving enemy target. The real breakthrough came in late 1915 when the German Fokker E2 monoplane appeared, with a forward-firing machine gun that was synchronised to fire through the plane's propellers without hitting them. It was an ingenious invention that enabled the German Fokkers, cruising at high altitude, to dive steeply down on the Allied aircraft, aiming and firing from the front of the plane. This technical breakthrough galvanised the start of aerial combat. Before long, faster Allied fighter aircraft were designed in order to keep the German fighters away from the slower observation aircraft. Then, more advanced German fighter aircraft were built to keep the Allied fighters away from *their* positions. In the see-saw air war of 1914–18 aerial supremacy shifted from one side to the other as new aircraft were produced and, in turn, better aircraft and weapons were designed to defeat them. 'Dogfights' between groups of Allied and German fighters became a common sight in the skies above the trenches. A new branch of warfare was born.

In August 1915 Lieutenant-Colonel Hugh Trenchard was appointed commander of the RFC. Trenchard's Army service had mostly been in India and Africa although he had learned to fly before the war at Brooklands, at his own expense. He was a tall, broad-shouldered man with a thick moustache, a loud foghorn of a voice (his nickname was 'Boom') and a naturally commanding nature. Trenchard began to plan for the massive expansion in the size of the corps from four squadrons to several dozen. He pushed for the development of faster aircraft with more powerful engines, equipped with better weapons, along with the widespread use of radios. And, envisaging an additional use for aircraft in war, he wanted to develop larger aircraft with an improved capability to carry bombs to drop on the enemy. Trenchard recognised that at the heart of this new arm of warfare was the need for aerial reconnaissance and he put thirty-year-old Second Lieutenant John Moore-Brabazon in charge of air photography. Moore-Brabazon was a motor racing driver, a balloonist and, in May 1909, the first Englishman to fly in a heavier-than-air powered machine in England. A dashing, glamorous young man who always tried to find new solutions to problems, he took over the first of the RFC's experimental photographic units.

Working along with Moore-Brabazon was Sergeant-Major Victor Laws, the only photographic specialist the RFC was able to call on at that point. Laws, who had worked on aerial photography before the war, noticed that movement by men or vehicles crushed the grass or soft ground in a way that was still visible for a couple of days, appearing on a black and white aerial photograph as a patch of shading. This was the beginning of photo interpretation and the science of reading movements across land by the study of aerial photographs. The need to train dozens and then hundreds of aerial observers was a top priority. Laws became head of a new RFC School of Photography at Farnborough, where officers and NCOs were trained in all aspects of developing and printing glass plates, making enlargements, maintaining aerial cameras, and preparing maps from photographs. A new class of photo interpreters were taught innovative techniques of using shadows to measure the scale of objects on the ground. They learned to find and identify machine gun positions, artillery posts or the location of unit headquarters and to analyse the movement of enemy troops. They were soon able to assess enemy strongpoints and recognise trench dugouts and passages through the wire.[13] Before long every front-line squadron had its own small photographic unit to process and interpret aerial photos. The photographers were known as 'stickybacks', as the photos were often still wet and sticky when handed out. And Army trucks were fitted out as mobile darkrooms, with additional facilities to carry out photo interpretation.

As fighter planes proved their superiority over observation aircraft, so the reconnaissance aircraft had to fly higher to avoid interception. And the higher the observers flew, the greater the need for better cameras with longer lenses. Furthermore, the lower temperatures prevailing at higher altitudes caused moisture to condense in the cameras, fogging lenses and cracking glass plates.[14] So Moore-Brabazon and his team continued to advance the development of aerial cameras. A new wide angle camera was produced, its 10in lens capable of photographing an area three miles by two from twenty thousand feet with good, clear results. In early 1916 the E-type camera was introduced. Made of metal instead of wood, it also had an improved remote control facility for the pilot. Later came the L-type, with a long 20in lens and improved mechanisms for feeding the plates through the camera gate.

On 1 April 1918 the RFC merged with the Royal Naval Air Service and a new military service was born, the Royal Air Force. Its commander was Hugh Trenchard, now promoted to major-general. But the RAF was created at a time of crisis on the Western Front. The Germans had transferred huge numbers of troops from the Eastern Front after Russia dropped out of the war following its Revolution in 1917. On 21 March 1918, the Germans launched a mighty offensive that threw the French and British armies reeling back. It began during a long period of foggy weather when aerial reconnaissance was impossible and so the location of the attack, along the Somme, came as a surprise to the Allies. Within a few weeks the British Army had lost more than a hundred thousand men and by the second week of April the British commander-in-chief, Sir Douglas Haig, viewed the situation as highly perilous. Then, on 12 April, the weather cleared and the RAF reconnaissance aircraft brought back detailed, accurate information about the German positions for the first time. More photographs were taken that day than on any other since the beginning of the war. From the intelligence picked up via these photos, the Allies could again shell German positions with accuracy. Haig noted in his diary the 'satisfactory results of today's work in the air'.[15] When the Allies launched their counter-offensive in July, aerial photographs provided their commanders with detailed outlines of the German positions, greatly aiding the Allied advance. In the course of 1918 over ten million aerial photographs were taken in Belgium and France.[16]

The First World War had not been fought entirely on the Western Front. A hugely successful campaign had taken place in Palestine during 1917 and 1918, when a combined army led by General Allenby advanced from Egypt across the Sinai and defeated the Ottoman Turks at Gaza. Allenby then advanced north, captured Jerusalem and occupied all of Palestine, and by the war's end much of what is today Syria. A good deal of the area over which the Allied armies marched had never been properly mapped. Lieutenant Hugh Hamshaw Thomas of the RFC was to change all that. Hamshaw Thomas had been a leading palaeo-botanist before the war, well known for his study of fossils, and he was a Fellow of Downing College, Cambridge. He was a quiet, unassuming and studious young man who now brought to bear on aerial photography the painstaking approach he had previously applied to the study of Jurassic fossils. From late 1916 he led an aerial reconnaissance unit in Egypt that produced huge mosaics – sets of photos that were stuck together to produce an aerial view of a large area. From these photo mosaics, the unit produced detailed maps of more than five hundred square miles of Egypt, Palestine and Syria, and these maps greatly helped the advancing armies as they moved into uncharted territories that had been controlled by the

Ottomans for centuries.[17] Hamshaw Thomas's work demonstrated yet again the importance of aerial photography to military intelligence.

By the end of the war enormous strides had been made in the science of aerial reconnaissance. Cameras with lenses of long focal length could produce detailed images of large areas from as high as twenty thousand feet. Flexible roll film had begun to replace fragile glass plates. And the process of interpreting information from these photographs and of producing detailed maps of up to about 1:20,000 scale had been perfected. Most of the nations who had fought the war had developed their photographic reconnaissance arms, but the British Army and the RAF had taken these skills to new heights. Unfortunately, over the next twenty years, much of what had been so painfully learned would be forgotten.

In the peace that followed the cessation of fighting in November 1918, many of the military systems created during the war were wound down or disbanded. Moore-Brabazon left the RAF, went into politics and became a Conservative MP. He remained a major figure in British aviation for the rest of his life, encouraging Frank Whittle in the development of his jet engine in the Second World War. Hamshaw Thomas was involved in an ambitious plan to survey the whole of India from the air. But the plan was never carried out. Having lectured on the value of aerial photography to map making at the Royal Geographical Society in 1920, Hamshaw Thomas returned to Cambridge and to botany, where he spent the next twenty years. He founded the British Ecological Society and in 1934 he was elected a Fellow of the Royal Society.[18] But he would return to the world of aerial photography later.

Flying had advanced beyond all recognition in the four years of war and aircraft were now faster, more reliable and far more powerful, able to carry large bomb loads. Bombers and, to a lesser degree, fighters became the principal aircraft of the inter-war years and the role of aerial reconnaissance became a sideshow to the core purpose of the RAF. As photography lost its status within the RAF, pilots and navigators preferred to specialise in the glamorous subjects in which promotion was more probable, like engineering, armaments or radio communications. The RAF abandoned the science of photographic interpretation and photos were interpreted solely by Army officers attached to RAF units.[19] A new camera, the F-24, was introduced in 1925. Using 5in by 5in roll film, it could take up to 125 exposures. The camera was particularly suited to aerial surveying and during the 1920s the RAF carried out a variety of air surveys along the Nile valley and the Indian border with Afghanistan, and of the Anglo-Persian Company's oil refineries in Iraq. Later, these sorts of projects were taken on by specialist commercial air mapping companies. Within the small, inter-war RAF, aerial photography became the forgotten poor relation.

While the RAF turned its back on aerial photography, the subject attracted the interest of artists as well as explorers. In the 1930s, the artist John Piper became fascinated by the totally different perspective provided by viewing landscape from the air. Writing in the avant-garde art journal *Axis* in 1937, he observed that traditional painting from the Renaissance onwards had worked to a flat horizon and a vanishing point. But with aerial photography there was no right way up, no foreground and no rearground. Photographing the world from the air had freed the artist from the familiar patterns surrounding us. Hills no longer had steep inclines but were flat shapes. This sense of abstraction, Piper believed, was a genuinely liberating force for the artist, a sign of the modern and the new. Aerial photography for the artist was the opposite of what it was for the photo inter-preter. It was not a rational world to be understood and decoded. It was an abstraction of fields, lanes and lost buildings. Piper wrote that the Ordnance Survey photographs of Wessex were 'amongst the most beautiful photographs ever taken'.[20] This was another way in which aerial photography captured imaginations and suggested a new way of interpreting and understanding the world.

Despite this broader public interest in aerial photography, Victor Laws grew more and more disillusioned with the RAF and when he returned to Farnborough in February 1933 as group captain he wrote that RAF photography was 'at a dead end'.[21] Seven months later he left the service and went to take charge of a photographic survey in Western Australia. This was a low point not only for aerial reconnaissance but for the RAF itself. Very few technical advances had taken place since the end of the war and the RAF still flew biplanes that looked just like the aircraft that had fought against the Red Baron's Flying Circus above the Western Front. The bombers were still painfully slow at about 150 mph and virtually nothing was done to improve the quality of bombs or to develop naviga-tional aids to direct pilots and crews to their targets.

There were dramatic developments in aviation that did suc-ceed in capturing the public's imagination, like the winning of the Schneider Trophy in three successive races from 1927 to 1931. The winning aircraft were the streamlined monoplanes of the Supermarine company, designed by Reginald Mitchell. His modernistic designs and the use of new liquid-cooled engine technology took maximum speeds from 200 mph up to 400 mph. But this sort of thing passed the RAF by. Years of gov-ernment cuts in military spending had kept the RAF small and plans to expand had been repeatedly postponed. Most of the achievements of the First World War had become a mere memory, and with the loss of skills and lack of public investment the RAF had fallen seriously behind. It would take a major shock to the nation for that to change.

1

Secret Missions

Alarm bells did not initially ring out in Britain when Hitler was elected Chancellor of Germany in January 1933. But as he took on dictatorial powers, his bully-boys increasingly terrorised the streets of the main German cities. When they launched a violent and threatening campaign against the Jews some observers began to voice concern. In Britain, Winston Churchill was one of the first to warn about the threat posed by Hitler and his Nazi Party. One of the factors that caused alarm was Hitler's re-armament of Germany in defiance of the terms of the Treaty of Versailles. The rebuilding of the German air force was an impor-tant part of this rearmament. Only a few months after Hitler came to power an Air Ministry was formed in Berlin, ostensibly for civil aviation only, but soon the number of aircraft factories started to increase and a secret air force began to develop, based around flying clubs up and down Germany. In March 1935, while the western powers were diverted by tensions with Italy, Hitler publicly announced the formation of a reborn German air force, the Luftwaffe. The training of hundreds and then thousands of flyers began and thousands of aircraft started to roll off the German factories' production lines.

The British government maintained its public policy of appeasing Hitler rather than standing up to him. It was a policy that commanded general support among the British people, who had no desire to fight another war with Germany. The losses sustained in the Great War had scarred public consciousness too deeply. But in secret, from 1934 under Prime Minister Stanley Baldwin and then under Neville Chamberlain who became Prime Minister three years later, the British government did begin a process of building up the RAF. The Air Ministry commissioned the production of a new generation of monoplane fighter aircraft. These were the Hurricanes and Spitfires of Fighter Command that would come into service by the end of the 1930s. Churchill and a few others worried that this was too little, too late. But at least the first preparations for a possible war against Germany had been made. And the Secret Intelligence Service, also known as MI6, began to investigate what was really going on in Germany.

It was in this context that one of the most extraordinary personalities in the entire story of aerial reconnaissance entered the stage. Sidney Cotton was the son of a rich Australian landowner and businessman. He had come to England to attend school in 1910 and as a fifteen-year-old had visited Brooklands, the track in Surrey where both motor cars and aeroplanes were raced. It was here that young Cotton developed an obsession with aircraft. At school in Cheltenham he built a six-foot model aircraft which he flew across the cricket pitch. In 1916 he joined the Royal Naval Air Service and finally achieved his ambition of learning to fly. For a time he flew bombers from an airfield in France, but the science of bombing was still primitive and on most missions he and his fellow pilots either got lost or had to turn back. It was during his time as a pilot with the RNAS that Cotton made his first major contribution to the development of aviation when he invented the modern flying suit. Cotton noticed that when he flew wearing the overalls that most flight mechanics wore, he was kept warmer than other pilots wearing their naval uniforms. So he got a London outfitters to make up a single-piece flying suit, lined with thin fur surrounded by a layer of silk and with an outside layer of a light Burberry material. When sealed at the wrists and the ankles, the suit kept the flyer warm, and it had deep pockets below the knees for maps which the pilot could easily reach down to when sitting in the cockpit. He modestly called the new flying suit after himself – the 'Sidcot'. After much testing it became standard issue by the RFC and the RNAS. Even the Germans adopted the Sidcot flying suit and Baron von Richtofen was wearing one when he was shot down.

Cotton might have been a natural flyer and an imaginative airman but he was not suited to life in a military organisation. He came up with all sorts of ideas, such as a way to improve the cooling of aircraft engines and a plan to bomb Berlin. But he had a firm streak of obstinacy in his character and could not abide what he saw as inept leadership. His supreme self-confidence ensured that he always believed he was in the right and whoever disagreed with him was in the wrong. In May 1917 an incident blew up over the attachment of an extra water tank to an aircraft to cool the engine. When he was ordered to send a plane without the extra water tank on a mission, Cotton went straight to the Admiralty and protested. His commanding officer, Commodore Paine, accused him of refusing to obey orders. Cotton felt he had no option but to resign his commission there and then. He said he could not remain in a military unit 'where men at the top brought disaster by refusing to accept the advice of those they put in command'.[1] He returned to Australia, where he sat out the rest of the war. Although he had come up with all sorts of brilliant innovations, he had barely survived eighteen months in uniform.

For the next two decades Sidney Cotton was engaged in a variety of unusual and challenging jobs. He spent many years based in Newfoundland, making flights to scout out and identify migrating seals for sealing companies, and then to map much of the island using aerial photography. He organised a rescue mission for a team of explorers who were stranded on an ice-cap in Greenland. And during this period he became wealthy speculating on the Stock Exchange and buying and selling land. But many of his projects ended up in a clash of wills and the result of almost everything he tried his hand at was a falling-out with his business partners. He even fell out with his father, with whom he refused to talk for many years.

Cotton's fascination with photography led him to develop an interest in a new colour film system called Dufaycolor. He threw himself into this new project, which involved much travel, and he grew accustomed to flying in his own plane across Europe and America. But, after a few years, this resulted once again in a trail of disputes and collapsed companies. In September 1938 he was contemplating the failure of his colour film venture when he was contacted out of the blue by an old friend, A.J. Miranda.

Miranda put Cotton in touch with a mysterious gentleman in London by the name of Fred Winterbotham. After several meetings it appeared that Winterbotham was working for the British Secret Intelligence Service (SIS) and had been monitoring the growth of the German Luftwaffe. Winterbotham was using some excellent agents in Germany and had even personally met Hitler and many of the other Nazi leaders.[2] In the shadowy world of the SIS, Winterbotham also had close links at home with RAF Intelligence. During the same month that Winterbotham and Cotton met, the British Prime Minister signed an agreement with Hitler at Munich intended to preserve peace between the two nations. But it was increasingly obvious to many that war with Germany was now becoming not just a strong possibility but almost a dead certainty. Winterbotham was not alone in realising that the need for information about German military and industrial installations had suddenly become imperative. The British and French secret services started to look for a businessman with his own plane who was used to flying around Europe, as a cover to carry out aerial photography in secret over German military installations.

Cotton seemed to be the ideal candidate and he was taken on to the payroll of the SIS. He suggested that a Lockheed 12A would be best for the purpose. This American six-seater two-engined aircraft was used extensively as a corporate transport by big companies or wealthy businessmen. It was roomy enough that he could fit it out with cameras but not large enough to attract attention. It was crewed by a pilot and co-pilot. Miranda got a Lockheed sent across from the United States to the airfield at Heston, to the west of London not far from the site of what is now Heathrow. Heston was the home of many small flying clubs and it was Cotton's base. The initial idea was that pilots from the Deuxième Bureau, the French secret service, would actually fly the Lockheed under the pretence that it was Cotton on one of his business flights. However, Cotton soon ruled this out and insisted on flying the aircraft himself. He took on an enthusiastic Canadian named Bob Niven, who was finishing a short-service commission with the

RAF, to assist as engineer-pilot. When Niven heard that the flights might involve an element of risk his enthusiasm grew.

The Lockheed was fitted with a large French aerial camera nearly six feet long. An opening was cut in the floor of the aircraft's cabin where the camera was attached. In an emergency everything was to be thrown out of the aircraft through this opening. It was ready by the end of February 1939 and with a French secret service agent on board to operate the camera, Cotton flew his Lockheed on a series of flights above the Siegfried Line, the German defensive positions, in the area around Mannheim. On one of these first flights the Germans sent up a fighter to intercept the Lockheed, but Cotton headed for the French border and managed to lose the fighter. It was clear from the beginning that spying from the sky above German military sites was going to be a dangerous game for Cotton and his small team.

To Cotton's annoyance, the Deuxième Bureau were in charge of these initial flights. He thought they were bungling the operation and when they finally showed him the photos he had taken, Cotton was extremely disappointed. He had missed many of the key locations by flying an erratic course up and down over the target area, as instructed by the French agents. Cotton came up with a plan to use three cameras in a line, one pointing directly down, one angled slightly to the right and one to the left. By the use of these oblique cameras it would be possible to photograph an area ten miles wide from a single flight path at twenty thousand feet. The cameras Cotton wanted to use were newer RAF models that were much smaller than the six-foot French monster, each one fitting inside a domestic suitcase. However, the French said no to this plan and after a series of heated exchanges Cotton decided to walk out on the whole project and leave it to the French. He concluded, 'If worthwhile results were to be obtained I must have my own aircraft and operate in my own way.'[3]

British Intelligence wanted to continue with the spy flights and so paid for another Lockheed for Cotton, who this time fitted it out exactly as he wanted, with the three cameras all operated by a cable from the flight deck. The cameras came from the RAF and all reference numbers were carefully filed off in case they were captured by the Germans. They could be brought on board in suitcases without attracting attention. One of the key innovations was that warm air from the cabin of the aircraft flowed across the cameras, preventing condensation from forming on the lenses and ruining the photographs. This meant that the Lockheed could photograph from a far greater height than was customary for other photo reconnaissance aircraft of the day. Cotton and Winterbotham realised this was a significant step forward in aerial photography.[4] Cotton also devised a Perspex pear-shaped window, built into the side of the aircraft cockpit, to enable him to look straight down to see what he was photographing. Somehow he found time to patent this window and license it to Triplex, who produced more than a hundred thousand of them during the war.

By June 1939, with the aircraft ready and fitted with extra fuel tanks to give additional range, Sidney Cotton and Bob Niven set off on a long Middle East trip photographing Italian military installations across Sicily and from Libya to Ethiopia. Flying up and down the Red Sea photographing Italian naval bases, Cotton put out the story that he was surveying a new route for Imperial Airways. In ten days they were able to photograph key parts of the Italian empire that had been exercising the minds of the British and French naval and air staffs for years. And on the way back they flew across Cyrenaica, photographing for the first time Italian bases like Benghazi, Bardia and Tobruk that would in a few years become household names.

During this trip Cotton had a fortuitous meeting with an RAF pilot who had experience of flying photo reconnaissance missions. Flying Officer Maurice 'Shorty' Longbottom was based in Malta when he met Cotton. They got on well and shared an enthusiasm for aerial reconnaissance, which they both believed would be the key to future intelligence gathering in war. Cotton asked for Longbottom to be assigned to his spying flights over the Middle East but the RAF refused. Nevertheless the two men spent some time together talking through their ideas about how best to carry out photo reconnaissance and which aircraft were most suited to the task. The conclusions of these conversations would have a major impact on developments over the next few years.

Back at Heston airfield, the SIS decided to resume spy flights over Germany as the organisation was desperate for up-to-date information about German military preparations. This would clearly involve considerable risk, but Cotton had the ideal cover as a businessman trying to sell his Dufaycolor system in Germany. The German business agent he was dealing with invited him to Berlin in July. When they landed at Tempelhof a dozen jackbooted Nazi soldiers marched towards the plane. Cotton thought the game was up but the soldiers simply formed a line and saluted him when he disembarked from the Lockheed. It turned out that the German agent had laid on a welcoming party to impress Cotton with how well connected he was inside Nazi Germany! Cotton was received royally and met several of the Nazi regime's aviation bigwigs.

Cotton spent the last few weeks of peace in the summer of 1939 acquiring valuable aerial photographs of Nazi Germany's military preparations.[5] But he had to be careful, as the German authorities were suspicious of flights near military bases and routed civilian flights well away from them. By now he had fixed his cameras in the Lockheed's wings so they were not visible inside the cabin. At the end of July he flew to Frankfurt to attend an air fair. With extreme bravado he invited the commandant of Tempelhof airfield for a joyride in his Lockheed to see how the American aircraft flew. Cotton suggested flying down the Rhine to Mannheim and the area that he had unsuccessfully photographed for the French earlier in the year around the Siegfried Line. Knowing that the commandant was on board, the authorities gave permission for the flight and Cotton was able to fly up and down the river showing off the sites. As his distinguished German guest sat back and admired the aircraft, Cotton flicked the switch and the cameras in the wings clicked away, photographing the Rhine and the Siegfried Line below.

Cotton pushed his luck right to the wire. He was in Berlin in late August when, suddenly and unexpectedly, the German and Russian foreign ministers announced the Nazi-Soviet Pact. War seemed imminent. All civilian flights were grounded and the skies above Germany were full of Luftwaffe fighters and bombers heading east to the Polish border. Cotton and Niven boarded the Lockheed and waited for permission to depart, but they had no permit to fly and feared that Nazi fighters might attack them if they tried to leave Germany. At the very last moment permission was given and they took off. As they approached the Dutch border they looked right and saw in the distance the German port of Wilhelmshaven. There, glinting in the sun, was a line of ships which they realised must be the German fleet, maybe planning to put to sea. Out came the cameras and with a final flourish Cotton photographed the fleet from a distance.[6] When he passed on the photos, the Admiralty was delighted with the information they could learn from them. But Cotton had been lucky. His was the last civilian plane out of Berlin. When he landed at Heston the customs officer greeted Cotton and Niven with the usual question, 'Where from?' Cotton answered, 'Berlin.' The officer looked at them in astonishment. 'Left it a bit late, haven't you?'[7] One week later Hitler invaded Poland. Within days Europe was at war once again.

At the beginning of the Second World War there were only seven trained photo interpreters in the entire RAF, and the Army had barely a handful of photographic experts. The rundown of aerial reconnaissance since the end of the First World War had been almost total. Even more worrying was the fact that at the outbreak of war there were only two types of aircraft earmarked to carry out aerial photography. The first was the single-engined Lysander, intended to carry out tactical reconnaissance for the Army by seeing what the enemy was up to just ahead of its front line. The Lysander was very manoeuvrable but it was hopelessly slow for this task, with a cruising speed of only about 90 mph. The aircraft assigned by the RAF to carry out strategic reconnaissance behind enemy lines was the Blenheim, a two-engined light bomber with a top speed of about 260 mph. Most of the lessons about the need for speed and height painfully learned in the First World War had been entirely forgotten.

The RAF believed aerial photography with the existing cameras and lenses could best be done from about ten thousand feet. This was supposedly the only way to obtain photos of sufficient scale and detail to yield any useful military intelligence. But at this height the photo recon aircraft were at great risk, both from anti-aircraft fire and from attack by enemy fighters. The Lysander relied upon its manoeuvrability to evade enemy fighters and to dodge back behind Allied lines. But the speed of German fighters like the Messerschmitt 109 had made the poor old Blenheim effectively obsolete by 1939. The slow-moving aircraft, loaded up with its cameras, was an easy target for the German fighters, which were more than 100 mph faster, and the Germans began shooting down Blenheims in alarming numbers. Out of eighty-nine missions in the first four months of the war, sixteen Blenheims were shot down and each of their three-man crews were killed or – if they survived being shot down – captured. This was way beyond an acceptable loss rate.[8] Despite the losses, there was such a great need for aerial photography that the RAF carried on sending out Blenheims on reconnaissance missions. They would fly as high as possible to reach their location and then drop down to ten thousand feet to take their photographs, but at the high altitude the cameras seemed to freeze up. So, even when a mission survived interception, the photographs brought back were almost always useless. Of the eighty-nine missions in the first four months, forty-four failed to produce any usable photos. The crews began to feel that they had been assigned a mission impossible, but still they bravely carried on flying sorties deep into German territory in the slow, lumbering Blenheims.

The Admiralty had been pleased with Cotton's photos and assigned him to fly a couple more sorties over neutral Denmark and Holland to get cover of various German naval bases and out-stations. Ian Fleming of Naval Intelligence, later the author of the James Bond books, was Cotton's principal contact at the Admiralty at this point. Fleming tried to persuade Cotton to leave the Secret Intelligence Service and work directly for the Admiralty, with the rank of captain and with all the assistance he required. But two weeks into the war, on 15 September, Fred Winterbotham, Cotton's secret intelligence controller, called him and told him the Air Ministry wanted to see him urgently. Fearing that he was going to be reprimanded for the flying he was still doing despite the war, Cotton met Air Vice-Marshal Richard Peck, who to his surprise asked him what special equipment he was using to get his aerial photos. Cotton replied that he was using only standard RAF cameras provided by the RAF itself. Peck said that the RAF were disappointed with the photos they were getting as the cameras were freezing at the high altitudes they were flying to avoid the enemy defences. Cotton explained that the cameras were not freezing but that condensation was the problem, and that he had solved it during the Lockheed's spy flights by directing warm air from the engine ducts to pass around the cameras.

Peck asked Cotton to come back the following day, and at their second meeting there were many more RAF specialists present. However, they pooh-poohed the condensation theory and Cotton felt he wasn't being taken seriously. It became clear that the Admiralty were calling for aerial photos of two areas along the Dutch coast, at Flushing and Ymuiden, but that the RAF could not get photos of sufficient quality. Cotton offered to fly a mission in one of the RAF Blenheims to show them how to operate the cameras correctly. But there was outrage at this suggestion. The RAF could not possibly allow a civilian to fly a military aircraft on a wartime mission. Cotton protested but it was clear this wasn't on. The meeting broke up but they agreed to meet again the following morning.

Cotton went back to his office in St James's Square in London's smart West End. Utterly fed up with officialdom, he stared out of the window. It was a beautiful, clear autumn day. Cotton hit on a plan. He would show the RAF what was possible. First he called Niven at Heston and told him to prepare the Lockheed. Then he made a call to the photographic unit at

Farnborough and asked them to be on standby for a rush job. Finally his chauffeur drove Cotton to the airfield and he and Niven took off and flew out to the Dutch coast. At Flushing and Ymuiden there were big gaps in the cloud cover and the cameras started rolling again. When the Lockheed returned, the photographs were processed at Farnborough. They proved to be excellent. Good 12in by 12in enlargements were printed up and assembled in an album.

On the following morning at ten o'clock Cotton returned to the Air Ministry for the next meeting with Peck and his team. Peck was full of admiration when Cotton showed off the album of photos, but said that of course it was impossible to take photos of such quality in wartime. When Cotton explained that he had taken the photos at three o'clock the previous afternoon the meeting erupted. The senior RAF officers were utterly indignant. Voices were raised and accusations flew around the room. 'You had no right to do such a thing' ... 'flaunting authority' ... 'what would happen if everyone behaved like that?' One officer even suggested that Cotton should be arrested there and then. After a few minutes Cotton could bear it no longer. He walked to the edge of the room, left the RAF officers in their high dudgeon and slammed the door behind him.[9]

But the pressure was on the RAF to deliver to the Admiralty good quality aerial photographs of German naval movements. When war was declared Winston Churchill had returned as First Sea Lord and he personally became involved, demanding appropriate photographic cover of German naval bases. So a crucial decision was taken at the highest level of the RAF. They called Cotton back to the Air Ministry, where this time he was introduced to none other than Air Chief Marshal Sir Cyril Newall, Chief of the Air Staff, the head of the RAF. Newall opened the conversation by saying, 'So you're the man who's giving us all this trouble.' 'No, sir,' replied Cotton. 'His name is Hitler.' Newall laughed and they shook hands.

Newall had a completely different approach from the antagonistic attitude of some of the other officers. He took Cotton to his club in Pall Mall and over lunch they made a deal. Newall asked Cotton to set up an experimental photographic unit outside the formal organisation of the RAF. Cotton agreed to form a special unit as long as he was given carte blanche in the choice of men, machines and equipment. Newall agreed and it was decided to base this top secret experimental unit at Heston, the civil airport where lots of private flying was done and where no one would suspect secret military work was taking place. Cotton felt the conversation was going well and he was getting everything he wanted, so he decided to soft-pedal and assured Newall that he would try to work within the existing red tape and organisation of the RAF. 'For God's sake don't do that, Cotton,' said Newall. 'Your value to me lies in your continuing to do things in your own unorthodox way. I want results.'[10] Cotton's unconventional methods seemed to be winning through. He was at last going to get the opportunity to put his own ideas into action.

2

Sid Cotton's Air Force

Over the next few weeks, Sidney Cotton's top secret unit was
set up at Heston airfield, reporting to RAF Fighter Command
but as an experimental group outside the RAF's formal structure. It was known at this stage as the Heston Flight. Maurice
'Shorty' Longbottom and Bob Niven were the first operational
pilots. A photographic officer and about twenty others –
including Sergeant 'Wally' Walton, who had been through the
pre-war Farnborough training – made up the team. Cotton
himself was commissioned as a squadron leader with the
acting rank of wing commander. But Cotton's difficult personality inevitably led to tensions with the RAF authorities and
despite Newall's injunction to be unorthodox, Cotton's uncom-
promising ways soon won him many enemies. As the Heston
unit grew in size a senior and much respected RAF officer was
seconded to it as administrator. This was Wing Commander
Geoffrey Tuttle, who would play a major part in the development of aerial reconnaissance. Tuttle was a former fighter pilot

and an aeronautical engineer. He was charming, diplomatic and a very effective operator. As an RAF 'insider' he was the perfect foil to the unconventional Cotton and in the months to come he managed to get many of the new innovations translated into practical improvements.

Meanwhile, Shorty Longbottom had considerably developed the ideas he had discussed with Cotton when they met in Malta. Longbottom submitted to the Air Ministry a paper titled 'Photographic Reconnaissance of Enemy Territory in War'. In the paper he argued that the ideal plane for aerial photography would be the fastest available, one that could fly at great height, above the range of the anti-aircraft defences, and could escape from enemy fighters sent up to intercept it simply by virtue of its speed. There was only one aircraft that fitted the bill, the new Supermarine Spitfire, which had a top speed of 360 mph. If the guns were removed to lighten the load, a photo-reconnaissance Spitfire with cameras added might be able to fly even faster. Longbottom's paper was nothing short of revolutionary. And like many radical proposals, it was quietly filed away and ignored.[1] In any case, it was purely academic because at the beginning of the war there was a desperate shortage of Spitfires. Production was way behind schedule and RAF Fighter Command was screaming for every Spitfire it could get hold of.

Cotton picked up on the idea of using the Spitfire for his experimental unit and put in a request. He was told in no uncertain terms that this would be impossible. Not only were no Spitfires available for experimental purposes, but also he was assured that it was technically impossible to equip Spitfires with cameras. So he carried on working with the Blenheim light bomber. The team at Heston got to work streamlining the Blenheim by smoothing surfaces, blocking holes, removing projections and making the tail wheel retractable. As a result they were able to increase its speed by 18 mph. Soon word that Cotton could improve the speed of the Blenheim reached Air Chief Marshal Sir Hugh Dowding, the chief of Fighter Command. Dowding wanted to use the Blenheim as a fighter and was delighted to hear that Cotton's team were able to get an extra few miles per hour out of each aircraft by their modifications. He asked to meet Cotton, summoning him to Fighter Command headquarters at Bentley Priory in north London.

According to Cotton's account of the meeting, Dowding casually asked over tea if there was anything he could do in return. Cotton took the plunge and asked for two Spitfires, explaining his ideas about using them for high-speed photo reconnaissance. Dowding thought for a moment and then asked when he would like them. 'Yesterday,' replied Cotton. 'Would nine o'clock tomorrow morning do?' responded Dowding. According to Cotton, two Spitfires were flown to Heston the following morning.[2]

Although this is a splendid story, one which Cotton told in order to relate how good he was at getting what he wanted from the RAF, it is completely contradicted by the record. In fact, the two Spitfires came not from Dowding's Fighter Command but from Maintenance Command, where a few spares were held. And it was not Cotton who obtained them but Peck. Dowding's position was the exact opposite of that described by Cotton. In fact, on receiving the request for Spitfires he sent a message: 'Earnestly request that my Spitfire resources may not be trenched upon for any purpose other than home defence fighting.' He was at first totally opposed to the use of Spitfires for photo reconnaissance.[3]

Cotton's engineers removed the two Spitfires' guns and took out other excess weight. By polishing and streamlining the aircraft they managed to increase their speed from 360 mph to 396 mph, faster than any other aircraft known at the time. Cotton then wanted to fit an extra 29-gallon fuel tank, increasing the plane's range to about 650 miles at thirty thousand feet, and to install a 64lb camera just behind the pilot's seat. The RAF boffins said this could not be done as it would shift the aircraft's centre of gravity too far to the rear. After another battle with the authorities, Cotton, whose instinct in aviation matters often proved to be right, got his way. And the Spitfires flew beautifully with no problems.

At the same time Cotton's team did much experimental work with cameras and lenses of different focal lengths to find the optimum lens for aerial photography, and with different mountings to minimise vibrations and the blurring of pictures. There were many other problems to overcome. Nobody had ever flown for hours at a time at high altitude in an unpressurised cabin and it was not known how the human body would respond to such strains. But the technicians worked out a way of providing adequate oxygen and found a solution to the problem of freezing batteries. There was a great esprit de corps among the team, who were able to concentrate unimpeded on the job in hand. There was a relaxed attitude to discipline; pilots wore their caps at a jaunty angle, there were no parades or kit inspections and not much saluting of officers. Cotton now had the aircraft he wanted, fitted with the equipment he needed, and he was building up a team of experts around him. The Heston Flight was getting ready to prove itself in action and the men in this growing unit were proud to call themselves 'Sid Cotton's Air Force'.[4]

The first photographic sortie flown by a Spitfire took place on the afternoon of 18 November 1939 when Shorty Longbottom took off from Seclin near Lille. The objective was to photograph sites in neutral Belgium, where it was suspected (rightly as it turned out) that key engagements would take place in the event that a German invasion bypassed the great French defensive position called the Maginot Line. But the Belgians were unwilling for flights to take place over their territory in case it provoked the Germans into a reprisal attack. So this sortie was the first in a series of what were called 'X missions', flown by the Heston Flight in total secrecy over Belgium and Germany.

Cotton had succeeded in transforming the first stage of aerial reconnaissance. He had two aircraft that were now able to photograph safely from high altitude and bring the photographs back for analysis. But the Air Ministry were still not happy with the photographs themselves. They regarded photos taken from thirty thousand feet as too small-scale to be of any military use. The photographs were roughly on the scale of 1:70,000. The Air Ministry still wanted photos taken from about ten thousand feet, giving a scale of about 1:10,000, even though the serious loss rate of the Blenheims showed that this was not going to be possible. One RAF internal report vehemently condemned the Heston unit's photographs, claiming that 'the scale of the photographs taken ... defies interpretation, reduces the effort extended to futility and the writer to tears. There is absolutely nothing to be gained by the activities of these aircraft.' Maybe the writer was jealous of Cotton's team and its success, but he still concluded venomously, 'The sole achievement is a waste of petrol, time, paper, energy and imagination.'[5] As ever, Sidney Cotton found an answer. Lemnos Hemming, an old friend of his from the days when he had been involved with the aerial mapping operation in Newfoundland, was now running an aerial survey business with the name of the Aircraft Operating Company on Beresford Road in Wembley. Cotton paid him a visit.

During the 1930s, when aerial reconnaissance had become the poor relation within the RAF, most of the developments and the build-up of expertise in aerial photography and surveying had taken place within private companies. All over the world there had been a demand for the use of aerial photographs in mapping, and also for mineral and oil prospecting. In the Middle East, oil companies used aerial imagery to interpret the geology of the landscape and to decide where to drill. The Aircraft Operating Company was one such company. Its technicians had developed considerable skill in the interpreting of aerial photos, using new 3D stereoscopic devices to give the photographs greater depth. By this means even tiny items on a photo could be accurately measured, greatly aiding their identification.

The Aircraft Operating Company was also the first British company to import a Swiss machine called the Wild (pronounced *vilt*) A5 Stereo Plotter. This was a huge machine weighing several tons but it magnified to a level of nine times in the optical field and a skilled operator could produce from photos taken at thirty-four thousand feet a detailed map at a scale of 1:25,000. The technique was known as photogrammetry.[6] This vast piece of apparatus would soon take on a starring role in the drama of spying from the sky. Not only did the Wembley company have a Wild machine, it also had a skilled operator in Michael Spender, one of three brothers who would all have distinguished careers. Stephen Spender was a poet who served in the Auxiliary Fire Service in London during the war, Humphrey Spender; a leading photographer who used his camera to study real life, was one of the founders of Mass Observation in 1936. A few years later Humphrey would join the Army section at Medmenham as a photographic interpreter. Michael had studied physics at Oxford and then had taken part in a series of geographical expeditions in Greenland and on Everest. He had been at the Aircraft Operating Company for many years and he had a flair for interpreting and understanding aerial imagery.

Even before the start of the war the directors of the Aircraft Operating Company had offered their expertise to help the RAF in interpreting aerial photographs. And when war was declared they once more offered their services to the war effort. But on both occasions the Air Ministry turned them down, arrogantly assuming that they had nothing to learn from a private civilian enterprise. Now, having obtained his first high-level, small-scale aerial photographs, Sidney Cotton approached his old friend Lemnos Hemming and asked for assistance in interpreting the photographs to find items of military interest. Hemming agreed to help on the basis of a personal guarantee from Cotton that the company's bills would be paid. Both men were outsiders to the formal military structures and their work was complementary – Cotton's unit could take the photographs and Hemming's company had the skills to interpret them. They became natural but completely unofficial allies. The staff were sworn to secrecy and the stage was set for the next act in the development of aerial reconnaissance.

On 7 December Cotton delivered the first set of 5in by 5in prints to the Aircraft Operating Company in Wembley. With minimal technical details about the photographs, in two and a half days Michael Spender and his team produced a detailed map of the area photographed and found thirty items of interest to military intelligence. This was despite the fact that the photos had been taken at thirty-four thousand feet. A few days later Cotton delivered to the Wembley photo interpreters a second batch of photographs. Taken from above the Siegfried Line in Germany, they were the first successful photos of this area of the country taken since the war had begun. This time the interpreters at Wembley were able to identify German gun positions, airfield assembly points, evidence of troop and tank movements, and even underground telephone systems (traced by indications on the surface). Over the next few months the numbers of photographs arriving at the Aircraft Operating Company grew considerably. Sometimes the photo interpreters worked for thirty-six hours at a time, without rest, to deliver their reports. They gave the Admiralty detailed information about German naval movements, plotted details of many Luftwaffe airfields and made precise measurements of aircraft lined up on the ground. But all of this was being done by civilians, with minimal input from the RAF.[7]

Cotton, meanwhile, had moved his two Spitfires and the Lockheed from Heston to France, from where it was easier to fly missions over Germany and continue the secret coverage of Belgium known as the 'X' sorties. Having found it difficult operating his secret missions from RAF bases where local commanders resented not knowing what was going on, he preferred to base his small flight at French airfields where no questions were asked. He soon grew closer to the French school of photographic interpretation at Meaux, where officials were more open than the RAF had been and more willing to exchange information and ideas. Cotton thought even the team at Wembley could learn from what the French were doing and it was agreed that one of the civilians from the Aircraft Operating Company should spend some time at Meaux. Douglas Kendall, an experienced photo interpreter who had been in the aerial survey business for some time, was sent across from Wembley and picked up valuable experience with the French interpretation team.

With the volume of requests for both aerial reconnaissance

flights and reports from the interpreters growing continually, Cotton asked in January 1940 for resources to expand his small and still secret experimental operation. Again things moved slowly and, perhaps inevitably, Cotton felt that the authorities did not fully recognise the invaluable service he was providing. Particularly, he argued that the Air Ministry did not understand the need to train specialist photo interpreters. It was still official policy that any intelligence officer could work on analysing aerial photographs. He made it his business to bombard the Air Ministry with 'requests for actions and reminders of the work we were doing'.[8] No doubt this did not make him any more popular in Whitehall.

In mid January 1940, Cotton and his French counterpart prepared a summary of progress in the first four months of the war. They concluded that the RAF had photographed 2500 square miles of enemy territory for the loss of forty aircraft, including many Blenheims, while the French had photographed 6000 square miles of enemy territory for the loss of sixty aircraft. The Heston team had, by contrast, photographed 5000 square miles of enemy territory using the high-altitude Spitfires without a single loss.[9] Even the Air Ministry couldn't ignore the glaring disparity between the performance of the Blenheims and that of the Spitfires and on 26 January the Air Council decided to expand the Heston Flight with the addition of new Spitfires, new pilots and new support staff. But once again the Deputy Chief of the Air Staff, Air Marshal Sir Richard Peirse, declined the offer to take over the Aircraft Operating Company and its staff. Cotton had got some of what he wanted but by no means all. He had to go on using the team at Wembley covertly. And his brash, assertive behaviour had not won him any more friends at the Air Ministry.

Cotton's reputation for delivering quality imagery with

detailed analysis rapidly spread through the Admiralty, where he had been much respected since taking the photos of the German fleet at Wilhelmshaven just before the outbreak of war. In February 1940, the Admiralty asked Cotton to see whether he could find out if the *Tirpitz*, the heavy German battlecruiser, was still in dock at Wilhelmshaven or if, as a report had suggested, it had headed out to sea. The Admiralty relied upon the RAF for aerial reconnaissance but they had failed to confirm or deny the report. Cotton, who was working for the RAF, began to play a tricky game by taking on missions directly from the Admiralty. But the reliable Shorty Longbottom agreed to fly a sortie over Wilhelmshaven and on a clear February afternoon took a series of excellent photos. When the interpreters at Wembley examined them it was clear that the *Tirpitz* was still in dock. The Air Ministry insisted on making their own interpretation of the photographs and valuable days were lost. Going completely outside his brief, Cotton personally delivered a set of prints to the Admiralty, who were delighted to know that the *Tirpitz* was still in dock. The head of Operational Intelligence, Lieutenant Ned Denning, went down to Wembley to see the equipment that the interpreters were using. It was the first visit by a senior member of the intelligence staff from any of the armed services and he was hugely impressed with the Wild machine, which he thought 'would help us tremendously in identifying enemy naval units'.[10]

On 12 February 1940, Cotton was taken in person to see Admiral Sir Dudley Pound, First Sea Lord at the Admiralty and the chief officer in the Royal Navy. Pound explained how vital it was that the Admiralty should get regular, up-to-date reports of the whereabouts of German naval units, otherwise many British warships would be tied down, wasting their resources trying to cover parts of the North Sea where they were not needed. Cotton explained that one of his Spitfires, with extra fuel tanks, could photograph all the main German naval bases in question in a single flight. Pound asked Cotton to join him in a meeting at the War Room that evening with the top members of the Air Staff. Realising that this could be embarrassing for him, Cotton hesitated. Pound told him that Winston Churchill, First Lord of the Admiralty, wanted to meet him in person and would be at the meeting to smooth over any difficulties with the RAF chiefs. So Cotton agreed to attend the meeting and arrived at the Admiralty at 9.30 that evening, only to be told that Churchill had been called away at the last moment.

Cotton was still deciding what to do when the senior Air Staff officers arrived. They included Air Marshal Peirse, who had crossed swords with him earlier. Peirse was astonished to see Cotton, an RAF officer, waiting with the naval chiefs for a meeting which was at a higher level than he was authorised to attend. The situation was made even worse when Pound asked Cotton to sit in the chair next to him, in the seat usually reserved for the most senior RAF officer present, and asked Peirse to move down to the next chair. This was hugely embarrassing to Cotton and humiliating to Peirse, who could barely control his anger. Pound's terrible gaffe made for a tense atmosphere between Cotton and his RAF bosses.

At the meeting, Longbottom's photographs were passed around, as were the interpretations carried out by Michael Spender's team at Wembley. The naval staff agreed that the photographs were excellent and that they provided all the information needed. Peirse asked how the results were obtained. Cotton said the interpreters had used a special photogrammetric instrument. 'Then why weren't the Air Staff told about it?' Peirse demanded to know. 'We would have requisitioned it at once.' Cotton didn't like to say that this was the very same equipment at Wembley that the RAF had failed to take over despite being offered it three times. But Peirse was still fuming at Cotton's presence and refused to accept that his plan to fly Spitfire reconnaissance flights over the German naval bases was viable. He grilled Cotton for twenty minutes, until Admiral Pound intervened and insisted that Cotton's unit be allowed to give it a try. Peirse reluctantly agreed. The status of the Aircraft Operating Company was left unresolved.[11]

On the following day, Winston Churchill followed up the meeting with a letter to the Secretary of State for Air. Believing that the equipment at the Aircraft Operating Company and the skills of its operators were just too important to leave in civilian hands, he wrote that 'Major Hemming's organisation ... including the expert personnel, should be taken over by one of the Service Departments without delay.' Churchill concluded by forcefully asserting the Admiralty position that 'if for any reason the Air Ministry do not wish to take it over, we should be quite prepared to do so.' Finally stung into action, the Air Ministry agreed to requisition the magnification equipment at Wembley and to take over the Aircraft Operating Company with all its personnel lock, stock and barrel.[12] This was what the two outsiders, Hemming and Cotton, had wanted all along.

There were still delays in achieving the takeover and Cotton felt his relationship with the Air Ministry was deteriorating rapidly. Bearing in mind his actions of the previous few months this was hardly surprising, but of course Cotton didn't see it that way. Instead he perceived it as personal obstructiveness against his plans to expand his unit. As more and more requests for air cover came in from the Royal Navy and the RAF, Cotton felt that he was fighting on two fronts, against the Germans *and* the Air Ministry. At the end of March he wrote in his diary, 'The attitude of the Air Ministry appals me. God help the Allies unless our leaders wake up or we get new leaders.'[13] Meanwhile the Air Ministry staff began to hold meetings to discuss what to do with Cotton. He infuriated the RAF bosses when, for instance, he went direct to the manufacturers of the Spitfire at Supermarine in Southampton to try to obtain more aircraft. By doing this, the officials thought he was endangering the Spitfire's entire production flow. In a memo at the end of March, Peck concluded: 'The first and fundamental question is whether we go on with Cotton enduring such tribulation for the value of whatever further ideas there may be – and I think there will be good ideas – or whether we regularise everything and dispense with Cotton.'[14]

Finally, on 28 March Hemming received a letter informing him that the Air Ministry was going to take over his company. Slowly, over the next few months, air force officers arrived at Wembley and the unit was incorporated into the RAF. Michael Spender and his team began to learn RAF procedure and in turn started to teach the RAF officers the use of the Wild machine and the basics of photogrammetric methods. The Air Ministry had belatedly accepted that there was a science behind photographic interpretation that had to be learnt like anything else. The expanded unit at Wembley became known as the Photographic Development Interpretation Unit and was to work hand in hand with Cotton's unit, now renamed the Photographic Development Unit. The RAF had at last put aerial reconnaissance and interpretation on a proper war footing. And not a moment too soon.

At the beginning of April 1940 a new, long-distance version of the Spitfire was delivered to Sid Cotton's Air Force at Heston. Fitted with an additional thirty-gallon blister tank under the port wing, counterbalanced by a blister under the

starboard wing containing two cameras with 8in lenses, the aircraft had a range of over eight hundred miles. On 7 April
Shorty Longbottom set off in this Spitfire and photographed
the German naval base at Kiel for the first time. When they
examined the photos, the interpreters noted that a large
amount of shipping could be seen around the port and numerous heavy Ju 52 transport aircraft had been parked on a nearby
military airfield. Two days later, Hitler launched his attack on
Denmark and Norway, a combined operation using paratroopers carried in the transport planes and ships that had been
leaving Kiel harbour when Longbottom had flown over. The
invasion came as a complete surprise to the British and French.
The information gleaned from the aerial photos had been put
to no use, for the simple reason that, as these were the first
photos of Kiel taken in wartime, the interpreters had nothing
to compare them with. They had no way of knowing if the
activity was exceptional. It was a further reminder that photographic interpretation was only effective if there were repeated
previous covers with which to make comparison.

On 6 May 1940 a Spitfire from Cotton's unit flew along the
Luxembourg–German border. When the photos had been
developed they were examined by Douglas Kendall, who spotted a series of German tanks nestling in the woods of the
Ardennes. In photographs from a low-level follow-up sortie,
the interpreters could see four hundred tanks in the woods,
supported by ammunition dumps, armoured vehicles and oil
depots. Cotton personally rushed to London with the photographs, but nothing was done. Once again Cotton felt this was
a personal affront. In the early hours of 10 May 1940 Hitler
launched his invasion of northern Europe through the
Ardennes forest.

Cotton raced back to France where the military leaders were

calling on his unit to provide regular reconnaissance flights. Speed of interpretation was now vital. Information about the latest German movements in their blitzkrieg or lightning war had to be passed on within hours or it was useless. Such were the pressures that Douglas Kendall began to interpret directly from the wet negatives before they had dried or been printed up, phoning his interpretations straight through to headquarters.

On 16 May, as the Dutch surrendered and the French army began to retreat, the Air Ministry sent orders to evacuate the Photographic Development Unit. Cotton appealed to Air Marshal Sir Arthur Barratt, the man in charge of the RAF in France and one of the unit's main customers. They stayed put, continuing to fly sorties and make urgent interpretations, but the German advance was too rapid for air intelligence to be of much value. Cotton must have looked an unlikely military figure at this time, flying here and there in his Lockheed and seeking personal meetings with senior British and French military figures. Kelson, his personal valet and chauffeur, still accompanied Cotton everywhere, and one day out driving during an air raid Cotton instructed Kelson to pull in at the side of the road under some trees. He told Kelson to be ready to jump into a nearby ditch if the raiders returned. 'Will you be jumping in too, sir?' asked the ever-polite chauffeur. Cotton admitted that he would. At this the chauffeur went back to the car and began to rummage around. Asked what he was doing, he replied, 'I'm going to place the rug in the ditch, sir.'[15] Such was the style of the never-to-be-ruffled gentleman's gentleman.

Convinced, as always, that he knew best, Cotton had defied orders in not evacuating his unit. But as the German onslaught continued, on 9 June the men were forced to evacuate south with RAF headquarters to an airfield near Orléans. Wally Walton set up a photo processing unit in a little mill on the

Duke of Orléans' estate where they washed film taken during the sorties using water from a local trout stream. But the unit was too far from the battle zone and from now on provided little or no intelligence of value to the Army, which had already evacuated from Dunkirk. And unfortunately one of the Spitfires was left behind and captured by the Germans with all its camera gear intact, giving them a clear understanding of what RAF aerial reconnaissance was capable of.

Cotton flew south to Marseilles to organise reconnaissance sorties against the naval bases of Italy, which had now joined the war against the Allies. Then, on 14 June, he returned to Orléans and organised a further evacuation 120 miles south-west to Poitiers. Here the unit was forced to abandon all its vehicles, including the valuable mobile photo processing trailers, which were set on fire to prevent them from falling into the hands of the enemy. Although still loyal to Cotton, some of his team began wondering if they had left it too late and would not be able to get out of France back to Britain. In the chaotic scramble that followed, some of the remaining men reached a small grass airfield near La Rochelle and, amid the chaos of the total French defeat, finally escaped the country in whatever aircraft they could find. A few even commandeered some tiny Tiger Moths and headed off carrying spare petrol cans in the front. In Brittany they managed to land and refuel before the flight across the Channel. Several men piled into an abandoned Fairey Battle aircraft that had crashed into a tree. With the men lying alongside each other in the bomb bay, the pilot managed to get airborne and evacuate. Some of the team were able to escape by boat and eight others, including Douglas Kendall, hitched a ride in a troop carrier that was rounded up for the evacuation.[16] With the unit's precious equipment now abandoned or destroyed, on 17 June Cotton left in his Lockheed, picking up several stragglers including a civilian secretary who would not leave France without her collie dog. It seems he spent some time offering to evacuate various French dignitaries for large sums of money, which naturally didn't go down at all well in the Air Ministry.[17] In the end, more by improvisation and luck than by judgement, every member of the unit succeeded in getting back to England.

As Cotton stepped out of the Lockheed at Heston on his return, an RAF orderly handed him a letter from an official in the Air Ministry. The letter said simply and clearly that there had been a review of the future status of the Photographic Development Unit, and that it was now regarded as no longer being experimental and would therefore take its place within the organisation of the RAF. It also informed Cotton of the decision that Wing Commander Tuttle would be the unit's new commander, concluding that the Air Council wanted to record 'how much they are indebted to you for the work you have done and for the great gifts of imagination and inventive thought which you have brought to bear on the development of the technique of photography in the Royal Air Force'.[18] It was the day after his forty-sixth birthday and Sidney Cotton had been sacked.

Cotton was not unnaturally distraught at receiving this letter. Coming as it did at the end of a long period of intense stress during the fall of France it seemed particularly brutal. Cotton felt that the many enemies he had made in the senior echelons of the RAF had finally had their revenge. His team, which now consisted of well over three hundred men, recommended him for the Distinguished Service Order. This was turned down but he was later awarded an OBE.

Cotton played no role in the rest of the war. After the Battle of Britain came the nightly Blitz on the cities of Britain. London was bombed every night for weeks on end. Although the RAF fighters, Churchill's heroic 'Few', had done well against the Germans during the daytime battles in the skies above southern England, they had little to help them in tracking down enemy bombers at night. Cotton tried to develop a searchlight that would enable the fighters to find the German bombers, but the RAF had already turned down a similar scheme and they rejected Cotton's new version. He and a colleague patented a system but it never got going and he came up against constant hostility from his old adversaries in the Air Staff. In March 1941 he was asked to resign his commission in the RAF. He went to the Admiralty to offer his services there, but again the Air Staff intervened and the Admiralty told him they had been asked not to work with him. He tried to interest the Americans in his searchlight project but was then threatened by RAF security with passing on information to a foreign power (at this point the USA was still not in the war). Everywhere he turned, Cotton felt blocked. This feeling was probably exaggerated by Cotton's own sense of paranoia. But without doubt the Air Ministry treated Cotton badly. Officials felt him to be a loose cannon and a threat to their own authority, wasting time trying to set up projects and to explore ideas they had already rejected. Cotton ended the war trying to rescue for his wealthy French friends racehorses that had been captured by the Germans. Without doubt a brilliantly inventive mind had been lost to the war effort.

Sidney Cotton had helped to lay down the fundamental principles of aerial reconnaissance, principles which held good for the rest of the war. The RAF had been entirely wrong in thinking that slow-moving, low-flying fighter-bombers were the aircraft best suited to taking aerial photographs. The high loss rate of the brave crews bears witness to this. In the end, each Blenheim sortie became almost a suicide mission, a state of affairs that should have been foreseen and prevented. Cotton had established that aerial reconnaissance had to be carried out only by the fastest planes available, flying at the highest possible altitude. He had improved the systems for operating cameras and for avoiding condensation or the freezing up of camera apparatus. He had made it clear that photo interpretation relied upon frequent repeated sorties over the same territory, so that every change taking place on the ground, every construction, almost every new movement, could be tracked and plotted.

Cotton was a maverick who had battled with the bureaucracy of the Air Ministry and had proved his point through a set of spectacular faits accomplis, from the pre-war photographing of the Siegfried Line to the photographing of Wilhelmshaven which had so delighted the Admiralty and so annoyed the RAF. He had been the right person at the right time as the military in Britain geared up for all-out war. The early days of the war were marked by typically British, amateurish muddle and improvisation. But Cotton laid the foundations for the highly professional skills that would later characterise photo reconnaissance and photo interpretation. This was a huge achievement. But he was absolutely not the right person to lead a military unit in war. The eccentricities that enabled him to rattle the cage of the RAF during the phoney war were the very characteristics that made him unsuitable for command in a real war. He saw everything as a personal crusade and everyone who disagreed with him as representing the forces of evil, out to undo the good he was doing. He insisted on doing things his way regardless of the bigger picture. In the chaotic evacuation from France he risked losing nearly everything he had succeeded in building up, both men and materials. The Air Ministry had been absolutely right to dump him after the Battle of France. Now it was time to move on.

3

Crisis

As the Battle of France raged and Sidney Cotton tried to organise the evacuation of his unit, the Joint Intelligence Committee, the central intelligence coordinating committee that reported directly to the War Cabinet, met in London. They agreed that if Britain was threatened by invasion then 'regular and systematic air reconnaissance over all areas in which the seaborne expedition might sail will be vital'.[1] It was clear that the RAF bosses urgently had to resolve the situation regarding aerial photography. On 10 June, a joint meeting of senior RAF and Royal Navy officers took place at the Air Ministry to discuss the future of photographic reconnaissance (PR) along with that of photographic interpretation (PI). In addition to the decision to bring Cotton's experimental unit within the structure of the RAF, to dispense with Cotton and to replace him with his deputy Geoffrey Tuttle, it was also decided to move photo reconnaissance from Fighter Command where it had initially been situated. This brought into focus the ongoing debate as to where

PR should sit within the RAF, as well as how it should relate to the Royal Navy and the Army.

Bomber Command, which already had its own small photo reconnaissance and interpretation unit, strongly made its own case for taking over Cotton's PR unit to give priority to a bombing campaign against Germany. On the other hand, the Admiralty reiterated its demand for top priority to be given to keeping a watch on the enemy's ports and naval yards. After several hours of debate it was decided, wisely, that PR and PI should not be 'owned' by any of its principal customers. Instead a new unit would be created out of what was left of Cotton's team inside the administration of RAF Coastal Command. The immediate threat to Britain in the summer of 1940 came from the coastal ports and airfields of Nazi-occupied Europe and it was entirely appropriate that the slender resources of aerial reconnaissance should largely be dedicated to the observation of these sites. Had Bomber Command taken over, then aerial reconnaissance might have been focused entirely on finding suitable targets and on damage assessment missions. Such tasks had to be a secondary priority at this time of crisis. The official RAF record of the meeting notes that the Air Staff had put up with a 'dynamic individualist' in the form of Sidney Cotton as long as the unit was experimental, but adds that 'At this point the smooth working of the Unit demanded first and foremost the qualities of command and organisation too seldom associated with the qualities of imagination and initiative needed in the initial stages.' The changes made in bringing aerial photography under operational command and the replacement of Cotton by a regular RAF officer, Wing Commander Tuttle, 'were recognitions of the gravity of the situation and of the importance and immediacy of the role which photographic reconnaissance was expected to play'.[2]

Geoffrey Tuttle formally took over Cotton's unit in June and it was renamed the Photographic Reconnaissance Unit, commonly referred to as the PRU. Tuttle was the right man for the job, a popular, efficient leader with a wealth of valuable flying experience. He was determined to keep the 'Flying Club' atmosphere that Cotton had created at Heston, where relaxed dress and an informal attitude to discipline were tolerated. The number of Spitfires available to the PRU soon grew to twelve and constant improvements in their range and in the cameras they carried enabled them to scout further and further across occupied Europe. Following the Nazi triumphs of April and May there was now a vast area to cover, from the Arctic Circle in Norway to the Franco-Spanish border. So in July Tuttle expanded the range of the flights he could operate. 'A' Flight was moved to an RAF station at Wick in the north-east of Scotland. From here its pilots could carry out photo reconnaissance flights over the Norwegian coast. 'B' Flight was moved to an RAF airfield at St Eval in Cornwall to cover the west coast of France. 'C' and 'D' Flights remained at Heston, from where they could cover enemy ports along the Channel as well as parts of France, Belgium, Holland and Denmark. There was now hardly anywhere in occupied Europe within about 350 miles from England that the spies in the sky could not look down on and photograph.

At the same time, the old Aircraft Operating Company in Wembley also became a part of the RAF and was renamed the Photographic Interpretation Unit, better known as the PIU. The executives of the company all received honorary commissions but many of the specialists like Michael Spender retained civilian status. The offices in the industrial unit were now renamed Paduoc House (a peculiar anagram devised from mixing the initials of its previous title, the Photographic Development

Unit, with those of the Aerial Operating Company). The PIU consisted of nineteen RAF officers and eighty-eight men and women of other ranks, including photo processors and librarians. Appointed to command this new unit was Squadron Leader Peter Riddell, who had led the specialist Bomber Command photo interpretation unit for a year. He was a brilliant and efficient administrator and brought tremendous energy to the task of organising a disparate but talented group of men and women, in which four out of ten of the photo interpreters were still civilians. Riddell proved to be well up to the task of integrating the unit and inspiring it with the challenges ahead. Tuttle and Riddell would now set about creating the operating structure of the two halves of aerial reconnaissance, the taking of aerial photographs and the interpreting of them. What they did next would shape the development of photo intelligence for the rest of the war.

After Cotton's removal, during the summer and autumn of 1940, the photo intelligence community faced its first real test. During this time Britain stood alone in Europe – while of course still receiving considerable support from its vast empire. Up against it was a Nazi enemy who within ten weeks had conquered Norway, Denmark, Holland, Belgium and France. Churchill quickly rebuffed any suggestion of a negotiation with Hitler. So, in mid July, the Führer issued a directive calling for an invasion of Britain.[3] But his generals and admirals argued between themselves as to how they should carry this out. The Germans had made no plans for an invasion of Britain before now and they lacked the resources, especially the landing craft, necessary for such an ambitious cross-Channel operation. Herman Göring, head of the Luftwaffe, suggested he could solve the dilemma by destroying the Royal Air Force. With Britain's air force wiped out, he claimed, the Royal Navy could not function effectively and the British would probably give up. Then there would be no need for an invasion.

In mid August the Battle of Britain began in earnest as the Luftwaffe launched its attack on RAF airfields in southern England. The Hurricanes and Spitfires of the RAF held their own against the regular forces of German Dornier and Heinkel bombers, supported by fighters like the Messerschmitt 109. The country soon came to believe in a heroic version of events whereby the British David magnificently held off the Nazi Goliath. But RAF losses were heavy and it was clear to those who knew the reality of the struggle that this level of attrition could not go on much longer. In a famous account, Churchill described a visit he made to the headquarters of 11 Group Fighter Command at Uxbridge at the height of the struggle. As wave after wave of German bombers were picked up by radar crossing the Channel, and squadron after squadron of RAF fighters were scrambled and sent up against them, Churchill turned to the anxious Group Commander and asked, 'What other reserves have we?' The answer came, 'There are none.'[4]

It took some time for the reorganisations of the PRU at Heston and the PIU at Wembley to take effect. But time was not on Britain's side in the summer of 1940 and soon reconnaissance Spitfires were out recording the location and strength of the Luftwaffe airbases scattered along northern France. There were four hundred bases from where the Luftwaffe launched its daily raids against Britain and it was a tough challenge trying to monitor what was happening in so many airfields.[5] Walter Heath was in charge of interpreting these photos, and by observing the extension of a runway or the construction of new hangars he could calculate which aircraft would soon be arriving at a particular airfield. By measuring the size of aircraft on the ground, an operation for which the Wild machine was ideally suited, he could establish what aircraft were flying out of which bases. From this painstaking work his team could draw up a detailed plan of the Luftwaffe bomber bases and the airfields from where their fighter escorts flew, along with an estimate of their numbers.

The War Cabinet had established a new group of intelligence chiefs to assess the likelihood of a German invasion. Called the Combined Intelligence Committee, in early July – when the German army was fresh from its dramatic victories in Europe – its members felt there was a strong possibility that Germany would be 'making preparation for raids in force, or for [the] invasion of the British Isles'.[6] However, for the next few weeks, reconnaissance flights over the ports of northern Europe reported nothing unusual. As fears grew that an invasion fleet might sail instead from Norway, the RAF carried out recon flights there as well, but they too concluded in late July that there was 'no significant grouping of shipping and compara- tively little movement'.[7] By late August, as the Battle of Britain raged between the Luftwaffe and RAF Fighter Command, there was still no sign of preparations in the ports along the Channel. On 23 August the Combined Intelligence Committee was able to report that 'no serious threat of invasion yet exists from Netherlands, France or SW Norwegian coasts'.[8] So far, so good.

But from the end of August the photo interpreters at Wembley began to spot an increasing number of barges assembling in the major ports of Antwerp, Rotterdam and Amsterdam. These were conventional barges, of a type used in huge numbers to trans- port cargo up and down the main arteries of Germany like the Rhine. Some of them were self-propelled. Others were towed two at a time behind a tug of some sort. The photo interpreters were now counting the barges and on the next reconnaissance over the same area it was possible to see how their numbers had

changed. On 31 August, as the Battle of Britain entered its crucial phase in the skies above England, it was noted that fifty-six
barges had disappeared from Amsterdam and a hundred more
had left Antwerp. It appeared that they were being moved south
and west to the Channel ports. On this same day eighteen barges
were spotted for the first time at Ostend. Over the first six days
of September every new photograph revealed more and more
barges assembling in the Channel ports of Boulogne, Calais,
Dunkirk and Ostend – only twenty or thirty miles from the
English coast. But there was no sign of the movement of any
German warships from their bases and still on 6 September, the
Combined Intelligence Committee was able to conclude that
'there is little evidence other than the movement of small craft
towards the Channel ports to show that preparations for invasion or raids by sea on UK are more advanced than they have
been for some time.'[9] Light bombers were despatched to bomb
the concentrations of barges, but their numbers grew ever larger.

At this point Göring's Luftwaffe was still battling it out with
Fighter Command. Cursing the number of British fighters that
were being sent up against his aircraft, on 7 September Göring
committed the blunder that we now know cost him the Battle
of Britain. He shifted the attack from the RAF airfields to the
city of London. By going for civilian targets, Göring gave the
RAF the respite it desperately sought. No one, of course,
realised this at the time, and over the next ten days the number
of barges being counted in the Channel ports grew and grew.
The interpreters counted 255 barges at Calais; 192 at Dunkirk;
230 at Boulogne; 140 at Flushing; and 227 at Ostend. At
Antwerp photo sorties revealed that another 600 barges and 200
merchant ships were assembling.[10] Was this Hitler's invasion
armada? At Wembley, Michael Spender using the Wild machine
noted that a few 130ft barges at Rotterdam had modified bows.

It seemed that some sort of landing ramp to ease loading and unloading was being added. Were the Germans building makeshift landing craft using the Rhine barges to which they had access in large numbers?

In the House of Commons on 17 September Churchill reported that the enemy's invasion preparations were steadily proceeding. When the House went into secret session, he gave further detail. Using the figures he had received from aerial reconnaissance he reported that 'upwards of 1,700 self propelled barges and more than 200 sea-going ships, some very large ships, are already gathered at the many invasion ports'.[11] On that same day, Michael Spender was re-counting the number of barges that had gathered at Dunkirk. One hundred and thirty had arrived in the last four days. Suddenly he threw down his optical viewer, exclaiming, 'We don't want these,' and sprang to his feet saying, 'They'd better give us rifles instead!' He discussed with another colleague the inevitability of invasion and came up with the idea of going down to Kent to shoot at least one German before no doubt being shot himself.[12]

However, it turned out that the number of barges in the Channel ports reached its peak on the following day, 18 September. From then on their numbers began to diminish. And this was reported daily back to the Combined Intelligence Committee. Hitler had failed to win mastery of the skies over England and as summer turned into autumn the weather became less suitable for an invasion. By the end of September, the photo interpreters at Wembley noted a change to the look of the docksides along the Channel ports. The amount of activity had dramatically decreased. They could report that the barges were being sent back to their Rhineland homes. The potential invasion fleet was clearly dispersing. By the end of October the number of barges had dropped to less than half the number that had been there six weeks before. Photo intelligence was the first to confirm that as the autumn progressed the threat of invasion was passing. Britain had survived to fight another day.

Historians have frequently questioned whether Hitler ever seriously considered an invasion of Britain. At the time, with the signs of the assembling armada and the daily onslaught from the air against Britain's cities, this question was rarely asked outside senior Intelligence circles. Few people doubted that this was a moment of national crisis when, for the first time in three hundred years, Britain faced the prospect of invasion by a determined enemy. However, by analysing the photographic evidence today, it can be seen to tell quite the opposite story. The number of barges and warships gathering in the Channel ports was far from sufficient to allow Hitler to carry out an invasion. The assembly of the landing fleet had begun late, at the end of August, and was not very far advanced by the middle of September, the last sensible moment to mount an invasion. Moreover, the number of barges with ramps fitted to their bows was tiny. At Wembley, in the end, the interpreters could only find a total of six barges modified by the attachment of landing ramps.[13] And there were no signs from aerial photography that the German navy had deployed. Its main capital ships were still being observed at Kiel and Wilhelmshaven. Only motor torpedo boats and six destroyers had been spotted in the Channel ports. Of course, the big warships would only join the invasion fleet at the last minute. But there was no sign of any preparations. The pathetic fleet in the Channel would have been no match for the Royal Navy, which would have deployed in force against an invasion armada.

When the Allies mounted their invasion of northern France, four years later, the invasion fleet consisted of three thousand warships and more than four thousand landing craft, many of them specially constructed to carry tanks, trucks and the supplies that any invading force would need. The number of vessels gathered in northern France in September 1940 was only a fraction of this number. The D-Day invasion armada took a year to organise and months to assemble. The barges in the Channel ports built up to their peak in a couple of weeks. The aerial photographs prove today once and for all that Hitler was going through the motions in assembling vessels in the Channel ports but was not seriously considering an invasion of Britain with this puny, ill-equipped force. Possibly he had taken Göring at face value when he said his Luftwaffe would bring Britain to its knees and there would be no need to invade. In London, the Combined Intelligence Committee recognised that their assessments were based 'so greatly upon aerial reconnaissance'.[14] And today the photographic evidence is clear. Hitler did not seriously plan to launch an invasion of England. However, it certainly did not feel like that at the time.

The threat of invasion had put photographic reconnaissance and interpretation through its first real wartime trial. The number of missions flown and the detail picked up from the photos taken provided the Intelligence chiefs with almost a daily barometer of the likelihood of invasion. But there were still fears that this daily reckoning was not the full story. Some senior figures in Intelligence believed that because the Germans knew there was no aerial reconnaissance over the Baltic, as it was still out of range to the PR aircraft, they were assembling an invasion fleet there that would take only a couple of days to reach Britain. There were urgent demands for longer range Spitfires that could reach the Baltic and the first of these flew in late October. Reassuringly, the interpreters were able to report that there were no signs of unusual activity.[15] With an increase in the number of Spitfires available and using the skills of the interpreters at Wembley, aerial photography had passed its first test with flying colours, and the sense of urgency and the detail of the reports that they were able to deliver gave an uplift to the whole organisation.

Under Peter Riddell at the newly formed Photographic Interpretation Unit, a sophisticated system evolved for the process of interpretation. This became known as the three-phase system. 'First Phase' interpretation was immediate analysis of any urgent intelligence required from a photo. This could be the identification of a ship to see if it was still in harbour, or finding out if aircraft were gathering at an airfield or if troops had been deployed, or the making of a quick assessment of the extent of bomb damage after a raid. First Phase interpretation was usually carried out on the airfield where the reconnaissance aircraft had landed. As soon as the aircraft touched down, the ground crew removed the film from the cameras and rushed it to a processing unit where it would be developed and prints made. This would usually take about an hour from touchdown. A First Phase interpreter would then look at the images and immediately describe any key pieces of information, sending this intelligence by teleprinter to head-quarters or any other agency that needed to know the results. The intention was that such intelligence would be despatched within three hours of the plane's return to base although it could be done even quicker in an emergency, for instance if the Admiralty and the RAF were eager to know the location of a German warship so a bombing raid could be quickly launched against it.

'Second Phase' interpretation was to be carried out within twenty-four hours of the film being processed. This allowed for a more coordinated analysis, after all the day's photographs were in, and for the revelation of far more detail than was possible in the urgent First Phase work. This interpretation was carried out not at the airfield but at the main PIU, initially at Wembley and later at Medmenham. Photo interpreters were on hand twenty-four hours a day. The Second Phase interpreters issued activity reports every twelve hours, summing up the key intelligence they had gathered from the photographs.

The aerial photographs were then passed on to 'Third Phase'. This was where specialist interpreters got to work to provide detailed analysis for recipients or 'customers' who required it. So there were units that specialised in enemy aircraft, in shipping, in railway traffic, in industrial activity, in damage assessment and so on. As we shall see, these specialist units produced some of the most important interpretations of all and were able to provide the military chiefs of all three services with incredible detail about almost every activity within Nazi-occupied Europe of relevance to fighting the war.

The PI work carried out by the RAF was regarded from the summer of 1940 onwards as high grade specialist intelligence work and it was performed by specially trained interpreters, all of whom were officers. Supporting the photo interpreters were teams of non-commissioned men and women from the RAF and the Women's Auxiliary Air Force who kept the communications going, using teleprinters that sent telex messages by telephone cable or radio link. Along with them were the photo developer technicians, the librarians and the administrative staff to keep this rapidly growing Intelligence operation functioning efficiently.

There are three aspects to military intelligence during war. First, information has to be acquired. Then it has to be interpreted or analysed. Finally it has to be passed on to those who need to know it or who can act upon it. The systems developed during the second half of 1940 at the PRU at Heston and the PIU at Wembley were created to do precisely this. Some of them had been started by Sidney Cotton. But his legacy was refined, improved on and advanced by Geoffrey Tuttle and Peter Riddell. And the three phases of photo interpretation were designed to extract maximum value from each photograph for different military uses. It was a complex and growing operation but one that at heart was brilliantly focused and fit for purpose.

Douglas Kendall was one of the first leading photo interpreters of the new wave of wartime RAF officers. Before the war he had been in aerial survey work in East Africa as part of the Aircraft Operating Company. Back in London when war began he had become part of the Heston Flight and it was he whom Cotton had sent to Meaux to learn from the detailed work being done by French photo interpreters. Kendall had a questioning mind and a natural ability for deductive reasoning which made him well suited to this specialist intelligence work. He also had an immense capacity for hard work and the determination to carry on even when no obvious conclusions could be reached.[16] Having returned to London in one of the last flights out of France during the chaos of the evacuation, he was at the centre of photographic interpretation at Wembley.

The cast of characters that gave the PIU its unique character now began to appear on the scene. Lemnos Hemming had for some time been trying to persuade Claude Wavell, an old colleague and a brilliant mathematician, to join them from South America, where he had been doing pioneering work in an air survey of Rio de Janeiro. After the evacuation at Dunkirk, Britain's perilous state was clear for all to see and Wavell rallied to the flag. He sent a telegram to Hemming: 'If you still want me, I'll come.' Hemming replied, 'Come at once.' Wavell started

by helping Kendall and then went into Third Phase work, specialising in enemy radar. He proved a genius at spotting and
identifying mysterious radio installations and within a few
months had found one of the transmitters of the Knickbein
beam, used by the Germans to guide bombers to their targets at
night. In November, Wavell identified one of the so-called Freya
radar stations near Auderville on the Cherbourg peninsula.
Finding and identifying an aerial only a few feet in size in
photo covers from the whole of occupied Europe really was
akin to finding a needle in a haystack. And Wavell was brilliant
at it.

Michael Spender, the first user of the Wild magnification
machine, had many contacts within the academic world and
the RAF recruitment programme now drew some of these figures into the world of photo interpretation. Glyn Daniel was a
young archaeologist and a Fellow of St John's College,
Cambridge. After Dunkirk, he too decided it was time to leave
academia and do his bit. He volunteered for the RAF, explaining in his application letter that from his archaeological work he
had experience of interpreting aerial photographs. He was
summoned by return of post to a meeting at the Air Ministry.
Asked how soon he could be available, he replied that he was
available immediately. So he was told to go to Horne's
menswear shop in Regent Street and buy an RAF officer's uniform there and then. As he walked down the street in his new
uniform, to his surprise two airmen saluted him. He hadn't
even been told how to salute back.[17] Three days later he went
with a group of other men to an office where they were told
there was no time for basic training or drill practice. The others
were allocated to postings all around the world – from
Reykjavik to Singapore and from Washington to Cairo. To his
utter amazement, Daniel, on the other hand, was given a travel

voucher for the Underground and told to report at once to Wembley. On his arrival at Paduoc House, which he described as a 'broken-down looking suburban factory', Peter Riddell, who was working in his shirtsleeves and braces, greeted him with the words 'Thank God they are sending us some men at last.'

Glyn Daniel and Claude Wavell were quickly trained up by Douglas Kendall. Daniel enjoyed the work immensely despite the struggle he had with understanding how to use a slide rule. Everything moved so quickly that within three weeks Daniel was in charge of a shift of photo interpreters. He spent eight months at Wembley in what he described as 'the splendid inspired madhouse of civilians and RAF and WAAF officers interpreting air photographs, making photographic mosaics, writing reports, [and] sending out annotated photographs'.[18] He was the first but would not be the last Cambridge archaeologist to spend his war interpreting aerial photographs.

Most of the new arrivals that summer were young men who were still building their careers, but in the early autumn of 1940 a quietly spoken, elderly figure arrived at Wembley. One of the founders of aerial reconnaissance in the First World War, Flight Lieutenant Hugh Hamshaw Thomas had eventually returned to Cambridge. Having built a reputation as one of the country's leading palaeo-botanists, when war was declared again in 1939 he offered his services to the Air Ministry and, with his background in PI, tried hard to get to work in that field. But with the Air Ministry giving a low priority to photo interpretation at the time, Hamshaw Thomas was allocated to general intelligence work in Lincolnshire. Eventually he managed to cut through the red tape and secured a posting to the interpretation unit at Wembley. There he began to revise the *Manual of Air Photography*, which was by now seriously out of

date. Having done this he started Third Phase work, specialising in German factories, and built up a vast card index with
photos of German war factories, along with detailed reports of
what they produced, the technologies involved, their volume
of output, and so on. As the basis of the Industry Section, this
became an invaluable resource over the next few years for the
identification of factories to be bombed. It was a long way
from the study of fossils, but it relied upon the same level of
patient observation and deductive reasoning. Soon after the
Industry Section got going, Kendall took Field Marshal Smuts,
the South African leader, on a tour of the site. Hamshaw
Thomas explained to him what he was doing and afterwards
a somewhat astonished Smuts turned to Kendall and said,
'Do you know that man is one of the best botanists in the
world.'[19]

The Photographic Interpretation Unit was always intended
to be a multi-service operation and in September 1940 it was
decided that the Army photo interpreters who had evacuated
from France after Dunkirk should join forces with the RAF
under the same roof at Wembley. Just over twenty Army interpreters with their specialist knowledge of military matters
arrived to join the growing band of brothers at the PIU and they
would form an important part of the future establishment.

But PI was not just a band of 'brothers'. A real innovation
was that women were also recognised as being particularly
skilful in the patient, detailed work of photo interpretation, and
so a group of eighteen women from the WAAF were sent to the
new unit. Up to this point women had worked as clerks, wait-
resses or in other administrative positions. They were now
asked to plot the route aircraft had taken on maps spread out
across large trestle tables. They would mark with a square each
run of photographs taken over the target area, enabling them

to plot on the map the location of each image recorded. These 'plotters' were pioneers for the many remarkable women who would be recruited into photo interpretation over the following years.[20] In these pre-PC days, Sidney Cotton had made the appallingly patronising remark that women were ideally suited for this type of work because 'Looking through magnifying glasses at minute objects in a photograph required the patience of Job and the skill of a good darner of socks.'[21] Fortunately, with the labour shortage meaning there were always too many jobs for the numbers of trained men available, the RAF were genuinely enthusiastic to recruit women as photo interpreters. On a cold, damp December morning in December 1940, a group of five WAAFs and a young and rather embarrassed Army officer arrived at Wembley to begin their two-week training course in PI. One of the WAAFs was a young journalist who had already spent some years as a female in a male environment at *The Aeroplane* magazine. Her name was Constance Babington Smith and she would go on to be probably the most famous of all the photo interpreters of the Second World War.

At Wembley, and even more so at Medmenham, women would work alongside men doing identical work. Several women, like Constance Babington Smith herself, would run their own units and were placed in command of men. Today this would not seem in any way exceptional but in 1940s wartime Britain it was nothing short of revolutionary. Women usually did menial or administrative jobs and were rarely put in charge of men in a professional setting. When they married it was standard practice for most women to leave work in order to raise a family, which counted heavily against their chances of being trained in specialist skills. Even somewhere as unusual as Bletchley Park the vast majority of women were employed as machine operators, typists or filing clerks. Women fulfilled these functions at Medmenham too, but there was an equality in photo interpretation that was absent in almost every other aspect of the war.[22] It was yet another of the features that would make Medmenham unique.

Following the Battle of Britain came the Blitz of British cities. In the suburbs of London, situated right next to major railway marshalling yards at Wembley Junction, the PIU buildings became an easy target for Luftwaffe bombers. There is no evidence that the Germans knew of the vital war work that was going on here but rogue bombs intended for the railway yards and nearby factories became an increasing risk. In the early morning of 2 October the PIU received a direct hit from a German bomb. Two weeks later the building was hit again, this time by the blast from a 500lb high-explosive bomb that landed only fifty yards away. The roof was severely damaged, and a surveyor's report noted 'serious structural damage' and that one of the external walls was at least nine inches out of line. It was predicted that another bomb might bring the whole building down.[23] The Phase Three interpreters on the top floor had to wear raincoats and put up umbrellas over their desks. In wartime people were used to putting up with discomfort, and there was relatively little moaning, but Paduoc House was no longer an appropriate location for secret intelligence work so vital to the war effort. It was clear that a move was imperative.

Heston, although it was still officially a civilian airfield, also became a target during the autumn of 1940. Doubtless the Luftwaffe had spotted the presence here of the reconnaissance Spitfires and in mid September up to a hundred incendiaries were dropped on the airfield, causing widespread damage. Later in the month the Germans dropped a delayed-action

magnetic mine, which hit with terrifying accuracy the main
hangar used by the PRU. Five valuable Spitfires, a Hudson and
a Wellington were destroyed, along with Sidney Cotton's now
legendary Lockheed that was still parked there. During
October, the Germans blitzed Heston almost nightly. The processing and printing sections where the First Phase
interpretations were carried out were three times dispersed outside the airfield but still they were hit more than once. The
room used as the officers' mess became too dangerous for the
pilots and so Geoffrey Tuttle found them accommodation in a
village a few miles away. Every evening the female night shift
plotters would carry out their work in an air raid shelter for
protection. But Tuttle stayed at his post during the raids and
when the German bombers came over he would sit alone in the
officers' mess, playing Ravel's *Bolero* loudly on the gramo-
phone.

Wembley and Heston had become too vulnerable to the
bombing and it was clear that a move away from London to a
quieter and more remote location was necessary. In addition
there was still rumbling discontent about the reorganisation of
aerial photography earlier that year following Cotton's
removal. Bomber Command felt that its specific demands for
photo reconnaissance were not being met and the Admiralty
wanted far more extensive coverage of German ports than it
was getting. As the civilians endured the bombs of the Blitz, the
planners at the Air Ministry began to devise a scheme for
organising a centralised photographic reconnaissance service of
sufficient size to meet the requirements of all the services and
of all the groups within each service. Until the autumn of 1940
the growth of photo reconnaissance had been limited by the
availability of Spitfires and trained pilots. Now more Spitfires
were coming off the production line and pilots were coming

forward. The unit that had begun with just two Spitfires had
more than twenty by September. Arguments about the precise
organisation of the service still went back and forth, but a
search began for a new and much more practical base for the
reconnaissance flights and for a far bigger home for the photo
interpreters.

After considering several airfields, the Air Ministry decided
to transfer the PR operation to RAF Benson in Berkshire.
Centrally located near London and the headquarters of Coastal
Command at Northwood in Middlesex, it was believed to be
relatively secure from air attack. In December 1940 the Spitfires
and back-up aircrews began the move from Heston to Benson
and operational flying began from there at the end of the
month. Benson would remain the home of RAF photo reconnaissance for the rest of the war.

Having settled on the move to Benson, the next task was to
locate a suitable home for the growing number of photo interpreters. This would ideally be near Benson and not far from
London. Due to the scramble of several ministries and military
establishments to find premises outside London, finding such
a site proved to be far more difficult. In November 1940, after
photo intelligence had proved itself during the invasion scare,
the military made a decision of immense long-term significance. This was to form a new Central Interpretation Unit with
the mission 'to act as a central clearing-house to which air
photographs from all sources should be submitted for interpretation and from which interpretation reports should be
issued to [all] the various ministries and service formations
concerned'.[24] This new unit was to house the PIU from
Wembley as well as the Modelling Section, based until now at
the Royal Aircraft Establishment at Farnborough. It was to produce from aerial photos all the maps, charts and models that

were required. Navy and Army photo interpretation was also to take place under its roof. Additionally, it was to take responsibility for the training of new photo interpreters and to provide a central library of all aerial photos from all sources. The new site would have to be large enough to house about four hundred men and women to start with and the intended size of the unit made finding a suitable home even more challenging.

There was still a demand from Bomber Command to retain its own separate interpretation centre at High Wycombe, and so a compromise was agreed upon at the Air Ministry. Bomber Command could interpret its own damage assessment photos but it could not report on other activities and all its photographs, once interpreted, had then to be passed on to the Central Interpretation Unit for Second and Third Phase interpretation. It was a fudge and it wouldn't survive for long. The logic of having a Central Interpretation Unit was that it had to include *all* functions. Finally in September 1941 everything came together and the specialist bomb damage interpretation unit joined the CIU. The Deputy Chief of the Air Staff commented wryly at the time, 'This takes us full circle. Originally PRU was the "Cotton Club" and a law unto itself. This was unsatisfactory so it went to Coastal Command – and was a law unto Coastal Command. Then Bomber Command naturally demanded a better share and got a PRU of its own. Now the proposal is to concentrate it again. A laborious process to rid ourselves of Cotton. But very probably the only way!'[25] The Central Interpretation Unit was to be placed under a new RAF Directorate of Intelligence that would coordinate the work of PR and PI and prioritise requests made by the various commands and government departments, as well as demands from the Joint Intelligence Committee and through it all information required directly by the War Cabinet. It would be a massive task and a vital piece in the jigsaw that made up wartime intelligence.

The search for suitable premises went on for some time. Thame Park in Oxfordshire was inspected but then the Army requisitioned it as the HQ of Southern Command. Properties in Henley and at Saunderton in Buckinghamshire were visited. But when the requirement was increased to house a staff of four hundred it was realised that all these sites were too small. Eventually the RAF requisitioned Danesfield House, a large mock-Tudor mansion overlooking the Thames from a bend in the river between Marlow and Henley. It was a peculiar structure of local white chalk with castellated towers and tall brick chimneys. The site also contained about sixty-five acres of formal gardens. The house was the third built on the site and had been finished in 1901 for industrial magnate Robert Hudson, the manufacturer of Sunlight soap. The building was already in use by Colet Court School, which had been evacuated from Hammersmith at the beginning of the war. The masters and schoolboys were now unceremoniously thrown out and the RAF moved in. Some people within the RAF thought it was unnecessary to requisition such a large property, but before long it proved not to be large enough and a crop of brick huts had to be built in the grounds to accommodate the unit's rapidly growing needs. Like all RAF stations it was named after the nearby village and therefore it was called RAF Medmenham. Moving in equipment began in early 1941 but it was very difficult to find an engineering company that, in the middle of the Blitz, had the spare capacity to dismantle and lift the delicate machinery from Wembley, particularly the huge Wild Stereo Plotter. Everything took longer than was intended. But when it was finally ready, in April 1941,

Medmenham became the base for the interpretation of aerial photographs for the RAF and later the United States. It was to remain at the centre of photo interpretation for the rest of the war.

4

Medmenham

RAF Medmenham, the newly requisitioned home of the brand new Central Interpretation Unit, opened for business at 9 a.m. on 1 April 1941. Wits enjoyed the fact that a vital resource for the intelligence war was starting up on April Fool's Day. But the move from Wembley, with its bomb-damaged buildings and leaking roofs, had taken longer than anticipated. Most of those who now settled in to the mock-Tudor mansion house with its superb gardens and spectacular views over the river Thames were overjoyed with the move. The house was spacious, very grand but also modern. It had central heating, which was pretty rare at the time. Officers were at first billeted in splendid homes all across the smart stockbroker belt between London and the Chilterns. Glyn Daniel was one of those who found himself billeted in a grand house just outside Marlow, where he was looked after by a butler who had formerly been employed by a duke. The butler brought him early morning tea each day. The owner of the house, who only reluctantly shared it with strangers, told him severely, 'I hope you are a gentleman.' Apparently, the previous lodger had been found late at night drunk in the rockery and was told to leave. He obviously was not a gentleman. Daniel knew how to behave and spent several months living there in luxury. It was about as far removed from living in London in the Blitz as could be imagined.[1]

The creation of the Central Interpretation Unit at Medmenham was a milestone in the development of photographic interpretation for military intelligence. The muddle and improvisation that had characterised the early days of PR and PI, and the confused structure that led to overlaps and rivalry, was now replaced by a large, single unit. As the official record noted, from now on 'the procurement and interpretation of air photographs became an exact science and an essential component of our intelligence organisation'.[2] From the beginning it was clear that RAF Medmenham was going to be an unusual place. The strange mix of RAF and academic qualities made it unique in the wartime military.

RAF Medmenham had been set up with an initial establishment of 114 officers and 117 other ranks. Of the hundred or so photo interpreters about one quarter were women from the WAAF. This proportion would stay about the same as the unit grew in numbers. The young WAAF officers at Medmenham, in their smart blue uniforms, became renowned throughout the military for their glamour.[3] Far more important, however, was the fact they were doing a superb job and over the next few years some of the most important work at Medmenham would be carried out by these women.

Peter Riddell remained in charge of the photo interpreters. The services of Lemnos Hemming, who had been given an honorary commission when the Aircraft Operating Company was taken over by the RAF, were now dispensed with. A new establishment needed a new commanding officer and the first to be appointed was Wing Commander Carter. There would be continuing tension between the academic nature of the place and the requirements of military discipline. But all this lay in the future and in the early days it was heads down for business.

In the early months of the war, there had been difficulty in finding the best people to become photo interpreters. It was felt that civilians were likely to possess the most useful skills but their ignorance of basic military information meant they needed a period of training in which they could learn to identify what was relevant for military intelligence. And although Riddell later tried to bring retired officers back into service, it was found that 'as a rule it was only among younger individuals that the requisite adaptability, keenness of eye and the stamina necessary for rush work were found'.[4] So there was an urgent need to train more specialist photo interpreters. Douglas Kendall had initially been given the task of setting up a school to train potential photo interpreters as quickly as possible. The relatively short two-week course that he established, like everything else, developed and changed over time, but almost everyone who worked at Medmenham needed to pass it before qualifying as a photo interpreter.

From the autumn of 1940, Pilot Officer Alfred 'Steve' Stephenson ran the training school and would do so for the rest of the war. Stephenson was in many ways typical of the new breed of photo interpreter recruited by the RAF to this rapidly expanding arm of intelligence. He had read Geography at Cambridge and was tutored by the man who had been surveyor on Scott's ill-fated expedition to the South Pole in 1911–12. Within weeks of taking his finals, Stephenson joined an expedition to survey the Arctic region of Greenland. For the next few years he explored the polar regions and even had a mountain named after him in the Antarctic. Often he would use aerial photographs to carry out the surveying work and he became familiar with the principles of photographic interpretation for mapping. He was elected a Fellow of the Royal Geographic Society, and by the age of thirty he was already a distinguished explorer when he came across some old friends working at the Aircraft Operating Company. In the winter of 1939 he expressed interest in the work they were doing and was told to get himself into an RAF uniform and to join them on the following Monday. After several months in the unit he took over the training school and by the end of the war he had run fifty-eight courses and trained some 1300 photo interpreters from all three services, setting the highest standards for the work they would go on to do. Stephenson was later awarded an OBE in acknowledgement of his enormous contribution to the science of photo interpretation.[5]

Everyone selected for work at Medmenham had first to go 'back to school' and attend the two-week course run by Stephenson. At first these courses were held at Medmenham. Later they moved to a nearby RAF establishment at Nuneham Park, another grand old house known for its marble bathroom. The course involved learning to identify objects seen from the air. Stephenson taught his students to search continually for new features that could give away evidence of what was happening on the ground below, and to be 'curious in the unusual'. Familiar objects become unfamiliar from a bird-like angle of view and everyone was taught to recognise by their size and shape what they were. Railways had to be distinguished from roads. Railways usually ran in long lines with gentle curves while roads often followed the contours of the landscape. Fighter airfields with grass runways had to be distinguished from bomber bases with more permanent taxiways. Merchant vessels had to be recognised by their oblong shape as being different from warships, which were usually sleeker, more elongated and shaped like a cigar.

Next came an introduction to the principles of stereoscopic viewing. The method of viewing two photographs slightly out of alignment created a 3D effect that made an object look real and rendered it far easier to interpret. There were several ways of creating a stereoscopic effect, but the most common was that when a reconnaissance aircraft was over its target and the pilot had turned on his cameras, they would expose the film at regular intervals calculated to allow for an overlap of 60 per cent. Every single object would therefore always be photographed twice, and in the short interval between the taking of the first and second photos the aircraft would have travelled forwards and its angle in relation to the object would have slightly changed. The photographs were then viewed in pairs through a stereoscopic viewer made up of two magnifying glasses, like a pair of spectacles, in a small frame. Using this simple device the interpreter could fuse the two images, which would almost literally come alive.

This technique took some time to learn and to perfect but it was at the core of photo interpretation. Many interpreters spoke of the 'childish thrill' when they succeeded in shuffling a pair of aerial photos into the correct position in the viewer. 'It might have taken a little time, and you felt convinced that something was wrong with your eyes, and you strained the muscles and tried squinting and then magic!'[6] Viewing a bridge or a gun emplacement, a ship or an aircraft in 3D not only made them easier to identify but also enabled the interpreter to take detailed measurements of the size of the object. The simple viewing frame with its two magnifying glasses was always called a 'Stereo', and the two matching photographic prints were referred to as a 'Stereo pair'. Stereos were the basic device used in nearly all PI. Almost every photo ever taken of interpreters at work shows them hunched over a Stereo examining a print.

The photo interpreters had a lot of fun showing off the 3D effect obtained by using a Stereo viewer. One of the interpreters had on standby a Stereo pair looking straight down on the Eiffel Tower. Whenever a visitor passed who wanted to see how they managed to interpret images he would show them these paired photos through the Stereo. He would always know when visitors got the effect. They would almost leap back from the viewing table when the Tower came into 3D, seeming to project right out of the photograph and almost poke them in the eye. When the King and Queen paid a visit to the Wembley site on 22 July 1940 for an inspection, Idris Jones demonstrated to the royal couple how a Stereo viewer worked. The Queen clearly jumped backwards when the Stereo pair came into focus and the 3D effect was achieved. She called the King over, and he spent some time moving the Stereo around to get the 3D simulation before finally announcing that he was very impressed with the effect. But Jones could tell from his body language and his failure to react on seeing the object in 3D that he had not achieved the basic requirement of the photo interpreter. Of course, Jones was discreet enough not to reveal this until after the war.[7]

The next lesson for trainee interpreters was how to work out the scale of the photographs they were examining. This was done by measuring the distance in the photograph between two identifiable objects and then comparing this to the distance between the same two objects on a map of the area with a known scale. If this was, say, 1:25,000, the comparison between the two distances could then be used to calculate the scale of the photograph. Many candidates found this arithmetic too complex to grasp. In an era long before the microprocessor and the pocket calculator, the device that was used to assist in such calculations was the slide rule, which was based on the use of logarithms. Again many photos of interpreters at Medmenham show them using slide rules. Even top professors who were not used to mathematics struggled with the use of the slide rule and one young WAAF officer wrote a 'Child's Guide in the Use of the Slide Rule (Simplified Version)' to assist her colleagues.[8] But once the scale had been worked out, then the size of every object in the photo could be measured and calculated. This was fundamental to all photo interpretation.

The interpreters went on to learn how to identify objects of key military significance from the air. In reports they were always to use a strict dictionary of military terms. 'Planes' in civilian parlance had to be classed as 'aircraft' or 'an aeroplane'. No lyrical language was to be employed. Descriptions had to be short and factual. Interpreters were encouraged to look again and again at the image to search out tell-tale signs of the enemy's activities. Disturbed areas of grass, for instance, would show up as lighter in tone than their surroundings and it was possible to see paths across a field that had been made by the constant movement of feet. Where were these feet walking to? Was there a gun emplacement in the hedges or trees where the paths led? Track activity could be spotted easily from the air, and it might reveal the existence of tanks or armoured vehicles, perhaps sheltering below camouflage. Shadows had a particular fascination for photo interpreters. They could reveal the detail of objects that could not be recognised by looking vertically down on them. For instance a radio mast or pylon seen from directly above might look like nothing much, but the shadow it cast could reveal a great amount about what it was and what it was used for. Ships that might look alike from the vertical would by their shadows reveal a detailed profile that made their identification much easier. A lot of aerial photography was carried out in the early morning or late evening, when the shadows would be at their longest. Of course, it was easy to misidentify what was happening on the ground. Many reports describing agricultural landscapes mentioned gun batteries that were in fact no more than cattle or tethered goats grazing and munching the pasture in circles. But good interpreters were able in time to distinguish between harmless farming activity and the preparations of an army at war.

Specialists would come and speak to the trainee interpreters. Michael Spender, the great expert user of the Wild machine, told the interpreters they had to learn to know at a glance what was normal so they could quickly identify what was abnormal – like the Rhine barges appearing in the Channel ports which he had identified in the summer of 1940 as a possible invasion threat. He used to tell the trainees, 'An interpreter is like a motorist driving through a town, who suddenly sees a rubber ball bouncing across the road from a side street. He can't see any children playing but he knows in a flash they are there and his brake is on. You must know what is normal, but you must also know the significance of what you see when you see it.'[9]

At the end of the short training course everyone had to take a test. Many interpreters spoke of how, by the time it came to take this test, they had learned enough about photo interpretation to feel that they really knew nothing about this complex science. In the early days, Peter Riddell used to run the exam as an oral test. Half sitting on a desk, wearing his flying boots and smoking a cigarette in a long holder, he would ask questions of each candidate in turn. When someone could not answer he would fire the same question to the person sitting next to them.

The fear of being shown up in front of your colleagues terrified everyone taking the exam, although in later years the process became more formal.

The passing-out exam put everyone under pressure. Sarah Churchill, the Prime Minister's daughter, who took the course in 1941, was in floods of tears after the exam, convinced that she had failed and let her whole family down.[10] In fact she passed and spent the next four years as a highly successful photo interpreter at Medmenham. No one who had not taken the course and passed the test was allowed to work as a photo interpreter.

What were the qualities of a good photo interpreter? Douglas Kendall believed that while the necessary skills only developed over time and it took some years for a good photo interpreter to learn his or her trade, a first-class brain was essential. This was why he recruited so many academics to the world of photo interpretation. Clearly patience, attention to detail and a strong visual memory were vital. The need for acute powers of observation was essential if an interpreter were to spot anything unusual. Along with patience came the sort of mindset that enjoyed solving problems. Elizabeth Johnston-Smith believed that photo interpretation was 'like doing a crossword puzzle – if you can solve the first one or two clues then it gets easier'.[11] Other interpreters saw it as being like a jigsaw. All the pieces of the puzzle were there in front of you on the photographs, you just had to find out what the main picture was and then you could put all the pieces together. As aerial photography involved a lot of guesswork and deductive reasoning it was rarely possible to see the whole picture. But as Kendall put it, 'in the jungle it is not necessary to see the whole elephant to know that the elephant is there.'[12]

The photo interpreters were an inventive lot, who in developing their new secret science came up with all sorts of ingenious contraptions to aid their calculations. One section responsible for the close monitoring of radio and radar towers needed to be able to measure with great accuracy the height of masts identified on aerial photos, as this often determined what sort of transmitting, jamming or radar operation the tower was used for. To do this with real accuracy required the performance of a complex mathematical sum that included knowing the latitude and the exact time of day when the photo was taken. Squadron Leader Claude Wavell, who led the section, put together an ingenious device for calculating the height of a tower from the shadow it cast on the ground. It was like a small globe made up of concentric circles of wood. The interpreter set the exact latitude of the tower and the precise date and time the photo was taken. The device then calculated first the angle above the horizon of the sun's rays. When the azimuth of the sun – that is its angle in relation to the equator – was factored in, along with the exact scale of the photograph, the device was able to calculate the height of the object by comparison to the length of its shadow. The apparatus was much admired and Wavell proudly named it an Altazimeter. He said it was as useful as a slide rule and used the basic principles of spherical trigonometry. Wavell reckoned that, crude though it was, its results – obtainable within a few minutes – were accurate to within 1 per cent of those available from detailed computations that, in the pre-computer era, could take up to thirty minutes. A poem was even written about the wonders of the Altazimeter. It began:

O wonderous spheroid gadget, now complete
With scales and whatnots properly adjusted;
Designed to help when e'er the brain with heat
From calculating heights is nearly busted ...[13]

After the war, Wavell asked the Air Ministry for some sort of recognition for the success of his invention. After several years he finally received a cheque for £25![14]

Often on good clear days pilots would fly several reconnaissance sorties. At their peak, in the run-up to D-Day, eighty sorties were being flown each day. This level of activity required a large production capability and to support this a huge team was assembled. After each reconnaissance flight the original rolls of film, with up to five hundred exposures on each roll, would arrive at Medmenham. The route of every sortie and outline plots of each set of photographs taken were traced on to small-scale maps so there was always a record of each part of occupied Europe that had been photographed or re-photographed. From this record, air cover of any part of Europe could quickly be called up at any time for comparative purposes. All the tracing was done by WAAFs and this was one of the original tasks performed successfully by women. It was precise work that required great skill and total attention to detail. A good tracer could plot about a hundred photos in an hour. The plots were then cut out and mounted on a master map for later reference. All the original photographic prints then went into the main Photographic Library. This grew at the rate of about one million photographs *each month* at the height of the war. All requests for access to this vast and growing aerial archive came to the library, sometimes up to 350 requests each day. The librarians were proud that they could find prints of cover from almost anywhere in Europe in just a few minutes.

The long rolls of film negative taken from the reconnaissance aircraft were stored in the film library. It was possible to make a new set of prints from the original negatives at any time and a huge Williamson Multiprinter from Kodak was installed to do this, printing up to a thousand photographs per hour.[15] With the war at its height the staff of the Photographic Section grew to 275 and they were producing up to 140,000 duplicate photos per month. At the end of the war the library reportedly held about seven million photographic prints from eighty thousand sorties across all parts of the world.

Communications to the airfields from where the reconnaissance aircraft flew was usually by teleprinter, an early form of instant typed written communication or texting. There was naturally a substantial top secret secure communications unit at Medmenham to receive and pass on all forms of urgent messages. A large typing pool bashed out the multitude of daily, weekly and monthly reports produced by the Central Interpretation Unit. In the era before photocopying, reports that had to go to multiple sources were usually typed out on a stencil and then printed off on circular rotating printers or duplicators. Up to one hundred copies of some reports were duplicated this way.

Backing all this up was a Central Library of reference material that any of the interpreters could refer to. This ranged from Jane's catalogues of shipping and aircraft, through detailed accounts of industrial processes, to pre-war travel guides to Germany, Italy, France and the rest of occupied Europe. It took a small army to sustain this vast operation, to feed, house and support the people and to keep the whole unit operational. By the end of the war, when the Americans were also present in force at Medmenham, there were about 550 officers and 3000 other ranks working on photo interpretation.[16]

Photo reconnaissance and interpretation was, of course, only one source of wartime intelligence. Several others were available. Prisoners were interrogated, or were left in groups and

their conversations recorded. This could reveal all sorts of valuable information. But inevitably this was random. Most of the
German prisoners in Britain in the early part of the war were
aircraft crews that had been shot down. From these POWs it
was possible to learn all sorts of valuable technical information,
for instance about the navigational aids that the Luftwaffe were
using to guide their bombers to targets on night raids. But there
was relatively little intelligence about the activities of the
Wehrmacht or of the German navy.

The most familiar form of human intelligence (HUMINT)
came from the dark world of undercover agents. They were
managed by the Secret Intelligence Service, MI6, under the
command of Sir Stewart Menzies. With the whole of northern
Europe under Nazi occupation there were many opportunities
for British Intelligence to gather information from Europeans
opposed to Nazi rule. This was the type of intelligence the SIS
preferred. Agents would approach resistance groups and an
immense amount of valuable information about German
deployments or planning was smuggled out to London. The
SIS also used the more dramatic, cloak-and-dagger method of
dropping British agents into occupied Europe, but the intelligence gained was not always as of such critical importance as
recent novels and movies might suggest. The Special
Operations Executive (SOE) was a separate arm of intelligence
that trained agents as saboteurs or assassins and dropped them
behind enemy lines to cause as much disruption as possible.
Overall, the amount of information gathered from agents was
not as much as might be imagined. And agents were notori-
ously vulnerable to the planting of false information that had
been fed to them by the enemy. The British home intelligence
arm, MI5, was spectacularly successful in this, in 'turning'
German agents in Britain and feeding back false information to

deceive the enemy. So it was necessary to cross-check in some way most intelligence gathered from agents before it could be verified.

In addition to Human Intelligence there was Signals Intelligence (SIGINT), and the SIGINT best known today came from the code breakers at the SIS Code and Cypher School at Bletchley Park. At the time this was the most secret operation of the war, and the activities of the code breakers were kept under wraps for more than thirty years, into the Cold War. Stories about their achievements only began to leak out in the mid 1970s. Now, ironically, the work carried out at Bletchley Park is one of the most famous operations of the war. The German military, the police and even some of the German railways and transport organisations used a device known as an Enigma machine to send communications in code. Although the various German organisations used different versions of the Enigma machine, they all followed the same basic principles. The operator set a series of rotor blades at the back of the machine to a different configuration every twenty-four hours. He then typed out his message and every letter was sent as a different coded letter by an open radio link. Another operator who had set his rotor blades to the same configuration would then pick up and decode the message. To decrypt the signal a code breaker would have to run through millions of possible permutations.

During the First World War British Intelligence had done brilliant work in cracking German signals but in the post-war years, like so much else, the skills built up had been run right down. In the late 1930s Polish intelligence had learnt much about the operation of the German Enigma machines and the Poles passed this information on to the French and British on the eve of war. This provided the foundation for the wartime work of the code breakers. In September 1939 the Code and Cypher School moved out of central London to a country house near the main railway line to the north that had been acquired at Bletchley Park. Here the work of code breaking and of listening to high level German communication could carry on in secret. The unlikely group of mavericks, mathematicians and other geniuses gathered at Bletchley Park devised complex electronic machines to help them decode the German signals – and along the way laid the foundations for the post-war computer industry.[17]

The intelligence gathered from breaking these codes was generically known as Ultra and it started to come on line in late May 1940, soon after Churchill became Prime Minister. He regarded the work at Bletchley Park as of enormous importance and by the end of the war ten thousand men and women were working there. The number of people who knew about the code breaking was however tiny, probably only about thirty top people in the government and the military. Even those closest to Churchill thought the yellow boxes that arrived for him almost daily and for which only he had the key, were full of information gathered from secret agents abroad. They had no idea of the existence of the code breakers at Bletchley Park. There has been much debate about the importance of the intelligence learned from Ultra over recent years but at several critical points of the war, especially in the titanic struggle with the U-boats in the Atlantic, it proved to be vital.

By comparison to the human intelligence from prisoners and agents, and the signals intelligence from the code breakers, the intelligence derived from photographic evidence had an overwhelming advantage. It was clear, objective and provided a visual record not of what was said to be going on but of what actually *was* going on. In one sense, as the old cliché has it, the camera never lies. Aerial photographs of occupied Europe recorded in detail what was really happening on the ground. Of course, it was necessary to read or interpret them correctly and both sides developed ingenious ways of trying to deceive the spies in the sky. But over the next few years the RAF excelled in developing the extraordinary skills of photo interpretation. And aerial imagery could be used to check out intelligence gathered from all the other sources. If an agent or a resistance worker reported the construction of a strange new building at a certain place, the RAF could carry out an aerial sortie over that precise location to photograph what was going on. If the description of the new building proved to be correct then the source of the information could be regarded as reliable. If signals intelligence reported the amassing of ships in a harbour, then a reconnaissance sortie could be sent over the harbour and the photographs would record whether or not the report was correct.

It had taken a huge challenge to the established way of thinking to bring about a revolution in aerial photography within the RAF. But the air force now developed some of the most sophisticated techniques for recording and interpreting aerial photography in the pre-satellite era. And at Medmenham, the RAF had created one of the most extraordinary establishments of the war. As inventive as Bletchley Park and as thorough as a university research establishment, the men and women who arrived at Medmenham were to play a vital role in the intelligence war.

5

The Mad Men of Ham

Everyone remembers their first impressions on arriving at Medmenham. To most newcomers it seemed like a hive of quiet but intense activity. The splendid rooms of the house with their high ceilings and dark wood-panelled walls were divided into separate sections into which different units were packed, creating a busy, at times frenzied atmosphere. Despite the attempts of the RAF commanding officer to impose strict discipline and smart dress, a more relaxed feeling prevailed than in many military establishments. And many of the officers working there were older than was usual in the military. They had left successful careers to do their war work with a Stereo and a set of photographs. To nineteen-year-old Elizabeth Johnston-Smith the whole place had a 'fuddy-duddy', middle-aged feel to it which she didn't like at all.[1]

Geoffrey Stone remembers that it didn't feel like a 'regimented military establishment', that it was 'much more like an academic institution full of civilians in uniform'. He noticed that no one seemed to work to the clock but that everyone was totally absorbed in their work and carried on until whatever they were doing was finished.[2] Everyone remembers this academic feel to Medmenham. When Toby Hick arrived, straight from Cambridge, the first person he saw there was his old college botany tutor.[3]

There were certainly many scholars recruited to work on PI during the war. They brought vital specialist skills, and many geologists and archaeologists had specific experience of working with aerial photography before the war. Peter Kent, for example, was a young geologist who helped to locate and assess oil storage tanks. The number of explorers working at Medmenham meant that had there been time, the RAF station could have mounted a very effective geographical expedition. Archaeologists were valued for their ability to piece together intelligence from tiny scraps of information. Glyn Daniel, the first Cambridge archaeologist to work at Medmenham, helped to recruit Dorothy Garrod in 1942. She was extremely eminent in her field and had done important archaeological work in Palestine in the 1930s. Her excavations had cast new light on the origins of *Homo sapiens*. In 1938 she was appointed Professor of Archaeology at Cambridge, the first woman ever to become a professor at either Oxford or Cambridge. At fifty, she was initially refused admission into the RAF as being over age. But when Daniel pointed out that she had been in the armed forces in the 1914–18 war an exception was made for her. She started at Medmenham in 1942 and became an expert on the movement of troops and supplies by train. But the recruitment didn't stop with her. By the middle of the war the entire Archaeology Department at Cambridge had been recruited. Along with Daniel, another of Garrod's post-war successors, Grahame Clark, also worked at Medmenham.[4] In addition, there were many botanists and engineers, as well as a Coptic scholar from Sudan.

Medmenham was also able to call upon the specialist skills of those such as Constance Babington Smith, known to friends and colleagues as 'Babs'. Having travelled to air shows all around Europe in her pre-war role as a journalist on *The Aeroplane* magazine, she would head the section on aircraft identification. Her brother, Bernard, was a brilliant mathematician who became a specialist at Medmenham in night photography. Bertram Rota, the owner of an internationally famous second-hand bookshop in London specialising in rare manuscripts and first editions, was responsible for putting together the briefing folders of aerial photographs before each bombing operation.

Douglas Kendall as Technical Control Officer was at the centre of the Medmenham operation. He was quietly spoken and many people found him quite shy. But he was a charismatic figure. Most remember him as always having a telephone in his hand. He was at the central point between, on the one hand, the customers of the Central Interpretation Unit, that is all the military units that required photo reconnaissance and interpretation, and, on the other hand, the staff and the teams of specialists at Medmenham. All requests for aerial photography, whether from the Admiralty, the War Office, the Air Ministry or from any of the operational command units of the Royal Navy, the Army or the Royal Air Force, went to the Joint Photographic Reconnaissance Committee, the JPRC. A subcommittee of the Joint Intelligence Committee, which reported to the Chiefs of Staff, this was the link between the work done at Medmenham and the direction of Britain's entire war effort. As Prime Minister, Winston Churchill would have known from the summary reports by the Joint Intelligence Committee about the key work going on with photo interpretation. The JPRC sifted and prioritised all requests, and having agreed what reconnaissance and interpretation was needed, then passed this on to Kendall. As the man responsible for the entire operational direction of Medmenham, he established the working methods and the organisation of the unit into specialist teams. Kendall was a round peg in a round hole. He had the authority to command and the skills to motivate a team of specialists. Immensely inventive in finding solutions to problems and in encouraging others to think creatively about the challenges with which they were presented, Kendall stayed in command of the operational side of the work at Medmenham until the end of the war.

The cast of characters that assembled at Medmenham were an unlikely group to be found developing a new secret science for military intelligence. Glyn Daniel described them as 'an ill-assorted collection of dons, artists, ballet designers, newspaper editors, dilettanti, [and] writers'.[5] Locals referred to the staff at Medmenham as the 'Mad Men of Ham' (a disservice to the many women present). Eccentrics seemed to abound. Villiers David was a colourful character who lived nearby and used to row across the river every day to get to work. He wore bright red braces under his blue RAF uniform. Lady Charlotte Bonham Carter, a member of the famous landed gentry family, was in her late fifties and one of the oldest interpreters at Medmenham. She managed to conform to military rules while bringing her own individual style to the RAF station. Although she wore the uniform of a WAAF section officer, she wore it in her own way with tresses of grey hair bursting out below her blue cap. Often she insisted on carrying a very un-military umbrella. Although people found her stern and forbidding, she was no snob. When instructed to visit London she would hitch-hike from Medmenham. On leaving the base and waiting for a suitable jeep, the corporal on the gate would ask her where she was heading and she would reply in her imperious voice, 'To the Air Ministry, please, young man.'[6]

Joining Medmenham as a young WAAF officer at the end of 1941 was the Prime Minister's second daughter, Sarah. She went by the name of Sarah Oliver, but everyone knew her as Sarah Churchill. Rebellious as a teenager, Sarah was nicknamed 'Mule' by Winston and Clemmie because of her stubborn nature. After two years at a school of dancing she had started to work in the theatre, to the concern of her parents who didn't think this was a suitable career. She appeared in a succession of West End shows and revues and in one performed as a dancing girl in the chorus line, wearing a short skirt and frilly knickers. In the finale she had to turn upstage and bow, presenting her frilly bottom to the audience. At one of these revues she met Vic Oliver, a Viennese comedian. They decided to marry but her parents were strongly opposed to the union. Oliver was nearly twice Sarah's age, his divorce had not properly come through and Winston was concerned that, as an Austrian, his nationality would be an issue if Britain went to war with Germany and Austria. They eloped to New York and after Vic's divorce was ratified they married on Christmas Eve, 1936. Returning to England, they continued with their stage careers. But it was not a happy marriage. By 1941, it had broken down completely and Winston accepted Sarah back into the family. Deciding she wanted to do her bit in the war, she chose the WAAF because of the colour of the uniform. She worked as a clerk for several months before being commissioned and then, aged twenty-one, took the PI course at Nuneham Park. At first she worked in the section that monitored enemy shipping but she went on to work successfully in several other sections during the war.[7]

Sarah was a redhead, lively and popular but in no way grand, and she never seems to have pulled rank on the other PIs. She appears to have genuinely enjoyed the companionship she found at Medmenham. Working intensely hard there she discovered a job satisfaction that was new to her and she felt valued and appreciated by her peers. She wrote to her father in September 1942 that 'they have allowed me to understand at Medmenham, that I am beginning to be useful to them', concluding quite humbly, 'I love the work and feel I have a real job.'[8] She still kept up her social life, making several trips to London to visit theatrical friends, and on Sundays she sometimes joined her parents at the Prime Minister's country retreat at Chequers, not far from Medmenham. On one occasion she asked Len Chance, a young photo interpreter who had a Hillman sports car, for a lift. He said he would love to drive her but he had no petrol. She took him to a nearby garage that was used by the Prime Minister's car on its journey to Chequers and told the garage owner, 'Give him two of Daddy's!' Len got his petrol and Sarah got her lift.[9]

With so many artists working at Medmenham it's perhaps not surprising that there was a lively social life, with many concerts and theatrical evenings put on by the interpreters themselves. Often the composers working at Medmenham – these included Humphrey Searle and Robin Orr, the organist at St John's College, Cambridge – wrote the music for the concert shows. Sometimes the choreography was organised by the dancer Frederick Ashton, who spent his war years at Medmenham and later founded the Royal Ballet. Almost everyone remembers the shows as being of a very high standard. Sometimes the theatrical revues managed to satirise the leading figures at Medmenham in a comic, entertaining way.[10] The actress Pauline Growse was also there and in early 1944 a strikingly handsome

young man named Derek van den Bogaerde arrived. He went on
to become probably the most famous of the Medmenham
alumni after the war as the movie star Dirk Bogarde.

Occasionally there were concerts featuring famous performers who were known by one of the photo interpreters and
had been invited to come down from London. Sarah Churchill
invited several leading figures from the West End theatre, as
well as classical musical performers like Sir Malcolm Sargent
and the celebrated Ukrainian-born pianist Benno Moiseiwitsch.
Before one of his concerts, the piano at Medmenham was
judged to be inappropriate for the maestro after too much
rough handling by amateur performers. Lady Charlotte
Bonham Carter offered the use of one of her own grand pianos
that was in store for the duration. The piano duly appeared and
was tuned by Robin Orr. Soon after the beginning of the concert
one of the piano wires broke, waving in the air precariously
while Moiseiwitsch carried on to the end of the piece. Several
people thanked the Ukrainian for his superb playing. 'Thank
you for ruining my piano,' said Lady Charlotte. Moiseiwitsch
shrugged his shoulders, implying that, sadly, such things
happen in war.[11]

Not everyone found life at Medmenham appealing. The
hours were long, the work was hard and the pressure was
relentless. The station worked day and night, twenty-four
hours a day, every day of the year. The standard shift pattern
was twelve hours on and twenty-four hours off. Those who
were regularly required to work nights worked on a shift pattern of twelve hours on from 8 p.m. to 8 a.m. and thirty-six
hours off, so they would be fresh for their next night shift. There
was always a sense of urgency about completing reports.
Howard Pickard, a geology graduate from Leeds University
who had worked with aerial photographs, was 'snapped up' by

Medmenham in the autumn of 1943. He went into First Phase and enjoyed the work, but he found the pressure too much and after a couple of months asked for a transfer abroad. Sent to the PI operation in India, he worked on First Phase interpretation in Calcutta. He went on to lead a distinguished career in RAF Intelligence after the war, serving in the Far East, in Britain, Germany and the Middle East. Medmenham had just not been for him.[12]

Mostly, the interpreters at Medmenham ate in the officers' mess and the non-commissioned staff in their separate mess. Meals were produced using rationed food and no one recalls them as being anything special. Bacon and sausages were a treat. Lady Bonham Carter seems to have found the rations particularly meagre. Many PIs remember her as always being hungry. She would gather up any food left over at breakfast in a string carrier bag and keep it for her elevenses or mid-morning break. She had the carrier bag with her at all times, even when on parade.[13] A rare luxury was tea on one of the terraces of the old mansion house overlooking the river. But everyone put up with the conditions. There was no alternative.

Drinking was an important part of RAF culture and the local pubs, the Dog and Badger and the Mace and Hounds, were popular haunts. But of course no one was ever allowed to talk shop in the local for fear that enemy informers were listening in. Everyone was told not to talk about their work to others, they were to 'Keep Mum' as the wartime phrase had it.

Security at Medmenham was paramount. As a vital arm of military intelligence no one could discuss with anyone else the work they were doing. PIs in one section had no idea what those in another section did. In this, Medmenham was again like Bletchley Park. One Sunday in early November 1942, Sarah Churchill went to Chequers on a short leave. She arrived in the early evening and as she was in uniform she did not have to dress for dinner like the others. Her father was keen to see her and summoned her up to his bathroom, where with a large fluffy towel discreetly wrapped around him he was getting out of the bath and his valet Sawyers was helping him dress for dinner. As he combed the few hairs across the dome of his head, the Prime Minister reflected out loud that the Anglo-American landings in North Africa known as Operation Torch were about to begin. 'At this very minute,' he said gravely, 'sliding stealthily through the Straits of Gibraltar under cover of darkness, go five hundred and forty-two ships that are carrying our troops for the landings in North Africa.' 'Five hundred and forty-three,' interrupted Sarah. 'How do you know that?' asked Winston in astonishment. 'I've been working on Operation Torch for three months,' replied his daughter. 'Why didn't you tell me?' asked the Prime Minister. 'Because we were told not to mention it to anyone,' replied the photo interpreter. 'I believe there is such a thing as security.' Churchill was much impressed with his once wayward daughter.

As an epilogue to the incident, the Prime Minister often repeated the story as a sign of how secret was the work being done at Medmenham. He told the story to Eleanor Roosevelt, the US First Lady, who was as impressed as Churchill himself had been. She in turn repeated it in America during a speech about women's war work in Britain. When the speech was reported in Britain, Sarah was called in before officials for a reprimand for breach of security. Asked who had revealed to Mrs Roosevelt that top secret work on the Torch landings had been done by photo interpreters, she explained that it was her father who had passed on the story. The officials decided that no further action should be taken against her.[14]

Despite the mix of talented and eccentric people working at

RAF Medmenham and the studious or academic atmosphere that everyone who worked there describes, the station was still a military establishment playing a vital role in the top secret world of intelligence. There was a constant underlying tension between the discipline needed to run a unit working for military intelligence and the relaxed culture of the specialists who brooded for hours staring at aerial photographs with their Stereo viewers and came up with brilliant devices to aid their interpretation. Group Captain Carter, Medmenham's first CO, wanted to run the place like a regular RAF establishment – an impossible task given the eclectic nature of many of the specialists who worked there. He soon became unpopular with many of his men. After a heavy night shift, Glyn Daniel had gone down to the Dog and Badger for breakfast one morning and was sitting on the local churchyard wall with his uniform open and not wearing his hat when the CO happened to drive by. The next morning he was called in to Carter's office and reprimanded, being told that discipline and the proper dress code must at all times be observed.[15]

But despite the occasional flare-up, life at Medmenham largely rolled along happily, focused on the primary task of PI. Wing Commander Peter Stewart replaced Carter as station commander in early 1942. Stewart made himself unpopular with the Air Ministry, and at Medmenham he was known to have had various liaisons with WAAF officers, which was of course considered entirely inappropriate. So it was decided to appoint a new CO in August 1943. Group Captain Francis Cator, the new station commander, had a record of bringing proper RAF discipline to bear in the units he ran. The Chief of Intelligence at the Air Ministry summoned Cator from Training Command and, as Cator wrote later, charged him with the mission of 'sorting out' Medmenham.[16] It was a strange brief as

only in the eyes of the staunchest, died-in-the-wool discipli-
narian could it have been perceived that Medmenham was
broken and therefore needed fixing. But Cator set about trying
to make the PI centre operate a bit more like an orthodox military establishment.

When he arrived, Cator was surprised to be met by an
'extremely comely WAAF officer' who introduced herself as his
personal assistant. He was used to being attended to by male
ADCs or batmen and enquired what her duties would be.
These, he later recalled, struck him as being 'of a rather personal nature and not, as far I could see, closely connected with
my job as Station Commander'. He told the WAAF officer that
his wife and daughter would soon be joining him at
Medmenham and that they would look after him. He sent her
back to PI work, to which she returned, he remembered, without 'any noticeable enthusiasm'.

Cator was surprised to learn of the remarkable work being
carried out at Medmenham, of which he had known nothing
before arriving. He was impressed by the mix of characters
working on PI but realised on meeting them that his ideas of
discipline and theirs were very different. Everywhere he
seemed to sense that people were slacking and trying to get out
of hard work. Cator is pretty well the only person ever to have
felt this about the people and the amount of work being done
at Medmenham, where long shifts often meant people worked
up to fifty-four hours per week. Most interpreters remained on
duty until they had finished what they were doing, taking little
notice of time, and if on the following day the workload was
lighter they would arrive a little late for the next shift. Cator
was definitely not happy about this arrangement and lectured
the dons and PI experts on the need for punctuality. He
instructed the RAF Police on the main gate to take the names of

latecomers. Anyone absent for duty was ordered to be brought before him. Cator remembered, forty years later, how much this was 'resented'[17] – hardly surprising, bearing in mind that most photo interpreters were civilians in RAF uniforms who had left successful careers to do their bit for the war effort.

Another of Cator's first actions was to organise a station parade and march past. Kit inspections and parades were regular fare at most RAF stations but were unheard of at Medmenham. For the Army and Navy personnel on the station this posed no challenge. They had all been through basic training and knew how to march and how to parade. But most of the RAF specialists had been called out of universities or industry and, in the RAF way, had been given no basic military training at all. Civilians one day, they were RAF officers the next. As the day of the parade approached, rising levels of panic spread among many of the RAF officers. Lady Bonham Carter was one of those particularly alarmed by the prospect. She told a young officer, Len Chance, who had been through basic training, 'I've got to do a parade.' Len showed her exactly what she had to do to organise her team. Filled with a new confidence she got her section together, instructed them to 'Fall in' and with great enthusiasm announced she was ready to go on parade.[18] It is not recorded whether she had her umbrella with her or not.

When the morning for the station parade came there was a dispute as to how the different units should line up. The Royal Navy, as the senior service, insisted on leading the parade. The Army officers present, who were very cynical of the ability of the Navy and the air force to 'do military', insisted they should be second. The RAF teams began to line up in third place. The Army quickly formed in sections behind their section leaders. In no time they had reported to the adjutant, 'All present and correct, sir!' At which point, the adjutant replied, 'Very good, carry on.' The Army officers took this as an instruction to begin and ordered their men to march off. This they did, but the adjutant realised that no one else was ready and ran after them to call them back. It was at this moment that Group Captain Cator happened to come round the corner, to be greeted by the sight of the adjutant running after the senior Army officer, calling his men to come back and start again. He was not amused.

But the misunderstanding with the Army was only the beginning. When everyone had finally formed up, the parade began. However, so many people were there, including the many other nationalities present, Norwegians, Danes, Dutch, Poles and of course by this time a large contingent of Americans, that they could not all assemble in the field that had been set aside for the purpose. So the Americans and some of the others had to form up separately in a lane through a nearby wood. The main contingent marched forward on the command and when it entered the grounds of the camp turned down the north drive to march around to the front of Danesfield House. Unfortunately, they had chosen the wrong direction. The dais on which Group Captain Cator stood, ready to take the salute, had been set up at the end of the south drive. So when the first section of the parade marched up they passed by the saluting base from the rear. When the Americans who had formed up down the lane approached the house, they took the correct south drive. And so, adding insult to the injury of the confusion, they crossed the first group in front of the dais, on which Cator had by now turned around bravely trying to take an orderly salute, and had his back to them.[19] Cator was furious.

There were no further parades for some time. Fortunately,

parade ground prowess was not a requirement for PI skill. Once the fiasco was over and the giggles had died away, the specialists returned to their work, and life at Medmenham carried on as normal.

6

Boffins at War

After the instant First Phase interpretation to pick out any urgent military information, within twenty-four hours aerial photographs were taken to Medmenham where the interpreters gave them a more detailed Second Phase analysis. Second Phase at Medmenham soon grew into a large team situated in one of the palatial halls. It operated around the clock, producing daily summary reports of activities on enemy airfields, on the railways, in the shipyards and anywhere else that was a military priority at the time. Only when the Second Phase interpreters had finished with the photographs were they passed on to the specialised Third Phase. This was broken down into many different sections. A Section dealt with the analysis of enemy shipping. This had been vital to the work of photographic interpretation from the beginning of the war in establishing the whereabouts of the German fleet. Indeed, the Admiralty's appreciation of photo reconnaissance had been a great boost in the face of RAF indifference. By 1941 the CIU had built up a team of dedicated specialists who could not only identify the enemy's warships but also keep a detailed tally of the patterns of merchant shipping in occupied Europe. Medmenham was charged with watching a long list of ships that included the battleship *Tirpitz*, the battle cruisers *Scharnhorst* and *Gneisenau* and a range of cruisers and smaller ships. The interpreters also had to report on torpedo boats, E-boats, minesweepers, escort vessels and five separate classes of destroyers.

David Brachi, one of the original employees of the Aircraft Operating Company, became a key figure in A Section at Medmenham. He spotted a new class of German destroyer, the Elbing class, which was smaller than the other classes, 330ft rather than 410ft. Moreover he noted in his report that this new class of vessel had an additional gun between its two funnels. The Admiralty simply disbelieved this claim, as the use of a gun between the funnels had been tried in the First World War and had proved ineffective. So the Admiralty told Brachi he had made a mistake, and invited him to amend his report and remove the reference to the gun. Brachi refused, insisting that he had photographic evidence proving the gun was there and that he could not change his report to reflect the views of the admirals, 'as to do so would undermine the integrity of photographic interpretation'.[1] He was brave to insist on his interpretation, and he was soon proved correct when a French photograph taken at sea level proved the existence of the new gun, just where Brachi said it was.

Merchant ships were another category and were divided into five classes, from large passenger liners down to small tramps and coasters. The interpreters put together a card index of drawings and photographs of every known merchant ship and recorded details of regular shipping routes. In today's world of powerful databases this might seem a cumbersome way of collecting data, but through such painstaking, careful work it was possible to follow specific merchant ships as they chugged back and forth along their regular trade routes. From 1941, every port in Europe was photographed at least once a week if possible. The interpreters kept charts of the movement of ships, and by observing which part of the port was used by each ship they could usually tell what commodities the ship carried – food, fuel, armaments, or whatever. Even if the name of the ship wasn't known it could be given a number and closely monitored. The science of photographic interpretation was in knowing what was normal in order to be able to spot what was unusual. If a ship loaded with coal left one port for another every week and then it was noticed that two ships a week were making the same journey, the question had to be asked, why? What was going on near the second port that required a doubling of its supply of coal?

David Brachi soon developed a specialism in watching and monitoring the building of U-boats in the various German shipyards at Kiel, Hamburg, Bremen and elsewhere. He could identify each stage in the building of the standard five-hundred-ton U-boat in use at the beginning of the war. The process began with the laying of the keel, which had a characteristic long, narrow shape that was always a giveaway. Then followed the construction of the superstructure, and finally the launch of the vessel and its fitting out. The Germans used the same methodical production process in every shipyard and although parts of the process were camouflaged, this too was clearly identifiable from the air. Brachi knew that each U-boat took about eight months to build, from laying the keel to launch. There were then about three months of trials before the U-boat passed into service. So Brachi was able not only to monitor the U-boats' progress but also to forecast the output of U-boat construction, from the moment a keel was laid down, for nearly a year ahead.

Brachi couldn't see every yard where the submarines were built, but in early 1941 he noticed a doubling of production capacity in the shipyards he could observe. Knowing that this was likely to be matched in the other yards, he wrote a report in February 1941 predicting that production of U-boats would double by the end of the year. This went straight to Admiral Godfrey, the Head of Naval Intelligence, and from him to Admiral Dudley Pound, the First Sea Lord, who brought it to the attention of the Chiefs of Staff. And so the Prime Minister soon got to hear of the alarming forecast. Churchill was extremely worried about the U-boat threat to Britain, as he knew the nation relied on the import of raw materials like fuel, chemicals and foodstuffs for its very survival. He later wrote, 'The only thing that ever really frightened me during the war was the U-boat peril. I was even more anxious about this battle than I had been about the glorious air fight called the Battle of Britain.'[2] When he received the report on the huge increase in U-boat production, Churchill created a special War Cabinet Committee of scientists and senior naval staff to tackle the challenge of what he now called the Battle of the Atlantic, declaring that this battle would be as important to Britain as the Battle of France or the Battle of Britain had been.[3] David Brachi's photographic intelligence report was a key element in sparking off this new campaign.

Another ingenious discovery by A Section was how to calculate the speed of a ship by analysing the waves it created in its wake. Bryan Westwood was a young naval lieutenant who had spent years at sea in convoys before joining Medmenham. He contacted the nearby University of Reading, who found in the papers of a nineteenth-century physicist a study of wave patterns and their relation to the speed of vessels through water. At whatever speed it travels at, a ship's wake sends out waves at precisely the same angle. Using this old research Westwood was able to calculate that the spacing of the waves within the pattern created in a ship's wake would increase in the ratio of the square of any increase in speed. As the waves of a ship's wake could clearly be seen on an aerial photograph, it was possible to calculate its speed by taking the square root of the measurement of the spacing of the waves and then applying this to a table of speeds that could be calculated beforehand. Westwood was able to prove his theory by obtaining aerial photographs of a Royal Navy cruiser on its speed trials.

This could have been of immense value in identifying, say, from a photo of a group of warships heading out to attack a convoy how long it would take for them to reach their target. The only trouble was that the Admiralty was very sceptical of Westwood's findings and made little use of this brilliantly clever innovation. That was until the whole process had been taken over by the Americans and proven in Washington after far more extensive trials and assessments than had been possible at Medmenham. It was yet another example of the inventiveness of the teams who worked on photo interpretation, and Westwood was pleased that his theory had been proved correct. But he was outraged that the Admiralty had only believed the Americans and not their own staff.[4]

F Section did for the railways of occupied Europe what A Section did for shipping. It was started by Ron Moody, an Army captain from the Royal Engineers who had worked for the LNER (London and North Eastern Railway) before the war. He gathered as much reference information as he could about Europe's railways by collecting timetables, guides and maps. At Medmenham the section soon grew and was filled with railway experts who were able to identify the special types of railway trucks used for carrying items such as chemicals, coal, fuel, arms or naval guns. Other members of the team worked on roads and waterway transport. Again the team were able to build up a detailed understanding of the patterns in which freight moved around occupied Europe. They were also able to study the vulnerability of marshalling yards, depots, bridges and viaducts, and analyse the effect of bombing on the railways. They could follow how quickly the railway system was able to recover from a raid or how effective a bombing mission had been in causing congestion. It was soon discovered that the Germans were very quick at repairing damage to marshalling yards, but that it took much longer to repair a bridge or viaduct, and so bombing these led to greater disruption. It was joked that F Section could tell you anything you wanted to know about the railways of Europe – except the time of the next train from Marlow to Paddington!

Both A and F Sections worked closely with the model-making team. Model making had started in the Camouflage section at the Royal Aircraft Establishment in Farnborough but joined the Central Interpretation Unit when Medmenham opened for business. Initially the section was based in the basement of Danesfield House. The wine cellar, the stores and other accoutrements of the basement of a grand country house were moved out and tables, fret saws, hammers and all the workings of a carpenter's workshop were brought in. The team who made up the small Model Section had mostly been sculptors or artists before the war. They were led by Geoffrey Deeley, a successful sculptor, and he was supported by several painters, engravers, a medical illustrator and a famous silversmith, Leslie Durbin. The presence of these well-known and talented artists added further to the colourful life at RAF Medmenham.

This section interpreted aerial photographs in a different way from the rest of the photo interpreters, by creating 3D models from them. They made models of ships, aircraft, tanks, military vehicles, buildings, military installations, even railway engines and trucks, which gave life to the 2D photographs and were used as recognition models to help new PIs identify the objects concerned. But the section soon began to produce models of whole landscapes that could be as big as twenty feet square. These included models of beaches and cliffs to be used in preparation for amphibious landings, of ports and harbours in the planning of air raids, or of specific places, buildings or radio transmitters for use in the detailed planning of a commando raid.

Each terrain model was made by building up the contours of the area using hardboard cutouts, mounted layer by layer on the model's base board. Accuracy was essential if the model was to be of any use and aerial photos or pre-war maps provided the detailed outline of the contours. The model makers prepared everything to a precise scale, carefully calculating the size of each part of the model. Then they laid a plastic or rubber surface over the crude layered hardboard model to smooth the landscape and make it look real. Sometimes they used new plastics like PVC or polystyrene. Next they would lay a mosaic of vertical aerial photographs over the contour model, an extremely skilful job as several photos usually had to be cut out to give the 3D model its photographic skin. This would then be painted to turn the black and white photographs into a real colour landscape with roads, rivers, trees, woods and fields. Finally small models of key buildings or installations were made separately and stuck on in position. Everything more than about four feet high was modelled and added in. Anything below this height, like a hedge, was simply painted on. On the surviving models the buildings appear like matchsticks on their side and every single building has the exact proportions of the original. At every stage, specialists from the Third Phase were called in to ensure that the model was as accurate as the interpreters could make it.[5]

The section made more than 1400 models during the war, and they were used extensively in the briefing of pilots, seamen, soldiers and special forces before missions. Sometimes the models were photographed, often with a lighting rig that replicated exactly what a location might look like, for instance, to a bomber pilot on a moonlit night. Sometimes, as in the build-up to D-Day, multiple copies of the same model had to be made, so a plastic mould was taken from the master model and duplicates were produced from this. The highly specialised work was very time-consuming and soon the section grew from a dozen or so artists and sculptors to a team of eleven RAF and WAAF officers and fifty-five other ranks. It rapidly outgrew the basement and after a brief stint in an outstation by the river at Henley, moved back into large workshops in the grounds of Danesfield House. In the run-up to D-Day the requests for models were so numerous that the section grew even larger, but always the work was checked and double-checked to ensure accuracy. Ninety-seven separate models were made in preparation for the Normandy invasion and General Eisenhower paid special tribute to the work of the model makers in their contribution to the victory.

The Model Making Section brought together craft skills with the imaginative talents of professional artists on an industrial scale of production. Its work represented not only one of the most delightful and detailed but also one of the most artistic, tactile and creative manifestations of the interpretation of aerial photography. Today the work could be carried out in a virtual form in a matter of hours with computer-generated imagery, but in wartime Medmenham the models produced were real, beautiful and remarkable tributes to the creativity and inventiveness of wartime Britain.[6]

C Section was devoted to the study of the enemy's airfields, its interpreters gathering detailed information about all of the Luftwaffe's airfields across occupied Europe. There were four hundred bases from which German aircraft could attack Britain. And there were hundreds more in the Mediterranean, both for the Luftwaffe and the Italian air force.

Fighter aircraft usually flew from smaller bases with grass landing strips, while concreted runways usually signified the presence of bombers or heavy transport aeroplanes. The interpreters built up a record of the aircraft flown from each airfield, along with their battle order, and carefully tabulated the serviceability and readiness of the aircraft. The result was that at any point the team at Medmenham could provide photographic cover of a specific airbase or could report on the preparedness of the enemy to mount air activity in a particular region.

The interpreters kept a close watch on the expansion of airfields, recording the extension of runways or the building of new hangars or taxiways. Interpreters had to know their aircraft types, again measuring in detail tiny outlines to confirm the type of aircraft at each base or to identify new types as they were introduced. Often the introduction of new aircraft was anticipated by changes to airfields. For instance, in late 1943 when the Germans began to prepare for jet aircraft, it was necessary to lengthen runways and to adapt the fuelling facilities. The interpreters spotted all of this on aerial photographs and were able to make predictions as to the location and approximate numbers of new aircraft that would be deployed on each

A-type camera handed to the observer in a Vickers FB5. He had to lean out the side, take the photo and then change the glass plate before taking another.

Aerial photo mosaic of the Passchendaele Front, 1918. The infantry never went forward without a trench map made from a photo mosaic.

Sidney Cotton in Wing Commander's uniform, right, with Air Marshal Sir Arthur Barratt, in France, 1940. Cotton revolutionised photo reconnaissance but fell out with everyone.

A reconnaissance Spitfire alongside F52 cameras fitted with 36-inch lenses. Each photo taken by these cameras at 30,000 feet covered an area of about a square mile with such detail that vehicles could clearly be seen on the ground.

The Swiss-built Wild A5 Stereo Plotter. A big machine that was able to measure the smallest detail.

Aircraft Operating Company offices in Wembley. The sandbags did not protect the building from major damage when the bombs began to fall.

Barges gathering at Dunkirk harbour, September 1940. The photo interpreters were duly alarmed. But was it evidence of a real threat of invasion?

Danesfield House, RAF Medmenham, photographed in 1945. See all the huts and buildings at the back and to the west of the house.

Model makers at work at Medmenham on a model of Kiel harbour. See the incredible detail of streets and houses.

Constance Babington Smith who ran the Aircraft Section – she and her team found the V-1.

Sarah Oliver, right, better known as Sarah Churchill – the Prime Minister's daughter who found job satisfaction as a PI.

Claude Wavell with magnifying glasses – he found the key enemy radar and radio masts, some of the smallest objects discovered from aerial photos.

Kay Henry with the Altazimeter – Wavell's invention to measure the shadows of tiny objects by working out the angle of the sun.

Adrian 'Warby' Warburton – as usual, looking casual in Malta.

Tony Hill – famous for his low-level dicing sorties.

Maurice 'Shorty' Longbottom – he came up with some of the ideas that helped to transform photo reconnaissance.

The cockpit of a PR Spitfire – the camera controls are where the gunsights would have been.

Michael 'Babe' Suckling – the pilot who found the *Bismarck* and *Prinz Eugen* hidden in the Norwegian fjords.

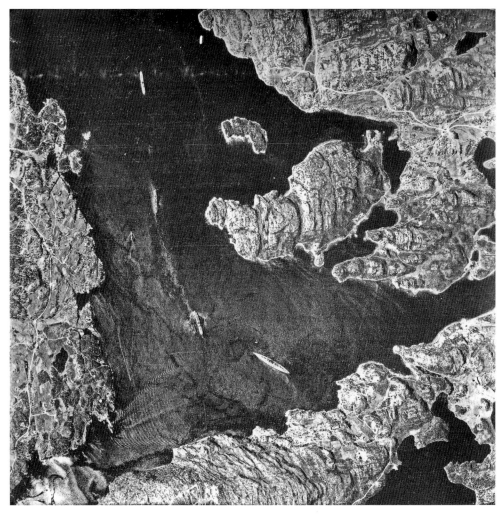

Michael Suckling's photo of the *Bismarck* with support ships in Grimstadfjord, south of Bergen, 21 May 1941. This was called 'the picture that sank a battleship'. (All photographs courtesy of the Medmenham Collection)

airfield. This section was initially led by a WAAF, Flight Officer Hammerton, before coming under the command of another WAAF officer, Ursula Powys-Lybbe. She remembered that very little information about the broader implications of German airfields was ever passed on to her section because Air Ministry Intelligence wanted to keep news of all developments top secret. As a consequence, Powys-Lybbe later said she and her team felt they were often working 'in the dark' when it came to developments in German aviation that would have helped them interpret what they were seeing. After a visit to the Air Ministry she managed to improve the flow of information, but yet again this was a sign of the often unfriendly attitude of the intelligence world to the still very new science of photographic interpretation.[7]

The work of the airfield team was closely linked to that of L Section, or the Aircraft Section. Formed just before the move to Medmenham, this was put under the command of another formidable WAAF officer, Constance Babington Smith. Having been an aviation journalist before the war, she had wanted to specialise in aircraft identification. But there was no special unit dedicated to the subject, only the team devoted to studying German airfields. She soon picked up the skills necessary to identify enemy aircraft from an aerial photograph, even fighters, which sometimes showed up in the photos as no bigger than a pinhead. She bought her own special Leitz magnifying glass from a jeweller in order to examine such tiny objects. In early 1941 she wrote a report on Italian military aircraft and on the following day was summoned to see Squadron Leader Peter Riddell. Fearing that he was about to reprimand her for some terrible gaffe, she cautiously went in to see her senior officer, who surprised her by saying that her report had made him realise how important aircraft recognition was going to be. He asked her to head a new aircraft team, and the Aircraft Section was born there and then.[8]

At Medmenham, L Section was based in the west wing of the house, which was covered with a mass of mauve wisteria. Its sweet scent drifted in through the windows in spring and summer, filling the air with a very un-warlike perfume. The work done by Babington Smith's team soon provided an important contribution to the war effort. They spotted new types of aircraft, often while still in prototype, following them through their air trials and making predictions as to when they would become operational. The interpreters kept a close watch on the hangars at Rechlin, the German equivalent of Farnborough, where experimental aircraft were stored. They also carried out identification and close monitoring of the factories at which different aircraft were made. Every month the section produced a report on new aircraft types and the activity at the aircraft factories, along with a prediction of future aircraft output.[9]

In 1941, fearing an airborne invasion of Britain, Babington Smith and her team were told to look out for enemy gliders. They soon discovered the existence of a new type of glider, approximately twice the size of those that had been used in the blitzkrieg the year before. It was estimated that this new giant could probably carry a small tank or armoured vehicle. With good aerial cover and the use of the new camera lenses available from 1941, an interpreter could usually measure the wingspan of an aircraft on the ground to an accuracy of one or two feet. So it was usually possible to spot a new model. And when jet aircraft trials began it was possible to see where they were carried out, as they left tiny strips of burnt grass behind where the engines had been tested. From 1943 Babington Smith and L Section would play a vital role in the discovery of the Nazi V weapons programme (see Chapter 15).

Of course, all of this aerial observation did not take place without the Germans knowing that Allied aircraft were looking down into their backyard, and they made extensive attempts to camouflage what was happening on the ground. Lines were drawn across runways to make them look like hedges, in an effort to disguise the area around an airfield as farmland. Factories or ships were covered with vast nets, sometimes painted in the shape of a suburban housing estate or something equally harmless. Designed to work using the colours of the local landscape, these techniques were often successful in disguising what was below to Allied aircraft flying overhead. However, in black and white photographs the shapes and camouflage designs could be spotted more clearly, as they had a different tonal quality from the neighbouring 'real' landscape. Often in time the paint began to wear or to peel off and gave the game away to the photo interpreters, although the camouflage was still effective to a pilot looking down while flying by at high speed. Comparative covers of an area also revealed the use of camouflage – in one cover there would be, say, an armaments factory and a month later the same site would apparently be green fields or a forest. Pilots overhead would never know this, but the PIs could easily spot the pretend transformation.

Camouflaging or disguising ships rarely deceived the trained eye of a photo interpreter, although it was very effective in concealing them from pilots or other mariners, whether at sea or below the sea, looking from the periscope of a submarine. Dazzle camouflage was particularly effective in disguising from other vessels a ship moving fast at sea. In February 1942 the *Prinz Eugen* was at Brest harbour lying up with the *Scharnhorst* and *Gneisenau*, preparing for their dramatic dash up the Channel. The RAF flew reconnaissance sorties over Brest almost daily to keep a watch on the German warships. In an effort to confuse British Intelligence, the Germans built a dummy *Prinz Eugen* which was to remain behind after the real warship had slipped away at night. They used an old French cruiser, with two additional vessels attached at the stern to add the extra length. The effect was to create a reasonable imitation when viewed from directly above, although the joins in the hull could still be seen and an oblique photograph of the harbour gave the whole game away. A lot of work went into the disguise, but in vain.[10]

E Section at Medmenham was devoted to identifying the different types of camouflage and to advising pilots what to look out for. It was headed by another WAAF officer, Molly Thompson, nicknamed 'Tommy', who would often brief other interpreters how to spot German camouflage after studying their latest techniques. According to Douglas Kendall, camouflage rarely misled the photo interpreters and an experienced PI could quickly spot the different types used by the Germans, so its use would do nothing except draw attention to the importance of a location.[11]

However, it took longer to spot a more successful form of mirage. One afternoon Kendall, then in charge of Second Phase, was studying aerial photos of some open fields near the German town of Soest, to the east of the heavy industry of the Ruhr valley, when he spotted something new. He showed the photo to his colleague Geoffrey Dimbleby, a cousin of Richard Dimbleby, the founder of the Dimbleby media clan and at the time a famous BBC war reporter. The photo showed dozens of bomb craters across empty fields. 'What do you think?' asked Kendall. 'One of the Ruhr raids gone wrong, isn't it,' suggested Dimbleby. Kendall realised the bombs had been dropped on the wrong site but he had spotted something else. In the corner of the fields were three shapes, each about the size of a large barn. Kendall had found a decoy. The shapes were three fire sites, set ablaze when bombers approached to draw off their attention from the industrial targets to the west. Many bombers simply dropped their bombs where they saw fires raging. In Britain, the same technique had been used during the Blitz to draw enemy bombs away from city centres. Dimbleby got to work studying the photographs and found that each of the three rectangles was without a roof and was surrounded by a wall five feet high – this could be measured from the shadows. Inside were quantities of what looked like straw, which was set alight during a bombing raid. From twenty thousand feet at night this would make the area look like a mass of burning buildings and attract the attention of the passing bombers, who would then direct their bombs to what they took to be their already burning target.

Dimbleby began to study the countryside around all the major industrial targets and soon identified dozens of decoy sites. Most were surrounded by bomb craters, illustrating how successful they had been in attracting the bombers. A new section – Q Section – was created to hunt out decoy sites and Dimbleby was put in charge of it. In the area around Cologne, this section identified seventeen separate decoy sites. Dimbleby and his team marked up maps and aerial photographs for air crews, enabling them to identify what were the real targets and what were the decoys, briefing some of the bomber crews in person to tell them what to look out for. The crews seemed to find the briefings very helpful. But Bomber Command put a stop to them, claiming that the photo interpreters were upsetting the morale of the crews by showing them photos of craters in empty fields.

German decoy attempts grew more and more sophisticated as the bombing offensive continued. Oil depots and storage tanks are particularly obvious from the air. So the Germans would roof over a whole site with camouflage nets to disguise the location as open fields. Then they would build a complete dummy site some miles away with simple wooden structures. As with other camouflage, the dummy sites were easy to identify in photographs but more difficult to spot from a bomber flying at altitude overhead.

Towards the end of the war, the Germans increasingly used smoke to disguise sites from the air. When radar picked up approaching aircraft they would trigger huge smoke screens to obscure a potential target area. Sometimes these were very effective, obliterating the view of bombers or hiding the ground below from the prying cameras of a reconnaissance aircraft. But of course smoke could easily be blown off course by a change in the wind and was difficult to control. Before long the interpreters were able to identify the generators where the smoke was set off. Although they were visible on the photographs only as tiny dots, they left small white circular marks where the surrounding grass had been scorched. But the game of deception became even more ingenious when the Germans launched decoy smoke screens. When Kiel was attacked in March 1943 a smoke screen was raised, but another decoy screen also went up around another town to the north-west that looked similar from the air. Keeping one step ahead in the decoy war was never easy.

There were several other specialist sections at Medmenham, who built up expertise on industry, on army sites, on targeting and damage assessment. These will be explored as the narrative unfolds over the next few chapters. One final section, however, deserves mention at this point. Although important work was being done at Medmenham, the intelligence gleaned from aerial photography still had many detractors and there were

senior people throughout all three services who mistrusted the
PIs' conclusions. In modern parlance, photo interpretation had
an image problem. In the spring of 1942, Peter Stewart, then station commander at Medmenham, delivered a report in person
to Bomber Command. As he sat in the officers' mess at Bomber
Command in High Wycombe, he noticed that most of the senior
airmen were reading the *Illustrated London News*, *Picture Post* or
other magazines filled with pictures, rather than the newspa-
pers. It suddenly occurred to him that what was needed was a
picture magazine to show off the stunning photographs that
were pouring in to Medmenham daily to promote the work of
photo interpretation. So he proposed to produce a monthly
magazine containing some of the photographs that came
through Medmenham.[12]

Initially there was much hostility at the Air Ministry to the
idea of promoting what was going on at a top secret unit. It
took Stewart six months of arguing and persuasion to get
permission to produce a prototype magazine. The decision
went right up to the Chief of the Air Staff, Sir Charles Portal,
who finally gave the go-ahead to produce a single trial issue. It
came out in October 1942, acquiring the name *Evidence in
Camera*.[13] Although not classified as confidential or secret, it was
only given clearance to be circulated to RAF officers' messes,
where it was left around for officers to pick up and look
through. It proved such a success that it became a regular feature produced by a dedicated team at Medmenham. The
principal editor was Shirley Eadon, a WAAF officer with jour-
nalistic experience. It had a distinctive blue cover and consisted
of forty or fifty pages of aerial photographs with short explana-
tory captions. The aerial images perfectly capture the sense of
awe gained by looking down on the world from above. In addition to promoting the field of aerial photography and what

could be learnt about factories, military installations, shipyards and railway marshalling yards, *Evidence in Camera* also introduced airmen to images of new tanks, ships or enemy aircraft. The photographs were selected to show off the most dramatic effects of Allied bombing and *Evidence in Camera* proved particularly popular on bomber airfields.

The magazine contained regular features like the 'Problem Picture' – an abstract image that made no sense until explained in the next issue. The tone was always light and where possible humorous. As a further reminder of the talent available at Medmenham, there were also regular cartoons from artists such as Julian Phipps, who later became cartoonist for *The Daily Telegraph*, Maurice Pownhall, and Albert Edgar Beard of *Punch*. Continual battles took place with the Air Ministry, who instinctively felt unhappy about promoting secret intelligence work – although Medmenham was never mentioned by name. And when there weren't battles about security there were arguments about the shortage of paper during wartime that threatened to bring the whole project to an end. But *Evidence in Camera* survived and 114 issues were produced in all. Today, they are still wonderfully absorbing. They present a unique collection of aerial imagery that records the range of photographs that the PIs at Medmenham worked with.[14]

The organisation of Third Phase interpretation at Medmenham was unique in the Second World War. No other participant in the war developed such a sophisticated system for strategic photo interpretation. In the first two years of the war, all German military activity had been offensive. The only need for aerial reconnaissance during a blitzkrieg was for tactical information about the deployment of enemy troops. And this became ingrained in the thinking of German photo intelligence. Photos taken of Britain in 1940 prior to bombing raids were marked up

to show the location of anti-tank ditches, barbed wire entanglements and machine gun bunkers. But the interpreters entirely
missed the large Chain Home radar towers and never identified
key factories, for instance the factory in Derby where Rolls Royce
produced the Merlin engine or those in Southampton where the
Spitfire was built.[15] This lack of strategic interpretation was the
single biggest failure of German photo intelligence. As the war
progressed and the need for strategic intelligence of Allied operations grew, the German military had other priorities and failed
to reinvent its photo intelligence operation.

Along with this, the Germans did not give much status to
their photo interpreters. They, like their Allied counterparts,
worked in stereo and had good quality instruments, but most
interpretation was done by NCOs and not by officers. A lot of
their work was not centralised or shared between different
units. This essential failure to make strategic use of aerial photography probably meant they did not understand how much
information the Allies were gaining from aerial reconnaissance.
The Germans began industrial programmes without understanding how they could be followed and studied from the air
because this was a technique they had not pursued themselves.
After the war, many senior German officials were amazed at the
extent and the quality of the information the Allies had learned
about so many aspects of the Nazi war machine.

Medmenham was only a few miles from RAF Benson, the
airfield from where the pilots flew the reconnaissance missions
that produced all the photographs available to the interpreters.
There was not much communication between these two arms
of photo intelligence. Occasionally, dances were held in which
the glamorous WAAF officers at Medmenham could meet with
the dashing young pilots from Benson. The pilots always had
a fund of stories from their daring missions with which to

amaze and impress the female officers. But in truth, the two aspects of photo intelligence called for very different sets of skills. The work of the photo interpreters involved teamwork, hours of patient study and painstaking analysis. It took place in a quiet, studious atmosphere. That of the reconnaissance pilots was more solitary. It involved hours of flying over occupied territory, potentially up against enemy fighters and anti-aircraft fire. The reconnaissance pilots' culture of daily risk taking was a world away from the challenges faced by the ground-based photo interpreters. It takes a special sort of individual to be able to fly for hours at a time, unarmed, over enemy territory simply in order to take a set of photographs, perhaps of a single factory or shipyard. And then to get back home again.

7

A Rare Form of Bravery

During the summer of 1940 it was essential to maintain regular reconnaissance cover of the Channel ports in order to report on the state of the potential invasion barges. The problem was that whenever the weather was bad and clouds had set in, it was impossible to carry out the usual high level aerial reconnaissance. So the pilots had to fly low level sorties below the cloud to take their pictures. This meant the aircraft were within easy range of anti-aircraft fire, known as 'flak', and it was also more likely that they would run into enemy fighters. The pilots called these low level reconnaissance missions 'dicing' – an abbreviation of 'dicing with death'. Wing Commander Geoffrey Tuttle, the officer in charge of flying at Heston, briefed his pilots in advance of a dicing mission to keep low to avoid enemy radar and to memorise all the key visual landmarks. Split-second reactions would mean the difference between life and death. Tuttle told the pilots, 'Switch on your cameras in good time before you whistle past your target. You've got to be right first time because there isn't going to *be* a second time.' He believed it was almost suicidal to try to photograph the target twice on a dicing sortie.[1]

Flying Officer Alistair Taylor was a dab hand at dicing. He would prepare meticulously for every sortie, memorising the route and the landmarks, noting the location of the known flak batteries, calculating his precise time of arrival over the target area. He made sure he was fully informed on all the enemy fighters he was likely to meet, on how they would probably respond, what speeds they were capable of and what guns they were armed with. On one mission on a cloudy day in July 1940, Taylor set off in his Spitfire on a dicing mission over Flushing. He had just finished taking his photographs when he spotted a twin-engined Ju 88 only three hundred yards behind him. The instinct of most RAF pilots would be to engage the 'bandit' at once. But this was not an option for a reconnaissance pilot, whose guns and armour plating had been removed to create extra speed and enable him to attain extra height. There was only one yardstick of success in a recon mission, to return with all your photos intact. And so, having spotted the Ju 88 on his tail, Taylor made a right turn and climbed as fast as his Spitfire could take him. The German followed him, climbing too. Having gained some height, Taylor turned sharply to the left, out across the sea, and headed straight for the Kent coast at full speed. Despite its two powerful Jumo engines, the German fighter couldn't keep up with the Spitfire and the next time Taylor looked in his mirror there was no sign of it. Taylor arrived back at Heston with all his photos, and another report was available to feed into the analysis of the German invasion plan.

By then stories of the escapades of the aerial reconnaissance pilots were spreading throughout the RAF, and the Photographic

Reconnaissance Unit began to build a reputation as a place for some of the best fliers. Three reconnaissance pilots received the Distinguished Flying Cross (DFC) that summer, including Maurice 'Shorty' Longbottom and Bob Niven, who had done so much to set the pattern for aerial reconnaissance.[2] This was the first recognition of the gallantry of the unarmed recon pilots.

More and more volunteers now came forward to join the PRU. Tuttle had his pick of these pilots. He had a knack of choosing the right men. Although he laid down the rules for flying recon missions he was also looking for individuals who would learn their own techniques for each mission. Navigation was critical. And managing the flow of petrol was a vital skill. The risk of running out of fuel was always high on such long sorties. Tuttle used to tell his pilots that it was much better to have fuel than to have guns. 'If you stopped to fight you'd be using up even more fuel,' he told them. 'You don't need guns when you're flying the fastest planes in the sky.'[3] New pilots would be allocated a first operational reconnaissance flight over one of the Channel ports, known as 'the milk run'. Then they would move on to a sortie flying farther afield over, say, Rotterdam. And finally, if they had the right stuff, they would graduate to a flight over Germany and several hours of flying alone over occupied Europe.

It was quickly realised that fighter pilots, posted to the unit on account of their familiarity with Spitfires, were usually unsuited to the work of photo reconnaissance, whether by temperament or training. Sidney Cotton had expressed this view in a letter as early as 2 February 1940, when he wrote, 'It is much easier to teach a man to fly a Spitfire than to teach a Spitfire pilot with the wrong temperament to do the work we are doing.'[4] Indeed, the two pilots who had blazed the trail for photo reconnaissance were not Spitfire pilots – Longbottom was from a flying boat squadron and Niven had flown bombers.

In June 1940 Air Chief Marshal Bowhill, the head of Coastal Command, laid down three qualifications for new pilots joining the reconnaissance unit. First they must have considerable experience; second, a real ability to navigate; and third they must have what he classed as an 'above average classification as a pilot for Common Sense'. He was keen to see pilots transferring from bomber and army coordination squadrons but not from fighter squadrons, summing up the situation by saying that 'the work called for a rare combination of conscientiousness, daring, self-reliance and initiative'.[5] All pilots transferring to photo reconnaissance went on a training programme to learn the new skills required. The course lasted two to four weeks, during which pilots also converted from twin-engined aircraft to single-engined ones like the Spitfire.

The fact that reconnaissance aircraft were stripped of their guns and armour plating was fundamental. For some pilots, like Flying Officer Gordon Hughes, PR work almost became a religion. This was partly because he had pacifist leanings from his Methodist background as a boy. Although he was not a conscientious objector, he felt strongly that photo recon was the only way in which he could do a front line job in the war without being asked to kill people. He made it a virtue that he did not have guns to fire and felt that photo recon pilots benefited greatly from this, later saying, 'If you have guns the temptation to use them is tremendous and you say to yourself "I'll have a bash – I'll have a go".' Without guns the recon pilot only had one objective to concentrate on, taking his photographs and bringing them home. Hughes thought that getting everything right to achieve this objective was the purpose of his work.

This would also not provoke the enemy in the same way as

going in guns blazing. Richard Cussons, another experienced PR pilot, remembered: 'The general idea was to fly fast and high and nip in, take the photos and nip out again before the enemy realised what was happening.'[6] Hughes summed it up in a metaphor: 'If someone slips into your garden and picks some flowers and slips away again quietly you may feel annoyed but you may not do anything about it. But if someone, in order to pinch some of your flowers, breaks down the gate, smashes the fence, and tramples down half your garden, you certainly *do* do something.'[7] It was a good philosophy to operate by.

Of course many reconnaissance pilots did not return. Usually they were simply posted as missing, since no one knew what had happened to them on their long, lonely flights. Many pilots went down in the sea and nothing was ever heard of them again. Occasionally, if a plane had crash landed, reports would later come back from resistance groups in occupied Europe, and it could be established from the registration number of the aircraft which pilot had gone down. But whether it was from mechanical failure or from having been shot down was rarely ever known.

A few pilots who had crashed managed to send word back. Flight Lieutenant James Smalley DFC was shot down over Kiel in October 1940 and from his prisoner-of-war camp he managed to get a letter through to Geoffrey Tuttle, his commanding officer. He wrote, with characteristic RAF understatement: 'Sorry I couldn't finish the job, Sir! Don't quite know what happened – big bang and fireworks. I just managed to get out, a bit battered but safe and sound and as happy as can be expected. Very good treatment, good quarters, food and company here – but of course I'm worried about and anxious for all my friends back home and long for news and long to be back with you all again. My love to all the boys, Sir – thank you for a very happy stay in your unit.'

Another pilot, Flying Officer Peter Dakeyne, also wrote to Tuttle from the same POW interrogation centre. His account probably sums up the fate of many reconnaissance pilots. He had a momentary lapse of concentration while on a low level flight over the Belgian coast in September 1940: 'I rather foolishly ran into AA [anti-aircraft] fire whilst preoccupied and also distracted by a third factor. A direct hit stopped the prop, so rolled and fell out to land among troops! The machine made a spectacular crash full out! The prospect of a year or two here is infuriating but I hope that I will see you again – the last month or two had been to me – ideal! The best of luck!'[8]

Two vital developments took place in the spring of 1941. With the bombing of Heston in the autumn and winter of 1940, what was now called No. 1 Photographic Reconnaissance Unit was relocated to RAF Benson in Berkshire. This airfield had recently been used as a training base but had spare capacity and room for expansion.[9] Its central location made it ideal. Second, Supermarine produced a new version of the Spitfire specifically for photo reconnaissance.

The model in use up to this point had been the Spitfire PR ID, also known as the 'flying petrol bowser' since it carried extra fuel tanks in its wings, along with an additional tank behind the pilot in the fuselage. This gave the Spitfire a super long range of about 875 miles. Flying Officer Samuel Millen took one of these aircraft on a flight over Stettin and Rostock in the Baltic. The sortie lasted five hours twenty minutes and earned Millen the DFC. Tragically, he died on a mission a month later. Another pilot took one of these super long range Spitfires on a direct flight to Malta to photograph the Italian battle fleet. He too was shot down a few weeks later, this time over Genoa, although he survived and became a prisoner of war. In April 1941 a new version of the Merlin engine, the Merlin 45, was added to this Spitfire, making it slightly faster. This version, known as the Spitfire Mark PR IV, became the standard model used by the photo reconnaissance squadrons for the next two years, and more than two hundred were produced.

There was probably no such thing as an average day for a reconnaissance pilot. But certain common features characterised the flying routine.[10] Most pilots would rise early and go straight to the station Met Office to get an idea of the day's weather and prospects for flying. If flying was 'on' then the pilots would take a light breakfast. They had to be careful what they ate before a long, high altitude flight and avoid anything that might give them wind or make them blow up like a balloon during the flight. After breakfast it was to the Operations (Ops) Room, where the day's programme was chalked up on a blackboard. Some of the flight commanders would abruptly hand out instructions and get straight on with the day's missions. At Benson, however, one of the flight commanders, Tony Hill, would talk his younger pilots through the sorties clearly and enthusiastically, helping them to understand what they were about to face. Wing Commander Tuttle would often come in to the Ops Room and discuss the sorties with the flight commanders. Although he didn't do much flying himself any more, he was an inspiring leader who knew instinctively how far to push his pilots and how to help them plan a sortie.

Then the pilots piled into the blue Humber Snipes that carried them around the airfield and went to the Intelligence Room for the formal briefing. The pilots would mark up their own course on their maps and finally, back in the Snipes, drive out to their aircraft which the ground crew had prepared and whose engines they had already warmed up.

Some pilots now leapt into the cockpit and nervously rushed into action. But most took this final stage of preparation more slowly, knowing that if they hurried now they might overlook something. Many pilots would walk around their aircraft, examining it carefully. The ground crew were happy that the pilot was both inspecting and appreciating their work. There was one last formality at this point: the pilot had to sign a 'Form 700' accepting the aircraft from the ground crew.

Once inside the cockpit the pilot was handed his helmet, with goggles attached and an oxygen mask swinging from it. The pilot checked his controls, attached his oxygen mask and took a few deep breaths to check the flow was working. Oxygen was breathed from take-off to landing on reconnaissance flights. PR pilots were the first to use oxygen throughout their flights and Dr Robson, who was based at Benson, used the missions as an opportunity to study the effects of breathing pure oxygen for long periods of time. Once when Gordon Hughes was doing his checks he found that the oxygen tube was faulty and was about to come apart. This could have proved fatal. The airman who had failed to spot this was put on a charge for twenty-eight days.

If all was well, the pilot would call 'OK Flight' to the flight sergeant and then switch on the engine. Two airmen would hold down the tail as the pilot tested the engine to full throttle. With the engine running smoothly the pilot would give the thumbs-up sign from side to side, the chocks would be pulled away and the pilot would taxi to the end of the runway and take off. The sortie was on.

A Spitfire or any other recon aircraft was likely to be heavy with petrol at the start of its flight and the pilot would need the longest possible run to get airborne. Then he would climb slowly to the outward altitude, maybe 25,000–30,000 feet, increasing his oxygen supply every 5000 feet. At the heights the reconnaissance aircraft flew it was bitterly cold and cockpits were unheated. Most aircrew didn't like to wear electrically heated outfits but would dress for the intense cold. Over warm underwear and a long-sleeved vest they would wear a thick white sweater. On top of this came their RAF battledress with heavy flying boots over thick woollen socks. Some pilots wore gloves but most felt this restricted their movement and preferred not to, despite the freezing cold of everything they touched. Some wore thin silk gloves known as 'inner liners'. In a few places the heat of the engine was conducted back into the cockpit and the pilot could try to warm his hands there.

Once they were approaching enemy territory, pilots would need to keep a constant lookout for enemy fighters. They called this 'rubber necking' as it involved continuously turning their heads to look to each side and then behind them. Aircrew tried fitting rear-view mirrors but these were not successful. A pilot became too reliant upon the view from the mirror and would miss an aircraft approaching from a blind spot. There was nothing for it but to keep searching the sky, and many pilots wore silk scarves to prevent their necks from becoming sore.

At great height a pilot's main problem, apart from preventing his hands from freezing, was stopping his Perspex canopy misting up. If this happened his clear vision was severely impaired. One pilot who suffered from sinus trouble used sometimes to suffer extreme pain at altitude. But he would carry on and open his canopy slightly to freeze the side of his nose in order to kill the pain.

Once over the target, if the sky was free of clouds the pilot would begin his aerial photography. Aiming the cameras was not easy and required experience. They were mounted behind the cockpit, so the pilot had to bank the aircraft steeply, straightening out only when the target was disappearing under the nose, and turn the cameras on as it passed below the aircraft. Most pilots got used to this quite quickly and the results were surprisingly accurate. When the pilot had passed the target area he would turn the cameras off. Pilots were briefed on finding their principal target, an airfield, factory, shipyard or whatever it might be. But if there was a problem, or the target was obscured by cloud, then they were told to look out for a series of secondary targets on which information of a lower priority was needed. Each camera could take up to five hundred separate exposures, although it was rare for pilots to take that many photographs on a single mission.

Finally, when the photographs were taken, the pilot would turn for home. Navigation was done by dead reckoning. The pilot calculated the angle of a direct line between where he was and his base and he flew on that angle. He had to adjust the angle for the wind speed, so the Met briefing was a vital part of every sortie. And if he started to take evasive action for whatever reason he had to factor that also into his reckoning. All this was done by simple mathematical calculations and most pilots would keep a map and some basic instruments in a pocket or pouch on the side of their knee that would enable them to do this. The Spitfire was a favourite aircraft to fly. Most pilots said it fitted you like a coat and the aircraft almost became a part of you by reacting to your every move. But the flights were a long, lonely business.

As the pilot returned to base, the aircrew were waiting. As soon as the aircraft came to a standstill they would immediately remove the film magazines from the camera and rush them straight to the film developing and processing unit. The pilot would climb out, point out any technical problems to his flight sergeant and then head back to the briefing room for a quick debrief and to report anything he had seen in order to alert the photo interpreters in advance. Most pilots felt a strong sense of elation on returning, having flown, sometimes for hours, over enemy territory and having brought their pictures back to base.

The life of RAF pilots in any part of the service was an intense one and in line with other pilots, the recon crews liked to work hard and play hard. Drinking was an important part of this and no doubt provided a sense of release for many young men who didn't know if that evening would be their last. Whether it was in their mess or down at the local pub, RAF pilots were known to be heavy drinkers. Many commanders saw drinking as a good way for a squadron to bond together. Crews would not drink on flying days, but on other days putting away several pints was part of the routine.[11] Many RAF stations had a tie-in with their local. The White Hart was the favourite drinking hole for the PR pilots at Benson and the landlady, Mrs Clements, known as Clemmie, always had a special welcome for her 'RAF boys'. Tony Hill's father ran a brewery in Hertfordshire and so Tony would always claim that he had a professional interest in trying local beers to check out the competition. Most pilots didn't need such an excuse.

During the winter of 1940–41 much photo recon was devoted to recording German naval activity. Winning the war at sea and keeping the Atlantic sea lanes open was of critical importance not only for Britain's war effort but for the country's very survival. Along the French Atlantic coast giant pens were constructed for the U-boats to base themselves before their deadly missions out in the Atlantic. The watchful eyes of the spies in the sky closely monitored the building of these pens and the movement of vessels in and out of them. But when it was noticed that two of Germany's big battlecruisers,

Scharnhorst and *Gneisenau*, had left their docks at Kiel at the end of December 1940, a major alarm was sounded. Once in the Atlantic, these two German ships, known as the 'ugly sisters', with their 11in guns had a field day hunting the convoys and unescorted merchantmen. In three months the *Gneisenau* sank fourteen British ships and the *Scharnhorst* eight. Then, on 28 March 1941, they were spotted once again by the photo recon teams, this time in Brest harbour refitting. The PRU flew almost daily sorties over Brest to watch and report on what was happening to the ships, despite the heavy presence of German naval anti-aircraft gunners. The gunners used a system of box firing, by which they would track an aircraft and then fire five simultaneous bursts of flak into a box of airspace around that aircraft. It was frightening to be on the receiving end of this type of anti-aircraft fire.

The recon flights led to several attempts at bombing the ships but none of the bombs hit their targets. However, an unexploded bomb that had landed nearby forced the German navy to move *Gneisenau* from the safety of its dry dock and on 5 April the ship was photographed in the more exposed position of the inner harbour. It was decided to try to torpedo the ship before it was moved again and at dawn on the following day, a squadron of Beaufort torpedo-bombers was ordered to attack the ship. There were 270 anti-aircraft guns protecting *Gneisenau* but one aircraft, piloted by Flying Officer Kenneth Campbell, got through the hail of gunfire at mast height and his torpedo scored a direct hit. The German battlecruiser was left with a forty-foot hole in its side and was out of commission for eight months.[12] However, Campbell's aircraft was shot down by the massive anti-aircraft fire and he and the three other members of his crew were lost.

Campbell was awarded a posthumous VC for leading the

attack. It was a classic case whereby patient, daily observation by the photo recon teams had found just the right moment for the attack aircraft to go in and hit their target, despite the strength of the ship's massive defences.

On 19 May 1941, Germany's newest battleship, *Bismarck*, slipped its moorings in the port of Gydnia in the Baltic and accompanied by its escort, the heavy cruiser *Prinz Eugen*, sailed across the Baltic and through the Kattegat towards the coast of Norway en route to the Atlantic Ocean. The *Bismarck* was the most powerful battleship in the German navy, with eight 15in heavy guns. Despite its size it was faster than any battleship in the Royal Navy. Its mission was to create havoc with the convoys in the Atlantic and to distract the Royal Navy from its work in the Mediterranean, just as a major German operation against Crete was about to be launched. On crossing the Baltic, the two ships were spotted by a Swedish warship and the Swedes passed on information of the sighting to the British naval attaché in Stockholm. He immediately alerted the Admiralty in London. At this point it was not known which ships had been spotted – only that they were large.

The PRU outstation at Wick was located at a wild and lonely spot, on the top of the Caithness cliffs at the tip of north-east Scotland, only a few miles from John O'Groats. The base housed a handful of pilots and a small team of First Phase interpreters, led by David Linton and a WAAF officer, Eve Holiday, who specialised in naval matters. Alerted by the sighting of the German ships, the Air Ministry realised that if they had now reached Norwegian waters they would be in range of the PR flights out of Wick and so the base was scrambled. The senior flier there, Flying Officer Greenhill DFC, decided to send out two planes immediately. He himself would fly along the Norwegian coast near Oslo, where it was thought the German ships were most likely to be, and Pilot Officer Michael Suckling would fly further north along the coast near Bergen in western Norway. Suckling, although the junior of the two fliers, was still an experienced PR pilot. Photographs of him reveal a youthful-looking figure with fair hair, blue eyes and a radiant smile. His nickname was 'Babe'. Suckling took off just after 11 a.m. on 21 May, on what proved to be one of the most famous PR sorties of the war.

At almost exactly the same time as Suckling took off from Wick, the *Bismarck* quietly slipped into Grimstadfjord, south of Bergen, to rendezvous with supply ships and a refuelling vessel. Suckling's Spitfire hit Norway just below Bergen and he flew along the coast at high altitude, banking left every few minutes to look down on the grey fjords below. It was difficult to know exactly where he was with the unending flow of islands and inlets surrounded by steep mountains. Then he spotted the German fighter base at Herdla. He turned on his cameras for a few seconds and carried on flying along the coast.

On one of his many banks to the left he suddenly saw something that made him nearly leap out of his seat. He threw the Spitfire into a steep vertical dive to get a better look. Far below him, he could see in the fjord the specks of one, two, three, four, five ... six ships. One was large, probably a cruiser, and it was surrounded by destroyers and a large merchant ship. Suckling levelled off, turned his camera on and flew across the fjord, carrying on to Bergen and photographing the port there. He was just turning for home when he spotted another group of ships in a fjord below. Here was another large ship and three more merchantmen, with a host of smaller ships bustling around. At 1.15 p.m. Suckling turned on his cameras again, flew the length of the fjord and then turned west. He had got what he came for.

But to complete his mission he had to bring his precious

cargo of photographs safely back to base, which entailed navigating across three hundred miles of grey, empty, featureless sea with just a compass as a guide. This was no simple matter. High level winds, or a slight error in calculating his direction, could easily drive a pilot off course. And on the long journey from Norway it was vital to pick up the Shetland or Orkney islands below and turn south for the mainland. If they were obscured by cloud, or if, due to the wind, he had made a slight miscalculation, a pilot could easily miss his base, run out of fuel and be forced to ditch in the sea. Even if the pilot survived the photographs would be lost and the whole mission would have been in vain.

On this occasion everything went well for Suckling, who flew straight back to Wick and landed at about 2.30 p.m. The aircrew were waiting for him as he taxied into his parking slot, and immediately they began to remove the camera magazines and rushed them to the film processing and developing unit. Eve Holiday drove out to meet Suckling, who excitedly called out to her as he climbed out of the cockpit, 'I've seen them! Two of them!' She drove him to the officers' mess where David Linton was waiting. 'Come in,' called Linton, realising Suckling's excitement. But the pilot was still in his flying gear and it was strictly against regulations to enter the mess in a flying suit. 'I can't,' he called out to Linton. But he repeated what he had told the WAAF officer, 'I've seen them, two of them, and I think they're cruisers, or one might be a battle-ship.'[13]

News of Suckling's sighting was immediately phoned down to Medmenham, but it took an hour before the photographs were processed and David Linton was able to examine them. When he looked closely with his Stereo and magnifying glass he could barely believe what he saw. He hesitated for a moment to check his identification then sent out a teleprinter message. The first ship that Suckling had photographed was the heavy cruiser *Prinz Eugen* and in the second fjord was none other than the most powerful ship in the German navy, the *Bismarck*. Not only had they found the *Bismarck* but Linton was able to confirm that there were no booms around the ship to protect it from torpedoes. It looked like they were about to sail.

In fact there were no protective booms because the ship had only just arrived in the fjords around Bergen two hours before. But Linton's surmise proved to be correct. Only four hours later, in the early evening, Captain Lutjens gave the order for the *Bismarck* to sail and, escorted by *Prinz Eugen*, the pride of the German navy headed north on a course to enter the Atlantic Ocean through the Denmark Strait between Iceland and Greenland.

Coastal Command headquarters wanted to see the prints immediately to verify the sighting of the German navy's principal battleship. But there was a problem: no planes were available to fly the prints south except for Suckling's Spitfire, and he had just returned from his long flight. Nevertheless, the recon pilot refuelled, clambered back into the cockpit and headed south. After a couple of hours he was approaching Nottingham but was running out of fuel. By now it was evening and darkness had set in. He landed and knocked up an old friend who owned a garage in the area. Together, they set off by car through the night and the blackout, reaching Coastal Command headquarters north-west of London in the early hours of the morning. Here it was soon verified that Suckling had indeed photographed the *Prinz Eugen* and the *Bismarck*.

Suckling's photographs and Linton's identification began one of the most famous chases in naval history. Royal Navy cruisers and battleships set off in pursuit of the German vessels.

In its first engagement with the Royal Navy a lucky hit from the *Bismarck* struck the ammunition store of HMS *Hood*, and the ship went up in a huge explosion and split in two. It sank in a matter of minutes and only three of its crew of 1500 men survived. The order was sent out from the Admiralty, 'Sink the *Bismarck*.' Pursued for several days by cruisers and Swordfish aircraft of the Fleet Air Arm from HMS *Victorious*, the *Bismarck* was finally hit and its rudder was so severely damaged that it could do no more than sail around in a circle, listing heavily to port. The battleships HMS *Rodney* and *King George V* closed in for the kill and, six days after being identified by the PR team in Scotland, the *Bismarck* finally went down with the loss of nearly two thousand crew.

For finding the German battleship, Michael 'Babe' Suckling became a hero within the RAF. The work of the photo reconnaissance and interpretation teams suddenly became famous. But Suckling's days of glory did not last long. Two months after his famous flight over the Norwegian fjords he was flying another mission, this time from St Eval in Cornwall, over La Rochelle. He did not return and was never heard from again. No one ever knew what happened to him. Such was the life, and death, of a pilot in photo reconnaissance.

During the course of 1941 various technical developments took place that were to improve considerably the work of the PR pilots. In November the first camera with a 36in lens was used. From a height of thirty thousand feet this could produce photos to a scale of 1:10,000, enormously improving the detail that could be seen and the degree of interpretation that was possible. And the following month saw the introduction of the first entirely new camera of the war. Called the F-52 – coincidentally it had taken just fifty-two days to design and construct – it could be fitted with lenses of up to 40in length for high level photography and, most importantly, it used a larger film format, 8½in by 7in. A larger negative enabled the pilot to record more information on the photograph and the new long lenses were far better suited to high altitude photo reconnaissance.

Arguably more important still was the introduction of a new aircraft into the armoury of the photo reconnaissance squadrons. As far back as September 1939, Sidney Cotton had predicted the demand for a two-seater photo recon aircraft with a range of at least 1500 miles. The De Havilland Mosquito was the answer to this prayer. Geoffrey de Havilland had years of experience of designing and building high speed aircraft and many of these had fuselages made of wood, which – perhaps surprisingly – has similar structural properties to lightweight aluminium. With metals in very short supply in wartime Britain, the De Havilland team set about building a fast bomber that could outfly enemy fighters, with a shell built out of birch plywood filled with lightweight balsa wood. Designed with two engines for a crew of two, a pilot and navigator-bomber, it was a brilliant piece of engineering. Later models could carry the same weight of bombs as the B-17 Flying Fortress while still being 20 mph faster than the Spitfire. With the power of a bomber and the speed and agility of a fighter, the Mosquito was a winner. In its trials in early 1941 it established itself as the world's fastest operational aircraft. It would remain so until the era of jet-powered fighters.

The Mosquito would perform many different roles, including those of a light bomber and a night fighter. But with the Joint Intelligence Committee calling for photo cover of ever more distant targets in northern Norway, the eastern Baltic, south-eastern Germany and Poland, its initial role was in photo reconnaissance. The first ten aircraft off the production line were allocated for PR flying and Geoffrey de Havilland Jnr, the eldest son of the firm's founder, flew the first Mosquito to RAF Benson on 13 July 1941. Flying trials continued throughout the summer. Carrying no bombs, the PR version of the Mosquito could easily accommodate the larger cameras with the longer lenses. The first ever successful PR flight of the Mosquito took place on 19 September 1941 when Squadron Leader Alistair Taylor and his navigator, Sgt Sidney Horsfall, flew a reconnaissance flight over Bordeaux.

Despite some early teething problems the Mosquito proved an ideal aircraft for photo reconnaissance. The twin Merlin engines gave a maximum speed of nearly 400 mph, the plane could reach 35,000 feet and had a range of 2180 miles. The presence of the second crew member, the navigator, revolutionised aerial photography. The pilot could concentrate solely on flying the aircraft over the target area while the navigator could keep watch for enemy aircraft and operate the camera. The navigator could also use the new VHF radio designed to aid navigation, especially on the return journey to base.

The first flight of three Mosquitos were allocated to Wick in the autumn of 1941 under command of Squadron Leader Taylor. Each of the three aircraft he led was named after a drink, 'Whisky', 'Vodka' and 'Benedictine'. With the arrival of these long range aircraft, however, the impracticalities of the base on the clifftop at Wick soon became apparent. It took ages to get prints back to Medmenham and days for spare parts to arrive. So the Mosquitos were moved down to RAF Leuchars, a more established base outside St Andrews and near Dundee. It was from here that Taylor and Horsfall set off on a routine flight over Trondheim and Bergen on 4 December 1941. There was nothing special about the sortie. But the Germans had a new long range anti-aircraft gun and it seems that Taylor's Mosquito was hit at altitude. It took some time for the story to unfold of what happened next, but observers on the ground remember seeing a new type of twin-engined aircraft hit by anti-aircraft fire. It was said that the pilot could have brought the aircraft down and crash landed. But, of course, Taylor knew that to do so would mean letting the Germans have access to the RAF's newest arrival. So it seems he headed out to sea and crashed there, knowing that rescue would be almost impossible but that his Mosquito would not fall into German hands.[14] It was a tragic but heroic end for the pilot who had already achieved the RAF's highest accolade, being the first man to be awarded a double bar to his Distinguished Flying Cross. He had flown more than a hundred PR sorties and his success brought tremendous prestige to the reputation of the photo recon pilots. His death was a great loss to the entire PR and PI world.

The *Bismarck* had a sister ship, the *Tirpitz*, built to a different design with a broader beam but also armed with eight 15in guns. Having completed her sea trials in the Baltic, the *Tirpitz* set sail from Wilhelmshaven in January 1942 heading north with an escort of four destroyers and an ice-breaker. Her mission was to attack the Russian convoys in which American and British supplies were being shipped to Soviet Russia on a route from Britain to Murmansk in the Arctic Circle. The supplies were a vital lifeline for the Soviet Union, fighting for its survival against the German army on a huge five-hundred-mile front from the Arctic to the Black Sea. A secret report sent by a Norwegian agent claimed that the *Tirpitz* had been spotted in the fjords near Trondheim. But it was up to the photo reconnaissance pilots to verify if this was correct, and if so to find the exact location of the German ship.

Two experienced pilots from Wick flew out and searched for the *Tirpitz* but found nothing. Maybe the report had been wrong. On the third day, 23 January 1942, Flight Lieutenant Alfred Fane Peers Fane (known simply as 'Fane Fane'), a pilot who had only just arrived at Wick from Bomber Command, was asked to take a look. He flew the long journey to the Norwegian coast near Statlandet, but the weather was poor so he turned north for Trondheim. He was flying over Aas fjord when he spotted something like a ship in the shadows. He later wrote down in his diary the sequence of events that followed. He began by thinking, 'No, too big, must be a small island – better make sure. By God it's a ship – it's *the* ship – rolled on to my side to have a good look and remember saying out loud – "My God I believe I've found it". Could not believe my eyes or my luck – did three runs over it and next fjord and turned for home.'[15]

But Fane's journey home was not straightforward. He flew for hours, until by his reckoning he should have crossed the Scottish coast. He dropped through the cloud to six hundred feet but could see nothing except a vast expanse of water. He began to get worried as he had only twenty gallons of fuel left. Then at last he spotted land. But he realised he was flying over an island. Reckoning it must be one of the Orkney Islands, he turned south for the mainland. Having passed John O'Groats he soon spotted a short runway, circled around and with a bare ten gallons left in his tank came down with immense relief, only to find he had landed at the satellite or emergency reserve landing strip for Wick. He was so new to the area that he didn't even know Wick had a satellite strip. He made the final hop to his home base just a few miles away and handed over his film. There was panic on at Wick as he was so late, and sea rescue teams had already been briefed. But he was able to report that he thought he had found the *Tirpitz*, or the 'Rowboat' as it was nicknamed.

Then, with his adrenalin still flowing, he had to wait for the photos to be processed. His diary beautifully captures the atmosphere: 'Hopped about on one foot and then the other waiting for the photos to be developed. When film was ready tore in to look at the negatives. Maybe I'd missed the b— thing. NO! There it was – no doubt now it was the *Tirpitz* all right.'

An almighty 'flap' went up on confirmation that they had found the German battleship. Fane continued the story in his diary: 'I adore flaps, they always make me laugh. Group rang up. Coastal Command rang up – the Admiralty rang up. Poor Eve [WAAF officer Eve Holiday] was up all night. Next morning signal of congrats from Butch [Air Marshal Harris, soon to be appointed commander-in-chief of Bomber Command].' Fane clearly enjoyed his fifteen minutes of fame.

Just as the *Bismarck* had presented such a threat to Atlantic shipping before its sinking, so the *Tirpitz* was now perceived as a huge threat, not only in the Atlantic but also to the Russian convoys. Two days after the *Tirpitz* had been found, Prime Minister Winston Churchill told the Chiefs of Staff, 'The destruction or even crippling of this ship is the greatest event at sea at the present time. No other target is comparable to it ... The whole strategy of the war turns at this period on this ship ...'[16] The PR units were ordered to give top priority to monitoring the *Tirpitz* and its support ships in order to try to attack and sink it.

But keeping watch on the *Tirpitz* posed a massive challenge to the photo recon teams. Not only was the trip a thousand miles there and back, but the Norwegian fjords offered perfect shelter for large ships, which could remain hidden from the air by high cliffs and deep shadows. And the Germans had strung huge camouflage nets across the *Tirpitz* to make the ship look like an extension of the wooded slopes that ran down to the sea.

A hundred PR sorties were flown over Trondheim and its sur-rounding area in a fourteen-week period, each lasting between four and five-and-a-half hours. Not only was the pilot alone, with radio silence imposed, relying on his own navigation to find Trondheim and then to get back, but at these northern latitudes the cockpits were even colder than usual. Sometimes the dials began to freeze up. And few of the pilots were as lucky as Fane had been in clearly identifying the battleship in the waters below.

Richard Cussons had flown Spitfires on missions over Germany, Holland and France when he was posted to Wick in April 1942. He described flying these long sorties to Norway with fuel tanks 'filled to overflowing'. Each flight had to cross four hundred miles of sea until Cussons could pick up a recog-nisable point on the Norwegian coast. On 13 April he flew his first mission over the fjords and in perfect, clear conditions took a brilliant set of photographs of the *Tirpitz* with other German big ships including the *Prinz Eugen*, the *Von Scheer*, the *Admiral Hipper* and the tanker *Altmark*. But his beginner's luck didn't last. In thirteen further sorties that month, only four times did he successfully spot any German ships.[17] Later in the month, partly on the basis of Cussons's identification, Lancaster heavy bombers tried repeatedly to bomb the *Tirpitz*, but without suc-cess.

The *Tirpitz* and its support ships moved further north, out of range of Spitfire photo recon flights. Sheltering in the northern fjords around Alta the German raiders posed a great threat to the Russian convoys sailing around the north of Norway to the port of Murmansk. In July 1942, the mere possibility of the appearance of the *Tirpitz* caused those in command of convoy PQ17 to order it to scatter, resulting in the loss of twenty-four out of thirty-five merchant ships to U-boat attacks. It was the heaviest loss a Russian convoy had yet suffered, and in the Admiralty questions were asked about the viability of continuing to supply the Russians by this means. The disastrous decision to break up the convoy had partly been taken because there was no accurate photo recon intelligence as to where the *Tirpitz* and its fellow ships were or what they were doing. Something more had to be done to track the German warships and protect the Russian convoys.

The only option was to keep a daily watch on the German capital ships in northern Norway. So it was decided, in August 1942, that the RAF should open a PR station in Soviet Russian territory on the Kola peninsula, not far from Murmansk. From here it would be possible to follow the movements of the German ships in their northern anchorages more closely. The unit would have to be self-sufficient, so in mid month a ground party of riggers, electricians and photographers set off by ship with crates of equipment and chemicals for processing and developing film. At the beginning of September three Spitfires led by Flight Lieutenant Tim Fairhurst left Scotland for the long flight across Norway, Sweden and Finland to the Kola peninsula. They landed at Afrikanda and were directed to the officers' mess by a Russian girl in uniform who spoke excellent English. But they were told that the landing strip was subject to attack by German tanks. So the next day the three PR Spitfires flew on a further eighty miles north to Vaenga, a small airfield cut out of a silver birch plantation, which would become the photo reconnaissance base for the next six weeks.

The intention was for the RAF personnel to work alongside Soviet air force teams. But although the recon unit received a hearty welcome, cooperation proved difficult. The RAF team was billeted in a red brick country house that looked grand from the outside but, it was soon discovered, was overrun with mice. It was also a frequent target for German air raids, and so the British team asked to be moved into underground facilities. The Russians gave them a shelter to live in, which seemed an improvement until it was discovered that it had until recently been the morgue.

The three Spitfires, along with a First Phase interpretation team, began to operate at the airfield at Vaenga and from mid September flew sorties over the Norwegian fjords. They spotted many of the German ships but could not find the *Tirpitz*. It was an anxious period as the next convoy, PQ18, was en route and vulnerable to attack. But the *Tirpitz* had gone missing. In fact, as we now know, Hitler feared that an Allied invasion of Norway was imminent and the battleship was posted south near Narvik ready to fight off an invasion force. It was eventually spotted and photographed there by a Mosquito flying out of Leuchars in Scotland. The RAF pilots continued to fly sorties from Vaenga every day that the weather permitted but they often had to drop below the cloud, to between three thousand and four thousand feet, to get any photographs. One aircraft flown by Pilot Officer 'Sleepy' Walker was shot down at low altitude, probably by ground fire.

The Russians were puzzled by the whole operation. They couldn't see the point of missions to photograph the German navy that didn't go on and bomb the ships they found. And the routines of life on a Soviet air base were alien to the RAF team, especially the gun drills that were called at unusual times and apparently without warning. At one point Russian gunners shot through the propeller of a Spitfire just after it had taken off and it took all the skill of the pilot to bring the plane back in to land. The Russian food was dull and monotonous. Communications were poor. And the local mosquitoes bit everyone relentlessly. The weather two hundred miles inside the Arctic Circle, along with the poor level of cooperation from the Soviets, turned the tour of duty at the base into a rough assignment. By the end of October the winter darkness began to close in and the PR and PI teams were withdrawn from Russia, leaving the Spitfires behind as a gift for the Russians.[18] The experiment had not been a success. But future convoys could now sail under the cover of the Arctic night until daylight returned the following spring.

For much of the winter of 1942–43 the *Tirpitz* remained in its berth in Kaa Fjord, but by the spring it had moved to an adjoining fjord where it was spotted in May 1943. On 22 September Royal Navy midget submarines made an attack on the *Tirpitz*, and aerial photographs showed that it had been badly damaged. The ship returned to its berth at Kaa Fjord for much of the following winter and when it was spotted again in March 1944 it was still being repaired. Several attempts to bomb the ship during 1944 were only partially successful, but in October it was towed to Tromsö harbour. It was there that a raid by Lancaster bombers on 12 November finally managed to hit the ship with three giant 'Tall Boy' 12,000lb bombs.

Within a few hours of the raid a Mosquito recon flight was on its way to Tromsö. When the pilot arrived he found great activity going on below and he could see a large patch of oil floating in the harbour. His photographs revealed that the huge German battleship had capsized and its entire superstructure was under water. This one mission to take pictures of the overturned battleship lasted seven hours fifty minutes.[19] The long saga of the *Tirpitz* had finally come to an end.

The Allies had allocated a vast amount of photo reconnaissance resources to finding and watching the ship, and had made many attempts to sink it. But one result of the attention dedicated to pursuing the *Tirpitz* was that it spent most of the war in hiding. Unlike the *Bismarck* it never once ventured out into the Atlantic to attack the convoys, although its presence still seemed to pose an immense threat. Nevertheless, it must have been a relief to the photo recon pilots to know that the long sorties along the Norwegian coast had at last produced the desired result.

The pilots who flew the photo reconnaissance sorties were often seen as a sort of elite within the world of single and twin engined RAF crews. Dedicated to their mission, most, like Gordon Hughes, were happy to be performing a vital wartime job that did not entail being asked to kill. Dickie Blyth had a classic trailing air force moustache and spoke with an effete hunting-and-fishing-type accent which the Americans loved. Alistair Taylor had a steely intensity to him and he is remembered as a strikingly handsome, tall, lean figure with a natural air of authority. Some of the female photo interpreters spoke of how they 'worshipped' Taylor, so strong was the sense of charisma around him.[20] Others found him a cold fish, totally professional in the way he approached a mission, calculating for every possible eventuality, but without humour or interest in those around him. Gordon Hughes had a natural sense of leadership and was a popular flight commander. He was promoted through the ranks as the war progressed but ensured that he was still able to keep flying.

Tony Hill was every schoolboy's idea of a hero: modest, self-deprecating, willing to try and keep on trying until he accomplished a difficult task. After the bombing of the Le Creusot works in France in October 1942, Bomber Command was extremely keen to obtain damage assessment photos. When a couple of attempts to take the photos resulted in failure, Hill led the third attempt himself, as he thought it was too dangerous to ask any of his pilots to fly the mission. This time the

German anti-aircraft gunners were waiting, and while making a low level pass to get obliques he was shot down. He survived the crash but had broken his back. So badly was he missed that the French Resistance were asked to rescue him from his hospital and an aircraft was prepared to fly out to bring him back. Tragically, Hill died in the rescue attempt.

In the latter stages of the war, both Spitfires and especially Mosquitos equipped with drop tanks to supply extra fuel, could fly tremendously long missions. It was not unusual for a pilot and navigator to leave the UK early in the morning, cross the Dutch coast, photograph perhaps four or five separate sites in the Baltic, then fly south across Germany to photograph factories around Munich, head on to photograph Italy and land at the San Severo airbase used for Mediterranean PR. After a six-hour flight and a quick dip in the Adriatic, the crew would fly back across northern Italy the following day and photograph maybe half a dozen sites in France before returning to the UK. In October 1942, one Mosquito crew flew four thousand miles in three days of sorties to the Mediterranean and North Africa, most of it across enemy territory.[21] PR sorties were hard missions, physically draining and mentally very demanding. The crew had to keep alert, navigate with pinpoint accuracy and constantly try to avoid enemy fighters or flak from the ground. The pilots needed a rare combination of skills even by the standards of wartime flying.

8

The 'Warby' Legend

One of the most celebrated photo reconnaissance pilots of the war was probably the most unusual and individualistic of them all. Adrian Warburton had an unhappy childhood growing up in England at boarding schools and living with his grandparents in Bournemouth. It was typical of the upbringing experienced by many children of parents working abroad in the Empire. Known as a loner at school, he refused to participate in the team games that were so encouraged in the British public schools of the time. He was seen as something of a misfit, and although he was good at swimming and enjoyed a fascination with flying he spent an unremarkable few years at St Edward's School, Oxford where he happened to be a contemporary of Guy Gibson, who later went on to lead the Dam Busters raid (see Chapter 9). Douglas Bader, the Battle of Britain ace, had been at the school earlier. On leaving school Warburton was articled to a firm of city accountants, but he longed to get away from dull office life to fly, and with war clouds gathering in late 1938 he volunteered for the RAF.

However, Warburton proved to be no natural flier and when he got his wings in May 1939 his flying skills were classed as 'below average' – anything worse than this and he would not have qualified. He began what looked as though it was going to be an undistinguished flying career and hardly flew at all in the early years of the war. During the months when the nation's fate was being decided in the skies above southern England in the Battle of Britain, Warburton was on a navigational course and took no part in the fighting.

Along the way Warburton had married a barmaid at a pub he frequented, The Bush. Her real name was Eileen but for some reason she was known as 'Betty of the Bush'. He did not appear to love her and they spent virtually no time together before he was posted away, after which he never seems to have seen her again. Warburton built up substantial debts which meant he could no longer pay his mess bills – a major crime in the 1940s RAF.

Warburton's schoolboy 'misfit' label seemed to scar his flying career as well. His squadron commander eventually came up with a plan to get him out of the country and out of trouble by sending him to Malta. His squadron had been allocated three Glenn Martin Marylands, a twin-engined American light bomber that, because of its high ceiling and fast speed, also had potential for photo reconnaissance work. Fitted with cameras, the Marylands had to be flown to Malta for urgent PR work there. Warburton mapped out a route for the aircraft to follow right across occupied Europe and on 6 September 1940, with the Battle of Britain still raging, he flew as navigator with his fellow officers to Luqa airfield on Malta. Here, his life rapidly began to change.

The small island of Malta was to play a central and heroic role in the next phase of the war. Centrally located in the

Mediterranean, which Mussolini claimed as an 'Italian lake', Malta was home both to a major Royal Navy base at Valletta Harbour and to an increasingly important RAF station at Luqa. From here reconnaissance aircraft could overfly all of Sicily, most of Italy as far north as Genoa, much of Greece and many parts of North Africa. These regions would become central to Britain's war effort as Churchill chose to take on the Italians, the one way he had to hit back at Hitler.

It was a successful policy, as Mussolini's failed expeditions in Egypt and Greece resulted in Hitler despatching German troops to pick up the pieces left by his ally. In early 1941, General Erwin Rommel was sent to rescue the Italians in Libya and North Africa. The small unit that he commanded was to grow into the Afrika Korps. There then began a war of advance and retreat between Rommel and the British forces based in Egypt. In the spring of 1941 Hitler's troops invaded Greece and occupied the country. Later the German leadership felt that the Italians should have conquered Malta and taken over the island in the way they had occupied Crete.

Immense pressure was put on Malta and the Luftwaffe bombed the island ceaselessly. For Britain, it was vital to hold on to Malta, but the island was reliant upon supplies being shipped in. The German navy and air force attacked convoy after convoy, sinking large numbers of merchant vessels. The siege of Malta nearly succeeded in starving out the island, but somehow it still clung on to act as a thorn in the side of the Axis military machine in the Mediterranean.

The extreme circumstances of life in Malta, the endless pressure of air raids and the spartan rations, did not suit many. But they did suit Adrian Warburton, known universally as 'Warby'. Great demands were soon placed on the Marylands of Flight 431 for photo reconnaissance of what the Italian navy was up to and where its modern fleet of battleships and heavy battle cruisers were positioned. With the confidence of his flight leader, an outgoing Australian named Tich Whiteley, Warby was encouraged to emerge from the shadows. When the other pilots went down with stomach upsets known as the 'Malta Dog', he took up flying again. Warby could manage only another shaky start and he never quite mastered the art of taking off and landing in two-engined aircraft. But he rapidly proved a master of everything in between, quickly grasping what was needed to photograph effectively from the air. His Maryland was equipped with oblique as well as vertical cameras and he would employ the obliques on daredevil low level passes, using surprise to fly quickly over a fleet at anchor. But unlike most of the 'dicing' pilots, if something went wrong and he felt he hadn't got the pictures needed, he would go back again for another pass despite the mass of anti-aircraft fire that would soon be turned on his single plane. Sometimes he would go in as low as two hundred feet. On occasions, flying even lower just above the waves, rather than use the cameras mounted in the aircraft he would take pictures with a handheld Leica camera he had borrowed from a wealthy Maltese marquis who also happened to be a photo enthusiast.

Warburton's first notable flying achievement was to photograph the Italian fleet at Taranto harbour. The naval commander in the Mediterranean, Admiral Cunningham, was planning a daring carrier-borne Fleet Air Arm attack on the Italian fleet and needed regular recon reports of the ships moored at Taranto. On 10 November 1940 Warburton flew with his favourite crew, navigator Sgt Frank Bastard and wireless operator/gunner Sgt Paddy Moren, through dreadful weather to Taranto. In two low level sweeps he noted down the names of five battleships, fourteen cruisers and twenty-seven destroyers, along with their precise location. He had flown so low over the Italian ships that when he returned a ship's aerial was found caught up in his aircraft, trailing behind the tail wheel.

On the following day he flew again over Taranto and took high level photos which helped to identify the location of torpedo nets and barrage balloons and were used to brief the pilots on board the aircraft carriers HMS *Illustrious* and HMS *Eagle*. That night, twenty-six Swordfish aircraft attacked the harbour, sinking three battleships and a cruiser and damaging many other warships. The attack on the Italian fleet fundamentally swung the balance of naval power in the Mediterranean in favour of the Royal Navy and allowed Allied convoys to reinforce Egypt. Admiral Cunningham paid specific tribute to the work of the reconnaissance pilots in the success of his daring strike. Warburton seemed to be fearless in the face of the enemy and within six months he had won his first DFC for gallantry in the air. This was quite a turnaround for the 'below average' flier of eighteen months earlier.

The Marylands at Malta were not formally part of the PR command based at Heston and later at Benson. Bearing in mind the extreme difficulties of life on the island, the authorities turned a blind eye to the more relaxed atmosphere that prevailed. It was one that Warby needed in order to flourish. Officers and men worked together closely. With the absence of spare parts all sorts of improvisation was needed to patch up damaged aircraft and to keep them flying. At times everyone joined in the repair work. Unlike other PR flights, the Marylands were armed with machine guns for defence and sometimes with incendiary bombs that were simply kicked out of the lower hatch of the aircraft. If intercepted by Italian fighters, Warburton would often turn on them and he soon began to shoot them down. After a few months he became the top Malta 'ace', shooting down more enemy aircraft than even the fighter pilots based on the island. This was the only time the pilot of a light bomber ever achieved such a feat.

In April, two Hurricanes arrived in Malta fitted out with twin F24 cameras. Warburton flew these on shorter recces, keeping a watchful eye as Axis convoys loaded up to sail from Naples, Messina or Palermo to take supplies to Rommel and his troops in North Africa. His knowledge of the Italian fleet soon proved invaluable. He grew to recognise the principal Italian warships and to know where they regularly moored. He could quickly spot if one of them were absent from its normal home. He even began to identify some of the merchant vessels used to re-supply Rommel's troops. Occasionally, the Navy would question his identification, after which on at least one occasion he flew back again, going in even closer and photographing the ship's name plate to prove his point.

Soon the stories about Warburton's fearless flying grew into quite a legend. On one occasion, the Army wanted the entire coastal road from Benghazi to Tripoli to be photographed as this was the sole road used by the German and Italian armies to bring supplies up to the front. It was estimated that it would take about a week of regular PR flights to cover the full five-hundred-mile stretch. Despite being pursued by enemy fighters on four separate occasions, Warburton managed to photograph the entire road in a single sortie using a wide angle lens, saving several days of dangerous PR flights. On another occasion he was flying low over a new Italian airfield to photograph it when the control tower gave him the green light to land. He went in even lower, lined up at a group of transport planes on the ground and opened fire with his front-firing machine guns. There must have been some amazed Italian faces on the ground that day.

The extraordinary displays of flying soon made Warby a famous figure in Malta, and in desperate times when stocks of food, fuel and everything else were so low and defeat or conquest was staring the island's people in the face, his exploits provided a great boost for morale. In 1941 he began a relationship with an English cabaret dancer by the name of Christina Ratcliffe, who had been stranded on Malta the previous June and had no means of getting away. She and several other stranded dancers formed a troupe called the Whizz Bangs that went around to entertain Army, Navy and Air Force personnel in their messes. Christina was thought to be the best-looking English girl on the island and Warburton soon impressed her with his thin, athletic figure, his flowing blond hair (grown much longer than would have been allowed by RAF regulations in Britain) and his blue eyes. She later said 'He looked like a Greek god.'[1] She also noticed the smart colours of the DFC on his uniform and clearly recognised him as a war hero. They began to live together in a flat on the island and were soon known as the most glamorous couple in Malta – the flying ace and the beautiful cabaret dancer. Christina seems to have offered some sort of stability for Warburton and although he was not a show-off in the usual sense, she certainly provided him with a sense of self-worth which he might not otherwise have gained even from his flying achievements.

In May 1941 a new commanding officer arrived in Malta to take charge of the RAF operation. Air Vice Marshal Hugh Pughe Lloyd, usually known as 'Hugh Pughe'. He soon realised the value of Warburton's star status on the island and allowed him pretty much a free hand to do things in his own way. Warburton rarely wore approved flying kit, preferring to dress in grey flannels, although he always wore his blue RAF cap, which slowly became worn out and tatty, on top of his long blond hair. Warburton was a great friend and supporter of his aircrew, the mechanics known by the officers as 'erks', who laboured for long hours to maintain and service aircraft and rarely received any thanks or recognition. He would spend many hours with the aircrew, either helping them out or simply sitting on the ground playing cards. As a consequence, although they admired him for his flying, many of the other RAF officers on Malta did not take to this eccentric figure who lived off base with his girlfriend, didn't socialise in the usual way in the officers' mess and preferred to spend time with his aircrew. But with support from the Air Vice Marshal, Warby was secure and his legend went from strength to strength.

There were still arguments, of course. Lloyd did not approve of photo reconnaissance pilots who got distracted into dog-fights with enemy aircraft. He wanted them back at base with their photographs intact, not taking risks and showing off. Lloyd later remembered how he would say to Warburton, '"Really Adrian, it's very naughty of you to go chasing these poor Italians," and he would answer a little shamefacedly "Well, sir, it was too easy." Then he would come into my office [on another day] and say rather sheepishly: "I've shot down another one". "You musn't do that Adrian," I told him: and so it would go on.'[2] Even allowing for the rose-tinted nature of memories recalled years after the event, the story still reveals the remarkably frank and informal way the most senior RAF man in Malta dealt with the junior flying officer. Lloyd jokingly called Warburton 'the King of the Mediterranean'. But the nick-name stuck. Some even saw him as the Second World War's equivalent to Lawrence of Arabia.

In the autumn of 1941, Ultra intelligence from German sig-nals decrypted at Bletchley Park regularly began to report on the plans for convoys leaving Italian ports to carry supplies to Rommel's Afrika Korps. Once this intelligence had come in, the photo recon pilots were able to follow each convoy as it set sail. As a consequence, the RAF achieved great success in attacking and sinking the supply convoys in the western Mediterranean. In one month, they sunk 77 per cent of Axis shipping heading for North Africa.[3] In a fury, Hitler despatched three air corps from the Eastern Front to reinforce the Mediterranean and from the end of December 1941 the bombing of Malta went up a gear. Sometimes, coming from bases in nearby Sicily, there were up to eight air raids in a single day.

With the Luftwaffe now flying in force over the Mediterranean, the happy days of shooting up the Italians ended. And the reconnaissance pilots were up against the formidable Me 109s, flown by pilots battle-hardened on the Eastern Front. Warburton continued to find himself in scrape after scrape but he used his superb flying to outmanoeuvre the enemy fighters. He would bank so hard that his aircraft would judder and shake, but the Me 109 usually went shooting past. During one flight over Taranto harbour the flak was so heavy that when a shell exploded near Warburton's aircraft (this time a Beaufighter specially adapted for aerial photography), it threw open the armour-plated door between Ron Hadden, the photo mechanic on board, and Warburton at the controls. Hadden later described what he saw: 'He had his hat on top of his helmet; cigarette hanging from his lips [both against flying regulations]; one elbow resting on the side of the cockpit, driving the plane with his other hand. His complete lack of fear and nonchalant attitude to the noise and from the flak was fantastic. Warby at his best. Fighters were chasing us, the port engine had failed but he pressed home his recce and safely returned.'[4] Warby seemed to be able to escape from every scrap, outperform every pursuer and survive every technical fault. He even walked away from two crashes.

Warburton's flying skills have never been fully dissected. When he left his first long posting on Malta at the end of September 1941 he had been awarded the DFC twice and had eight confirmed 'kills', with several more 'probables' and many aircraft destroyed on the ground. He flew photographic reconnaissance sorties from Egypt for some months before returning to Malta at the end of the year. As a reconnaissance pilot he had all the necessary skills. He was an individualist and a fine navigator. As a consequence, about every six months he would receive another medal, first the DSO and then a double bar to his DFC. In August 1943 he received a bar to his DSO. When he finally left Malta the following month he had clocked up about 390 operational sorties. He had truly diced with death on dozens of occasions, but no pilot survives all this because he is in some way 'protected', let alone because he is 'lucky'. Despite his devil-may-care flamboyance and his displays of bravado, Warburton could only have survived by applying a supremely professional approach to every mission. He did not take risks; he took *calculated* risks. And either instinctively or by detailed preparation, he knew how to calculate risk.

Warburton well deserves his reputation as a fearless reconnaissance pilot who prided himself that he would get his photographs back whatever the circumstances. But he cannot be summed up in a rosy, idealistic way as a pilot who could naturally outfly others. Malta had provided the opportunity for Warburton to do things his way and to discover what he and his aircraft were capable of. Never a natural flier, his inability to comfortably take off and land in two-engined aircraft remained throughout his career. Had he stayed in England he might have remained a good navigator, but the restrictions and regulations would have prevented him from becoming the star pilot he was celebrated as in Malta. Some people need extraordinary circumstances to enable them to achieve their best and will not excel in the confines within which others flourish. Maybe Warburton needed Christina; he certainly needed the informal atmosphere of Malta, and he needed a mission – to photograph the Italian fleet and the German and Italian armies. Only when all this came into alignment did his gallantry become heroic rather than suicidal.

In the spring of 1943, Warburton, now a squadron leader in charge of 683 Squadron back on Malta, photographed the beaches on Sicily where amphibious Anglo-American landings were to take place in July. After the successful conquest of Sicily in just a month, Italy capitulated. The pressure on Malta was off. The Allied armies crossed to the Italian mainland, now heavily reinforced with German troops, and began their slow march north, only liberating Rome in June 1944 – just in time to be eclipsed by the Normandy landings.

Warburton finally left Malta in September 1943. He was not wanted back in the UK. He had never been part of the more formal PR organisation based at RAF Benson. He had a reputation for taunting authority and challenging his senior officers while looking after those who worked for him. His maverick, unorthodox style would never have fitted in to what was now a huge operation of several squadrons of reconnaissance pilots back home. He had got on extremely well with the American fliers who had begun to appear in large numbers in the Mediterranean during 1943. Lieutenant-Colonel Elliott Roosevelt, son of the President, was in charge of the US Army Air Force Photo Reconnaissance Unit and he liked Warby hugely, writing later that he had never known a better flier.

No doubt with a little help from his high-ranking American admirer, Warburton, who by this time had been promoted to wing commander, was awarded command of the new 336 Wing. Made up initially of three squadrons, it was to be based at La Marsa near Tunis, the headquarters of the Allied Air Forces in the Mediterranean, but would move into southern Italy as soon as appropriate landing fields had been captured in the area around Foggia in the south-east. Warburton took to his new responsibility with vigour and began to select the best pilots and crews from across the Mediterranean theatre. Then, on 26 November, he had a car accident after what colleagues remember as a night of heavy drinking. He broke his pelvis and was taken to hospital, where he was put in a large plaster cast. He was in hospital for about seven weeks.

During this time Warburton seems to have gone into a decline. He was not one to endure being holed up in a hospital ward for long and while he was in hospital 336 Wing was moved to Italy. Moreover, to his intense frustration, he was replaced as its commanding officer by Gordon Hughes. Eventually, he discharged himself by climbing out of a hospital window and getting friends to remove the plaster cast. Then somehow he 'borrowed' a Spitfire and flew to San Severo, where his wing was now based. For a few weeks, Warby was a fish out of water, not sure which way to turn. Eventually, no doubt once again with the help of his American supporters, he was sent back to the UK and in the spring of 1944 appointed as liaison officer with the US 7th Photo-Recce Group, based at Mount Farm in Oxfordshire.

This job was a 'piece of cake', in contemporary parlance, and no doubt most officers after three years of operational flying, and after enduring the privations of Malta under siege, would have been delighted to do their bit for the war effort based on an American airbase, even able to enjoy the luxuries and extra rations that American soldiers and airmen in the UK enjoyed, in contrast to their British counterparts. But not Warburton. Friends noticed he had become severely depressed. On 12 April 1944, Elliott Roosevelt personally gave him authority to fly a long reconnaissance sortie over southern Germany to take damage assessment photos of the recent US bombing raids on ball-bearing factories. Roosevelt clearly thought that letting him fly again would cheer his friend up. In strange circumstances that have never been fully explained, two US F-5 aircraft (the photo reconnaissance version of the Lockheed Lightning, a two-engined fighter-bomber) took off, one flown by Captain Carl Chapman, an American, and the other by Warburton, who was not at the time allocated to operational flying. They flew together to a point north of Munich and there went their separate ways to photograph the two bombed factories. Chapman went on and landed at an airbase in Sardinia, as had been the flight plan. Warburton was never heard of again.

As he was such a legend, the Warburton rumour machine soon went into overdrive. Some believed that, rather than fly to Sardinia as arranged, he might have decided to head for his old wing in southern Italy and simply ran out of fuel. Others thought he had got into such trouble with the authorities in England that he had decided to come down in neutral Switzerland in order to opt out of the war altogether. Strangely, when the US authorities finally passed on his possessions to his mother there was hardly anything in his billet, so some suggested he had taken them with him and headed for Malta. Some even thought he had made it to Malta and was there living incognito with Christina – although she always denied ever seeing him again after he had finally left the island the previous September. The mystery seemed a fitting end to an enigmatic life.

Decades passed and no definitive evidence came to light. The discovery of the crash site of an F-5 Lightning in Comiso, Sicily suggested that if this had been Warburton's plane, then maybe he was trying to get to Malta after all. Then, in 2002, thanks to the hard work of Frank Dorber, an enthusiast who refused to let the Warby legend die, the German authorities agreed to dig up the remains of an F-5 near the village of Egling, near Dunzelbach in southern Germany. The engine was removed and a roll of film was found in the wreck, showing that the plane had been on a photo recon mission. Later it was verified from the number on the engine plate that this was the plane Warburton had been flying. German records showed that it had been shot down by anti-aircraft fire at 11.45 a.m. on 12 April 1944.

The strange tale of Adrian Warburton ended with the removal of his remains from the wreckage and his burial at the Commonwealth War Graves cemetery at Durnbach on 14 May 2003. Christina Ratcliffe had died in 1989. But the Ministry of Defence tracked down his official wife, Eileen, 'Betty of the Bush', who had remarried in 1976 and, after living in Australia for many years, had just returned to the UK. Now in her nineties, she was flown out to Munich by the MoD to attend the ceremony. Warburton was given a funeral with full military honours. A trumpeter from the Central Band of the Royal Air Force played the Last Post and a lone piper played a lament. The last of the Second World War photo recon pilots was given a thoroughly twenty-first-century burial with the media in full attendance and television cameras following every step of the procession.[5] It somehow seems an appropriate postscript, not only for the strange story of Adrian Warburton but for the heroism and bravery displayed by every single pilot who flew across enemy-occupied territory for hours on end, day after day, week after week, month after month to capture those precious photographic images for the interpreters to study.

9

Finding the Targets

On the night of 19 March 1940, the RAF carried out its first bombing raid of the war on Germany. For the first six months of the war, Bomber Command had done little more than drop hundreds of thousands of leaflets calling for the nation to lay down its arms and seek peace. The Cabinet had frequently debated the propriety of bombing German territory. The war was still in what was called its 'Phoney' stage, and as there had been no German air raids on Britain many ministers felt that to bomb Germany risked provoking Hitler into ordering a huge retaliation. The Secretary for the Air, Sir Kingsley Wood, even argued against bombing Germany because bombs might fall on private property, which would never do.[1]

The target for this first raid was the seaplane base at Hornum on the island of Sylt, near the Danish border, from where German aircraft had been dropping mines in the North Sea. It was decided that this was a legitimate target as the mines were causing real menace to the Royal Navy and there was little risk of civilian casualties. There was much excitement about the mission and the Air Ministry released information to the press during the night the raid took place. Headlines in the following morning's papers shrieked out 'Land Target at Last for the RAF – Tons of Bombs Dropped' and 'Hangars and Oil Tanks Ablaze'. This was what the public wanted from the RAF, to go out and show the Germans what was what. It was tremendous for morale to think that the RAF were hitting back at the Nazi war machine.

Hugh Hamshaw Thomas was, at this early point of the war, an RAF intelligence officer, debriefing bomber crews as they returned from missions. He later remembered how the commander of 5 Group, who had ordered the Hornum raid, carried out some of the debriefings in person as he was so keen to hear about the damage caused by the first raid on Germany. He was pleased when he got 'a good story' of blazing wreckage below and of buildings destroyed by bombs. But he was annoyed when some pilots 'wouldn't play up', as he wanted them to provide more vivid evidence than they were prepared to about the damage caused by the raid.[2] The commander's name was Arthur Harris and later in the war he would be appointed to take charge of Bomber Command. He became one of the great protagonists of the bomber offensive, acquiring the nickname 'Bomber Harris', or to his men 'Butcher' or 'Butch'.

With aerial photography playing a crucial role in damage assessment, on the morning after the raid a Blenheim reconnaissance aircraft flew over the Hornum base and took a series of photographs. When the aircraft returned and the photos had been developed and printed they were rushed to Bomber Command headquarters at High Wycombe. Bomber Command at this time had its own small photo interpretation unit run by Squadron Leader Peter Riddell, quite separate from the work that was going on at Wembley. The photos arrived mid evening and Riddell and three interpreters immediately set to work to assess the damage that had been done to the German base. All night they worked on the photographs. To their dismay, despite the dramatic reports from some of the bomber crews, they could see all the hangars still intact, the Heinkel seaplanes still on their slipways and the large oil tanks entirely undamaged. The interpreters went over the photographs again and again through the night but they could find no evidence of damage to the airbase. They could not even see bomb craters in the sand dunes around the site. The press were clamouring for photographs of the damage and Prime Minister Neville Chamberlain had announced in Parliament that the raid had been a terrific success. But for the PIs, it was not looking good.

Early the next morning Riddell received a phone call. 'Have you shaved?' the voice asked.'Yes,' said Riddell. It was a cheerful Air Vice-Marshal Norman Bottomley, who then said, 'Put on a clean uniform quick, as you've got to go to Buckingham Palace with some enlargements of the photos of Sylt.'

Riddell could not believe what he was hearing. He asked to see Bottomley immediately, and in his office explained that there was no evidence of any damage to the German base. There are different versions told by those involved of what happened next. But it is clear that the office where the photo interpreters had been working was then locked, with the PIs still inside. Some say that it was Riddell who locked them in, not wanting anyone else to see or hear about the photos, and that he then went to the head of Bomber Command, Sir Edgar Ludlow-Hewitt, who demanded to see the photos himself. Riddell laid out the photos on the floor of his office and together the two men crawled over them for thirty minutes. Ludlow-Hewitt had a magnifying glass and

Riddell showed him that the base had sustained no damage at all.

In other versions of the story, it was Harris who locked the PIs in their office and told them they were not to come out until they had found evidence of damage caused by the bombing raid. Whatever the case, the chiefs of Bomber Command were astonished. They simply could not believe the evidence from the aerial photographs. Various explanations were offered as to why no damage appeared to be recorded. The photos were not clear enough. The scale of the photos was too small and so it was impossible to see the damage. Someone even suggested that the Germans had brought in repair squads in the early morning to clear everything up so by the time the reconnaissance aircraft appeared, the damage had been covered over. However, the simple explanation turned out to be the most unpalatable one for Bomber Command. The RAF bombers had totally missed their target for that night. Although the implication was too painful to accept at this stage of the war, the fact was that with the navigation techniques then available it was simply impossible for RAF bomber crews flying at night over enemy territory to find and identify a small target as precise as a single airbase. In fact the bombers had not bombed Sylt at all. Instead they had bombed a similar looking island a few miles to the north-east. As if this was not embarrassing enough, the island turned out not even to be in Germany, but inside neutral Denmark.[3]

After a few days, when the dreadful truth had sunk in, the Air Ministry slipped out a press release that covered up the humiliating failure by saying, 'The photographs taken [after the raid] have proved to be of no value in indicating the extent of the material damage inflicted in the course of the heavy attack.' Later it was admitted that the damage caused 'was probably not as great as was originally estimated'.[4] The Germans meanwhile took groups of neutral journalists on tours of the Hornum base to show that their operation had suffered no damage whatsoever. It was a bitter blow to such a lauded bombing mission. And overnight, Bomber Command became hugely suspicious about damage assessment reports from photo interpreters.

In this case, the awkwardness over the Sylt raid was soon forgotten. The German invasion of Norway followed a few days later in April 1940 and all attention was focused on this new chapter in the war. It was left to the official history of the bombing offensive to conclude later that in the early stages of the war, 'Bomber Command was incapable of inflicting anything but insignificant damage on the enemy.'[5]

The story of the problems Bomber Command had with its aircraft, with the poor quality of its bombs and with the total absence of the sort of navigational aids necessary for flying hundreds of miles across blacked-out enemy territory at night has been told elsewhere.[6] The crews had not initially been trained for night flying as it had been assumed that the RAF would carry out bombing in daylight. But the heavy loss rate of up to 50 per cent in the first raids of the war made it clear that bombing would have to take place at night. In addition the crews were not used to flying at the height to which they were now forced by the heavy anti-aircraft fire coming up at them. This made it even more difficult to bomb with accuracy and a big difference began to grow between the expectations and the claims of great success, on the one hand, and the reality – as proved by the aerial photographs – that targets were being missed by miles, sometimes even by tens of miles.

This made for a tense situation between Bomber Command and the photo interpreters. Not only Bomber Command but the public at large wanted to hear that RAF bombers were hitting and destroying German targets as retaliation for the Blitz. There was a natural tendency for commanders to blame the photographs or the interpreters for failing to say what they wanted to hear, that a raid had been a striking success. More than once a negative report from the PIs would come back with words like 'I do not accept this report' scrawled across the top of it. As a consequence, at the end of 1940 Bomber Command insisted on keeping its own photo intelligence unit under its own command. The unit had its own reconnaissance Spitfires, flying out of RAF Oakington, an airfield on the edge of the fens in East Anglia. By controlling its own PR and PI, Bomber Command hoped somehow to limit or at least manage the flow of information about how hopeless these early bombing missions were. So, when all photo interpretation was centralised at Medmenham in April 1941, Bomber Command again insisted on maintaining control of its own separate unit. But this state of affairs could not last for long as it went totally against the purpose of Medmenham, to build a specialised centre of photo interpretation for the whole of the war effort. In September 1941 the logic of the situation finally prevailed. The Bomber Command PR and PI operation was disbanded and the unit was integrated with the work going on at Medmenham.

The unit employed various techniques to show the effectiveness of night bombing in a more positive light. One of the most challenging was the development of night photography from the air. Since it had been assumed that RAF bombing would be carried out in daylight, many bombers in the first years of the war were equipped with aerial cameras. When it was realised that bombing would have to take place at night, these cameras seemed redundant. But a lively young Scotsman who had been put in charge of Bomber Command's PRU unit,

Squadron Leader Pat Ogilvie, thought otherwise. He set about finding ways of obtaining useful information from night photographs and began a set of experiments with new, ingenious devices. The camera had to be synchronised with the explosion of a flashlight or flash bomb that was dropped with the main bomb load. The camera aperture would stay open for some time, maybe as long as five seconds, to ensure the film was exposed. The consequent image would show a series of white, wavy lines, like streaks of spaghetti across a black background.

Over time it became possible to work out how to interpret these lines and to distinguish what would have been the source of each light that would be shining bright on a night air raid. The fires burning below would give one sort of exposure that could be identified and tracked. The explosions of anti-aircraft shells or of tracer being fired up at the bombers would take on another distinctive appearance that could also be identified. Finally, within the few seconds of exposure there was likely to be something on the ground that could be identified by matching the photograph with daylight images – a river, a road or a building that would be lit up sufficiently by the flash to register. This would enable the interpreters to plot the precise location of an aircraft at the moment it dropped its bombs.[7]

Pat Ogilvie soon recruited an old friend to join him in tackling the challenges of interpreting night photography. This was Bernard Babington Smith, coincidentally the younger brother of Constance, the WAAF officer who was to lead the aircraft identification section at Medmenham. Ogilvie heard that Babington Smith was finishing his officer's training and thought he had just the right sort of enquiring, mathematical mind for his unit, so he asked for him to be posted to Oakington. Babington Smith arrived in December 1940 and began to collate the hundreds of night photographs that had been taken. By gradually working out what all the white streaks meant he could begin to calculate the intensity of anti-aircraft fire in different parts of Germany, the spacing and use of searchlights, and the layout of decoy fires. He was soon able to make some suggestions about the intensity and accuracy of the bombing raid itself from the glow of the burning buildings on the ground. There was still much scepticism that PI could accurately record how successful a bombing mission had been, so Babington Smith developed the practice of only passing on photographs that recorded successful missions.[8] This no doubt helped to make night photography less unpopular with his bosses.

When Bomber Command PRU finally moved into Medmenham, Babington Smith went with it, arriving in February 1942 along with his library of strange black photos covered with white streaky lines. He was put in charge of what was appropriately called N Section and was allocated to what had been the main bathroom of Danesfield House. Babington Smith was soon measuring fire tracks and assessing the concentration of incendiaries or high explosives at or near the target area. He could create a mosaic from all the images that had been taken at night and by identifying the centre of the blaze he could see from each aircraft's night photographs how near they were to the target area. Night photography developed into a sophisticated science at Medmenham and within a few years was offering valuable information about the accuracy of bombing missions that supplemented the damage assessment photography carried out on the day after a raid.

By the middle of 1941, the Prime Minister's principal scientific adviser, Sir Frederick Lindemann, was becoming seriously concerned about the effectiveness of Bomber Command's nightly forays over occupied Europe. Lindemann was a close friend of the Prime Minister as well as a senior adviser and it was certain that anything he felt concerned about would soon be passed on to Churchill. It so happened that Lindemann's private secretary, Bryan Hopkin, bumped into Glyn Daniel at around this time one evening at the Hare and Hounds pub, the local used by many of the Medmenham staff. They were old school friends and had been undergraduates at Cambridge together. When Daniel told his old friend he was at Medmenham, Hopkin replied, 'Aha, just the man we want,' and invited him to dinner the next evening. On his arrival, Daniel found Lindemann was there as well. The scientist told him, 'The Prime Minister and I want to know exactly what photo intelligence is learning about the war,' explaining that reports from Medmenham were only reaching the War Cabinet in an abbreviated and summary form. He and Churchill were both suspicious, he said, 'that information was being withheld from them, especially the right information about the extent of our bombing successes and failures'. Daniel told them what he knew but suggested they talk with Douglas Kendall, who as a more senior interpretation officer would have a better overall view on the matter.

Kendall arrived for dinner a few days later shaking like a leaf, as he had been commanded to attend by a direct call from the Prime Minister's office in Downing Street. After a while he relaxed and told Lindemann about the serious problems Bomber Command's aircraft were having in finding and hitting their targets.[9] By now, all Lindemann's fears and suspicions were raised to new heights.

Lindemann alerted Churchill, and the Prime Minister ordered him to carry out an independent investigation. As a consequence, David Butt from the War Cabinet secretariat analysed more than six hundred aerial photographs taken in June and July 1941. Most were night photographs taken from the bombers during raids. The Butt Report contained a full analysis of what these photographs recorded and it confirmed Lindemann's worst fears. Its main conclusion was that only about one in three bombers who claimed to have attacked a target succeeded in dropping their bombs within five miles of it. On a full moon this improved to about two in three, a disappointing success rate in itself. But the report found that on nights when there was no moonlight, only one aircraft in *fifteen* managed to drop its bombs within five miles of the target. Butt accepted that his report was not definitive, but he had analysed photos from a hundred raids and he was confident that his findings were broadly accurate. He made it clear that the bomber crews who came back nightly with stories of seeing the target in flames below them were not as reliable as the photographic evidence. He concluded: 'A camera cannot make mistakes and cannot like a human being under conditions of extreme strain be misled by appearances. Conclusions drawn from photographs should be completely reliable.'[10]

The report was an appalling indictment of Bomber Command's aircraft and techniques of navigation. Churchill was shocked by the conclusions. He was concerned that so little damage was being done to the German war economy and that so many crews were being lost for so little gain. He immediately forwarded the report to the Chief of the Air Staff, Air Chief Marshal Sir Charles Portal, with a note saying 'This is a very serious paper, and seems to require your most urgent attention. I await your proposals for action.'[11]

Needless to say the air marshals repudiated the accuracy of the findings, and a full-scale debate about the efficacy of the bombing offensive ensued. But the fact was that there was very little Bomber Command could do at this time to improve the accuracy of its bombing, until new navigational aids came in and the next generation of four-engined 'heavy' bombers replaced the two-engined light bombers with their tiny bombloads that were in current use. In November 1941, after a raid in which nearly one in ten of the bombers were shot down or failed to return, an unacceptable loss rate, Churchill ordered what amounted to a cessation of the bombing of Germany for the winter. He felt that Bomber Command risked frittering away its fleet of aircraft and crews in a series of small and ineffectual raids. Sir Richard Peirse (the man who in 1940 had fallen out with Sidney Cotton), Ludlow-Hewitt's successor as head of Bomber Command, was himself removed from his command. He was replaced the following February by Sir Arthur Harris and only then did the bombing offensive begin again.

When the offensive started up once more in earnest in the spring of 1942, it had a new champion in 'Bomber' Harris. New technology arrived with the use of 'Gee' and 'Oboe', the nicknames for different forms of radio signals used to help guide aircraft to their targets. And Bomber Command began to benefit from the arrival of the first of the new fleet of heavy bombers, the Halifax, the Stirling and the Lancaster. Again aerial photography played a vital role. After Bomber Command had selected the targets, each crew would be provided with a folder of photographs to study beforehand and to take on the mission to help them identify the target when they were overhead. A Target Section at Medmenham was set up to service these needs. Each target folder consisted of maps of the target area and two sets of mosaics of aerial photos, printed on exactly the same scale as the maps. One mosaic would be marked with key pieces of information and indicators to help identify the target from the air. There was also information about the target, any known flak defences and detailed information or aerial photos showing decoy sites. At the end of May the first of the

Thousand Bomber Raids was launched on Cologne. The amount of work involved in researching, selecting photos and printing mosaics for the target folders for each aircraft on missions of this scale was immense.

Bertram Rota, now one of the senior officers in the Target Section, was given permission to visit the bomber airfields and talk with station commanders, intelligence officers and the crews themselves to see what ideas they had about the folders and how they might be improved. In one of these sessions he overheard crews talking about 'watermark' aids. When he asked what this meant, it was explained to him that most crews used landmark features as visual idents of the ground below to assist their navigation and that the easiest of these to see from the air was water – rivers, canals, lakes. Rota realised that water features had to be marked more clearly on the aerial photos to help the aircrew find their targets. But the importance of 'watermarks' went beyond this. A WAAF officer named Loyalty Howard who was working in the Night Photography Section noted that bombs intended for the major Krupps industrial plant at Essen were frequently being dropped six miles to the east. On further analysis it appeared that Lake Baldersee, which was shown on the maps near the Krupps works, had been drained. The bomber crews were picking up a bend in the river six miles away and were aiming at that instead. As Rota and others in the Section noted, sometimes the centre of the target was less important than in establishing the means of getting to it.[12]

After the technology of navigational aids had improved with the introduction of 'Gee' and 'Oboe', there was a further development with the use of a form of aerial radar that mapped the terrain below the bomber. This was called H2S. Navigators could follow the outline of the landscape below and plot their route to the target area. Photographs could be taken of the H2S screen at the moment an aircraft's bombs were released as a way of identifying later exactly where it had been when it dropped its bombs. Again, this proved controversial with bomber crews and their bosses. It was difficult enough flying for hours over enemy territory under attack from night fighters and being fired at by flak batteries below, without having some snooping device on board that reported on you if the navigator had directed you to the wrong place. After one set of photographs seemed to establish poor navigation, Bomber Harris wrote to the head of Intelligence at the Air Ministry protesting at the 'criticism'. The tension between the bosses of Bomber Command and the photo interpreters had not gone away.

From 1943, the RAF began to use pathfinders – often flying in fast Mosquito aircraft, another role in which the plywood wonder excelled – as another way of trying to improve the accuracy of bombing. The role of the pathfinders was to identify the target and then drop target indicators, in the form of coloured flares, over the area to be bombed. The planes usually contained the latest navigational aids to help them precisely identify the target. The bombers following behind could clearly see the flares, indicating the location for their bombing run. The use of coloured flares led to the first employment of colour film in aerial photography. PIs could identify the flares and assess the accuracy of their placing, and were thus able to record the effectiveness of the bombing mission itself.

Colour film was in short supply during the war years and so a form of 'composite colour' was used in which only a few frames of colour film were superimposed on a roll of black and white film. It was an ingenious solution and colour began to play an important part in night photography. By the end of the war about 80 per cent of night photographs were taken in colour or in composite colour. Later in the war, 35mm movie cameras were installed and moving film of target areas was recorded. The use of onboard H2S screen cameras, colour film and movie film, all added to the complex science of night photography.[13]

Working alongside the damage assessment teams at Medmenham were the industrial specialists known as D Section. These experts needed to know in detail what factories were involved in work that contributed to the war effort. Most of the well-known aircraft or armament factories had been identified before the war. In the early days at Wembley and then at Medmenham, Hugh Hamshaw Thomas was in charge of building up a reference library of data about industry in Germany and the rest of occupied Europe. Card indexes were made for each factory with details of its exact location and a summary of everything that was known about it. Any aerial photos of that plant in the library were noted down. But the interpreters required a huge breadth of knowledge as to how different factories worked: what processes were involved in, say, iron or steel production, what technologies were involved in the production of synthetic fuels, which engineering plants produced which products, how the electric power industry operated and which plastics or explosives were produced at every single chemicals factory.

The PIs assessing the damage to industry would use whatever information they could find about the target factories. This might come from guide books, pre-war street plans or commercial directories. When the bombing offensive restarted in the spring of 1942, one of the first industrial targets was the vast Renault factory at Billancourt near Paris. The Ministry of Economic Warfare managed to obtain from Lloyds, who insured the factory before the war, detailed plans of the entire plant, including the layout of factory buildings, each vehicle assembly and engine shop, every forge and paint works, indeed every workshop on the site. From these it was possible to see exactly what the effect was of the destruction caused by the bombing, while from later aerial cover, it was possible to chart how quickly the Germans were able to rebuild the factory and to put it back into production. Ronald Gillanders from D Section became the PI expert on the Billancourt factory and he was able to advise against the re-bombing of the plant when the Americans proposed it as a target. He could see the factory was not yet back in production, that the stockyards were empty and that there were no lorries in the transport bay. His advice no doubt saved much wasted effort and probably many lives.

Despite the burgeoning number of photo reconnaissance flights taking place after bombing missions and the growing sophistication of damage assessment reports, the friction between Bomber Command and the photo intelligence teams flared up again in the autumn of 1942. Arthur Harris once more complained that he was not satisfied with the current system and felt the lack of control over recon flights was preventing him from adequately directing his bombing policy. Objecting to the fact that he was reliant upon another organisation for something so central to his operation he once again put forward plans for a reorganisation of photographic reconnaissance and for Bomber Command to take control of its own PR and PI. Once more the plans were opposed by Coastal Command, under whose authority PR still lay. They pointed out that such a reorganisation would reverse the whole process of centralisation and the development of specialist teams who could work together in the Central Interpretation Unit. Senior officials who had many other priorities once again spent more time discussing the organisation of PR. After much debate it was finally decided to leave it exactly as it was.[14]

The work of the photo interpreters received a rare moment of publicity when it was featured in the Crown Film Unit's documentary *Target for Tonight*.[15] The film was directed by Harry Watt, one of the most celebrated film makers to emerge from the 1930s documentary film movement in Britain. He had a reputation for making films of great realism, rarely using actors but instead casting real people playing themselves. Today his films would be called drama-documentaries.[16] *Target for Tonight* recreates the story of a Wellington bombing raid over Nazi Germany, explaining how such a raid was planned and carried out. It begins with a reconnaissance aircraft dropping by parachute a set of aerial photos which are then examined by a team of PIs.

There is no indication in the film of the existence of a Central Interpretation Unit in a grand Victorian country house in the Thames Valley. Instead, the PIs appear to work in a crowded room in an underground concrete bunker in the middle of nowhere. Glyn Daniel was one of those who appeared in the film, along with Constance Babington Smith, who is in the background happily counting the numbers of Me 109s on an enemy airfield. The aerial photographs reveal a huge industrial development by a river which is spotted by the squadron leader, played by Peter Riddell. He asks Daniel to get previous cover of the same location, and by making a quick comparison they can see that there are now railway marshalling yards, oil tanks and pipelines where there used to be open fields. This is all done quite convincingly. Glyn Daniel remembered that the script gave them some dreadful and inappropriate lines to say, which they managed to change.[17] The line that Daniel speaks in the film is 'It certainly is a peach of a target, isn't it sir!' The dialogue captures the wonderful tone of wartime RAF lingo, and the whole film is full of moments that in recent years have become comic clichés but which at the time gave the RAF a real cachet of being contemporary, with-it and hi-tech.

Having established what the next target will be, the film then follows a Wellington squadron preparing for the raid, concentrating on one aircraft, F for Freddie, as it takes part in the raid. The skipper of this aircraft, Squadron Leader Charles Pickard, became a star as a consequence of the film, at least within RAF circles.

The film was a huge success and seems to have convinced audiences that the RAF was dishing it out to the Nazi war machine on a regular basis. The phrase 'Target for tonight' entered regular parlance, particularly with BBC newsreaders. The film was voted Best Documentary by the National Board of Review and went on to win an honorary Academy Award in 1942. Of course, it gave no hint of the hopeless inaccuracy of most RAF bombing at this stage of the war, but for many viewers it did link aerial photography with the process of selecting targets for bombing.

The reality was that the selection of targets for the strategic bombing offensive came from a variety of sources. Reports from the damage assessment teams and by the industrial specialists at Medmenham fed back into the selection process. The Ministry of Economic Warfare wanted to lay down the overall objectives of the bombing offensive. But Bomber Command jealously guarded their right to select the target for their bombers each night. One of the clearest examples of the tension between them came in early 1943, when the Ministry pressured Bomber Command into attempting to breach the key dams that provided much of the water for the German heavy industry centred on the Ruhr valley and in addition generated some hydro-electric power for the region. The Ruhr, with its massive coke ovens, iron foundries and steel blast furnaces, produced many of the raw materials that kept the German war machine going. The problem facing Bomber Command was how to cause a big enough explosion to break the massive dam walls that held back hundreds of millions of gallons of water. Initial calculations suggested that a ten-ton bomb was needed. But at this time, no bomber was capable of carrying such a huge device.

The story of how the ingenuity and determination of an eccentric inventor came together with the bravery of a specially formed elite squadron is well known thanks to the hugely successful film *The Dam Busters* – one of the classic British war films of the 1950s.[18] The inventor, Barnes Wallis, developed a bouncing bomb that would skim along the surface of the reservoir behind the dam, sink when it came to the dam wall and explode at a depth of thirty feet, causing maximum damage to the wall. The canister bomb was dropped, spinning, from a four-engined Lancaster bomber that had to fly at precisely 220 mph at a height of exactly sixty feet over the reservoir. The unit put together to carry out the raid was 617 Squadron, reluctantly formed by Sir Arthur Harris, who was sceptical throughout that four-engined Lancaster bombers could fly low level precision raids. It was led by Wing Commander Guy Gibson, at twenty-four already one of the RAF's most distinguished bomber pilots with both a DSO and bar and a DFC and bar. Intensive training began in March 1943 with practice flights over dams in Derbyshire's Peak District and in North Wales, and in about six weeks Gibson reported that his squadron was trained and ready to fly a low level, night time precision raid.

Photo reconnaissance was vital to the success of the raid and recon Spitfires began flying over the dams above the Ruhr from early February 1943. Because of bad winter weather it took nine sorties to get effective photo cover of the principal dams. From these photos it was possible to assess critical information about water levels in the dams and about nearby anti-aircraft batteries. It was calculated that the ideal time to destroy the dams would be in May, when spring waters had filled them to their maximum levels. Ronald Gillanders was, again, the specialist at Medmenham who studied the dams and their reservoirs almost daily and got to know the countryside around them well. The skilled model makers quickly got to work producing two large 3D relief models of the Möhne Dam and the Sorpe Dam and the hinterland around them. Ready by mid May, these were used in the final briefings, enabling the aircrew to familiarise themselves with the exact topography they would find as they approached the reservoirs.[19]

The daring raid took place on the night of 16 May 1943. Nineteen Lancaster bombers set off in three waves timed to arrive over the dams one after another. They flew at sixty feet all the way across Holland and Germany, avoiding most of the flak and flying below radar but always at risk of hitting high trees or electric cables. Two of the aircraft did in fact hit pylons and crashed to the ground. The first target, the Möhne Dam, survived three direct hits, with giant fountains of water rising a thousand feet above the reservoir. The fourth bomb finally punctured the dam wall and the crews thought they had seen water begin to pour through the gap into the valley below. The next target, the Eder Dam, forty miles away, took three direct hits before a great earthquake appeared to shake the dam wall. The third target, the Sorpe Dam, was hit but its huge concrete and earth construction did not apparently break. Eight Lancasters failed to return from the raid, a loss rate of over 40 per cent. For his heroism in leading the raid Guy Gibson was awarded the VC. Thirty-three other crew members received gallantry awards, making 617 the most decorated squadron in the RAF. But Bomber Harris concluded that such precision missions were too costly in skilled crews. He decided to carry on instead with his policy of what the RAF called 'area bombing', but which was more colloquially referred to as 'carpet bombing'.

The Dam Busters raid was probably the most famous RAF bombing raid of the Second World War. As the official secret history of photo intelligence concluded, 'Bomber Command undoubtedly owed a considerable amount of its success [on the raid] to the cooperation and assistance rendered by the Photographic Reconnaissance Organisation.'[20] But how much damage had the raid really caused and how disruptive would it prove to be to German industry in the Ruhr? These were questions to which, once again, photo intelligence had to find the answers.

10

Assessing the Damage

At 7.30 a.m. on 17 May 1943, only an hour after the last Lancaster of 617 Squadron had touched down on returning from the Dam Busters raid, Flying Officer Jerry Fray took off in his PR Spitfire from RAF Benson to fly three hundred miles to the site of the dams. When he was still a hundred miles from the Ruhr he could see what looked like a bank of cloud to the east, but as he came closer he realised it was the sun glinting on the floodwaters that had filled the valley below the Möhne Dam. He estimated that the floodwater in the valley was about a mile wide and even now, eight hours after the raid, water was still gushing through a massive breach in the dam wall. The water level in the reservoir had fallen noticeably and great brown mud flats were showing around the edges. From thirty thousand feet Fray looked down on scenes which only a few days before had seemed so peaceful, but where now only the tops of trees and a few tall buildings and church steeples stood out above the floodwaters. He remembers being overcome by

the immensity of the scale of destruction below him and he
'wondered if the powers that be realised just how much
damage had been done'.[1]

In the Eder valley the destruction was even greater and more
than three-quarters of the water in the dam had escaped. The
pilot saw that the reservoir had almost ceased to exist as a landmark and had it not been for the water rushing through the
breach in the dam it would have been difficult to find what only
a few days before had been a huge lake. Fray had just taken a
second run of photos over the Eder valley when he spotted two
enemy aircraft approaching. He immediately turned for home
and pushed hard on the throttle.

When Fray landed back at Benson the station commander
was waiting to meet him and his immediate reaction was to
wonder if he was in trouble. Instead the group captain called
out, 'Have they hit them?' Fray replied, 'Yes, they've pranged
two of them properly. The floods are spreading for miles.'

Delighted, the commander rushed off to phone Bomber
Command headquarters with the news. Ronald Gillanders had
been sent from Medmenham to Benson and he began to interpret the negatives as soon as they were processed, not waiting
for prints to be made. All he could see on the first few frames
was floodwater, acres of it. Gillanders said, 'For a minute I did
not recognise the place. I feared for a moment that they had
bombed the wrong dam ... The place which I had studied for
many months looked completely different.' He examined the
negatives further but there was no sign of the power station
below the dam. It had completely disappeared. Then he saw the
curve of the dam wall with a crystal-clear breach right in the
middle of it. He estimated it was between 180 and 200 feet
wide. As he looked behind the dam he realised that the reservoir he had been studying for months was half empty.

Gillanders telephoned the head of Intelligence at the Air Ministry and gave his report while he was still looking at the negatives. When he realised that the Eder valley was flooded but that the pilot had turned for home before photographing the actual breach in the dam, the man from the Ministry said to him, 'Tell the pilot to go back and get it.' At this point Gillanders handed the phone to the station commander.[2] Another two sorties were flown that day to complete the cover of the Eder Dam and the Sorpe Dam, which was still intact. It was possible to see where explosions had damaged this third dam but the photos confirmed that, although weakened, it had not been breached.

The PIs were soon able to establish from the aerial photographs that the damage to the valleys was extensive. Mud and silt were building up in huge quantities, and further down in the Ruhr valley itself power stations had been damaged, cables were down and railway lines had been washed away. Below the Eder Dam a Luftwaffe airfield had been flooded and twenty-five road and rail bridges had been swept away. Initial estimates suggested that there had been thousands of civilian deaths although this was later reduced to about 1300. Tragically, it was later discovered that nearly five hundred of these had been Ukrainian slave workers who were living in the valleys below the dams.

The photo coverage was pin sharp and that day the Air Ministry released the aerial photo of the breached Möhne Dam to the press. It was a brilliant use of a superb reconnaissance photo and it featured on the front page of most of the papers on the following morning. Everywhere there were triumphant reports of the raid, with stories of the widespread devastation and paralysing of German industry. 'With one single blow the RAF has precipitated what may prove to be the greatest industrial disaster yet inflicted on Germany in this war,' declared the *Daily Telegraph* on its front page.[3] News of the raid was a huge boost to morale and a great fillip for Bomber Command after three years of questionable performance. And so the legend of the Dam Busters was born.

As the photo reconnaissance of the Ruhr continued that summer it soon became clear that German engineers were repairing the damage remarkably quickly. The disruption to electricity supplies was only brief as new power sources were rapidly redirected. Within six weeks water supplies to the Ruhr industries had been fully restored. Although steel production dropped in the Ruhr, the German economy as a whole saw increases in steel output over the following months. A massive effort went into repairing the breaches in the Möhne and the Eder dam walls and by the end of September both dams were operating near normally again. The Germans had clearly diverted huge resources to carry out the repairs but the photo interpreters watching the process of recovery were astonished at how quickly they were able to get back to something resembling business as usual.

The whole operation for the Dam Busters raid had been a classic exercise in photo intelligence. Other branches of the intelligence network had set the objectives but the interpreters had used aerial photos to analyse the targets in detail and to calculate the water levels – which they had done, as it was found out later, to within a foot of the actual level. Then aerial photography had helped to assess the damage to the dams, which was highly impressive in visual terms. Finally, the industrial experts had watched and recorded the whole process of recovery. The spies in the sky had been part of every stage in the preparation for the raid and in its aftermath from February to September 1943.

Damage assessment photography was at the heart of the analysis of bombing effectiveness. The photographs were always taken by reconnaissance aircraft flying over the target area as soon after a raid as possible, the following morning if the cloud conditions were right. Sometimes the pall of smoke from the bombing still hung over a city and there was a delay before usable aerial photos could be taken. These flights were always high risk operations, as the enemy knew to expect a recon flight over an area that had been bombed. But the pilots flew thousands of these sorties without questioning the danger. When a reconnaissance aircraft returned, the normal process of interpretation started with a First Phase summary of the damage within a few hours of the photos being printed, and a Second Phase, more detailed assessment a little later. But the real skill came when the experts in K Section at Medmenham, the Third Phase damage assessment team, got to work interpreting the photos.

The effects of fire were one of the most obvious signs of damage visible on aerial photographs. Fires left masonry with a whitened appearance and roofs usually collapsed before walls did, and so an area that had been devastated by fire looked like a 'honeycomb of lidless boxes'.[4] Often it was possible to see piles of furniture and other household debris that had been taken out of bombed houses and heaped up in the streets. On photos taken very soon after a raid the hoses of the fire brigades could usually be seen criss-crossing a damaged area, with pools of water surrounding them. Sometimes roads would still be blocked or trains held up, giving further evidence of the chaos on the ground in the hours following a raid. But the specialists at Medmenham were able to go beyond this. With factories, for instance, they could identify which parts of the plant had been damaged and which were still intact. From this they could calculate what the level of disruption to the factory output had been. Then it could be estimated how long it would take for the damaged areas to be restored and what output levels could be achieved over the following weeks or months. This was of immense importance in planning the strategic bombing campaign, as it was possible to predict when the optimum moment would be to bomb the factory again, that is after maximum effort had been put into rebuilding the plant and machinery and just before it was nearly ready to recommence full-scale production.

In addition to all this, it was possible for the experts of K Section to assess the effectiveness of different types of bomb on different types of building or installation. Distasteful though it might seem seventy years later, it was quite possible to calculate with some precision whether high explosive (HE) bombs or incendiaries were better able to destroy houses, and whether HE or some of the big specialist bombs were more efficient at destroying railway marshalling yards or bridges and viaducts. This might seem a particularly cold way of analysing the life and death prospects of the civilians below, but it was all part of the process of calculating the effects of area bombing.

In order to calculate such gruesome statistics, the boffins at Medmenham came up with another ingenious device that for reasons no one seems to remember was called a Damometer. Invented by Alec Heron, it saved interpreters huge amounts of time by calculating the proportion of a town or a factory that had been destroyed. The Damometer was able to plot the size of a target area either in acres or square yards. It did this by tracing to the millimetre the outside line on a photograph of an area to be measured. Once the exact scale of the photograph had been worked out, the Damometer calculated the precise size of the area. If the interpreter then traced around the edge of the area that had been bombed, a calculation could be made as to the exact size of this area and what proportion of the whole it amounted to. As the Damometer worked with Stereo pairs of photographs it was also possible to assess the height of buildings, identifying whether they were two-storey houses, blocks of high rise apartments, tall factories or towers. From this, the density of housing could be calculated and although the official record does not mention this, it was possible to estimate the density of population and even, very roughly, the numbers of casualties, or at least of civilians who were now homeless. Heron was particularly delighted when, after one raid, he had calculated the number of houses destroyed and a subsequent German radio report gave almost exactly the same number.[5] If a town or a factory was bombed more than once, then the zone devastated in the first raid might be highlighted in blue and that on the second raid in red, enabling the interpreters to record the cumulative effect of raids.

As the intensity of the bombing offensive grew, the number of PR sorties flown to obtain aerial cover for damage assessment grew equally rapidly. But by now there was a new threat to the reconnaissance pilots; a new German fighter had arrived on the scene. The Focke Wolf FW190 was one of the best German fighters of the war and could fly higher and faster than the Me 109. Capable of 400 mph, it threatened to outclass most Allied fighters and was a real menace to the unarmed Spitfires and Mosquitos.

On 4 September 1942 the first reconnaissance interception by the new German aircraft had taken place when two FW190s attacked a Mosquito soon after it had crossed the Dutch coast at 28,500 feet. As the enemy fighters approached, the Mosquito pilot carried out a series of steep vertical turns, causing his plane to judder badly as the enemy fighters shot past at speed. This put immense strain on the Mosquito, which experienced a high speed stall, causing it to flip over upside down. As it dived so it picked up speed, and the pilot was able to regain control. Coming under repeated attack, the recon pilot repeated this extraordinary technique five more times. He managed to throw off one of the FW190s, which went hurtling downwards, its pilot seemingly having blacked out trying to follow the evasions of the recon aircraft. But the navigator in the Mosquito suffered horribly from the aerobatics and was thrown on to the floor of the aircraft and badly bruised. The pressure of the G-forces caused him to vomit severely. After about twenty minutes of this extreme combat the Mosquito and the remaining FW190 were down to about two thousand feet when, to the immense relief of the recon crew, the enemy fighter turned for home. The Mosquito itself had sustained only minimal damage, a single bullet hole in the starboard tailplane and a Perspex wingtip broken by air pressure. But the crew's nerves had suffered considerably and they returned to Benson severely shaken.[6]

Two months later, a new mark of Spitfire known as the PR XI entered service. Its new supercharged Merlin 61 engine lifted its top speed by 50 mph to 420 mph and increased the height at which it could fly. But it was in desperately short supply, and so other aircraft had to be modified until more of the new Spitfires rolled off the production lines. With the threat from the FW190 in everyone's mind there was a debate within the reconnaissance community as to the relative advantages and disadvantages of the Spitfire and the Mosquito. Many senior officers preferred the Mosquito because its longer range enabled it to fly missions covering a much greater part of occupied Europe. A new mark of Mosquito, also fitted out with the Merlin 61, entered service at this time. It was proposed to the Air Staff that this aircraft should take over all reconnaissance work. But many pilots still preferred the Spitfire, whose quicker rate of climb and greater manoeuvrability made it easier to out-perform enemy fighters, even the FW190. The Chief of the Air Staff, Air Marshal Sir John Slessor, ruled that both aircraft should be kept in service. The new Spitfire PR XI was to replace the older models for short range tasks, and the new Mosquito was to be used for longer range missions.[7]

During 1943, as the adoption of these new reconnaissance aircraft was taking place, Berlin often became the target for Allied bombing missions. On 19 March, after a raid on the German capital, a reconnaissance Spitfire was able to circle the German capital for forty-five minutes, taking a series of out-standing damage assessment photos. But Berlin was always a difficult location for PR aircraft to cover and the enemy, as with all recon flights after an air raid, were often waiting. The recon-naissance pilots' only option was to fly higher and higher. Then, after a heavy raid at the end of November, one PR aircraft was intercepted at forty-two thousand feet by enemy aircraft and had to flee the scene. During the winter months, bad weather over the German capital was also a major problem. After another big raid in December, eighteen sorties were flown over Berlin before a single damage assessment photo could be taken. When Flight Lieutenant Brew flew over the city, he waited for the clouds to clear, constantly searching for any signs of enemy fighters. He finally got a set of photos but when he landed back at Benson he had barely twenty gallons of fuel left.[8]

Bomber Command and the American Eighth Army Air Force grew irritated by any delays in taking damage assessment photos. They were increasingly calling for photos to be taken within hours of a raid for instant assessments to be made. On bombing raids over Frederichshaven and Regensburg in the summer, the PR aircraft were above the cities before the bombers had landed, and Flight Sergeant Dearden accomplished the feat of photographing Kassel after a daylight raid within thirty minutes of the attack. But despite the courage of the PR pilots, it was impossible to take immediate damage assessment photos after every raid and Berlin still proved the toughest nut to crack.

On 16 September Bomber Command attacked a viaduct on the main railway line between Marseilles and Genoa at Anthéor, near Cannes. The viaduct carried the single railway link for supplies to Italy from occupied France. The Allies estimated that about fifteen thousand tons of military supplies were transported daily over this viaduct. On the day after the raid Mosquitos flew a high level reconnaissance sortie but it was impossible to see from the photographs whether the viaduct had been destroyed or not. The next day another Mosquito PR pilot took a series of low level obliques from eight hundred feet to get a side-on view. The pilot flew so low that he could see workmen on the ground filling the craters by the main road. But his photos showed that although there were near misses the viaduct itself had not been destroyed. So British and American bombers carried out further bombing raids in November. On 29 November, Mosquito reconnaissance aircraft took more low level oblique photos of the target and were able to record that the viaduct had indeed been hit and the railway link was broken. Aerial intelligence had tracked a key bottleneck in the enemy's supply chain and had provided a fruitful target to attack.

Meanwhile, David Brachi and the Naval Section at Medmenham were continuing to keep a close eye on the building of U-boats in the German shipyards. Early in the year Brachi had noted that fifteen U-boats were under construction at the submarine yard at Bremen and in March a bombing raid

was carried out. From the damage assessment photos the interpreters were able to see that eleven of the fifteen vessels under
construction had been hit. But it was calculated that the damage
would only put construction back by seven to eight weeks. A
further watch was kept on the shipyards and whenever the PIs
counted a sufficient number of nearly completed U-boats then
a new attack was made.

In July 1943 Bomber Command tried a new form of bombing
technique on the city of Hamburg. Thousands of small metal
foil strips – called 'Window' – were dropped in order to blind
the enemy radar. As a consequence the bombers hit Hamburg
without any fear of interception by night fighters. After a night
of bombing by the RAF, the Americans bombed the city for two
days in daylight and this was followed up by another night raid
by the RAF using incendiaries. Firestorms blazed across the city
with incredible ferocity, reaching temperatures of a thousand
degrees Centigrade. As the heat rose it sucked in oxygen, creating whirlwinds of flame in a terrifying inferno of fire.
Buildings simply disappeared. Bodies were incinerated. The
reconnaissance pilots who flew over the smoking remains of
the city were stunned by the destruction below. When their
photos came back, Alec Heron and his Damometer worked
overtime to calculate the scale of that destruction. The damage
assessment report completed in early August summed it up:

> The greater part of Hamburg, second largest town of
> Germany, is now in ruin. The general destruction is on a
> scale never before seen in a town of this size ... Blocks of
> buildings have been destroyed by high explosive bombs
> and it is evident that fire has spread uninterruptedly
> through whole districts of the town. There are large areas,
> extending for thousands of acres, especially East of the

town where every building in every street has been
demolished or left roofless and gutted. Many thorough-
fares are seen to be blocked with debris and parts of the
town have an appearance altogether deserted. It is estimated that in the fully built up areas the destruction and
damage to property amounts to over 77 per cent and is
close to that figure even in the more suburban districts ...
The storage capacity of the port has suffered severely.
Altogether nearly 500 dockside and railway warehouses
have been destroyed or damaged, besides many of the
older type of brick warehouses, used mainly for food storage.[9]

In its cool analytic style this report paints a gruesome picture of
the horror that must have existed in the firestorms, which lasted
for several days. It was later calculated that forty-two thousand
civilians had lost their lives and more than a million had fled
into the countryside. Twenty-two square kilometres of the city
had been razed to the ground. Joseph Goebbels confided in his
diary that the bombing was a 'catastrophe, the extent of which
simply staggers the imagination'. Albert Speer, the Minister of
War Production, told Hitler that if the Allies launched similar
attacks against six cities in swift succession, German war production might collapse.[10]

The morality of the bombing campaign has been discussed
elsewhere.[11] But for those involved with analysing the destruction there was no question that the bombing of German cities
was justified. The Germans had started bombing civilian targets
such as Warsaw, Rotterdam, London, Coventry and many other
cities. As Bomber Harris told the newsreel cameras in an oft-
repeated biblical quote, 'They who sow the wind shall reap the
whirlwind.'[12] So when Field Marshal Smuts, the South African

leader, paid a visit to Medmenham in August, soon after the
Hamburg raid, Ronald Gillanders was proud to show off the
huge mosaic they had laid out on a large table showing the city
after the massive destruction it had suffered. Gillanders
proudly waved his arm from right to left across the giant
mosaic, pointing out the scale of the devastation. But instead of
being elated, Gillanders saw Smuts slowly stroke his beard as
he looked at the evidence. He shook his head from side to side,
tears welling up in his eyes as he muttered the words
'Hamburg was a beautiful city, a beautiful city.' Gillanders said
he had never felt so completely deflated in his life.[13]

Most of the damage assessment reports produced by the
Central Interpretation Unit are now kept in the National
Archives and can be read today. The detail they contain and the
knowledge they display of the German war economy and how
it was damaged by Allied bombing are remarkable. It all hints
at a subtle but important shift in emphasis of the work at
Medmenham during 1943. Instead of using it defensively, as a
way of spying on what the enemy were planning to do to
Britain, to invade or to attack, the Allies were now using air
intelligence offensively, as a guide to the weak points in the
enemy's armour and how and where best to attack the Nazi
war machine. This was the true strategic use of photo intelligence.

The bomb damage assessment section at Medmenham had
become a vital adjunct to the bombing offensive and it
expanded rapidly from a team of thirteen in 1942 to a peak of
fifty-four specialist interpreters in mid 1944. As the American
daytime bombing offensive took off from early 1943 an increasing number of demands for damage assessment came from the
US Army Air Force, and as a consequence many of their PIs
came to work at Danesfield House. By May 1944 the whole

operation had grown too large even for Medmenham and there was debate at a high level about further reorganisation. In the spring of 1944 the decision was made to move K Section to the US Eighth Army Air Force headquarters at Pinetree in Buckinghamshire. But by this time the war had moved on, photo interpreters from Medmenham had moved out to create new units all across a world that was at war, and the frictions that had existed with Bomber Command had been replaced by a new threat – not from the enemy but from our principal ally, the United States Army Air Force.

11

To the Mediterranean and India

From the beginning of 1941, the one area where British troops were confronting German and Italian ground troops was the Mediterranean. With photo intelligence established as a key feature in the Allied arsenal there was a growing need for photo reconnaissance and interpretation in this theatre of battle, where a see-saw war was being fought in the western desert along the Libyan and Egyptian coastlines. The Italians' initial advance into Egypt was followed by a hugely successful British counter-advance that progressed five hundred miles and captured 125,000 Italian prisoners. Hitler sent his favourite general, Erwin Rommel, to the aid of his Italian ally. Rommel's unit, the Afrika Korps, soon went on the advance and recaptured all the ground conquered by the British.

Alongside this desert war, the Royal Navy was fighting a determined action to keep the Mediterranean open for British shipping. This involved taking action against the Italian navy and against the merchant ships that supplied the Italian and

German forces in North Africa with weapons, fuel and ammunition. The best way to organise and prioritise the many
demands made on aerial photography had constantly to be
revised and in July 1941 Peter Riddell left Medmenham on
what he jokingly called his 'world tour' to advise on the most
efficient means of running photo reconnaissance and interpretation overseas. He would help to create what were effectively
smaller versions of the Central Interpretation Unit, staffed initially by experienced photo interpreters from Medmenham.
Many knew them as 'mini-Medmenhams'.[1]

Riddell visited Gibraltar, Malta, Cairo, India, Burma and
Singapore, meeting everyone who worked with aerial photography. Most importantly he met with senior local commanders
in the Army and Navy as well as the RAF, acting as a sort of
salesman for photo intelligence.[2] Everywhere he visited he
found the Navy was keen on getting the best intelligence possible from air reconnaissance but the Army was lukewarm. The
RAF bases he visited were adapting for reconnaissance operations whatever aircraft were available and despite the lack of
resources there was a strong spirit of 'making do'.

Soon after the beginning of the war, the British government
had assured the Spanish government that combat aircraft
would not be flown out of Gibraltar. As Glenn Martin
Marylands regularly flew into Gibraltar it was decided to use
them as reconnaissance aircraft, as they would attract little
attention from the Spanish. The Marylands made reconnaissance flights from Gibraltar across the western Mediterranean
and the African coast. Technically they were based at Benson,
but they flew from Gibraltar for weeks at a time and a small PI
unit was based there as well.

We saw in Chapter 8 how Malta with its central geographic
position became a focus of the struggle for control of the

Mediterranean and how Adrian Warburton achieved legendary status as the fearless photo reconnaissance pilot who always got his pictures. So the Marylands, and two adapted Hurricanes, were well established at Malta at the time of Riddell's visit. On his arrival, Riddell met the newly appointed air officer commanding, 'Hugh Pughe' Lloyd, who asked for trained photo interpreters. It was on Riddell's recommendation that two PIs, Howard Colvin and Ray Herschel, were sent out to Malta. They occupied the office next to Lloyd's, built into the side of a medieval fortress with thick walls and a massive roof. Lloyd would pop in to discuss their latest findings and sometimes decided on targets for bombing raids in discussion with them.

Warburton used to come up to the office also to see the photos he had taken. The first time he visited, Ray Herschel was aware of a strange figure with an array of ribbons on his chest. The figure asked to see some photos and Herschel replied, 'Yes, I'll get them, sir.' 'Don't be silly,' replied Warburton, 'We don't "Sir" each other here.'

Herschel remembers that Warburton would never shoot a long run of photos, often coming back with only about fifty images exposed out of five hundred on a roll of film. But he was able to frame the target perfectly within his cameras. Herschel called him a 'natural air photographer'.[3]

The main reconnaissance being carried out from Malta at this time was of the Italian ports, watching the loading of each vessel that was bound for North Africa to reinforce the Afrika Korps. Recon flights over Naples and Taranto took place almost every other day. Herschel and Colvin would report on exactly what was being loaded into every ship. But the key requirement was to spot when they were about to sail. The PIs were able to do this by identifying when the small hatches on a ship had been battened down. This always meant that it would sail

within the next twenty-four hours. When a vessel was photographed at sea, the PIs could work out its speed using the
table that Bryan Westwood had calculated at Medmenham.
And although Herschel and Colvin did not know it, intelligence
about the convoys was also coming from German and Italian
signals that were being decoded at Bletchley Park. Code breaking, combined with photo intelligence, resulted in the sinking
of many supply ships before they reached North Africa. Royal
Navy submarines and Beaufort torpedo bombers flying out of
Malta achieved high hit rates, putting Rommel's Afrika Korps
under intense pressure. Ray Herschel loved the atmosphere in
Malta, despite the pressure and the constant German bombing,
and felt that everything afterwards was flat and frustrating.

Egypt was the location for the main British military headquarters of the Middle East Command, covering not only the
Western Desert where fighting was raging, but also Palestine,
Syria and Iraq. From Alexandria, the Royal Navy tried to control
the eastern Mediterranean and constantly demanded information about the deployment of the Italian navy and of German
shipping. There were only two trained PIs covering this vast
area, based at Heliopolis, the main RAF station near to Cairo.
Riddell met with Air Marshal Sir Arthur Tedder, the most senior
RAF commander in the region, to discuss the value of aerial
photography. Tedder had a genuine interest in scientific ideas
and would later become a great enthusiast for all forms of intelligence derived from aerial photos. Between them they agreed
to increase the number of PR aircraft in the region to twelve and
that this should rise to twenty the following year. Most of these
were to be twin-engined Mosquitos. However, when they were
deployed there were problems with their plywood frames in the
sandy desert conditions. And so twelve Spitfires were sent out,
which were to play an important role in the desert battles that

followed. It was also decided later in 1941 to create a Middle
East Central Interpretation Unit at Heliopolis, as a mini version
of Medmenham. The plan was to send out sixty-three trained
PIs from Medmenham, but this proved to be too ambitious and
it was months before Middle East Command got the full PI support it needed.

In the summer of 1942, as Rommel's Afrika Korps advanced
to within eighty miles of Cairo, initial orders were given for the
photo interpreters to evacuate Egypt for Palestine. The air was
thick with the smell of photos being burned but fortunately the
order was rescinded at the last minute and members of the unit
were told to stay put. The recon Spitfires regularly took photographic cover over Rommel's lines, and from this the PIs
produced large mosaics of the whole battle front, highlighting
the topography of the desert landscape and identifying enemy
positions. Army PIs went forward from Heliopolis and operated at divisional headquarters, advising commanders on the
detailed layout of the enemy's defences, where his armour was
based and the location of minefields.

Although it was sometimes difficult to spot individual tanks,
their tracks in the sand usually gave away their position and
large groupings of enemy armour could be seen by the mass of
tracks left behind. As so much of the desert was not mapped
these photo maps were plotted to show where the infantry were
planning to go next. The Eighth Army phrase for this was that
the 'going was plotted'. So the desert photo maps were termed
'going maps'.[4] Aerial imagery thus provided General
Montgomery with a great deal of the intelligence he needed to
plan his offensive at El Alamein in October. The battle turned into
a great Allied victory. General Freyburg, commander of the New
Zealand Division at El Alamein, said, 'I owe the success of this
operation to the air photographs.' Another general told one of his

PIs, 'You are the eyes of my division.' The battle was a turning point and aerial photography had proved invaluable.[5]

A week after the victory at El Alamein, a hundred thousand American and other Allied troops landed on beaches in north-west Africa in Operation Torch, the first combined amphibious operation of the war. Staff at Medmenham had worked over-time studying and preparing detailed reports on the enemy defences and providing more than forty models of the invasion beaches. The planners wanted to know precisely where the main defences were, the width of roads off the beaches, the size of airfields, the dimensions of key buildings, and so on. This was the work that Sarah Churchill had corrected her father about as he spoke of the imminent landings. Once the Allied armies had established themselves and negotiated their way through the complex politics of French North Africa, they set off on the thousand-mile trek eastwards across desert and moun-tains towards Tunisia, to link up with Montgomery's Eighth Army which was advancing westwards from Egypt. The inten-tion was to smash Rommel and his Afrika Korps and to throw Axis troops out of Africa in order to prepare the assault on southern Europe across the Mediterranean. Unfortunately, little thought had been given to photo intelligence in the planning for the land operation following Operation Torch. With no coor-dinated command for photo reconnaissance, there was confusion and duplication between the recon work carried out from Malta and in North Africa by the RAF and the Americans. It was a problem that would have to be solved in due course.

When Peter Riddell had arrived in India on his 'world tour' in the summer of 1941, he found no provision at all for aerial intelligence. Although aerial photography had been success-fully used for mapping in the 1930s little was known of strategic photo reconnaissance. In Singapore the military were aware of the threat from Japan but again there was no provision for aerial photography. Riddell agreed a target of sending six twin-engined reconnaissance aircraft to the Far East, but it was accepted that with priorities in Europe and the Mediterranean this would not be achieved for over a year and that current operational aircraft had to be adapted to carry cameras in the meantime. Everything, of course, was transformed when the Japanese attacked Pearl Harbor in December 1941 and simultaneously invaded Hong Kong, Malaya and the Dutch East Indies. It was decided to set up another 'mini-Medmenham' in India with a Central Interpretation Unit at Delhi.

Soon after Japan had entered the war, Glyn Daniel was called in one morning to Riddell's office. Out of the blue Riddell asked if he would like to go to India to set up a training school for photo interpreters and start a functioning photo intelligence centre that would scale up as the war with Japan progressed. 'You'll have a chance of seeing the last of the British Raj, it will interest you,' Riddell told Daniel, 'and when the Germans are defeated we'll take over what you have built up and you can go back to being a don at Cambridge.' Daniel accepted at once, and although sad to leave the frenetic activity of Medmenham he never looked back.

After an eventful journey by Imperial Airways flying boat across Africa and the Middle East, Daniel arrived in Karachi, where he set up a training school in Old Government House. Daniel found himself living a life of some luxury, enjoying gin and tonics and excellent curries in the cool of the whites-only Sind Club. He and two other colleagues from Medmenham ran three-week courses for Army and RAF intelligence officers. He thoroughly enjoyed the experience and felt that his teaching of undergraduates at Cambridge after the war greatly benefited from his experience of teaching officers in Karachi. After several months at the training school, Daniel went on to Delhi where he set up the Central Photographic Interpretation Section, a 'mini-Medmenham' for the whole of south-east Asia, complete with darkrooms, film library, modelling section and a growing band of photo interpreters. The section was located in the luxury of the Hyderabad Palace, the Delhi residence of the Nizam of Hyderabad. Some of the PIs were billeted in the Nizam's old harem. It was a far cry from the austerity, blackouts and bombs of wartime Britain.[6]

The whole operation of photo reconnaissance in the Far East posed immense problems. There was an appalling shortage of aircraft and to begin with four B-25 Mitchell light bombers taken from the Dutch were all that was available. Before long all four aircraft had been shot down and PR was carried out first by Hurricanes and then by Spitfires sent on from the Middle East. The huge distances over which cover was needed made it difficult for these single-engined aircraft to cope with all the demands made upon them. And the Anglo-American agreement to prioritise the war against Germany made it impossible for the Indian command to get suitable aircraft for PR until late 1943, when American Lightnings and British Mosquitos appeared in sufficient numbers and improved the range of the cover that could be provided. The military chiefs still protested that their lack of intelligence about Japanese deployments hampered their planning for offensive action. General Auchinleck as commander-in-chief asked for an additional hundred reconnaissance aircraft, but he was politely told that he had to make do with what he already had.[7]

When Lord Mountbatten was appointed Supreme Commander of the newly formed South East Asia Command at the end of 1943, he again pleaded for further PR aircraft. But in Britain everything was gearing up for the invasion of France and once more requests from the Far East fell right down the list of priorities. Eventually enough Mosquitos were sent to India for the unit to carry out a comprehensive aerial survey of Burma, and this proved an essential aid in the reconquest of the country which began in 1944. Aerial photographs, as in other theatres, were used in many different ways. PIs were able to identify fields behind enemy lines, enabling the Chindits to land by glider. A specialised group of railway specialists sent out from Medmenham tracked from the air railway lines and Japanese freight movements. On more than one occasion discussion took place about the use of aircraft carriers to transport PR aircraft in order to be able to provide cover of regions that were out of range from India and Ceylon (today Sri Lanka). But the Royal Navy refused to cooperate until the very last stages of the war. Howard Pickard, one of the PIs from Medmenham, worked on an escort carrier but was convinced that the cameras used by the Fleet Air Arm were not as good as those of the RAF.[8] It was only towards the end of the war against Japan that the photo reconnaissance capability finally caught up with all the demands being made upon it.

During these taxing years, the Delhi Central Photographic Interpretation Section had grown from a starter establishment of three men to the huge organisation necessary to cover the vast area of Mountbatten's South East Asia Command. There were soon outstations in Calcutta and forward units in Burma and Ceylon. The PIs had to learn from scratch almost everything about the Japanese war effort, from the types of aircraft they used to the size of their warships. By the end of the war there were several hundred intelligence officers and support staff working on photo interpretation. Initially the section was a genuine band of brothers, staffed only by men. But from late 1943, with the need for more and more experienced PIs, a party of about thirty WAAFs were sent out from Medmenham. Working closely with men who had enjoyed little female company led to the inevitable. A spate of engagements and marriages followed. Even the boss, Glyn Daniel, proposed to a WAAF officer, Ruth Langhorne, and they were married a year later, after the war.

Daniel, by then a wing commander, led the whole operation from Delhi and from Mountbatten's HQ at Kandy in Ceylon, at the end of the war. He was accused of having a tendency to promote old friends and fellow archaeologists, and his informal style of leadership was not always popular with the stiff upper lipped officers of the Raj. But by the end of the war his unit was impressively mixed, including RAF and Army officers, along with WAAFs, Indians and Americans. The work was tough in exhausting conditions but it had its luxuries, and was punctuated by drinks at the Imperial Delhi Gymkhana Club and, for Daniel, several visits to ancient historical sites across India.[9]

Back in the Mediterranean, the organisation of PR and PI was in a state of confusion. After many weeks of reconnaissance failings, in February 1943 Air Marshal Tedder himself made a further appeal for the supply of new Spitfire XIs for photo recon work, explaining the need for photo cover not only of enemy ports and the battleground in Tunisia but also over Sicily, Sardinia and southern Italy in preparation for the next phase of the Mediterranean war. London finally agreed to the request and four new Spitfires were sent out.[10]

At the time of the Torch landings only seven PIs had been based at Gibraltar and two in Malta. In early 1943, as the build-up of men and materiel in North Africa proceeded, it was realised that there would be a need for improved local photo interpretation. At the end of February 1943 another 'mini-Medmenham' was created, this time at Algiers. Called the

North African Central Interpretation Unit, it had a combined Anglo-American interpretation team with a single reconnaissance wing under American command. But the lack of trained PIs to cover the growing volume of work was a major problem, so during that spring it was decided to send out ten experienced WAAF officers from Medmenham. Among the women selected was Hazel Scott (née Furney), who had just celebrated her twenty-second birthday. She remembers arriving in Gibraltar from rationed Britain and being stunned by the stalls selling oranges, lemons and bananas. There was even chocolate cake available in the hotel.

The WAAFs then went on to Algiers and were excited by the French feel of the city with its pavement cafés, busy shops and a bustling street life that seemed to carry on despite the war. On the down side, they were at first billeted in a pokey cockroach-ridden hotel above the souk. So, overall, it seemed a mixed welcome to exotic North Africa. Aware that they would be a solitary group of young women surrounded by men who had enjoyed little female company for months or even years, the girls had discussed their situation before leaving Medmenham. They made a collective decision that, as they had an important job of work to do, they would definitely not encourage any male attentions; they would behave as officers and would not get themselves into trouble. They would all look 'as frumpy as we could with our hair tucked up, cap down'. But despite their best endeavours they were naturally the object of great male interest. Every time one of them stepped out into the street, the nearest jeep or transport vehicle would screech to a halt and offer them a lift. Rarely did they have to buy themselves a drink, and invitations to dinner were frequent. Combat troops on leave from the front would home in on them and tell them how lovely it was to hear the voices of English girls again. Not surprisingly, under this sort of pressure, one of the WAAFs, despite her pledge, was engaged within a week.[11]

At the end of May, the Allies finally defeated the Afrika Korps in the battle of Tunis. They captured 240,000 enemy troops, including nine generals. But Hitler ordered Rommel to escape. He wanted him to fight another day. The Allies now focused on the small Italian island of Pantelleria, situated midway between Tunisia and Sicily. The island was well defended with heavy coastal batteries, and a model of the island and its defences was made at Medmenham from aerial photographs and flown out to North Africa. The RAF began to bomb these batteries, and damage assessment photographs recorded the extent of the destruction. In an unusual sequence of events, the Allies now called in a prominent scientist, Professor Solly Zuckerman, who had produced detailed analyses of the effects of bomb damage both in Britain and in Egypt and Libya. Working alongside the PIs at the North African Central Interpretation Unit, Zuckerman assessed in detail the impact of each type of bomb, calculating how many bombs were needed to destroy a battery of guns. The Allies increased the number of raids, using different bombloads on Zuckerman's advice. They were found to be highly effective in targeting the coastal guns until all the essential targets had been destroyed. On 11 June Pantelleria surrendered, going down in history as the first heavily defended garrison ever reduced completely by air power. The experiment in combining aerial intelligence with a detailed analysis of the destructive potential of different bombs had proved a great success.[12]

Churchill and Roosevelt had agreed, at the Casablanca Conference in January, that the next Mediterranean objective would be Sicily. But there was precious little photographic cover of the island, so Tedder ordered a burst of aerial photography to identify the beaches for landing and then to aid the

advance across the island. With the limited supply of reconnaissance aircraft available the lion's share of this work fell on
the hard-pressed recon pilots at Malta. Adrian Warburton and
his crews rose to the task and within a matter of weeks provided extensive coverage of the beaches and inland routes
across the island. The photos were taken to Algiers for interpretation. Mosaics were produced, maps were made and plans
were drawn up for the invasion. Launched on 10 July, it was a
success and in five weeks the whole of Sicily was in Allied
hands. General George S. Patton, one of the American commanders, said that the low level oblique photographs supplied
to his landing forces had been 'essential to the success of the
operation'.[13] Mussolini was then ejected from power and the
Italian government surrendered to the Allies. The first of
Hitler's allies had been defeated. But the Germans responded
by effectively occupying Italy, sending battle-hardened troops
from the Eastern Front to reinforce the Italian peninsula.

In the next step, the Mediterranean war was taken to mainland Italy itself, and initially the campaign went well. Photos
were taken for interpretation to La Marsa on the coast outside
Tunis, where the tiny army of WAAFs had been transferred.
They were based in a convent just above a beautiful sandy
beach. In their free time they could swim in the Mediterranean
and picnic by the sea. At their mess, Italian POWs waited on
them. Another WAAF officer, Suzie Morgan (née Morrison),
remembers how the Italians would sing opera outside at night
and how lovely it was.[14] But the male attention continued, and
Hazel Scott had at least one proposal of marriage. She turned it
down, as she was much too aware of her 'rarity value', and she
was delighted when she was told that there was no gossip
going the rounds linking her with any bad behaviour.[15] Many
parties and dances took place to celebrate the Allied victories

and it was after one of these that Adrian Warburton, who was in command of 336 Wing at La Marsa, had the car accident that put him out of action for several weeks.

As the Americans advanced further into south-west Italy and captured Naples, the Eighth Army moved up the east of the peninsula, taking the Italian airbase of San Severo near Foggia. In December 1943, this was selected as the new base for photo intelligence, as long range flights from here could cover much of central Europe as far as Romania and Poland. Several units of American and British recon aircraft moved there, along with a squadron from the South African Air Force. With Adrian Warburton in hospital, Gordon Hughes took command of the RAF's 336 Wing and a new Anglo-American unit, called the Mediterranean Photographic Intelligence Centre, was formed. From San Severo all PR and PI activities for this theatre of war were controlled and the WAAFs from North Africa were transferred there in January 1944.

Having put up with the attentions of Allied soldiers and airmen for six months, these young women now had to face up to advances from macho Italian men as well. Hazel Scott remembers having her bottom pinched as she walked back to her billet after a late night shift and she and her friends decided they would only go out in pairs. She teamed up with Lothian Nicholas, who shared the same shifts as well as many common interests, and for the next two years they became inseparable. Scott remembers going to a café bar run by an Italian-American who spoke good English. The fliers from the airbase and the WAAFs were made very welcome there, but Scott was terribly embarrassed on one late-evening visit in the company of a pilot friend, when the bar owner announced with a knowing wink, 'We have rooms upstairs you know.'[16] Clearly the Italian men found it harder than the RAF to accept that women could work on an equal basis alongside their male colleagues.

For the rest of the war, all photo intelligence for Italy and planning for the invasion of southern France was based at San Severo. Ray Herschel from Malta also joined the team, which grew to about a hundred PIs. Herschel remembered studying the whole of the Balkans and Yugoslavia, as well as parts of Austria and southern Germany. One of his tasks was to locate Hitler's mountain retreat near Berchtesgaden, which the Americans intended to bomb. Under the umbrella of this combined unit he enjoyed working closely with the American photo interpreters.[17] After the capture of Rome and the advance into northern Italy, the Americans decided to establish an independent aerial photography operation and separate American Photographic Groups transferred to the 12th and 15th US Air Forces, while 336 Wing continued to fulfil the British military's reconnaissance requirements.[18]

After several more marriage proposals, Hazel Scott finally decided to ignore the dangers of getting 'hitched abroad' and became engaged to a South African reconnaissance pilot, Allister Miller. She was overjoyed at having finally found the right partner and looked ahead to a new life. The very next day, after her shift was over, she went into the officers' mess and everyone fell silent. A friend took her aside and told her that Miller had gone missing that morning. For days she hoped desperately for news that he had crash landed or been taken prisoner. But he was never heard of again. Scott picked herself up, as you had to do, and carried on with her PI work, broken up with short trips around Italy with Lothian Nicholas, to Pompeii and Sorrento, to Rome and to the Adriatic coast. She was on a gondola in Venice in May 1945 when news came finally through that German forces had surrendered. The city was full of New Zealand troops who had carried out its liberation and that evening a magnificent party took place in St Mark's Square. The Italians played music and danced wildly, the New Zealanders drank and enjoyed themselves. Hazel Scott and her friend looked on, happy that the war was over, but exhausted by years of intense work and of living on their nerves. Reflecting on the extraordinary things she had experienced and the tremendous people she had met, she decided that all in all, despite her personal sadness, she had not had a bad war.[19]

12

Arguments with Allies

In April 1942, four months after America had entered the war, US Army Major Elliott Roosevelt arrived at Freetown, Sierra Leone in a single B-17 Flying Fortress bomber. Roosevelt, the second son of the US President, had been in the US Army Air Force for two years. When the Japanese attacked the US Pacific Fleet at anchor in Pearl Harbor, he knew that he would be sent to serve overseas, but he was disgusted to discover that his assignment was to a mission called 'Rusty Project' in an obscure part of West Africa, thousands of miles from the scene of any fighting.

Before he left America he visited his father, Commander-in-Chief of US forces, at the White House. The President gave him a pep talk explaining that his job would be to carry out aerial photography of North Africa and that this had a vital function in clearing the Mediterranean, so supplies could be taken to the East. Roosevelt had a global view of the struggle and told his son that if the Germans fighting in North Africa broke through into the Middle East and met up with the Japanese in India, then the Allies would find it difficult to get support to the Russians and even harder to strike back at the Axis forces. 'The Nazis aren't in the Sahara just to get a sunburn,' the President told his son.

On his arrival in West Africa, Elliott and his team began the aerial mapping of North Africa, using a single American bomber kitted out with cameras.[1] They obtained useful experience in the science of air photography, and their work marks the beginning of US involvement in the process of photo reconnaissance and interpretation that was already well developed at RAF Benson and Medmenham.

A year before the son of the US President touched down in West Africa, and before America's entry into the war, another American Army officer, Captain Harvey C. Brown Jnr, had paid a visit to Medmenham. He toured the different sections, spending time with each one, and was very impressed with the range and detail of the work being done. He met Constance Babington Smith, who at the time of his visit was studying photos of the gliders which, it was feared, the Germans might use to mount an aerial invasion of Britain. She liked his easygoing, informal nature and his Virginia drawl, which at that time was still very unfamiliar. Captain Brown watched her making detailed measurements of the gliders' wingspans and was extremely impressed. He told her, 'If Goering knew how much you're finding out, I'm sure he'd put his wing loading up.'[2]

Until this point most aerial photography in the US military had been concentrated on survey work, as in the 1930s there were still many parts of the North American continent that had not been fully mapped – including by 1937 more than 46 per cent of the United States.[3] But the aerial surveys had been in the purview of the US Army and, remarkably, it appeared that in the years before Pearl Harbor, the US Navy had not one single photo interpreter. Now, senior military officials began to realise they needed to think differently about how to use aerial photography in a future war and there was a need to pick up new skills as quickly as possible. The one way they could do that was to learn from the Brits. On Brown's recommendation they made a request through the US Embassy in London in August 1941, four months before Pearl Harbor, for a group of American officers to be trained at Medmenham in techniques of photo interpretation. Permission was granted and eleven officers from all the services arrived. They went on 'Steve' Stephenson's course and then were attached to the CIU in order to gain practical experience in interpreting photographs. When Brown and the other observers returned to the US, they helped to set up a PI school for the US Army Air Corps at Harrisburg, Pennsylvania. The first graduates from this school went to work with Roosevelt and his team in North Africa.[4]

In the early stages of the war in North Africa, the Americans repeated some of the mistakes that the RAF had made earlier in the war. The slow flying B-17 bombers used for aerial mapping suffered from a high loss rate, just as the Blenheims had in 1939. A quarter of American reconnaissance pilots were lost in the first months of conflict. After the Torch landings in North Africa and the US troops' first direct contact with the enemy, there was a need for the creation of a new American photo reconnaissance unit in the Mediterranean. The US 3rd Photo Group was set up flying Lockheed P-38 Lightnings, American two-engined fighter bombers specially adapted for reconnaissance. The guns were removed and cameras positioned in the large nose of the aircraft, an ideal location for pilots to aim their cameras accurately. This variation of the Lightning, known as the F-5, became the workhorse of US reconnaissance in the Mediterranean.[5] The Lightnings were good at low level reconnaissance, at around five thousand feet, but sometimes suffered from engine failures at high altitude and were not fast enough to outfly the latest version of the Messerschmitt fighter, the Me 109G. Many American pilots openly said they preferred the Mosquito, but there were never enough of the 'wooden wonders' for the RAF, let alone enough to share with the Americans. The standard American camera was the Fairchild K17, which could be fitted with lenses of focal length ranging from a 6in wide angle to a 24in long lens suitable for use at high altitude.

The 3rd Photo Group was based at Algiers. Its commander was Elliott Roosevelt, now promoted to lieutenant-colonel and rapidly emerging as the leading figure in American photo intelligence. He was determined to keep American PR work under US command. Unfortunately, the RAF squadron sent to work alongside the Americans was hit in a bombing attack on its airfield at Maison Blanche and almost all of its aircraft and equipment were destroyed. Local commanders once again pleaded for replacements to be sent out urgently from England but with aircraft in limited supply, the Air Ministry was unable to fulfil their requests.

With the creation in February 1943 of the North African Central Interpretation Unit at Algiers, American flying units took over much of the reconnaissance work. But Roosevelt got to know some of the British fliers in the region, especially those based in Malta, and became a fan of Adrian 'Warby' Warburton, whom he admired greatly for his skill in taking photographs regardless of conditions and getting them back to base for interpretation. The American photo interpreters still had a lot to learn as they puzzled over aerial photos of mile after mile of open desert. On one occasion they set off an alarm that a convoy of tanks were advancing towards Allied positions. An RAF interpreter who got hold of the same cover realised that the supposed tanks were in fact a party of Bedouin with camels that had paused to rest. A famous corrective signal was sent out immediately: 'For tanks read camels'.[6] It was a sign of the lack of coordination between the British and American operations in North Africa under Roosevelt's command.

As early as the spring of 1942 plans had been laid in Washington for the heavy bombers of the US Eighth Army Air Force to operate out of England in order to take part in the bombing offensive against Germany. The American military soon resolved, on the evidence of the many senior officers who had seen Medmenham in operation, that it would be costly and unwise to duplicate the work of the Central Interpretation Unit. To copy all the photographs that had been taken and collected there, to fly sorties possibly in parallel with RAF reconnaissance flights, to start from scratch in building up a comparable level of expertise, would be a massive waste of effort. It was agreed that the Americans would provide four reconnaissance squadrons of eighteen F-5 Lightnings each. Whenever possible American PR aircraft would take reconnaissance photos needed for the American bombing campaign, supplemented by RAF aircraft when necessary. And RAF aircraft would in the first instance meet RAF requirements, supplemented by the Americans if needed. It was further agreed that there should be only one interpretation unit, that this should stay at Medmenham and that it should be an inter-service and inter-Allied operation. This was yet another facet of the combined military operation that America and Britain were committed to in fighting the war in Europe.

The first US bombing raids were launched from England in August 1942, but by that time no reconnaissance aircraft had arrived and the Americans were entirely reliant upon the RAF. Soon after this the first American interpreters arrived to join the CIU at Medmenham. Although they had been through the training school at Harrisburg they were, according to the secret official history, 'completely inexperienced in any interpretation of operational photographs'.[7] Some of the PIs at Medmenham were less polite. They thought the new American arrivals were brash and arrogant and some were 'pretty useless'. They certainly had a lot to learn. Accompanying the men were some female Air Corps interpreters, who it was thought were more open to picking up new ideas.[8] Nevertheless, the RAF PIs welcomed the new arrivals and were happy to share with them their own hard-won knowledge and expertise. An American historian later wrote how British PIs had helped the Americans get 'up to speed in record time'. He described Medmenham as the 'Mecca' of photo interpretation, where 'Allied photo interpretation was honed and passed on'.[9]

As the US bombing offensive slowly increased in intensity over the next six months, so the volume of demands for target identification and damage assessment increased proportionately and more and more PIs arrived from America. By June 1943 there were thirty American PIs at Medmenham and this increased to sixty later that summer, along with support staff. By the beginning of 1944 there were 163 Americans, including thirty Women's Army Corps interpreters, working alongside the RAF teams. Many worked in damage assessment, but there was a group of engineers making models alongside the RAF Model Making Section. Photos taken at Medmenham towards the end of the war show American officers engaged right across the spectrum of PI work, looking relaxed and totally at home in the mock-Tudor mansion on the banks of the Thames.

The first American reconnaissance unit arrived in Britain in

October 1942. It was based at Mount Farm, a small airfield that had been used as a satellite field to RAF Benson, an ideal location being so close to the RAF reconnaissance base. For several months the American operation was small in scale, but by March 1943, four squadrons of Lightnings had arrived, forming the 7th Photo Group under Lieutenant Colonel James G. Hall. All requests for reconnaissance cover went through Air Ministry Intelligence, where an America Liaison Officer now sat. Here the requests were prioritised and the work distributed either to the RAF or to the USAAF recon units. The American and British station commanders at Mount Farm and Benson worked closely together to coordinate their work. And all photographs were sent to Medmenham for Second and Third Phase interpretation either by British or American PIs, or sometimes both. A genuinely combined operation seemed to be working well, with minimum duplication of effort and maximum efficiency of operation. The official history later wrote of 'the smooth working and harmonious collaboration of the British and American organisations' as an 'outstanding example of Allied co-operation'.[10] It was all too good to be true.

Colonel Elliott Roosevelt admired aspects of the British way of doing things. For instance he was a great fan of the skills of Adrian Warburton. But there was something about the attitude of most British officers that got up the nose of the President's son. He found many Brits insufferably pompous and sure of themselves. Thanks no doubt to the fact that the RAF, the Army and the Royal Navy had been fighting the war for three years, many British officers felt that they knew how to fight the Germans and that the Americans had a lot to learn. However, Roosevelt seems to have shared the view of many American officers that the British were a bunch of stuffy, old-fashioned amateurs with a deplorable record in the war so far.[11] The sense of superiority that came from many of the Brits riled Roosevelt, and in the Mediterranean he wanted American operations to be entirely commanded by American officers.

In January 1943 he accompanied his father to the Casablanca Conference and took against many of the senior British generals, admirals and air marshals he met, thinking them to be like old-fashioned imperialists. He recounted later a private conversation he had with his father at the end of the summit. His father said to him, 'I've tried to make it clear to Winston – and the others – that while we're their allies, and in it to victory by their side, they must never get the idea that we're in it just to help them hang on to the archaic, medieval Empire ideas ... I hope they realize they're not the senior partner; that we're not going to sit by, after we've won, and watch their system stultify the growth of every country in Asia and half the countries in Europe to boot.'[12]

Elliott shared his father's dislike for the British empire but he lacked his father's tact and respect, coming to think that the British way was stuck in the past and dominated by the outmoded, imperialist ways of thinking. Roosevelt had a lot of energy and enthusiasm for photo intelligence, and the unit he ran in Algiers gradually built up to a strength of 2800 men. He wanted to organise things his own way. And as the President's son he was used to getting things done his way.

At the beginning of 1944 Roosevelt was recalled from the Mediterranean to take charge of US photo intelligence in Britain in the run-up to the invasion of Europe. By this stage of the war, the balance between Britain and the USA had fundamentally shifted. Britain's role was now eclipsed by the Americans. As the 'arsenal of democracy', America was building the ships, aircraft, tanks, vehicles, guns and ammunition for the Allied war effort. The numbers of US bombers and support aircraft in

England were growing daily and there would soon be a million GIs based in Britain preparing to launch the assault upon occupied Europe. The whole invasion was under the command of an American general, Dwight D. Eisenhower. Clearly, Elliott Roosevelt was aware of these shifts in the balance of power when he suggested, in early 1944, that a new American Reconnaissance Wing should be formed to control all American air force requirements. He refused to accept that American commanders needed RAF approval to fly their own reconnaissance aircraft. This seemed reasonable. But the corollary of this came when General James Doolittle, the commander of the Eighth Army Air Force, proposed that American photo intelligence should come entirely under US command as well. Roosevelt wholeheartedly backed this plan, and Doolittle planned to withdraw all American PIs from Medmenham and take them to Pinetree in Buckinghamshire, the headquarters of the Eighth. This went against the whole line of thinking that had prevailed since the United States joined the war, that to avoid duplication of effort both countries should work together within the CIU.

Roosevelt announced at a meeting with the Air Ministry in February 1944 that it would take forty-five days for his new organisation to become fully operational. British officials were horrified to hear this, knowing that the target date for D-Day was only four months away. They pointed out the huge duplication of effort that would be required. Photos from all new sorties would have to be copied for both Medmenham and for the American unit at Pinetree, as would hundreds if not thousands of reports from Medmenham, along with tens of thousands of photos from the library. PIs would be transferred from Medmenham just when one of the war's biggest and most ambitious operations was nearing its peak. None of this seemed to make any impression on Elliott Roosevelt.

Although an influential figure, Roosevelt was not without his opponents. One of these was James Winant, the Anglophile American ambassador in London, who regularly dined with Churchill and knew most of the British top brass well. Winant knew of the work at Medmenham and was an admirer of Douglas Kendall, effectively now the chief photo interpreter at the unit. The ambassador set up a lunch on 16 February at a private suite at Claridge's. Present were Sir Arthur Street, permanent under-secretary to the Air Minister, General Carl Spaatz, commander of all US air forces in England, and – on Winant's insistence – Douglas Kendall from Medmenham. It was remarkable for a mid-ranking officer of Kendall's status to attend such a high level meeting as this. But he was able to convince Spaatz of the important work going on at Medmenham and how it was progressing smoothly with both British and American officers working together. He explained how disruptive and potentially chaotic it would be to the war effort to split it up now. Spaatz revised the American military's demands and agreed that as long as he could control his own reconnaissance aircraft, he would be happy to continue the present arrangement of working through the combined interpretation centre at Medmenham.[13]

These conversations took place against the backdrop of a dispute at an even higher level over command of the Allied air forces in the run-up to D-Day. Eisenhower, as Supreme Commander of the invasion of Europe, wanted to control all air power and direct it to the needs of D-Day. 'Bomber' Harris objected to his bombers being diverted from their mission to smash German industry, arguing that this was still the best way to win the war. President Roosevelt sided with Eisenhower but Churchill was reluctant to hand over his bomber force to the Americans. Eventually Churchill proposed a compromise. Air

Chief Marshal Tedder, who had been recalled from the Mediterranean and appointed as Eisenhower's deputy, would take command of the air operation. This meant the bombers were committed to tactical bombing during the prelude to D-Day but that they remained under RAF command. This was acceptable to Eisenhower and to the Americans. In fact, everyone accepted it except Harris, who fumed at the diversion of his bombers for four or five months.

Elliott Roosevelt, no doubt aware of these high level arguments, at one point threatened to take the dispute about control over photo reconnaissance and interpretation to the President, his father. Having not been present at the Claridge's lunch, he was furious that he had been outmanoeuvred and continued to argue to Air Ministry representatives that nothing less than a fully independent, American-controlled interpretation unit was acceptable. The situation became extremely tense. At one point the US ambassador phoned to tell him that his course of actions 'might jeopardise the whole future of Anglo-American relations'.[14] This only enraged Roosevelt further.

Finally, at the end of March, it was agreed to set up a new body, the Joint Photographic Reconnaissance Committee, in which both Americans and British would decide the priorities for reconnaissance. The RAF would continue to fly their reconnaissance under 106 Group from Benson and the Americans under the Eighth Reconnaissance Wing from Mount Farm. It was also agreed to move the Damage Assessment Section from Medmenham to Pinetree. The section was so large that there was no longer room for it at Danesfield House. There was a problem in finding a suitable building for it near the American headquarters, but eventually the premises formerly occupied by a famous girls' school were turned over to the use of the photo interpreters. The old notices were still up in the school when the PIs moved in, and many lewd jokes circulated at the sign above a call button in one of the old dormitories that said 'Ring If Mistress Required'![15]

Right up to the last minute, Elliott Roosevelt argued his case for a separately controlled interpretation unit. But his battle had been lost. Kendall later said that Roosevelt did not speak to him for six months. Eventually though Roosevelt seems to have calmed down and he told Kendall later that he accepted the proposal.[16] He wrote after the war that he greatly admired the RAF men with whom he worked as 'consummately knowledgeable officers' who were 'thoroughly familiar with their job' and 'a constant credit to their country'.[17] It's impossible to know how genuinely he felt these words. But he did work alongside the British, remaining in charge of the American photo intelligence operation in Europe until in November 1944 he was recalled to Washington for an assignment at the Pentagon. No doubt Kendall and many other senior British officials were relieved to see him go.

In order to formalise the fact that it was now recognised as a joint Anglo-American operation, the Central Interpretation Unit, as it had been called since the opening of Medmenham in April 1941, was from 1 May 1944 renamed the Allied Central Interpretation Unit. Medmenham had survived its biggest challenge yet, not from German bombs or British official scepticism but from an American demand for control. It was now officially a combined unit. Just as well, for there was an immense amount of work to do, with the biggest combined operation of the war approaching fast. The countdown to D-Day, Operation Overlord, had begun.

13

Planning for Overlord

In May 1942, Major George Yool and a team of nine other Army photo interpreters were secretly withdrawn from Medmenham. The remaining Army PIs were told not to ask why they had left. Yool was instructed to report to Norfolk House, just off St James's Square in London's West End, where he was to form a new section of the Army Photographic Interpretation Service. Norfolk House was the headquarters of Home Forces Army Intelligence, and Major Yool and his team were given instructions to start working on a new top secret project. They were to begin searching along the entire coast of occupied Europe and up to thirty miles inland, from Den Helder in northern Holland all the way to south-west France and the Spanish border. Their task was to identify potential landing beaches for an invasion of Europe. The systematic photographing of enemy ports and harbours in northern France and the Low Countries began in order to assess the state of the coastal defences in anticipation of a future invasion.

At this point, progress in the war was far from clear and victory had not been won even in North Africa. There was no clear strategic decision as to when, where and how an invasion of occupied Europe might take place. At the highest level, Prime Minister Churchill and President Roosevelt, along with their Chiefs of Staff, differed as to when the best moment would be to invade. The Americans wanted to confront Hitler's armies as soon as possible. Churchill and the British argued that the invasion should only be attempted when the Allies had built up an overwhelming superiority in men and materiel. In the meantime, Churchill persuaded the Americans to keep fighting the Mediterranean war in order to sustain pressure on the Germans from what he called 'the soft underbelly of Europe'. The Americans reluctantly went along with this.

Critics of Churchill later claimed that he extended the length of the war by a year by concentrating so much effort on the Mediterranean. His defenders responded by claiming that, had the invasion been attempted any earlier, it would have been likely to fail, setting the Allied war effort back disastrously, and that it was only by the spring of 1944 that the Allies were ready to invade.[1] But the Army had to start planning ahead as the Allies were sure to invade one day. And there was a huge task ahead for the planners. The first question was to establish where the invasion would take place. Good photo intelligence would be vital in making that fundamental decision.

The Army had established its own photographic interpretation section in the summer of 1940. As the British Army rapidly regrouped after the disaster of Dunkirk and anxiously monitored signs of a possible German invasion, General Alan Brooke, then Chief of Home Forces, was concerned about the skills of the RAF photo interpreters working at Wembley. He wrote: 'The RAF interpreters are not trained in Army requirements nor in the recognition of objects of military importance, and the need for an adequate and skilled Army interpretation unit at Wembley has become apparent. I consider that an Army Section should now be formed.'[2] His principal concern was that there were specific objects of military significance, relating to the deployment of enemy troops, his armour and artillery, that were beyond the expertise of RAF photo interpreters.

Brooke got his way, and by the time of the opening of the Central Interpretation Unit at Medmenham eight months later there were about forty Army photo interpreters providing tactical intelligence for Army units, in the group known as B Section. The official title of B Section was the Army Photographic Intelligence Section (APIS). Wags noted that 'Apis' was also the name of the sacred bull of the Ancient Egyptians and wondered what sort of sacred cow the Army had created.

The Army PIs were part of the Army Intelligence Corps, led by Lieutenant-Colonel Tom Churchill (no relation to the wartime Prime Minister). Churchill had been the leading figure in army photographic intelligence in the 1930s and it was his task to recruit new PIs. Like the Air Ministry recruiters, he turned to civilian specialists including archaeologists, geologists and surveyors and sent them on the training course run by 'Steve' Stephenson. Everyone who passed the course was sent on a probationary attachment to Medmenham.

But whereas the RAF would accept anyone with specialist skills and get them into uniform and working as an officer straight away, the War Office insisted that no one could be commissioned within the Army who had not passed a War Office Selection Board. Unfortunately, some of those who had started working at Medmenham then failed their Army officer selection. A solution was found by appointing them as non-commissioned officers, and by this means another famous pre-war archaeologist, Stuart Piggott, was allowed to carry on working at Medmenham. Even more bizarrely, *Punch* cartoonist Albert Edgar Beard failed his War Office Selection Board but the Army gave him a senior sergeant-major rank in order to enable him to carry on his PI work. Sergeant-majors were known for their ramrod stature, their strict discipline and for shouting at young recruits. It was said that the quiet, self-effacing cartoonist was probably the most unlikely regimental sergeant-major in the British Army.[3] But his presence added to the rich mix of talents at Medmenham.

The Army PIs concentrated on finding objects of specific relevance to military needs. They were responsible not just for locating enemy artillery and identifying enemy armour, but also for plotting the layout of trenches, machine gun positions, minefields, barbed wire and so on. Barbed wire always signified that something was being guarded and could alert interpreters to the presence of a military installation. A field might be cultivated or under pasture but barbed wire would show up easily, as grass, nettles or shrubs always grew underneath and would stand out clearly on an aerial photograph as a dark patch. The PIs could also identify minefields from the air as tiny white dots would show up where the ground had been dug over and often the mines were laid out on a pattern that could easily be picked up on an aerial photograph.

Although it was vital information for the RAF, whose fliers had to cross enemy territory, Army PIs specialised in finding anti-aircraft batteries and produced maps of occupied Europe on which flak guns were marked. From the air, anti-aircraft guns looked quite different to artillery batteries. Flak guns had to fire directly up into the sky, whereas artillery weapons, which fired at a low trajectory, were roofed over or placed under camouflage. Heavy flak batteries were usually laid out in squares of four or six, the gun emplacements themselves being square or octagonal. There was usually an ammunition store, a hut for the gunners and a command post nearby. Light flak batteries were usually sited in groups of two or three and operated from a radio or telephone link without a command post.[4] It was extraordinary how much the photo interpreters could see, but they were lucky that the Germans were so systematic in the way they organised their military installations.

We have already seen how important tactical photo intelligence had proved to be in the run-up to the battle of El Alamein, as well as in Tunisia, Sicily and Italy. The photos for these operations were interpreted in Egypt and in North Africa by APIS units in the field. Army PIs worked closely alongside their RAF colleagues at Heliopolis in Egypt and in Gibraltar, as well as in the team that was sent to Italy. The different procedures and priorities of the Army and the RAF were a potential cause of tension between the PIs. But it seems that most of the time, and certainly when they were busy, the Army and the RAF PIs got along well with each other and mucked in together. Douglas Kendall, the senior RAF interpreter at Medmenham, was willing to adapt procedures in order to get a job done and much of the credit for the smooth working of the multi-service operation must go to him.[5] In Britain, there was also a squadron of Spitfires, either 140 or 16 Squadron, dedicated to photographing objects of importance to the Army. With relatively little Army activity in northern Europe in 1941, the unit remained small in scale but from 1942 it grew in size. By this time, the Army had a major new task to undertake.

One of the first operations of the new APIS unit at Norfolk House was to prepare for a large scale raid against the port of Dieppe on the north French coast. The military authorities decided that before any full invasion of occupied France could take place a smaller raid was needed as a sort of dress rehearsal to test techniques and equipment and to learn lessons in advance of the event itself. After many changes of plan, the Dieppe raid finally took place on 19 August 1942. Two commando units landed to the east and west of the town to disable batteries of heavy guns that otherwise might fire on the invasion fleet, consisting of 230 vessels. At the heart of the raid, five thousand men from the Canadian 2nd Division were to land and capture the port and hold it for twenty-four hours before withdrawing.

The raid certainly provided a steep learning curve for Allied forces. One of the commando wings ran into a force of German ships and was decimated at sea, leaving very few men able to get ashore. The main assault force found the enemy defences to be far more substantial than anticipated, with machine gun nests in the side of the cliffs providing a murderous enfilading fire on the troops trying to struggle across the beaches. The planned support from tanks due to come ashore from newly built Landing Craft Tanks (LCTs) went hopelessly wrong as a series of navigational errors resulted in their failure to arrive on schedule. After a few dreadful hours of slaughter on the beaches the raid was abandoned and all survivors were ordered to withdraw. The Canadians had lost two-thirds of their men and in all there were nearly four thousand Canadian and British dead, wounded or left behind and taken prisoner.

It was a bloody price to pay, but important lessons had been learned. The Allied commanders now understood that it would be almost impossible to capture a heavily defended port town as a way to bring supplies ashore. The landing force for a full scale invasion would be vastly bigger than that of the Dieppe raid, so they would have to find another way of delivering men and materiel. They also realised that landing on beaches over-looked by tall cliffs could be suicidal. Finally they accepted that the precise timing of all parts of a coordinated invasion force was essential for success.

Moreover, the intelligence for Dieppe gained from aerial photography had been poor. Interpreters had failed to spot many of the defensive machine gun positions, nor had the strength of defences around the town been clearly established. Aerial intelligence now had to go up a gear to find the right sort of beaches and to clarify the precise topographical conditions around the beachhead. It would be essential to track down and locate every single enemy machine gun position, minefield and artillery emplacement. These could not all be seen on photos taken by vertical cameras so there was a need for low level oblique photo cover of the landing areas. This information would be necessary to prevent the full invasion from being another fiasco.

Up to this point, Army PIs had been trained on Stephenson's RAF course. But with the immense growth in Army PI work from 1942, there was a need for a specific training course for soldiers. Such a course was started at the Army School of Military Intelligence at Matlock in Derbyshire. One of the early participants was Geoffrey Stone, who had been an instructor in field security at Matlock for two years and was a keen photographer. Stone remembers that there was great scepticism in the Army about photo interpretation. He recalls officers asking 'Why interpretation? If it's there on the photo, it's there.' He quickly learnt that it was not so simple. If you could see a gun emplacement, an interpreter had to ask what sort of weapon it was: an anti-aircraft weapon, a field gun or a heavy artillery battery? At a scale of 1:10,000 a tank would show up as little more than a speck on a photo taken from thirty thousand feet. But after examination with a magnifying measurer (a magnifying glass with a scale built into it), it was possible to work out the length and the width of the armour and so to identify the type of tank that had been photographed. Stone was keen on solving puzzles, especially crosswords, and he clearly had an aptitude for PI work. 'It's not only a case of recognising what you *could* see,' he said later, 'but of inferring what you *couldn't* see.'[6]

For Operation Torch, the invasion of North Africa in November of 1942, aerial photography played a part in the success of the landings. And in preparation for the invasion of Sicily in July the following year, significant strides forward had been made in the use of aerial intelligence. PIs learned how to measure the angle of a beach from aerial photos, and located the detail and extent of minefields both on the beaches and around the routes off them. Colonel Tom Churchill briefed the commandos who were part of the first wave landing force. Brigadier Laycock, the Commando Brigade commander, said later, 'Having air photographs of a strip of coast we were about to attack explained to us by Tom Churchill was the most interesting of all my experiences. His interpretation of air photographs proved accurate to a degree which I could not have believed possible.'[7] Churchill had claimed that sites that appeared to be coastal artillery positions were in fact machine gun posts. It was a risk to stick his neck out on something that could have proved fatal had he been wrong. But his interpretation was correct and the landings were a success.

By the time of the invasion of Sicily, the Army Photographic Intelligence Units had established their own small PI teams in the field. They often operated out of a truck or a caravan and carried out their own detailed interpretation of photos to establish what the enemy were up to just a few miles ahead of the advancing troops. Were they on the move? Were they drawing up armour or artillery? Were there strongly held fortifications

ahead? So rapid was the Allied advance in Sicily that when it
came to preparing for the crossing to the Italian mainland, the
model of the landing zone that had been made at Medmenham
had not yet arrived. So, just south of the city of Catania, two
Army PIs, Captains Bill Hall and Jack Robinson, made their
own floor model out of clay overlaid with aerial photos, using
inks taken from nearby offices to colour in forests, rivers,
houses and forts. It was a big model with large planks laid
across it so the officers planning the crossing could walk across
and look down on a depiction of what they could expect to find
when they reached the mainland. It was a marvellous piece of
improvisation in the field and served its purpose well. By the
time the model painstakingly made in Medmenham arrived,
the landings had already successfully taken place.

As the Allied forces slogged their way up the Italian peninsula, forward APIS units helped in briefing local commanders.
Before every assault, sixty photo-maps were produced for each
division so they could be distributed to every company and
artillery battery taking part in the assault. Mosaic photo-maps
were made at a scale of 1:50,000, and more detailed mosaics of
1:10,000 could be made of areas of particular importance. This
intelligence, combined with statements from prisoners of war,
from ground observation posts and from any intercepted
enemy communications, enabled divisional intelligence officers to build up a picture of the distribution of enemy forces
ahead. It was reputed that an order from a German regimental commander was captured near the Sangro river in
south-east Italy. It read: 'The enemy are taking air photographs
every day so that they know as much about our positions as
any one of us. To reduce this leakage of information you must
avoid making footpaths and you must carefully camouflage
your positions. In particular, you must avoid exposing your

bare backsides during the daytime as they would be clearly visible on the photographs and might pinpoint positions.'[8] There is no evidence of PIs identifying enemy units from spotting their bare bottoms. But the order remains a good one, just in case.

In mid August 1943, at the Quadrant conference between President Roosevelt and Prime Minister Churchill and their Chiefs of Staff in Quebec, the epic decision was made to go ahead with Operation Overlord, the invasion of Europe, along the Normandy coastline. The shortest crossing would have been to the coast along the Pas de Calais. But it would be almost impossible to capture any of the heavily defended ports along this stretch of coast and many of the beaches were lined with tall cliffs. Early research had identified the Normandy beaches as providing good landing conditions with only modest cliffs. The military had learned the lessons from Dieppe. The date set for the invasion was 1 May 1944, to be called D-Day.

The Army photographic unit at Norfolk House reporting directly to the Chief of Staff of the Supreme Allied Command was turned over to work exclusively on planning for Overlord. By the end of the year it had grown to a unit of thirty PIs supported by eighteen draughtsmen. Alongside them were colleagues in the Army and RAF at Medmenham and months of detailed planning now began. In addition to identifying gun positions and enemy strongpoints, PIs' attention was focused on beach defences and on underwater obstacles. The beaches had to be photographed with the tide both in and out. An important advance came after a stroke of luck when the PIs detected the existence of small mines attached to the end of underwater obstacles. During a bombing attack along one beach, a chance photograph revealed the simultaneous detonation of fourteen separate explosive devices under the sea, as the tide was in. But when the explosion points were plotted on a photo of the beach with the tide out, it was realised that each one corresponded to the exact location of one of the underwater obstacles. On other beaches, the recon pilots photographed giant curved steel stakes known as Hedgehog, and intended to destroy landing craft. Geologists looking at photos of the pebbles on each beach were able to estimate whether the shingle was sufficiently firm to enable tanks to cross the beach. Sometimes, when the photographs couldn't provide conclusive evidence, divers were sent in at night from submarines to bring back samples of the sand and the pebbles. The Army PIs also searched inland areas for sites that might be suitable as drop zones for Allied paratroopers and landing fields for gliders. The line of German defensive positions along the Atlantic and Channel coasts, defending what they called *Festung Europa* (Fortress Europe) was called the Atlantic Wall. It was a formidable defensive barrier and the Allies now had every metre of it under scrutiny.

In January 1944 Field Marshal Rommel was put in charge of further building up the Atlantic Wall and he threw himself into the task with immense vigour and energy. He visited beaches, supervising the construction of defensive machine gun and artillery positions that enabled the defenders to cover every part of each beach from at least two angles. Every field that might have been used for gliders was planted with iron and steel rods which the Allies called 'Rommel's asparagus'. Heavy guns were brought in from all over occupied Europe to build up artillery batteries along the coast and further inland. About thirty thousand anti-tank mines were attached to the beach obstacles along the many miles of coast. The PIs watched all this defensive build-up take place and for each action by the Germans, a counter-action was invented. As the Germans installed steel rods across potential landing fields, so the Allies trained engineers in landing with the right sort of explosives to destroy them. As the Germans constructed new artillery batteries, so the Allies made plans to bomb them, or for paratroopers to storm them.

In the spring of 1944 several Army PIs moved up to join the units that were waiting to invade. The British-Canadian 21st Army Group under General Montgomery, who was appointed Land Commander for Overlord, formed its own Army Photographic Interpretation Unit. They made daily First Phase reports on German positions to check if units had been moved or new positions had been fortified. By June 1944, the APIS unit in London had interpreted over a million photographs.[9] Everything was geared to having a maximum understanding of enemy dispositions and equipment as D-Day approached.

In order to deal with the huge demands being made on the unit as a result of the D-Day preparations, the number of Army interpreters at Medmenham was also growing. By the eve of the invasion, sixty-one army officers and thirty-three other ranks were working on PI under the command of Major Norman Falcon. Though he had a bad stammer that in a more conventional establishment might have disqualified him from a position of high command, Falcon had a clear, incisive, enquiring mind and never jumped to conclusions without testing every possible explanation from every angle. He proved a capable commander of Army PI and was highly respected by his RAF compatriots.

Geoffrey Stone, one of the Army PIs sent to Medmenham, was posted to the basement of Danesfield House, which he felt reflected the lowly position of Army PIs in the eyes of the RAF. One of his first jobs was to list all the quarries in northern France and to analyse what kind of stone each one produced.

An advancing army would require hardcore to build foundations, runways and gun emplacements and so would need to
know where to find every type of stone quickly. He then went
on to F Section, which specialised in railways and communications in occupied Europe. Stone built up from aerial
photographs and pre-war guide books a detailed plan of the
railways in Austria, with information about every station,
bridge and marshalling yard. As he later remembered, 'You
never knew after the invasion where troops would get to and
if they got to Austria they would need to know about the railways, about the strength of bridges and about the whole
network.'[10]

In January 1944, Air Chief Marshal Sir Arthur Tedder was
appointed deputy to the Supreme Commander of Operation
Overlord, General Dwight D. Eisenhower. As RAF commander
in the Mediterranean, Tedder had followed the research of a
team of top British scientists led by Professor Solly Zuckerman,
the specialist who had advised the RAF so successfully on the
bombing of Pantelleria. Zuckerman's research on North Africa,
Sicily and Italy showed that a disproportionate amount of
damage had been caused by hitting the enemy's railway communication links. Tedder eagerly took up this cause and, with
Zuckerman, came up with a 'Transport Plan' to bomb the main
lines and marshalling yards across northern France and
Belgium to prevent the enemy from moving up reinforcements
into the battle zone. The planners realised that one of the greatest potential threats to Overlord would come from the
Germans' ability to bring up massive reserves to counter-attack
the Allies as they struggled to secure their bridgehead. The
pressure on the railway team in F Section was intense. They had
to find all the major hubs, which when destroyed would immo-
bilise the railway network.

In March, RAF Bomber Command was diverted from its offensive against German industrial and civilian targets and, to 'Bomber' Harris's annoyance, was ordered to bomb six railway marshalling yards in France. The raids were a great success and marked the beginning of a major bombing offensive against targets that would be vital to the success of Overlord. But of course, it was essential not to give away the planned site of the landings, and so raids had to be carried out across a broad area of France and Belgium so as not to alert the Germans to the importance of Normandy.

In addition to the heavy bombing, a new Tactical Air Force was formed to assist the land forces in attacking specific targets of military significance. The flying of ground support missions had been very effective in North Africa and Sicily but now had to be organised on a far bigger scale. New reconnaissance squadrons made up of the latest Spitfire XIs and Mosquito XVIs were created with the specific objective of working closely with the ground troops. Experience had shown that armies in the field needed a continuous flow of aerial intelligence and this had become an integral part of every offensive action. Army commanders were encouraged to be 'air minded' and to use photo reconnaissance as much as possible.[11] Army PIs needed to work particularly on First Phase photo interpretation. There was criticism from the RAF of the way the Army organised First Phase PI, in three shifts of eight hours in each twenty-four. Most of the recon flying took place in the early morning and late afternoon, and so certain shifts were swamped with work while others had a relatively easy time. In practice, all PIs tended to work when they were needed. 'If it was a cloudy day and there were few sorties,' Geoffrey Stone remembers, 'RAF Benson would call and say "That's your lot" and we would pack up early. If it was a busy day you just had to be flexible and do whatever the job demanded.'[12] There were few moans about this. Everyone knew they were taking part in one of the most critical operations of the war.

In the six months before D-Day the Model Section at Medmenham went into overdrive, producing models that helped everyone from the planners at the Supreme Headquarters of the Allied Expeditionary Force (SHAEF) right down to platoon commanders. A large number of American model makers joined the unit to work on models for the American landing beaches. The models produced were of three types. Small scale model-maps of large areas of northern France showed the landscape and core communications. There were thirty-two originals of these, each 5ft by 5ft, and plaster casts were made enabling multiple copies to be produced and distributed. Then there were models of stretches of coastline going about twelve miles inland. Made at a scale of about 1:5000, these were very detailed, showing beach defences and gun emplacements along with roads, rivers and other communications. They were huge, about sixteen feet square. Sixty-three originals were made and at least three copies of each were produced. The models made for the airborne and glider landings were the most detailed of all, at a scale of about 1:900. Fewer of these were needed but they included the tiniest of details.[13]

When the troops were finally isolated inside their units in the last few days before D-Day and were allowed no further interaction with the outside world, the models were revealed to prepare them for what lay ahead. It was possible to point out the details of the beaches they would land on, the hinterland they would cross, the buildings they would see and the enemy fortifications they would face. Thousands of photographic maps were produced, annotated with details about the strength of bridges, the angle of anticipated enemy fire and the routes to follow. Hundreds of oblique low angle photos were printed. The coxswain of every landing craft was given a low angle photo, taken from an aircraft flying just above the waves, showing him what his beaching point looked like. Every platoon leader in the first waves of the invasion forces had photographs of his own particular stretch of beach.

Of course things still went horribly wrong. Strong currents in the wilder than expected seas drove landing craft on to stretches of coast far from their intended destination. Men were landed in entirely the wrong places. There are few recorded instances of soldiers struggling up beaches under fire stopping to look at aerial photographs. But this is not the point. It was a massive undertaking to prepare this amount of information and no army in history has ever landed on foreign soil with as much intelligence about what faced them, where the enemy were and what they were equipped with, and of the terrain ahead, as on D-Day.

The volume of work going through Medmenham peaked in the last weeks before the invasion. British and American reconnaissance aircraft combed up and down the beaches of France and Belgium recording last-minute troop deployments and any changes in defensive armaments. American Lightning F-5s with cameras in the nose were particularly good at these missions. In photos taken during extreme low level sorties, German engineers working on beach obstacles can be seen running for cover, such was the level of surprise. Again, the Allied aircraft covered a wide area so as not to alert the enemy as to the actual location of the invasion beaches. Even PIs interpreting the photos did not know which beaches would be used in the invasion and which were photographed simply as decoys.

In addition, a brilliant deception was organised with the establishment of a pretend 1st Army Group in the south-east of

England. Dummy landing craft, tanks and trucks were laid out in long lines near the coast and photographed. PIs at Medmenham studied the photos and changes were made to make the dummy machines look as authentic as possible. Then German reconnaissance aircraft were allowed to photograph them. This helped to convince General von Runstedt, the Commander of Army Group West, that the invasion was coming across the narrowest part of the Channel, the Pas de Calais. He continued to believe this for some time after the actual invasion had taken place 150 miles to the west.

The final stage of the preparations for D-Day was to identify all the radar sites that might pick up the approach of the invasion fleet. G Section under Claude Wavell, which specialised in identifying the many different types of radio, radar and wireless telegraphic apparatus employed by the Germans, produced more than 250 reports listing every device along 450 miles of coast and up to 20 miles inland.[14] A hundred separate German radar stations were located by the team at Medmenham, some of them consisting of several different types of installation. In May an experiment was carried out in firing rockets from Typhoon ground attack aircraft at the radar stations near Ostende. After damage assessment oblique photos had shown that this was successful, a huge operation by rocket-firing Typhoons and Spitfire fighter bombers was launched on 22 May to destroy as many of the radar sites as possible. Only a few radar stations in the Pas de Calais were left operating in order for them to be able to pick up the phoney signals of a fake armada crossing the Channel.

At the last moment, D-Day was delayed by bad weather and postponed by twenty-four hours. But intelligence reports from aerial photography continued up until the last minute. The last one was timed at 1600 hours on 5 June. Later that night about

27,000 British and American paratroopers jumped behind enemy lines into occupied France. At dawn on 6 June, a fleet of 3000 ships with 4000 landing craft ferried about 130,000 American, British and Canadian troops across the Channel to clamber ashore over the next few hours. The Americans on Omaha beach had a terrible time of it and suffered appalling casualties – not because the PIs had failed to spot the position of the German defences in the cliffs, as at Dieppe, but because the air forces had failed to destroy these emplacements before the first waves hit the beach. Elsewhere, the months of detailed planning paid off and casualty rates were far lower than anticipated. In some landing zones the only delay in advancing off the beach was caused by traffic jams with so many vehicles trying to progress inland. Reconnaissance aircraft flew the length of the invasion beaches approximately every two hours during D-Day, photographing the battle that raged below. The reason seems to be that Allied commanders wanted an hour-by-hour picture of what was happening in order to study in detail the course of the day in case the landings failed. But they didn't fail and D-Day proved a triumphant success. The photos taken make up a remarkable and detailed record of the battle for the Normandy beaches during the day that changed the course of the Second World War.[15]

Just a week after D-Day, the Supreme Commander, General Eisenhower, wrote to express his 'sincere appreciation' to the model makers for their work in the invasion preparations. Having paid tribute to their 'whole hearted co-operation and diligence' in producing from aerial photographs the models 'which considered collectively represent a construction programme of great magnitude', he concluded by thanking them for a task well done, saying, 'May they feel that theirs is a real contribution to our ultimate victory.'[16]

Having come safely ashore a huge build-up of men and materiel began inside the growing beachhead. But despite early elation, the fighting became bogged down for several weeks in the Normandy countryside. The Germans brought up rein-forcements, though much more slowly than they would have wished thanks to the destruction of the rail transport links and of the road bridges over the Loire. But two tough, battle-hardened SS Panzer divisions were transported across Europe from the Eastern Front and when finally deployed they helped slow the Allied advance to a snail's pace.

What was particularly alarming for the infantry was that they now found themselves in what the Normans call the 'bocage' country. Sunken roads ran between patchworks of tiny fields bordered by high hedgerows. These were not the sort of hedges that were familiar in Devon or Pennsylvania. They were centuries-old structures of mud banks and thick shrubby undergrowth topped with hedges or trees, rising perhaps to twelve feet. They were ideal cover for defenders and especially hard to advance through. A soldier never knew what he would find behind the next hedgerow. Despite all the preparations, no one had warned the troops to expect this. And, sure enough, the photo interpreters had not picked them out. Although they had seen the network of hedges, they had not anticipated that they would be such solid, dense structures. Eventually, the Americans adapted some of the steel obstacles they had found on the beaches as giant metal scoops that were welded on to the front of Sherman tanks. It took the force of thirty tons of armour behind these improvised forks to penetrate the ancient Norman hedgerows. By the end of June about one million soldiers faced each other across the Normandy countryside. But the Allied armies still had to break out from their beachheads. This would prove much tougher than expected.

Photo intelligence had played its part in one of the biggest operations of the war. But it also had a role to play in some of the smallest wartime operations, sometimes involving a few dozen men, sometimes only a single man or woman.

14

Special Operations

On the night of 27 February 1942 a team of more than 150 elite paratroopers were dropped a mile inland from the French coast in an area just north of Le Havre. After gathering their equipment, they quickly and quietly made their way up a valley to a villa used by the Germans on the clifftop near a village called Bruneval. Here they opened fire and overwhelmed the small German garrison. One of the men accompanying the paratroopers was an RAF technician, and he began to dismantle some sophisticated electronic equipment at an installation about fifty yards away. As he did so, German reinforcements arrived and a fierce fire fight raged. When he had loaded the equipment on to special trolleys, the technician gave the signal to the Airborne commander, Major John Frost, who ordered his men to withdraw down a coast path to the beach below. What was this strange operation all about? And why were men's lives being risked to seize electronic equipment from a clifftop in northern France?

From the early stages of the war there had been a debate within the RAF as to whether the Germans had been able to develop radar technology, as British scientists led by Robert Watson Watt had done. Radar had played a critical role in the Battle of Britain, guiding the Spitfires and Hurricanes of the 'Few' to the target areas where the German bombers were heading. Although radar had helped the RAF survive the battle, the consensus among senior intelligence officials was that the Germans did not have it. But one young scientist took a different view. His name was R.V. Jones and he had made a name for himself by arguing that the Germans had developed a system of beams to guide night bombers to their targets during the Blitz. He was in a small minority in arguing for the existence of the beams but he had been proved right. Finding out how the German system worked meant it could be jammed, and knowing this probably saved many British cities from even greater destruction.

As the loss rate among British bombers flying over occupied Europe increased during late 1940, Jones became ever more convinced that the Germans had developed a radar system. Signallers picked up strange high frequency signals but Jones was unable to confirm what they were. Then, aerial photographs of what was thought to be a radio transmitting station near Auderville on the north-west tip of the Cherbourg peninsula revealed the existence of two mast towers, each 20ft square. By looking at them in stereo in two photographs taken just a few seconds apart, Claude Wavell at Medmenham had been able to see that the shadows of the masts had moved slightly. The masts only showed up as minuscule specks on the photographs, but by taking tiny measurements of about one-tenth of a millimetre, Wavell was able to show that they were in fact rotating.[1] This was the proof that Jones needed. He was now convinced and, with the aid of information from intercepted Enigma messages from Bletchley Park, he was able to persuade the decision makers that the Germans did indeed have radar. The system in use was apparently called 'Freya' after an ancient Nordic goddess.

A new group at Medmenham, G Section, was formed under Squadron Leader Wavell to specialise in hunting down these radar towers, and before long several of them had been found along the occupied Channel coast. But Jones knew from further signals being picked up by the Allies that another, more accurate short wave radar system was also in operation. Decoded German messages referred to a system known as 'Wurzburg'. In November another shape was spotted on the French coast on the tip of high cliffs near Le Havre. The PIs were able to make out a set of footpaths worn into the grass, seeming to converge on a tiny object almost at the tip of the cliffs. The apparatus was near the village of Bruneval.

Occasionally, pilots from Benson would travel the few miles to Medmenham to talk with the photo interpreters. Gordon Hughes was one of those who enjoyed doing this. One autumn day in 1941 he and another recon pilot, Tony Hill, were off duty. Visiting Medmenham before going out for a few beers, they ran into Claude Wavell, who showed them a new photograph that was puzzling him. He thought the shape of the apparatus was a paraboloid, that is like a small bowl turned on its side. Was this the new type of Wurzburg station?

'You pilots annoy me!' joked Wavell. 'You go over this place time and time again and never turn on your cameras in time.' What he needed were low angle oblique photos of the curious installation. Hill immediately became fascinated and offered to photograph the apparatus the next day.[2] This sort of photography was extremely difficult. The oblique camera in a Spitfire was below the aircraft, pointing out to the left, and the pilot had to fly low and to the right of an object, turning on his camera when the target was under the wing. Flying at maybe only fifty feet but at 300 mph and probably under anti-aircraft fire made this really tricky, and the tendency was to turn on the camera too late, and so miss the target. Hill flew a dicing sortie over Bruneval the next day but his cameras failed. Nevertheless he got a good look at the apparatus, so he called Wavell that evening to tell him that it was about ten feet in diameter and looked like 'an electric bowl fire'. From now on the object was known universally as the 'Bowl-fire'. The following day, Hill went back again and this time managed to take one of the classic aerial photos of the war, showing the small villa and a path leading up to a squat bowl structure that looked out to sea. Finding and photographing a piece of apparatus just ten feet in diameter along hundreds of miles of coastline was an almost impossible task. But, thanks to a combination of scientific hunch, brilliant observation and magnificent flying, photo reconnaissance had succeeded.

Jones now requested that a raid be made on the installation in order to bring back some of the technology for examination. If British scientists knew how the new German radar worked, it might be possible to find a way to jam it. That is why Major John Frost and his men found themselves under fire in the small villa on the clifftop at Bruneval. Initially it had been thought that a commando raid from the sea would be the best way to carry out the operation. But it had been decided that the coastal defences were too strong to allow this and so an Airborne unit was sent to drop inland and come up to surprise the radar station from the rear. Photo mosaics and a model of the clifftops and surrounding countryside at a scale of 1:2000 were made at Medmenham, and were used in the detailed planning of the raid.³ Once the radar station had been stormed and the technology dismantled, the men and the captured gear would make their way down the cliffs and escape in waiting landing craft. Although not everything went smoothly that night, overall the raid was a great success. There were few casualties, and the paratroopers got away with the radar equipment. They even had the bonus of bringing back a German radar operator as a prisoner. As a consequence of the Bruneval raid the Germans increased the defences around all their radar stations, surrounding them with barbed wire entanglements. This had the unintended consequence of making them far easier to identify from aerial imagery as barbed wire stood out clearly on black and white photographs. Soon G Section at Medmenham had plotted dozens more Freya and Wurzburg stations.⁴

By this time, Jones and Wavell had built up quite a rapport and G Section began to identify more and more unusual radio communication stations. Not knowing what all of them did, they gave them nicknames: 'The Horse Bird', 'The Chimney' and so on. At one of these unusual sites, called 'The Basket', Wavell spotted trellis-type bowl structures about twenty feet in diameter. Recognising these as the sort of structures that had been used to make Zeppelin airships, he requested photo cover of the Zeppelin factory at Friedrichshafen. Sure enough, he spotted a pile of components that could have been used to make up the bowl. These changed on a regular basis, obviously implying that they were being used. Soon afterwards the Prime Minister happened to tour Medmenham on an official visit. Wavell showed Churchill what he had found and the PM was fascinated. 'Have we been there yet?' Churchill asked, meaning had RAF bombers visited the factory. Wavell said no, they hadn't. A few days later, he heard that the factory at

Friedrichshafen had been heavily bombed.[5] Churchill rarely missed a trick.

In early 1942, while the Bruneval raid was being planned, a new top secret unit was created at Medmenham to work with the recently formed Combined Forces – that is, the Commando Brigade and what today would be called Special Forces. One of their first big missions was against the dry dock at St Nazaire. This was the largest dock in France and the only one capable of carrying out repairs if heavy German warships like the *Tirpitz* were ever able to get out into the Atlantic to attack Allied shipping. The only Admiralty maps of the port were out of date and so a scale model was built from aerial photographs. It was constantly updated as the latest cover showed construction of new U-boat shelters and other buildings. The commando officers used the model to plan the details of the raid, and the model was photographed in daylight and darkness from various angles to simulate the exact view the attacking force would get. From the photographs it was also possible to identify the location of four heavy coastal batteries.[6]

On the night of 27 March the Royal Navy and the commandos attacked the port and came under heavy defensive fire. The Navy succeeded in ramming the dock gates with an old destroyer packed with explosives triggered by a delayed-action fuse. The raid was a success in that when the explosives went off on the following day the damage to the dock gates was so great that they were never repaired. Damage assessment photography over the next few months showed that the huge caisson had buckled and the dock was left unused until after the war.

Allied losses were high and more than half the commandos were killed, went missing or were captured during the raid. Five

VCs and dozens of other medals were awarded for gallantry in the action. But the objective of preventing the dry dock from being used to repair the Atlantic raiders had been achieved. As we have seen, the *Tirpitz* remained in her Norwegian hideaways, monitored by photo reconnaissance aircraft and harassed by the Navy and the air force, until successfully attacked by heavy bombers towards the end of the war.

Douglas Kendall was the only person at Medmenham with sufficiently high security clearance to know about the Enigma code-breaking work that was going on at Bletchley Park.[7] He was able to check intelligence from Ultra every now and again against information from aerial photos to put his interpreters on the right track or to avoid them wasting time pursuing something irrelevant. In early 1943, Kendall was sent for by R.V. Jones and told in strict secrecy about the construction of the atomic bomb in the United States. Winston Churchill was concerned that the Germans might be developing their own atom bomb and wanted a thorough search from the air of potential research and development sites. There had been various hints that research on potential atomic projects had been moved from the Kaiser Wilhelm Institute in Berlin, where pioneering work on nuclear physics had been done earlier in the century, to a range of sites in the Stuttgart area. If an atomic bomb project was under way, it would draw upon vast new water and power supplies. So, on his return to Medmenham, Kendall asked D Section, the industry team, to start looking at cover around Stuttgart, without letting on exactly why they were to do so.

It was a strange request and no doubt the interpreters of D Section puzzled over their task. The whole area was to be combed and all power lines plotted and compared with previous covers, to see if new lines into a factory or research establishment had been constructed. Water supplies were to be similarly checked. After a detailed survey the PIs identified nothing abnormal and Kendall was able to report that there was no sign that atomic research was taking place in the Stuttgart area.[8] This was another interesting case where photo intelligence was used to check out leads from other intelligence sources. Fortunately, it was true that Hitler was not building a Nazi bomb.

There was a scare in late November 1944 when photo interpreters at Medmenham detected a frantic rush of activity in the Hechingen area, about thirty miles south of Stuttgart. It was known that Werner Heisenberg, the most prominent of the German nuclear physicists who had remained in Nazi Germany before the war, was working here. Suddenly alarm bells sounded again. Were the Germans making a feverish last-minute attempt to build an atomic bomb as the Red Army approached the Reich from the east and the Anglo-American armies approached from the west? Churchill himself was alerted and a massive bombing attack was considered. Then Kendall spotted that all the work was going on at the same height, in a string of parallel valleys, and with a little research he found that before the war, low grade oil shales had been found in these valleys. With their oil supplies being hit, the Germans were simply looking for any source of oil they could find. The panic was over and there was no need to send the bombers in.[9]

Aerial intelligence was always part of the broader intelligence war. So, during 1942 Medmenham received a number of specific requests to identify sites in occupied Europe that conformed to certain rather unusual criteria. Usually the PIs were asked to find open fields of a particular size, without obstructions, near a specific town or village. There was no explanation as to why the requests were being made and the interpreters were puzzled and annoyed, feeling that if they knew the purpose of the requests they would be able to do a better job. But they were told that for 'security reasons' they could not be told. During 1943 the number of requests increased dramatically, to about forty per month, and a special unit within Second Phase, Z Section, was created to deal with them. Initially it consisted of six interpreters working in shifts, each shift supported by a Ground Information Liaison Officer, known as a 'Gilo'. Everything was absolutely 'hush hush', to use a phrase current at the time, and very few people at Medmenham knew of the existence of this group. Their findings were somewhat neutrally called 'Topographical Reports'. A special section of Air Ministry Intelligence known as A.I.2(c) was set up to process the requests and to receive the reports. And the volume of requests continued to grow.

After a while the penny dropped and the PIs at Medmenham realised what they were being asked to do. They had to find a patch of land about a thousand yards in length near a wood or forest, preferably even a clearing inside a forest. They realised that they were looking for sites where light aircraft could land in order to deliver secret agents into occupied Europe, or where agents could parachute in. Secrecy was of course vital in such matters, although the PIs continued to resent the fact that they were not being given the full picture. A series of coded prefixes were used to describe these missions. QH represented the use of a Hudson aircraft; QL a mission where a Lysander would land and drop off or pick up an agent, or evacuate someone with key information; QX a parachute dropping operation. A visit by Wing Commander Lockhart of Air Ministry Intelligence in July 1943 finally explained to the PIs what this was all about. After more than a year on the job, the members of 'Topographical' team at last felt that the veil of official secrecy had been lifted and they were allowed to understand what they were being asked to do and why.

The task called for extreme accuracy. Failure to spot some small obstruction like a fence, a pylon, a ditch or even a bush, or to report correctly the height of surrounding trees, might spell disaster. Alternatively, to exaggerate the extent of an obstacle might lead to the abandonment of a vital operation. Large scale cover of a potential landing ground was needed, but even then, if the shadows happened to fall awkwardly or the ground was dark, wire fences or telegraph poles might be invisible. To do a thorough job, it was important to obtain cover at varying times of the day when the shadows would be at different angles. It often proved difficult to know from aerial photographs alone what crops might be growing in a particular field, and so interpreters had to find out about the local geology and agriculture. PIs with knowledge of local farming conditions were well equipped for work in the 'Topographical' section.[10]

It was essential for the interpreters also to calculate the angles of slopes and gradients if a light aircraft was going to land on the fields they selected. Once again, some ingenious devices were created to measure these. The PIs used a Topographical Stereoscope to amplify the details of contour lines, which could then be traced through a gearbox system to a pencil that reproduced the lines traced by the operator at whatever scale was required. They also used the Abrams Contour Finder, along with a machine intriguingly called a Brunsviga Computer, a form of rotational calculator for making detailed measurements.[11] No one involved in any single element of these covert operations knew what anyone else in another part was doing. The work was so secret that even the history of Z Section, written at the end of the war, gives the wrong name for the airfield from where most agents were flown by RAF Special Duty squadrons into occupied Europe.[12]

Some of the agents dropped were working for the Secret Intelligence Service, MI6. Most worked for the Special Operations Executive, a shadowy organisation set up by Winston Churchill with the brief to 'set Europe ablaze'.[13] Its agents acted as saboteurs, assassins and explosives experts. They helped local resistance or partisan groups to stir up trouble for the occupying Nazi troops. There are numerous extraordinary stories of the courage, bravery and heroism of the agents dropped behind enemy lines at rendezvous points selected by the interpreters at Medmenham.

Some of the agents and their achievements have become famous. For instance, twenty-three-year-old Violette Szabo of the SOE was twice dropped into occupied France and helped to organise the Resistance before being captured and executed in Ravensbruck concentration camp. In 1958 her story was made into a feature film, *Carve Her Name with Pride*.[14] But most of the remarkable stories of these men and women have never been written up, and most agents preferred to remain anonymous for the rest of their lives. Eileen Nearne, who died in Torquay in September 2010 aged eighty-nine, was typical. Even her neighbours had no idea that in her youth she had served as a secret agent and had been dropped behind enemy lines, captured and tortured by the Gestapo. She simply never wanted to speak of it. When people found out about her past she was given a hero's funeral. A recent study of the subject lists an incredible 1400 agents who were flown or parachuted into occupied Europe.[15] The interpreters at Medmenham played a small but significant part in their remarkable exploits.

In February 1944 a unique mission was proposed to which

the interpreters at Medmenham were asked to contribute. The French Resistance had smuggled out information that a group of Resistance fighters being held at a large prison just outside Amiens in north-eastern France were about to be executed by the Germans. Others in the prison knew important information about Operation Overlord and it was essential to try to free them as soon as possible. So an unusual plan was hatched to carry out a raid, not to destroy the site but to breach the walls of the prison in order to enable as many prisoners as possible to escape. The mission was given the name Operation Jericho. In order to carry out the raid, photo interpreters carried out careful analysis of aerial photographs taken of the prison the previous December. Not only did the PIs prepare a plan of the layout of the prison, they were asked to provide detailed information about the height and thickness of the outer walls, the number of storeys in the main building, details of the wing where the guards were quartered and the position of machine gun posts. A model was quickly built and all these details were established. But it was going to take an extraordinary feat of flying to carry out a raid with the required precision.

Mosquitos from three squadrons, including an Australian and a New Zealand squadron, were called on to carry out Operation Jericho,. On the morning of 18 February, the pilots and navigators of all eighteen aircraft were briefed on the mission using the model. Each pilot was allocated a specific task. As there was no time to waste in mounting the raid, despite appalling weather conditions, the Mosquitos took off and headed across the Channel. Over northern France the weather cleared, but there was thick snow everywhere and using the long, straight road from Albert to Amiens to guide them for the last part of the mission, the Mosquitos came in low and fast to attack the prison. The raid had been timed for midday, when the maximum number of prisoners would be out of their cells while some of the guards were in their wing taking lunch.

The first wave, flying at 360 mph at a height of only about sixty feet, managed to hit the base of the outer wall with their bombs, making a huge breach. The second wave scored a direct hit on the barrack wing where the German guards were based. The third wave, due to arrive ten minutes later, were turned away by the raid commander as smoke now covered the whole site, making precision strikes impossible. They returned home without dropping their bombs. An additional photo reconnaissance Mosquito participated in the raid to provide an instant damage assessment record. Its photographs showed a breach of about twelve feet in the northern wall of the prison and recorded damage to the main prison buildings. Most importantly of all, it photographed several prisoners running across the snow outside the prison walls, where French Resistance fighters were waiting to whisk their men away.[16] The raid had been a success and 258 prisoners were able to escape, including seventy-nine Resistance prisoners. However, more than a hundred were killed in the raid and many of those who escaped, especially the common criminals, were recaptured later, but the raid had shown that the RAF could strike at almost any target, no matter how small or precise, anywhere in occupied Europe. But this had its limitations, as we shall see.

Throughout 1942 and 1943 alarming reports were coming out of Europe about large scale killings of civilians going on 'somewhere' in the East. From his earliest writings, Adolf Hitler had expressed a violent hatred of the Jews and his book *Mein Kampf* is infused with a hateful anti-Semitism. He spoke of the Jews and the Communists as the twin evils facing the world. But it was not until the war was well under way that planning for a campaign of genocide against the Jews began. In January 1942, senior Nazi officials held a conference at Wannsee, in a suburb of Berlin. Here they resolved to carry out 'the final solution to the Jewish question' by building camps with the specific purpose of exterminating thousands, then hundreds of thousands, then millions of Jews and other 'undesirables'. Ten days later, Hitler addressed an adoring crowd at the Sports Palace in Berlin and told them that the war would end 'with the complete annihilation of the Jews'.[17] Although his message was clear, the detailed information reaching agencies in Britain, America and elsewhere was still sparse and difficult to thread together.

From their earliest days in power, the Nazis had built concentration camps in which to gather without trial thousands of political opponents, homosexuals, gypsies and others judged to be hostile to the new social order. As the Germans captured hundreds of thousands of Soviet prisoners, they built more and more prisoner of war camps, along with new labour camps to marshal the millions of people who now found themselves living under the heel of the Nazi jackboot.

In the early months of 1942 the first of a new sort of camp was built, its principal purpose being the mass extermination of Jews. The name of this camp was Auschwitz. The first killings took place there that spring. Several thousand Jewish slave labourers were taken into a chamber thinking they were going into a large complex of showers. Instead, poison gas was pumped into the chamber. The dead bodies were then cremated. The process of killing at Auschwitz was conducted on an industrial scale. Trains from all over occupied Europe regularly delivered thousands of new victims. Fit-looking arrivals were selected by the SS and taken off to the work camp to begin a dreadful life of hard labour. Few survived for long. All the rest, the young, the old, the weak and infirm, were sent straight to the gas chambers and their bodies cremated. Once it had been expanded to include a huge camp at Birkenau, the complex was geared to the murder of up to twelve thousand victims every day. It was killing on a barbaric scale. But, of course, the existence of Auschwitz and the five other extermination camps built at Sobibor, Treblinka, Chelmno, Belzec and Majdanek was kept totally secret.

However, many reports of the killings were smuggled out to the west over the next few years, particularly to the Polish government in exile in London and to Jewish groups in Switzerland. They did their best to bring these reports to the Allies' attention. But officials found it hard to imagine that even the brutal and evil Nazi regime could undertake crimes of such appalling proportions. In early July 1944 the Jewish Agency, fearing that a huge rise in the number of Hungarian Jews sent to Auschwitz was imminent, formally requested to the British government that the camps, or the railway lines leading to them, should be bombed. Churchill approved the request but the Air Ministry raised many objections. It would involve reallocating aircraft, almost certainly Mosquito light bombers, to the task at a critical time in the war. The Allies had still not broken out of their beachhead in Normandy. Flying bombs were being fired on London daily and an immense effort was concentrated on tracking down the launch sites and destroying them. There simply was no spare capacity to allocate to an attempt to bomb the camps.

Bombing the railway lines was also ruled out as being impractical. Although enormous resources had been allocated to disrupt railway traffic in Normandy, just across the Channel, these railways in Poland were many hundreds of miles away.

Hitting prison walls in Amiens, forty miles from the Channel coast, was one thing. But hitting a relatively small gas chamber, or railway lines located in Upper Silesia or south-west Poland, was of a different order.

The Americans also rejected the same request. John McLoy, the Assistant Secretary of War, made similar points about not being able to divert considerable air support that was needed elsewhere in the war effort. He concluded that bombing the camps would 'in any case be of such doubtful efficacy that it would not warrant the use of our resources'.[18] Both British and American planners made it clear that there was in addition no definitive record of exactly where the extermination camps were located.

It was while these arguments were going back and forth, that the Americans had refocused their bombing strategy on hitting the dozen major chemical plants where oil was being manufactured for the Nazi war effort. One of these factories was the I.G. Farben complex at Monowitz, not far from Krakow in Poland. Reconnaissance aircraft flying out of San Severo in south-east Italy repeatedly took aerial photographs of the plant, which was only four miles east of the vast, sprawling complex at Auschwitz-Birkenau (indeed thousands of the forced labourers in the camp were sent daily to work at the chemical factory). On more than one reconnaissance flight over Monowitz, the pilot kept his cameras running and photographed, without realising it, parts of the Auschwitz-Birkenau site. So, the most evil extermination camp of the Holocaust was actually photographed on many occasions by Allied reconnaissance planes.

It is one of the extreme ironies of the war that Auschwitz-Birkenau was never analysed either by the photo interpreters at Medmenham or those at San Severo. Europe was full of different camps: concentration camps, prisoner-of-war camps, labour

camps, transit camps and deportation camps. It has been estimated that there were possibly a thousand camps scattered
across occupied Europe by mid 1944. The photo interpreters
were always looking for specific military targets and although
they were able to find a ten-foot radar tower or measure the
thickness of a prison wall, they were never tasked with assessing what was happening to the civilians in camps across
Europe. But in the summer of 1944, Allied planners did begin
to respond to the requests to try to attack the camps and questions were asked about where the death camps were located.[19]

In late July, the I.G. Farben factory at Monowitz was desig-
nated a target for bombing. It had been calculated from the
aerial photos that production of synthetic oil and rubber was
about to start here. The PIs made a list of specific target areas
like the gas generating plant that if put out of action would
prevent the entire factory from operating, and provided
photos and maps highlighting these targets. They included a
note that to the west and south of the plant were 'hutted
workers camps' which were not a target.[20] On 20 August, US
Flying Fortresses operating out of Italy bombed the factory,
dropping three hundred tons of high explosive bombs.
Damage assessment photographs taken immediately after the
raid showed that the damage was not as severe as the Allies
had hoped.

On 23 August another reconnaissance aircraft flew over the
plant. The day was clear and bright, and once again, from
twenty-nine thousand feet, the cameras photographed the
extermination camp at Auschwitz-Birkenau. Incredibly, on
these photographs taken in clear sunlight, a train can be seen
just to have arrived at the camp. Jews are being separated and
a line of people are being led to the gas chambers. The gas
chambers are identifiable by the vents in the roof. It is also

possible to see some of the five crematoria, and smoke is rising from an open pit used for burning bodies when their numbers exceeded the capacity of the crematoria. Once again, because they were not looking for such information, the photo interpreters picked up on none of it. Their task was simply to assess the damage at the chemical plant in order to calculate when would be the optimum moment to bomb it again. The killing grounds of Auschwitz-Birkenau had been photographed with remarkable detail, but entirely by accident.

In retrospect this appears to be almost criminally negligent. The Allies had evidence of mass extermination on aerial photographs literally in front of their eyes but did nothing with it. They were asked to bomb the camps but refused to do so. But this is to read back into events what only became fully clear in hindsight. The people who had the photographic evidence, the PIs, were not charged with assessing it. One PI based in San Severo explained that as they were not looking for evidence of mass killings, they wouldn't have known how to differentiate between barracks, labour camps and death camps. Another wrote much later that when they had seen images of camps they had not been 'a hundred per cent convinced'.[21] They were not the people who had been receiving, from the Poles and from the Jewish groups, information about the existence of the death camps. The British and American planners believed it would be almost impossible to bomb the camps with any accuracy. They feared the loss of innocent life if their bombs went astray. They were unaware that Jews in Auschwitz had rejoiced at hearing the bombers overhead attacking Monowitz, believing they had not been forgotten. Many said that they would have preferred to be killed by Allied bombs than by Nazi thugs.[22] This, of course, only came out much later.

As a curious endnote to the story, the aerial photographs that had so clearly recorded the killing process at Auschwitz-Birkenau were filed away in 1944 and not referred to again. That is, until 1979 when two CIA photo analysts were looking at wartime cover of Poland as part of a Cold War operation.[23] When they found and published the photographs a huge controversy erupted. If the Allies had been able to photograph the camp so clearly, surely they could have bombed the camps, or at the very least the railway lines running up to them? Surely someone should have done *something* to stop the Holocaust? Scholars and others have argued over this ever since. The subject was not on the agenda of those running aerial intelligence and photo interpretation at the time, but it has become a heated aspect of more recent debate about the crimes of the Holocaust.[24] Although the PIs can hardly be blamed for not finding what they had never been asked to look for, this is certainly not one of their proudest chapters in the war. When the Allies were trying to find out if the stories of the death camps were true and trying to discover any information as to their location, startling evidence was already available to them from aerial photographs on file.

The story of these Special Operations points up how integral aerial photography was to the intelligence operation. Sometimes a mission started when a sharp-eyed photo interpreter picked out something unusual or strange. Sometimes, another branch of intelligence asked the PIs to hunt something out. Frequently, the interpreters had to search vast areas of occupied Europe, unsure of what they were looking for. But whether aerial intelligence alerted the other branches of intelligence or responded to requests, it was used extensively on an extraordinarily wide range of tasks, whether to find a tiny radar mast somewhere near the Channel coast, or to establish whether Hitler's scientists were developing an atom bomb. However, the biggest single task ever undertaken by the photo interpreters was the hunt for Hitler's special vengeance weapons, the weapons of mass destruction that he hoped would reverse the course of the war and force the Allies into a negotiated peace.

15

Hunting the Vengeance Weapons

On 15 May 1942 a reconnaissance pilot, Flight Lieutenant Donald Steventon, was flying in his Spitfire high above the Baltic. He had already taken photographs over the big naval harbour at Kiel and was en route to Swinemünde (today Swinoujscie, north of Szczecin in Poland) where there was another large German naval base. As Steventon crossed the long thin island of Usedom with its thick belt of woodland stretching almost north–south, he banked slightly, and looking down he saw what appeared to be major construction work going on around an airfield at the northern tip of the island. He ran off a few of his precious photographs over the site and continued to Swinemünde, where he photographed the German destroyers in harbour. Then he turned for the long journey home.

When his photographs were processed and sent to Medmenham they produced some puzzlement. Alongside the airfield were three huge circular clearings carved into the thick forest and around these were vast cement cisterns. There were signs of other major construction works taking place and the airfield was being extended. There was also evidence of a dredging operation to reclaim land and extend the site into the shallow, sandy Baltic sea. The Second Phase photo interpreters simply marked the spot and noted 'heavy construction work'. In Third Phase, the PIs decided the airfield was not a threat as it did not appear to contain any German fighters that could oppose Allied bombers in the region. Flying Officer Constance Babington Smith remembers looking at the photos. As they were small scale and seemed to present no identifiable threat she assumed someone else must know all about the strange rings in the forest and passed them on to other Third Phase Sections for analysis.[1] No one picked up on the mysterious workings in the woods along the Baltic and, with their location noted for future reference, the photographs were filed away in the Medmenham library. In fact, Steventon had entirely by accident photographed the major German rocket research establishment at Peenemünde, where feverish work was taking place on developing some of the Nazis' most threatening and destructive secret weapons of the war.

The research establishment at Peenemünde had been opened in May 1937 as a joint German army and Luftwaffe site. Many German scientists had experimented with rockets throughout the 1920s and 1930s and the German military had soon become involved. The Treaty of Versailles had placed severe restrictions on the Germans' development of weapons, but had made no mention of rockets. So this became an area in which the army could take up the enthusiasm of civilian inventors and engineers and direct it for secret military purposes. In 1932, a twenty-year-old German aristocrat who had been fascinated with rockets since he was a boy, applied to the army for funding and began an extraordinary career of more than forty years at the leading edge of rocket science. His name was Werner von

Braun and the work at Peenemünde will forever be associated with him. On coming to power, Hitler allocated more resources to the development of rocket technology, and within a few years the remote site on the northern tip of Usedom island was selected as the location for this research. With 250 miles of open sea to the north and east, Peenemünde was highly suitable for use as a firing range. Heavily forested, the site could easily hide workshops, laboratories, hangars, test stands and the power plants needed for the top secret work. As an island it could readily be cut off and access to it controlled so its secrets could be kept from prying eyes – except, of course, from those of the spies in the sky.

From 1937, the Peenemünde site grew dramatically. Over the years the Germans built living quarters, shops and all that a self-sufficient community of research scientists needed. Surrounded by miles of sandy beaches along the Baltic coast, the researchers enjoyed almost a holiday camp atmosphere. Those who worked there remember feeling lucky that they had been assigned to such an idyllic spot where they could get on with their work uninterrupted by the war. On the other hand they realised that the Nazis had created 'a kind of ghetto for scientists'.[2] By the middle of the war there were four thousand scientists, specialist researchers and skilled workers living at Peenemünde. A railway link carried another eleven thousand workers to and from the island, all of whom were screened and checked for security daily. The entire establishment was under the command of army general Walter Dornberger.

The first rocket missiles developed at Peenemünde, the A1 and the A2, were small and rudimentary. The A3 was larger, 20ft in length, and used gyroscopes for stabilisation and steering. An engine was developed powerful enough to drive the rocket at speeds that would break the sound barrier. Impressed, the German army laid down specifications for a new rocket, to be known as the A4, that would carry a one ton warhead with an initial range of up to two hundred kilometres (130 miles). To achieve this, major new advances in rocket and propulsion technology were needed, along with the development of new fuels. Von Braun and his team dedicated themselves to the task of achieving these objectives, and for months and then years carried out research way ahead of its time on their remote island base on the edge of the Baltic.

In November 1939, the existence of the top secret experimental rocket establishment was leaked to the Allies in a document left on the windowsill of the British consulate in neutral Oslo. The document, known as the Oslo Report, listed several areas of advanced scientific development by German scientists. British Intelligence thought it was a hoax intended to deceive British scientists and ordered that all copies should be destroyed. R.V. Jones in the Air Ministry's scientific research unit was one of the few who kept a copy for later use.[3] But in the middle of 1942 the purpose of the work being carried out at Peenemünde was known only to very few. No one at Medmenham had been told anything about the Oslo Report or secret Nazi experimental rocket research.

On 23 October 1942, five months after the aerial photographs had been accidentally taken and filed away, the first ever ballistic missile, the A4, was successfully launched at Peenemünde. It flew in an arc up into the stratosphere and came down in the Baltic. It was a momentous event. German scientists had launched the Space Age.

Over the following months new reports about the secret weapons trials began to arrive in London. British Intelligence officials took seriously a report passed on in December by a

Danish engineer. Reports coming in from agents and labourers included a mix of stories about long range guns, rocket planes and shells the size of motor cars. Then in March 1943, two German generals who had been captured in North Africa were recorded as they spoke together in their prisoner-of-war cell. General von Thoma was recorded as telling General Cruewell, Rommel's second-in-command, that he had once seen an experimental rocket launch and that he had been told to 'wait until next year and the fun will start'.[4] The transcript of this conversation immediately set alarm bells ringing in British Intelligence circles.

It was realised that aerial photography could play a vital role in establishing what was going on and in confirming or denying the many rumours that were now reaching London. An Intelligence unit at the War Office sent Medmenham a directive noting that 'There have recently been indications that the Germans may be developing some form of long range projectors capable of firing on this country from the French coast ... There is unfortunately little concrete evidence on the subject available ... we should therefore be grateful if you could keep a close watch for any suspicious erections of rails or scaffolding ... ' On 19 March Medmenham received further details of the possible weight and length of the missile. Its range was thought to be about 130 miles. This new message concluded with the instructions, 'The obvious target for such a weapon fired against this country is London. That part of France within a radius of 130 miles from the centre of London should, therefore, be most carefully watched.'[5] The number of flights over Peenemünde and in northern France were increased immediately and the cover was carefully studied. The problem was that with such a vague description the PIs had little idea what they were looking for. It was, as one later wrote, like 'telling a blind

Möhne Dam the morning after the raid, 17 May 1943, showing the 200ft breach and water still flooding through. This was the aerial photo released to almost every newspaper and helped to make the Dam Busters raid the most famous of the war.

Nora Littlejohn, one of the team in Operation Crossbow – she has found a V-1 on the launch ramp at one of the heavily disguised Belhamelin sites. Her stereo viewer is on the right.

Prints and maps piled up in the photographic department at Medmenham. The photos were piled so high they called it the Siegfried Line. At its peak, one million prints were arriving at Medmenham each month.

The Wurzburg 'bowl fire' radar on the clifftop at Bruneval – the oblique taken by Tony Hill that led to the Para raid on 27 February 1942.

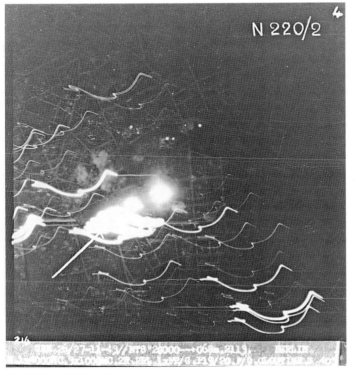

An example of a night photo taken over Berlin on 27 November 1943. The wavy lines show fires burning, anti-aircraft fire and searchlights. Night photos helped to establish the accuracy, or not, of the bombers.

Hazel Scott in Algiers.

Glyn Daniel in Delhi.

Derek van den Bogaerde at his desk.

Geoffrey Stone's APIS unit towards the end of the war. The interpreters' truck in the middle, supported by a jeep and a tent for the crew.

Peenemünde – the first sortie on 15 May 1942. No one knew what the strange circular sites were intended for.

Peenemünde – the first tiny image of a V-1 identified on a ramp (circled). Finding it was one of the greatest triumphs of photo intelligence in the Second World War.

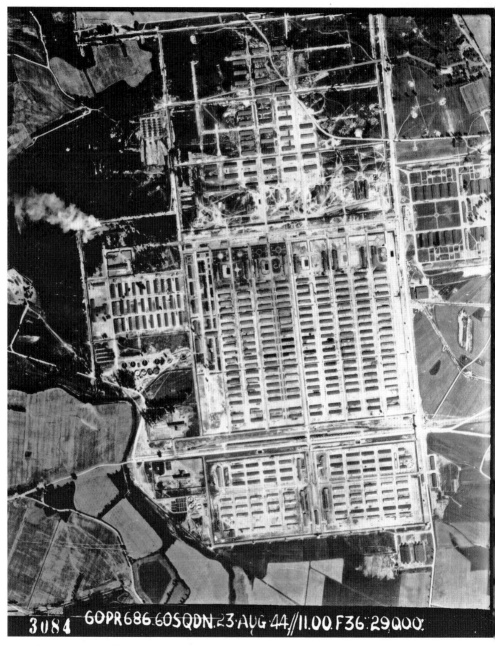

3084 6OPR686.6OSQDN.23.AUG.44//11.00.F36.29000.

Auschwitz-Birkenau camp photographed by accident on 23 August 1944. A train is in the station and new arrivals are being taken to the gas chambers. The camp was working at full stretch and smoke rises from an open pit on the left where bodies are being burned. This photo was just filed away in 1944 and not rediscovered until 1979.

Beach defences in northern France, known as 'Hedgehog'. Every obstacle was noted. Tens of thousands of low angle oblique photos like this were taken along the French coast.

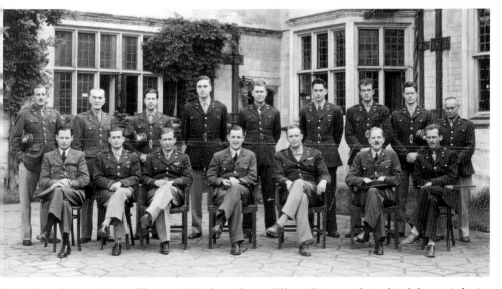

British and American officers at Medmenham. Elliott Roosevelt is third from right in the front row. Douglas Kendall is in the centre, to Roosevelt's right, and Hugh Hamshaw Thomas is on his left. After their falling out, Roosevelt didn't speak to Kendall for six months.

Photo interpreters, men and women, British and American, RAF, Army and Navy, pose on the steps at Medmenham towards the end of the war in the sunshine – this was the Second Phase section. (All photographs courtesy of the Medmenham Collection)

man to cross the road without a stick'.[6] There were no experts available in the entirely new science of rocket development to assist. It wasn't clear from the reports whether one weapons system was under development, or many. As another experienced PI has recently written of Medmenham's mission, 'finding something is immeasurably aided by knowing what one is looking for'.[7] And no one knew what they were looking for at this stage.

The Joint Intelligence Committee and the Chiefs of Staff decided to tell Churchill of the reports of experimental weapons and rockets at a meeting on 15 April. Churchill was concerned and it was agreed to set up a special committee to investigate the subject and assess the threat. Duncan Sandys from the Ministry of Supply, an expert on weapons development who also happened to be Churchill's son-in-law, was put in charge of the investigation. It was called Operation Bodyline, a name given by some joker after the term for an unfair form of bowling at cricket – obviously, by developing these secret weapons, the Germans were thought to be cheating in war.

One of Sandys' first actions was to visit Medmenham and view the aerial photographs, which were still puzzling the interpreters. He and his team looked at the three huge concrete rings and were persuaded that their purpose must be the testing of projectiles and explosives. They concluded that the site was 'probably an experimental station' but that 'the whole area is not yet in full use' and that 'a heavy long range rocket is not yet an immediate menace'.[8] It was an accurate summary of the current position, but the clock was ticking and the German scientists under Werner von Braun were working at full speed.

At Medmenham a new section was set up reporting to Wing Commander Hugh Hamshaw Thomas, who instructed Flight Lieutenant André Kenny to search for clues as to what was happening at Peenemünde. Both the RAF from Benson and the USAAF from Mount Farm flew reconnaissance missions almost daily and the whole investigation was given the highest priority. In another new unit under Major Norman Falcon, the chief Army interpreter at the CIU, Captain Robert Rowell was charged with looking at sites within occupied Europe at a radius of 130 miles from London. The Air Ministry sent a directive seeking evidence of 'a long range gun ... a rocket aircraft ... [or] some sort of tube located in an unused mine out of which a rocket could be squirted'.[9] The prevailing view was that a rocket would be launched horizontally from a cave or quarry, not vertically from a stand, but it was clear that no one really knew what they should be looking for.

Meanwhile an intense debate as to what the Germans were actually doing had begun within the British scientific community. Professor Frederick Lindemann, now Lord Cherwell and Churchill's closest scientific adviser, a man with immense influence over the Prime Minister, argued that, using conventional solid fuel, it was impossible to develop a rocket with sufficient propulsion to fly as far as 130 miles. Believing that any rocket capable of carrying a powerful enough warhead would be too heavy to propel into the stratosphere, he favoured the idea that the Germans were developing some sort of pilotless plane or bomb. Other scientists, including Dr William Cook and R.V. Jones, were convinced that German scientists were indeed capable of producing a powerful rocket that might weigh up to eighty tons inside a solid steel casing. It was suggested that such a missile could kill or injure up to four thousand people if it landed in the middle of a city.

As the scientific debate went back and forth, sorties over Peenemünde in the spring and early summer produced more and more evidence of intense activity at the site. The PIs observed giant crane-like structures at the centre of the round concrete clearings and noted that they seemed to be moving around. Possibly they were in some way linked with the test firing of the mysterious projectiles. There was even evidence of a flame emerging from a test bed, possibly that of a rocket being tested horizontally. But until the scientists had agreed what technology was being used the interpreters were not allowed to speculate on what they were looking at. They could only describe what they saw as factually as possible.

Then, in photographs taken on 12 June, came the first sighting of an actual A4 rocket, lying horizontal on its side on a railway truck, presumably waiting to be launched. The person who formally identified the rocket was not one of the PIs at Medmenham but R.V. Jones, who viewed the photos six days after they were taken. He calculated that it was a whitish cylinder about thirty-five feet long and five feet in diameter, with a blunt nose (it was later realised that the warhead was not fitted). It had fins at the other end. When he spotted the rocket on its transport he experienced a 'pulse of elation' and immediately passed on his finding to Lord Cherwell.

In Jones's own account, as in those of many others since, the PIs led by André Kenny at Medmenham were roundly condemned for failing to spot the rocket.[10] It was a failing in the sense that Kenny did not use the word 'rocket' to identify what he had seen. But the fact is that the photo interpreters still did not know what they were looking for and were not allowed to use descriptive words that had not been officially approved. In this instance, until the scientists had actually described the object for which they were searching as a 'rocket', the PIs were not allowed to use the word in their reports. Kenny and his team spoke of 'columns' standing upright of about forty feet in length, measured from the shadow they cast, which were A4 missiles on their launch pads. Kenny later said that they never doubted that these objects were rockets.[11] The realistic criticism of Medmenham should not be of the individual interpreters but of a system that did not pass on to the PIs all the information they needed. In this system it was logical that the first person to cry 'Rocket' should be one of the scientists who had some sense of what he was looking for.

While Peenemünde was being closely watched from the air, an extraordinary development had been spotted in northern France at the site of a former gravel quarry at Watten, near St Omer in the Pas de Calais. In April photo interpreters had noted some building work there but when new cover came in two months later they were aghast at the scale of the construction. Everything was on a gargantuan scale and involved thousands of tons of concrete. Initially it was assumed that this must be a form of command bunker for the Atlantic Wall, but the size of the structure seemed far in excess of anything needed for this purpose. As it was unlike anything that had been seen elsewhere, it was linked with the secret weapons that were being developed on the Baltic. Maybe it was the launch site for these new long range weapons? The French Resistance reported that thousands of slave labourers were working at the site with tens of thousands of tons of steel and concrete. Perhaps the Germans were far more advanced with the preparation of their weapons of mass destruction than had been anticipated. When Duncan Sandys and his team were made aware of this huge construction, they asked the Home Secretary to make secret plans for the evacuation of a hundred thousand women and children from the London area in fear of a massive and imminent missile attack.

We now know that Hitler had personally given the go-ahead for the construction of the Watten site. It was to be built with a gigantic concrete covering on the scale of the U-boat pens on the Atlantic coast that had proved largely impervious to Allied bombing. The Germans initially hoped to start firing missiles on London in late October 1943. Had the Intelligence chiefs in London known this they would have been even more alarmed than they already were.

A breakthrough came on 23 June when Flight Sergeant E. Peek, piloting a Mosquito out of Leuchars in Scotland, photographed Peenemünde again. It was the tenth sortie over the experimental rocket research site. This time it was a clear day, the sun was bright and the shadows were strong. The Mosquito, equipped with long lens cameras, made two passes over Peenemünde about half an hour apart. The images the pilot came back with electrified the PIs at Medmenham. They were able to spot two further A4 rockets, being carried horizontally on transporters. As the prohibition on using the word 'rocket' still applied, the PIs described them as 'torpedo-like objects'. They were measured as being 38ft long and 6ft in diameter, with a tail of three fins that were 12ft wide.[12] On the railway wagons the PIs also spotted high-pressure containers that were thought to be the fuel being used for the A4. These were later found to contain alcohol, liquid oxygen and hydrogen peroxide, information which proved to be of major significance in the days to come.

R.V. Jones and his team got to work analysing the photos and came up with estimates for the range of the rocket and the tonnage of explosives it could carry. Later, these estimates proved to be exaggerated. But, most importantly, the evidence of the fuel containers convinced Jones that the Germans had developed a form of high energy liquid fuel with which to power the rockets. The missiles could therefore be smaller and lighter than previous estimates of between forty and eighty tons had suggested. For the PIs, the advantage of these discoveries was that they could now recognise not just the rockets themselves but also what were called 'signature' objects around them – railway wagons, fuel containers and transporters. On future cover they were not looking solely for rockets. If they could identify any of these 'signature' items then they knew that rockets were there somewhere being prepared for launching. At last the photographic intelligence was making some progress.

But the 23 June cover had one further secret to reveal. The head of L Section, the Aircraft Section, 'Babs' Babington Smith, had been charged with looking for 'anything queer' at Peenemünde. When she studied the 23 June photos she noticed tiny burn marks in the grass around the airfield. This was the first ever identification of 'jet marks', where jet or rocket engines had scorched the grass while being run up to speed. Babington Smith then spotted four tailless aircraft of a kind she had never seen before. In the second set of photos, taken thirty minutes later, one of these tiny objects had moved and Babington Smith spotted it on the airfield being prepared for flight. She measured the wingspan as 30ft and named it the P-30 (this being the method for naming new aircraft: P for Peenemünde, the base where it was first spotted, and 30 for the wingspan in feet). It proved to be the first ever sighting of the Me 163, the rocket-propelled German fighter known as the Komet. When the Komet became operational a year later it was capable of flying at speeds of around 600 mph.

The sighting of the Me 163 on the airfield seemed to prove conclusively that Peenemünde was a research centre where the Germans were trying out all sorts of new technologies and high speed inventions. Babington Smith went back over previous cover of Peenemünde. When she had first looked at these photos, she said it had been like 'peering through an overlay of tracing paper'. But there, sure enough, around the same hangars, were the P-30s on the ground.[13]

When all the information was passed on, Duncan Sandys told Churchill, who called an urgent meeting of the War Cabinet Defence Committee at 10 p.m. on 29 June. Again there was intense debate as to what it all meant. Lord Cherwell still pooh-poohed the whole rocket idea and said that either the curious shapes were some new form of torpedo or else the whole thing was a giant hoax designed to deceive the Allies as to what was really going on, which he still believed was the development of some sort of pilotless aircraft. R.V. Jones was also at the meeting and although he had been Cherwell's protégé earlier in the war, he now blatantly disagreed with his old professor. Pointing out that the Germans had no aircraft big enough to carry a torpedo the size of these objects, he concluded that the evidence was compelling that Peenemünde was a research establishment where rocket technology was under development. Realising that this presented a significant threat to Britain, it was agreed to order a heavy bombing raid on Peenemünde as soon as conditions permitted. Churchill himself ordered the Central Interpretation Unit at Medmenham to make the maximum possible contribution to Sandys' investigation and insisted that all necessary facilities and manpower were to be made available to them.[14]

A model was made of Peenemünde, as was often the case before a major raid. After the sightings of the 23 June sortie, the PIs went back over the previous cover and found much that they had missed, or had seen but failed to understand. It was still not clear if the rockets were launched vertically or out of some sort of horizontal tube. So the model makers produced miniatures of what they thought the A4 would be like both flat on its transport and vertically at an imagined launch site. The prevailing view was that the rockets were so heavy that they would need to be transported to their launch site by rail, so the

PIs were instructed to look for sites near railway lines or new spurs of existing track.

Because Bomber Command needed a clear sky and a good moon to carry out the bombing raid, there was a delay of some weeks before Peenemünde was bombed. When the raid finally took place on the night of 17 August it was on a large scale, involving some six hundred Lancasters and Halifaxes that dropped 281 tons of incendiaries and nearly 1600 tons of high explosives. Well-executed feints over Berlin and Stettin kept the night fighters away from the bombing force until the end of the raid, enabling the bombers to go in lower than usual, at a height of seven thousand feet, in order to aim their bombs as accurately as possible. The raid caught Peenemünde completely off guard. It was directed most heavily at the housing area where it was believed the scientists lived as the British plan was to kill as many key scientists as possible. The factory workshops were a secondary target. Despite the distractions, the German night fighters still succeeded in shooting down forty bombers, causing the loss of nearly three hundred men.

The initial damage assessment photos were encouraging and it appeared that huge parts of the living quarters had been destroyed. The raid was classed as a great success. In fact we now know that the bombing was only partially successful. Many bombs had landed on the living quarters and at least one senior scientist, Dr Walter Theil, who had been in charge of building the A4 rocket's motor, had been killed. However, most of the bombs had hit the living camp of the foreign labourers working at the site and about 730 of these poor souls were dead. Many other bombs had fallen harmlessly in the surrounding forests. None at all had landed on the airfield or its facilities. And only one of the three main circular launch sites had been seriously damaged. Nevertheless the raid was a real shock to the research establishment and it proved that despite all the security, Peenemünde had been discovered. On the morning after the raid, Hitler and Göring raged at General Jeschonnek, the Luftwaffe Chief of Staff, for failing to protect Peenemünde effectively. In disgrace, Jeschonnek returned to his office, took out his revolver and shot himself in the head.

The raid put back the work at Peenemünde by at least a couple of months, possibly more.[15] A decision to move some of the secret testing work and manufacturing away from the site, which was no longer thought to be safe, caused further delay. The Germans now had to look for a new location to continue their research. There were thousands of square miles of occupied territory for them to choose from. And it would take Allied intelligence some time to catch up with their move.

Ten days after the raid on Peenemünde, on 27 August, heavy bombers of the US Eighth Army Air Force hit the vast construction site at Watten. The bombing was accurate and destructive. In a lucky break, the raid took place just after a quantity of wet concrete had been laid. Thrown about in the chaos of the bombing, the concrete then hardened over the twisted mass of damaged iron and steel girders. But the Germans brought up more heavy anti-aircraft guns to protect the site, and seeing this the PIs at Medmenham concluded that work was still continuing. Another raid, on 7 September, caused even more destruction. Sir Malcolm McAlpine, the leading construction specialist, was asked to look at the damage assessment photos after this raid and he advised that the Germans would find it easier to give up and start again somewhere else. The German engineers must have come to the same conclusion, as the PIs noticed that the anti-aircraft batteries were soon moved away and the huge construction was abandoned. But this was only the beginning. As Watten receded in significance, so new construction sites were spotted along the magical radius 130 miles from London.

In addition to the A4 rocket developed by Werner von Braun for the army, another secret weapon was being developed at Peenemünde by the Luftwaffe. They wanted their own weapon to rival that of the army. Erhard Milch, a senior Luftwaffe leader, believed that a flying bomb could carry a large payload over a substantial distance without risking any of his precious aircrew. In a separate project, a team of scientists began to work on this jet-propelled flying bomb, a forerunner of the Cruise missile. Cherwell had been wrong about the rocket but was right that the Germans were developing a pilotless bomb.

But neither the scientists in London nor the photo interpreters at Medmenham realised that the Germans were developing two quite distinct secret weapons for different branches of the German military. Despite the breakthrough in identifying the A4 rockets on the ground, the mass of information being gathered at Medmenham still did not make much sense and continued to frustrate the PIs. Constance Babington Smith described it as though 'two or three jigsaw puzzles had been jumbled together'. It was tempting, she said, to try to put one jigsaw together and simply to leave out all the pieces from the other puzzles that didn't seem to fit.[16] It was a couple of months before the key breakthrough was made. And this time it was the photo inter-preters who triumphed.

In September Wing Commander Douglas Kendall was put in charge of coordinating Operation Bodyline at Medmenham. As Technical Control Officer at the CIU, in essence the head of the photo interpreters, Kendall had an enormous burden of work already but in the evenings he would join the interpreters and look through the cover of the key areas of Peenemünde and the construction sites in northern France, searching for new clues that might help piece together the puzzle of the German secret weapons. Slowly, the emphasis shifted from *what* the Germans were doing to *when* the weapons would be ready to use. New sorties were flown almost every day and thousands of photos flooded in. These, along with hundreds of photos from previous missions, were examined and re-examined. There was a lot to take in: large scale building work in the Cherbourg peninsula, a new railway being tunnelled through a hill at Mimoyecques near Calais and signs of much new work in the Somme area of northern France. The hunt for the secret weapons moved up to a new pitch.

As we have seen, Kendall was the only senior officer at Medmenham with clearance to receive decoded Ultra messages from Bletchley Park. He also received information from MI6, including reports from agents and other news that was coming out of occupied Europe. So he was one of the few people who had a reasonable overview of the range of intelligence that was coming in. It was during one of his late night sessions with Norman Falcon, Robert Rowell, Neil Simon and others in the Army team who were scouring northern Europe for any unusual signs of new construction that the next advance came. An agent in France had sent a report that unfamiliar new structures were being built at eight new sites near Abbeville. When the sites were photographed at the beginning of November, Kendall noted that at all of them there were buildings that from the air looked like giant skis on their side. Around these were a pattern of other similarly shaped structures, including the foundations of what could be long, thin ramps. Work at all the sites seemed to have begun at about the same time. Unlike previous sites, none were near railway lines and most were located in woods for camouflage. When Kendall and his colleagues looked again, the most alarming feature of all emerged. Every one of the ramps was pointing directly towards London.

In one of his rare public speeches at this point of the war, Hitler hinted darkly in September that retaliation was coming against the British for the heavy bombing of German cities.[17] Joseph Goebbels, his Propaganda Minister, picked up on this theme and in several speeches to the German people spoke about the development of 'miracle weapons' that would turn the war in Germany's favour. He said the British would soon come to know once again what it was like to be on the receiving end of terror bombing from the skies. The British and their Allies were to be punished with what Goebbels called *Vergeltungswaffen*, vengeance or revenge weapons.

The internal scientific debate in London as to what the Germans were planning now reached a crescendo. Duncan Sandys believed that the evidence for rocket missile attacks was clear. But it was still far from clear as to how and from where the rockets would be launched, not to mention when they would come. And did the Germans also have another weapon up their sleeve? Lord Cherwell was still sceptical of the rocket threat and believed that an attack from a pilotless bomb was most likely. The War Cabinet asked Sir Stafford Cripps to survey the evidence and report back. On 8 November Cripps gathered all the scientific experts together for a meeting around a big U-shaped table in the Cabinet Office. At the end of the table sat the photo interpreters from Medmenham. The meeting began with a description of the agents' various reports. Some spoke of missiles, others of bombs. It was all rather vague. Other experts who had analysed Goebbels' speeches then pointed out that he would be highly unlikely to make up stories about secret weapons that did not exist, as the sense of disappointment among the German public would be too great.

Next it was time for the photo interpreters to present their evidence. André Kenny spoke first about developments at Peenemünde and the effect of the bombing. Then Neil Simon from the Army team spoke about Watten and the other large sites and the bombing there. Then it was Douglas Kendall's turn to speak. When Cripps asked him if he had any other evidence of secret weapons sites in northern France, Kendall replied that he had. He went on to describe the strange ski-shaped buildings they had only spotted for the first time a few days before, pointing out that they were unlike any other structures the interpreters had ever seen. When he explained that they all had a firing line directed at London the meeting fell silent. After a pause, Sir Stafford Cripps asked how many sites had been spotted. As the PIs had been working flat-out for the last forty-eight hours looking for these structures, Kendall replied that up until midnight they had found nineteen.

Cripps immediately adjourned the meeting in order for the PIs at Medmenham to complete their search. Two days later, when the meeting resumed, Kendall was able to report that they had found evidence of twenty-six such sites in northern France. They were named the Bois Carré sites after the location of the first to be identified. Although their use was still unknown, it seemed impossible that they could be used for launching forty-five-ton rockets, which would require much heavier handling gear. Nor were they near railway spurs, which were still thought to be essential for delivery of the rockets. Cripps reported back to the War Cabinet in a few days that the threat from some sort of pilotless bomb now seemed more immediate than that from long range rockets. He again stressed the need for continual reconnaissance cover and photo interpretation to monitor developments. Operation Bodyline was brought to an end. A new project, Operation Crossbow, was started, to hunt for a flying bomb.

Within two weeks Kendall's enlarged team, now focusing on the ski sites, had found ninety-six Bois Carré-type structures in differing stages of development across northern France. Identifying them was made easier by the fact that they were all laid out systematically according to a common pattern with buildings of the same shape and size. The three ski-shaped buildings on each site must be for the storage of the bombs, others were for the supply of fuel; a series of twelve concrete studs were thought to be the foundations of the firing ramp; and sunken buildings a short distance away were identified as living quarters for the crews. Although the local landscape called for minor differences in layout, Kendall thought that all the sites had been designed quickly according to a blueprint drawn up in Berlin.[18] But still no one knew what the mysterious flying bomb looked like.

After his reports to Cripps, Kendall asked Constance Babington Smith to take another look at the Peenemünde cover to see if she could find anything like a very small plane, possibly even smaller than the P-30 fighter she had already found. Babington Smith knew nothing of Bodyline or Crossbow, nothing of the discovery of rockets or of the ski sites, and nothing of the Cripps meetings. But, charged up by this new request, Babington Smith began to look again at the best cover available, starting with the 23 June imagery. Methodically, for day after day, she worked outwards from the obvious places to find an aircraft, the hangars and the airfield, and started to look further across the vast site. Then, towards the end of November, using her Stereo and her jeweller's Leitz magnifying glass, she spotted something outside a building that she assumed might be a place where engines were tested. It was a small cruciform object just visible from its white, reflective outline and its shadows on the tarmac. It was less than a millimetre in length on the aerial photo. She called out to her colleagues to come and have a look. Measuring it, she calculated that its wingspan was about twenty feet. Babington Smith had found Germany's secret weapon, the flying bomb. It was a tremendous moment for the whole team. A recent historian describes her discovery as 'one of the great PI achievements of the war'.[19] At last, Medmenham had found the secret weapon and photographic intelligence had discovered the missing link.

Now that the photo interpreters knew what to look for the next steps followed thick and fast. With a distinct shape to hunt for, the PIs were able to find the tiny object now named the P-20 on more recent cover of Peenemünde, where it had been missed before. They calculated that the midget plane was just the right size to power an expendable pilotless aircraft. The next crucial step forward came on 28 November when Squadron Leader John Merrifield took off on a Mosquito reconnaissance mission with his navigator, Flying Officer Whalley, intending to photograph Berlin. When they reached the German capital they were forced to turn back because of heavy cloud cover. Instead they flew north and took photographs of a series of alternative targets. Merrifield did not like returning with any of his film unused so they photographed not only Peenemünde but also a radio and radar experimental site at Zinnowitz, a few miles away along the Baltic coast. When the photos were processed the PIs at Medmenham spotted along the shore at Zinnowitz many Bois Carré-type buildings of the kind that had been identified in northern France. But this time the sites included a steel ramp extending out to sea. It was their first sighting of a completed firing ramp. Clearly this was a testing site for the flying bomb. Using their Stereos, the PIs were able to take three-dimensional measurements, and they calculated that the ramp was angled upwards at about ten degrees and was 125 feet long. The pieces of the jigsaw were slowly coming together.

Babington Smith and her team then had another look at what was going on at Peenemünde. Moving out from the airfield itself this time, Babington Smith looked further north, to the tip of the island. Here she could see dredging equipment that had been identified before as part of the island's reclamation scheme. But next to this were four ramp-like structures, again pointing out to sea. And this time Babington Smith, or possibly one of her team, found a tiny aircraft in position at the bottom of one of the ramps.[20] Others might have missed the minute cruciform object. But Babington Smith and her team now knew what they were looking for and recognised the shape immediately. They had found a flying bomb, which had miraculously been photographed just as it was about to be launched on a test flight. That evening, when Kendall got back from a meeting in London, he was told about the find and went straight to Babington Smith's office before even taking off his overcoat. He now realised that the ramps were a form of catapult designed to propel the flying bomb and get it airborne. They worked through the night looking at previous covers and spotted the ramps on the coast at Peenemünde as far back as May 1942.[21]

Piecing all this together was still a major challenge but after hours of discussion and working through the options, Kendall managed to deduce the complete workings of the flying bomb. The long, low concrete ski-shaped buildings were indeed thought to be storerooms for the bombs. The curve in the building was an anti-blast measure. The doorways were measured and found to be just wide enough to allow the bomb to be brought out and assembled by the square building with its wings on some form of base plate. The flying bomb would then be mounted on the firing ramp and under the propulsion of a powerful rocket booster, a catapult mechanism would fire it in the direction of London. All of this was written up overnight and Kendall presented it, along with detailed comparisons of the Peenemünde, Zinnowitz and the Bois Carré sites, in a report to the Joint Intelligence Committee dated 2 December.[22]

Finding out how the bomb was powered came later, after German aircraft had launched some glider bombs against naval ships. The Royal Navy picked up a number of these devices that had missed and ended up in the sea. When examined, they were found to be powered by a new fuel system mixing hydrogen peroxide with sodium permanganate. This was thought to be the fuel that would fire the catapult, giving the immense power necessary to get the flying bomb airborne. It was believed that the device could carry a warhead of between 2000lb and 4000lb (it was later found to be about 2000lb) and that this was powered when airborne by a pulse jet at a speed of about 400 mph. The engine made a very loud *putt-putt* sound which could be heard over a wide area and prompted Londoners later to call the weapons 'buzz-bombs'. A small automatic pilot in the fuselage kept the bomb at a height of between a thousand and two thousand feet, on a course directed by a magnetic compass. When the flying bomb had covered a certain distance (the number of miles from the launch site to London) the fuel supply was cut off. The engine stalled and fell silent for a few seconds as the bomb dipped and crashed to the ground. Londoners would later grow horribly familiar with the sound of the buzz-bomb over-head. As long as you continued to hear the engine putt-putting then you knew the bomb was passing by. If it fell silent, you knew you had about five seconds before the flying bomb would crash to the ground with a huge explosion. It was a terrifying, nerve-racking weapon.

Now that all the key information had been gathered, the ninety-six launch sites had to be destroyed. This began with a series of raids on 18 December, just over two weeks after Kendall presented his report to the Joint Intelligence Committee. The construction of each launch site was watched carefully and it was bombed at the point at which most of the work had been done but before the site was complete. The PIs allocated a certain number of points to each completed element – 10 for each of the ski buildings, 5 for the sunken building, 10 for the square assembly workshop, 10 for the launching platform, and so on. Half the number were allocated to a building that looked half complete. When a site totalled 70 points it was put on the list for immediate bombing.[23] Regular reconnaissance flights monitored the construction and recorded the damage to the bombed sites. By the end of December, fifty-two sites had been attacked and put out of action. Some had been attacked by heavy bombers, others by Mosquitos carrying out low level precision raids. By March 1944 all ninety-six sites had been bombed and eighty-eight were out of action. The Germans made some attempt to repair a few sites but none were ever used to fire flying bombs.

The number of sites has often puzzled analysts. Were there many more that the PIs had not spotted? In fact, because the flying bomb was operated by the Luftwaffe its initial operation was set up along the lines of a conventional squadron. There were six squadrons, each with sixteen firing sites. All ninety-six sites had been identified. There were no others, for now.

But there was no time for complacency. The Germans soon developed a much simpler launch site. The first of these new sites was identified near Belhamelin, which provided the generic name for the modified site. Most of the structures were adapted from farm buildings, or designed to resemble them

from the air, as the Germans knew their sites were being photographed by reconnaissance aircraft.[24] All that was laid down
were foundations and the interpreters realised that the buildings were therefore prefabricated and could be assembled very
quickly at the last minute prior to launch. There were no ski-
shaped storage buildings and the flying bombs were to be
brought in ready to fire. Disguised inside farms and concealed
within woods, the sites were extremely difficult to detect. In
Berlin, the Nazi leaders planned to start the flying bomb offensive on 20 April, Hitler's birthday, and to launch thousands of
the weapons against London in ten days. Hitler believed this
would bring Britain to its knees. But all the delays meant that
the launch sites were still not ready.

In May 1944, when twelve Belhamelin sites had been found,
the priority for photo reconnaissance and interpretation
shifted. Operation Overlord was barely a month away and all
activity had to be devoted to the invasion of Normandy. The
recon pilots and the PIs at Medmenham did not return to hunting down the flying bomb launch sites until nearly a week after
D-Day. On 11 June they found that firing ramps had been
installed at four Belhamelin sites and square buildings had
been erected at six. Early the following morning, Kendall
reported to the Air Ministry that the launch of the flying bombs
was imminent.[25]

The first ten flying bombs were launched on London in the
early hours of 13 June. Five crashed soon after launch. Another
went missing. Three landed in Kent and Sussex. Only one
reached London, landing in Bethnal Green. It was a slow start to
the promised offensive. But two days later, more than two hundred flying bombs were launched against England. Propaganda
Minister Joseph Goebbels announced that *Vergeltungswaffe
Eins*, Vengeance Weapon One, or the V-1, had been launched in

retaliation for the invasion of Normandy. The V-bomb campaign had begun.

Over the next few months the Germans launched 8617 flying bombs from sites in France. The British adopted all sorts of measures to try to shoot them down. High speed fighters like the Hawker Tempest tried to destroy them in mid-air. All of London's anti-aircraft defences were shifted to the south coast to try to hit the bombs while they were still out over the sea. Eight hundred guns, 60,000 tons of ammunition and 23,000 gunners were moved in one heroic forty-eight-hour period. An American gun-laying radar system was used to try to track and destroy the bombs. New proximity fuses set off anti-aircraft shells near the V-1s as they passed by, often turning a near miss into a direct hit.

As far as Medmenham was concerned the principal challenge was, if no stores of bombs were maintained at the modified launch sites, to find the bases where they came from and destroy the supply chain. This proved difficult to track down until, once again, reports from agents in France about underground storage depots provided the lead. The agents observed excavations taking place in the side of a hill near Beaumont. The work was carefully disguised under camouflage nets. Agents then identified similar activity at a set of caves at St Leu d'Esserent, north of Paris, which had been used for mushroom growing before the war. Again everything was being done under camouflage netting.

It was difficult to identify these developments from vertical photography, so low flying Mosquito PR aircraft, with forward facing oblique cameras in the nose, dived right down on to the site. From these photos it was possible to see that the caves were being strengthened and the entrance enlarged. A third site was found at a railway tunnel at Rilly-la-Montagne, near

Rheims in the Champagne district. All three sites were bombed. 617 Squadron, the famous Dam Busters squadron, was sent to bomb the site at St Leu, where an especially heavy bomb was required to penetrate the deep limestone caves. According to damage assessment photos, Barnes Wallis's massive 12,000lb 'Tallboy' bomb caused immense destruction around the site and it was thought that as many as two thousand flying bombs might have been buried in the rubble.

The V-1s were a truly terrifying weapon. They could arrive by day or night, in any weather. They were totally indiscriminate, crash landing anywhere at any time. Already exhausted by four and a half years of conflict, Londoners felt utterly helpless against the impersonal V-1 threat. There was no human enemy to shoot down, nothing to do but listen out for the rumbling of the noisy jet engine and hope it didn't fall silent when it was overhead. Sleep was disrupted. Nerves were on edge. People didn't know when they went to work in the morning if their families would still be alive when they came home in the evening. The rescue services were pushed to their absolute limits. At the peak of the campaign, a hundred V-1s got through to London every day. After the bombing of the storage sites this dropped to about seventy per day. But Hitler was wrong in his predictions. Londoners' resolve did not break.

However terrible the effects of the V-1s over London, it was nothing like as bad as it could have been. From the Bois Carré launch sites, at each of which twenty V-1s could be stored, the Germans had intended to fire two thousand V-1s in every twenty-four-hour period. From the new Belhamelin sites, where there was no storage facility, the maximum number that could be fired in a similar period was three hundred. And with the loss rate, barely a third of these actually got through. Yet in total, 2340 V-1s still landed on London. More than 6000

Londoners were killed and 18,000 wounded during the bombardment. Three-quarters of a million homes were destroyed or damaged. The V-1 campaign against England only ended when land forces captured all the potential launch sites in northern Europe. The last of the V-1s were launched from the air, and by the end of the year very few were coming over, although the last V-1 did not fall until March 1945. The whole experience was a horrible return to the dark days of the Blitz.

The most significant victory for photo intelligence was in delaying the start of the V-1 campaign by several months from early 1944 to mid June. This was a critical few months for the Allied war effort. Thousands of American, British, Canadian, French, Polish and other troops were assembling in southern England for the biggest and most ambitious operation in the war so far, the invasion of occupied Europe. The whole of southern England had become an assembly depot for endless lines of trucks, guns, jeeps and tanks. A huge armada of vessels were gathering in the ports of the south coast. It's impossible to tell what chaos could have been caused if V-1s had started raining down on this vast assemblage of men and materiel. The Supreme Commander of the whole operation, General Eisenhower, later wrote that 'if the Germans had succeeded in perfecting and using these new weapons six months earlier than he did, our invasion of Europe would have proved exceedingly difficult, perhaps impossible.' Eisenhower concluded that if the V-1s had been targeted on the Southampton–Portsmouth area, the centre of the principal assembly points for the invasion, 'Overlord might have been written off.'[26] In this case the war would certainly have gone on much longer and it's possible to conjecture that it might not have ended with the complete defeat of Nazi Germany but in some sort of negotiated truce. The stakes could not have been higher.

Taken in total, finding the launch sites, spotting the flying bomb, identifying the firing ramps and piecing together the workings of what would become one of Hitler's most feared secret weapons, was one of the great intelligence coups of the Second World War. Three thousand sorties had been flown and 1,200,000 photos had been interpreted. Dozens of reports had been written. It was a triumph for Medmenham, and the secret history later wrote that photo intelligence was 'the biggest single factor in the discovery of the flying bomb'.[27] If the Combined Interpretation Unit at Medmenham had done nothing else in the war, this discovery alone would have justified its existence and the years of work in developing the science of photographic intelligence. And the discoveries made by the photo interpreters, led by Douglas Kendall, had tumbled one upon another over just a few days at the end of November and beginning of December 1943. It had been a magnificent achievement.

Three months after the first V-1 landed, a new attack upon London began. Although by the end of 1943 the hunt for the German rockets had been eclipsed by the fear of flying bombs, the threat from Werner von Braun's rockets had not gone away. The bombing of Peenemünde in August 1943 had made it clear to the Nazi leadership that their research establishment had been discovered and that they needed to move the rocket programme to a new location to complete its secret work. The testing was relocated to Blizna, an artillery firing range formerly used by the Polish army. Deep in the dense forests of south-east Poland, the range was now run by the SS. From here, testing and rocket development started in late 1943. Von Braun and his team still had a lot of problems to solve, particularly with the propulsion of the rockets. There was a considerable way to go before the A4 would be operational.

In March 1944, underground reports reaching Scientific Intelligence at the Air Ministry claimed that some sort of rocket tests were taking place at Blizna and that the missiles created large craters. Though the site was out of range of photo reconnaissance flights from England, it was just within the range of Mosquito PR flights from San Severo in southern Italy. It was from here that photo recon aircraft had accidentally photographed Auschwitz. So, on 15 April, reconnaissance aircraft from Italy began to fly the nine hundred miles to south-east Poland to see what was going on.

At first the photographs did not reveal anything remarkable, but on 5 May a sortie recorded an A4 rocket lying in the open. The PIs were able to count four fins, as against the three observed in Peenemünde. But they could find no earthworks or any signs of a launch site. The general view had become that to launch a rocket vertically required a sophisticated launch pad with something to guide the weapon during lift-off. But there was still so much that the interpreters did not know about the A4. How was it transported to the launch site, and once it arrived how was it launched? There did not appear to be railway tracks at Blizna. Was it guided by beams to its target? If so, where were they controlled from? What size of warhead did it carry? Everything was easy to tie together in retrospect, but of course no one at the time had the advantage of hindsight.

It was at this point that a remarkable stroke of luck, combined with extraordinary bravery, led to a breakthrough. Unlike the rockets launched from Peenemünde, which came down in the sea, after each test launch from Blizna the missile landed somewhere in Poland. German engineers then went out and retrieved the crashed remains. After one test launch, a rocket crashed into the River Bug, north-west of Warsaw. The Polish underground managed to reach the remains before the

Germans did and they hid it. Working under the constant threat of discovery, Polish engineers examined the debris. Critical parts of the mechanism were packaged up, and on the night of 15 July a Dakota aircraft flew out from England to land in a field and collect the remains. Thanks to the daring mission, scientists in London had actual pieces of the A4 to study.

When another A4 exploded over Sweden, the authorities allowed the British to examine some of the parts. All the evidence now suddenly fell into place. In a single evening in July it became clear to R.V. Jones that the missile did not need any complex launch apparatus and could be assembled and fired from any flat piece of ground. It stood vertically on its four fins and would take off by itself, stabilised by gyroscopes and directed by jet rudders made of graphite that had been found in the remains brought to London. What's more, there was no need to transport the rocket to its launch site by railway. It was light enough to be carried on a purpose-built vehicle. So sure was Jones that he had discovered how the A4 could be launched that he wrote down the details and sent them to a colleague that evening just in case he fell victim to a flying bomb attack during the night.[28]

However, the PIs at Medmenham were not told of this and continued looking for a variation of the launch sites with firing ramps they had found for the V-1. Douglas Kendall, who was still involved with interpreting the photos on a day to day basis, later wrote that among the images of Peenemünde they already had a photo of an A4 standing on an area of asphalt by the sea. On it Kenny had identified a 'tower' approximately the same height as the rocket. In fact it was an A4 on its launch site, without any sort of firing ramp. But they had not realised the importance of this – that the rocket did not need any support but could be fired from any piece of flat ground. Kendall later saw this as a failing of the team at Medmenham, because the interpreters did not have completely open minds and were 'handicapped by the belief of our scientists that the rocket had to be guided by rails in a nearly vertical position'.[29] It is another example of how difficult it was to hunt for something completely new and unknown, and to think 'outside the box' of conventional wisdom.

With the pressure on to solve the mystery of the rocket missiles, tension between Kendall at Medmenham and R.V. Jones in Scientific Intelligence at the Air Ministry reached a peak. Jones thought the PIs were missing key elements in the photographs. Kendall complained that Jones was meddling in the work of the teams at Medmenham. The reality was that Jones had specialist scientific knowledge from a range of intelligence sources that were not available to the photo interpreters, so it is not surprising it was he who made the key breakthroughs. But for the PI team around Kendall, understanding how the rockets were launched remained elusive and their frustration grew.

The A4 rocket project had been a German army development programme. After the 20 July bomb plot, however, Hitler lost confidence in the army leadership and put all secret weapons programmes under the control of the SS. Werner von Braun now had to report to Heinrich Himmler. Himmler would hear of no more delays and was convinced that the scientists were being too cautious. Although the rocket development was far from complete, Hitler ordered the beginning of the missile attack upon England. On 8 September the first rocket was fired on London. It reached a height of about fifty miles before turning on its side and travelling in a perfect parabolic arc at a speed of around 3000 mph. After covering about two hundred miles it crashed into the ground, landing in Chiswick in west London. Three people were killed and seventeen seriously injured. The government, thinking people might panic if they knew the extent of the threat, put out a story that there had been an explosion in a gas main. Hardly anyone believed it.

This new weapon was named the V-2 and there was no defence against it. There was no hint of the missile's approach because it travelled faster than the speed of sound. The first thing anyone on the ground knew was of a huge explosion as the one-ton warhead blew up on impact. Only a few seconds later was it possible to hear the incoming missile. Cyril Demarne, a senior fire officer in the East End of London, recalled the sound as like a 'train coming in to a station'.[30] For Londoners still enduring the V-1 attacks, the V-2 campaign meant even further destruction and stress.

The photo interpreters at Medmenham found it almost impossible to identify V-2 launch sites, because the missile was entirely mobile and could be launched from anywhere. It was transported to its launch site on a specially adapted trailer wagon that could be hidden under trees until the last minute. With the failure of the Allied operation to capture the bridge across the Rhine at Arnhem, the Germans still occupied an area in the Hook of Holland less than two hundred miles from London. Radar plottings established that the first V-2s had been launched from near Rijs in Holland and, equipped with this lead, the PIs were able to spot the first launching areas among fresh clearings in woodland. But the photographic evidence was 'of no value' as by the time the rocket launchers had been identified they had moved on to new sites.[31]

Photo interpreters studied thousands of photographs but found no new sites. Then, on 29 December, they spotted thir-teen rockets in the Haagsche Bosch, a wood in the centre of The Hague. The Germans doubtless hoped that by siting the rock-ets in the middle of a city they could ensure that the Allies would not attack them. But the Allies sent fighter aircraft to The Hague to fire at anything they could see in the woods. Fighter attacks seemed to be more successful than conventional heavy bombing against the rockets, surrounded as they were by fuel and explosives. After a few days, the Germans abandoned the Haagsche Bosch and started firing the rockets from a racecourse just outside the city. Again this site was attacked and again the launchers moved on.

By January 1945 PR aircraft were carrying out an intensive search for V-2 launch sites, criss-crossing the zone from where the Allies thought attacks would come. More than a quarter of a million photographs were taken and studied, but there was no sign of the elusive launches. Then, after weeks of searching, on 26 February a pilot spotted a rocket in its vertical launch position with all the launch vehicles around it, at Duindigt near The Hague. The pilot photographed the only launch ever to be recorded. Ironically, with so many aircraft looking for the sites, this one site was photographed by three aircraft in less than five minutes. But, of course, by the time the photos had been brought back and processed, the site had already been dismantled and moved elsewhere.

The only way to stop the firing of the V-2 rockets was to capture their launch sites and to liberate all the territory within firing range of London. This eventually took place, but the Germans then launched a furious missile assault from inside Germany against Antwerp in Belgium, with further attacks upon Liège. The last V-2 fell on the south of England near Orpington in Kent on 27 March 1945, almost at the same time as the last V-1. About one in three V-2s had exploded in mid-air, probably as a consequence of Himmler's order to use the rockets before their development programme was complete. The heat generated during re-entry into the earth's atmosphere often ignited the warhead, causing the rocket to explode. More than 1100 V-2s were launched against England, and about half of these landed and exploded in the London area; 2054 people died as a consequence, with nearly 7000 seriously injured. Although the number was far below the early alarming predictions of 4000 deaths from each rocket, it was bad enough. Another half-million homes were damaged or destroyed. Even more missiles were fired on Antwerp, with a total of 1610 V-2s killing or injuring 30,000 Belgians.

As the war neared its end, the scientists who had worked on Hitler's jet and rocket programmes realised the game was up. With both the Soviets and the Americans recognising that these men had developed the technology of the future, there was a race to capture the German scientists and take them away. The Americans launched Operation Paperclip to round up as many of the brains behind the new weapons as they could. Werner von Braun and his team of 118 scientists surrendered to the Americans on 2 May 1945, a week before the final German surrender. They eventually were sent to the White Sands Proving Ground in New Mexico, where they helped to develop guided missiles for the American military. Thousands of other German scientists followed them.

The Soviets, on the other hand, captured around sixteen thousand German scientists and engineers who were taken to the Soviet Union and began work on the Soviet missile programme. Eventually Werner von Braun went on to lead the American missions in the space race of the 1960s and his rocket dream was realised when in 1969 the Apollo space programme finally landed men on the moon. It was just twenty-seven years after the first successful launch of the A4 rocket at Peenemünde.

The hunt for the Nazi secret weapons had initially been a race between two different forms of science and two intelligence systems, one attempting to come up with aggressive weapons of mass destruction and the other to discover and track what was happening. With the V-1s, photographic intelligence had shown what it could achieve. It was able to delay by many months and then very substantially lessen the blow of the V-1 flying bomb when it was finally launched against England. With the V-2 on the other hand, aerial photography and its interpretation had done little to help after the initial rockets had been found and identified. These two stories show both the strengths of photographic intelligence in the Second World War and its weaknesses. But while so much of the photo interpreters' time had been devoted to hunting down the V weapons, a new, potentially fatal threat had emerged to challenge the reconnaissance pilots. If reconnaissance aircraft were unable to fly over occupied Europe and take aerial photographs, then the whole process of photo intelligence would grind to a halt.

16

Towards Victory

On 25 July 1944, Flight Lieutenant Wall and his navigator, Flying Officer Lobban, were flying their reconnaissance Mosquito from Benson on a mission to photograph the chemical factories near Munich at thirty thousand feet when they spotted an interceptor approaching them at high speed. They went into a dive to gain speed but the enemy fighter soon caught up with them. They had been warned to look out for the latest product of German aviation technology, the new twin-engined Messerschmitt 262 jet fighter. When they realised that they were now being pursued by an Me 262 they thought they were 'gone for good'. Taking up position about two thousand yards behind the Mosquito, the jet caught up in less than ten seconds and opened fire.

Wall put the Mosquito into what he described as a 'rate 1 turn to port'. The Mosquito juddered violently under the strain as the Me 262 shot past at high speed, unable to turn as steeply as the Mosquito. Twice more the Me 262 came in to attack, and twice more Hall succeeded in holding on until the last second before turning violently to the right or left. At one point the Mosquito crew heard thuds on the underside of the fuselage and knew they had been hit. However, their plane flew on, and when Wall saw cloud cover ahead he dived and weaved into it, the Mosquito reaching about 450 mph in the dive.

They lost the Me 262 for a few minutes but when they emerged he was still there looking for them. Once again, Wall headed for a long line of cumulus clouds and managed to fly into the cover before the Me 262 got another chance to fire at them. They remained inside the thick clouds as long as they could and when they emerged, to their 'indescribable relief', there was no sign of the Me 262. The whole terrifying dogfight had lasted about twenty minutes.

Knowing that the Mosquito was hit, they decided to head south for Italy and the navigator kicked away the inside door in case they needed to bale out. Soon they spotted Venice below them, and then Ancona. They tried to pick up directions on their VHF radio but there was too much chatter, which only ceased when they called out 'Mayday'. They were then talked in to make an emergency landing thirty miles behind the Allied lines at Ferno, finally touching down and drawing to a halt on a recently bulldozed strip about twenty yards from the sea shore. Wall and Lobban had experienced the first ever inter-ception by the new German jet fighter. Because the pilot had kept a cool head throughout the dogfight, they had survived to tell the story.[1]

The German quest for new weapons and technologies had not been limited to flying bombs and ballistic missiles. In late 1943 reports started to arrive that the Germans were developing jet-powered aircraft. The Air Ministry in London had been slow to develop its own jet aircraft even though an RAF engineer,

Frank Whittle, had come up with a proposal for a jet engine back in the 1920s and had first patented the principles of jet technology in 1930. Rivalling Whittle's work was that of the German engineer, Pabst von Ohain, and when the Allies found out that the Germans were building their own jet, they began keeping a watchful reconnaissance eye on all the factories and airfields where they thought the jet might be in development. A hundred industrial plants and airfields were regularly photographed and studied. In February 1944 photo interpreters spotted the first German jet, the Messerschmitt 262 at Lechfeld airbase near Augsburg. Already, months before, in June 1943, Constance Babington Smith had found the tiny experimental rocket plane that was being tested at Peenemünde, the Me 163.

When these aircraft finally came into use, they posed a great threat to the lone photo reconnaissance aircraft flying for hours on deep penetration missions across Germany and occupied Europe. The Me 262 began operational flying in the summer of 1944. Soon afterwards the Me 163 also started to fly in combat. A fundamental aspect of the theory behind using unarmed reconnaissance aircraft was that they were faster than anything the enemy could send up to intercept. With the Spitfire and the Mosquito this had nearly always been the case. When the FW 190 first appeared it looked like it could outperform the Allied aircraft, but the newer models of both Spitfire and Mosquito maintained the RAF's advantage. However, the Me 262 could fly at least 50 mph faster than the fastest recon aircraft, and the Me 163 was even faster. This was very bad news for the photo recon pilots.

The first encounter with the Me 262 sent shock waves through the aerial reconnaissance community. Though Wall and Lobban had managed to evade the much faster jet fighter, other pilots were not so lucky and within days the first PR

Mosquito was shot down by an Me 262. In an even more terrifying combat on 4 September, a PR Mosquito was intercepted by two Me 262s who attacked in a combined operation. Again the pilot waited until the first approaching jet was only a few hundred yards away and managed to make a steep turn so the Me 262 shot by. When the second jet came in to attack, the Mosquito pilot used the same tactic. One after another the jets buzzed the Mosquito for more than twenty minutes and more than once the recon pilot risked a high speed stall through his drastic evasive action. Throughout the dogfight the navigator stood in the cockpit with his legs braced and his head forced hard against the blister at the top of the canopy. Looking backwards he was able to give the pilot a running commentary on what the enemy aircraft were doing. Losing height at about five hundred feet each minute, the Mosquito shuddered and shook during the high speed chase until it finally levelled out at nearly zero feet, at which point the Me 262s broke away. The Mosquito was so low it collided with a tree which destroyed the bomb-aiming window. The heroic pilot and equally cool navigator still managed to limp home, but this was flying at the absolute limit of the Mosquito's performance.

In yet another attack that month, the Mosquito pilot took such violent turns that the navigator's head 'was forced to his knees' by the G-forces. In this particular dogfight the pilot found himself racing head-on directly towards the Me 262 and turning slightly towards him as if about to open fire. Shaken, the Me 262 pilot veered away at speed. The bravado of making a dummy attack, even though he had no guns, had worked.[2]

The RAF decided only to fly Spitfires – and whenever possible the latest mark, the Spitfire XIX – on reconnaissance sorties over the areas where the German jets were known to operate. Although they were still not as fast as the Me 262 they were highly manoeuvrable. But as always, the new Spitfires were in short supply and while they were waiting for them, during September, the number of casualties to both British and American PR aircraft rose fivefold. Most of these extra losses were in the area around Munich where the Me 262s were flying. It appeared that the German jet pilots were using the Mosquito as a test for their own performance and tactics.[3]

The first attack on a PR aircraft by a rocket-propelled Me 163 does not appear to have taken place until March 1945, when a Mosquito crew at thirty-three thousand feet over Leipzig reported seeing two black trails coming up towards them at a phenomenal speed which they identified as about ten thousand feet per minute – which would be impressive in a modern jet fighter. The two Me 163s came in to attack from both sides simultaneously, at which point Pilot Officer Hays in the Mosquito did a half roll and went into a screaming dive at what he estimated to be an incredible 650 mph. When three more Me 163s appeared, Hays went into a spiralling dive down to the deck and managed to lose them. As if this wasn't bad enough, the Mosquito was then pursued by an Me 109. Once again the pilot managed to evade the enemy interceptor, but the Mosquito was hit by anti-aircraft fire and the navigator was wounded. Flying on without proper controls for nearly two hours, Hays made for the nearest friendly base in France. But when he came down to land, the landing gear, which had been hit by one of the enemy aircraft, collapsed and the Mosquito veered off the runway and crashed. Miraculously, although the navigator was badly wounded in the leg, Hays walked away from the crash unhurt.[4]

The Me 163 and Me 262 had both been designed with a view to attacking the formations of relatively slow-moving heavy Allied bombers that were then assaulting Germany almost every day. They were not made for high altitude dogfights with highly manoeuvrable aircraft like the Spitfire or the Mosquito. So although they presented a major threat in the final stages of the war, it was not the end of PR. The Allied bombers, meanwhile, relentlessly pressed home their attacks against the industrial plants and underground factories where the German aircraft were built, so they were never available in significant numbers. The Allied planners felt that they had the technology both to defend the bombers with aircraft like the Mustang, and to continue with reconnaissance flights using the Spitfire XIX. Had the war continued for much longer, then without doubt the RAF and the USAAF would have had to start using jet aircraft for aerial reconnaissance. It was another case where the war had seen the development of incredible new technologies that would point to the future of aviation. However, the first combats between jet fighters did not take place in the Second World War – it was not until the Korean War that aerial combat passed truly into the jet age.

By the last week of July 1944, about eight weeks after D-Day, the Americans had amassed the men and machinery necessary to break out from the Normandy stalemate. A huge offensive began that entirely overwhelmed the weakened German defences. Once the American tanks reached the open countryside there was nothing that could stop them. The British, under General Montgomery, finally captured the city of Caen and in a gigantic pincer movement, the Allied armies surrounded nineteen German divisions in the Falaise pocket. Ten thousand Germans were killed and another fifty thousand taken prisoner. The German commander, Field Marshal von Kluge, wrote a letter to Hitler saying that the war was as good as lost. Then he committed suicide.

Paris fell at the end of August. British and Canadian troops raced across northern France towards the Belgian border, capturing Brussels and Antwerp at the beginning of September. The PIs at Medmenham continued to focus on broad strategic objectives, while those in the APIS field units concentrated on immediate tactical targets. The mobile field units consisted of a thin-skinned three-ton wagon, in which the PIs worked, fitted with two desks and Anglepoise lamps, with a wooden rack at the end to store the prints; a jeep; and one or two tents. Each unit included two PIs, supported by a draughtsman, a clerk and two drivers. There was one such field unit for each division and several more at Army and Army Group headquarters. The photographs came from the reconnaissance squadrons of the Tactical Air Force and were rushed from the airfield to these forward units for interpretation.

Geoffrey Stone, who had been in the Army Section at Medmenham, was now transferred to one of these field teams at 2nd Army HQ. He remembers that leaving Medmenham and going to a forward unit was 'what you were expected to do' if you were an Army PI. But the pressure on interpreters in the field could be considerable. On one occasion Stone was called to see the general and asked if it would be possible to get tanks through a forest crossed only by narrow tracks. Stone asked for a few minutes to examine the aerial photographs and then went back to the general to say that he couldn't tell if the tracks were wide enough. The general exploded with rage and demanded to know if his tanks could get through, as he needed them to do so. As Stone recalled, 'you were often under pressure to tell a commander what he wanted to know. But in the field your advice often led to people going forward and risking their lives and you had to be absolutely sure that you hadn't missed anything.'[5]

A classic case occurred in September 1944. With the American General Patton advancing rapidly in the south,

Montgomery was keen on finding a British initiative that would bring the war to an early end. So, as the Allied armies advanced east across France and Belgium towards the German border, Monty came up with a daring plan to drop thousands of elite American and British paratroopers behind enemy lines, their mission being to seize three sets of bridges across the canals and rivers of the Netherlands. This would create a sixty-mile corridor down which land troops could charge through to the Rhine. If successful it would bring Allied troops into Germany months ahead of schedule and possibly even end the war by Christmas.

The US 101st Airborne, known as the 'Screaming Eagles', were to take the first bridges near Eindhoven. The US 82nd Airborne, the 'All-American', were to capture the next bridges at Nijmegen. British paratroopers from the 1st Airborne, popularly known as the 'Red Devils' after their maroon-coloured berets, were to land at Arnhem with the task of capturing the farthest bridge over the Lower Rhine, and then holding it until the armoured relief column could fight its way through from the Belgian border, supposedly only two days later.

The operation, known as Market Garden, had been carefully planned using a mass of aerial photography. At the last minute, the Chief Intelligence Officer of the Airborne Corps, Major Brian Urquhart, heard of intelligence reports that German armoured troops were refitting in a forest near the bridge over the Rhine at Arnhem.[6] Urquhart was a great fan of aerial photography and had done a lot of work with the PIs at Medmenham. He requested that low level oblique photographs of Arnhem should immediately be taken, and on 15 September this was done. Studying the obliques, Urquhart spotted large groups of tanks and armoured vehicles in the woods within easy range of the Red Devils' drop zone. He immediately reported this to General Browning, the tough, determined commander of the British Airborne Corps, and to other senior officers. But no one wanted to know. By this point at the eleventh hour, the momentum of the operation, Monty's great gamble, was unstoppable.

Urquhart had in fact spotted two SS Panzer divisions, resting and refitting in woods just to the north of the bridge the British paratroopers had been ordered to seize. But because the accidental presence of these tough German troops did not conform with the intelligence the commanders wanted to hear, it was ignored. According to Urquhart he was treated like a 'nervous child suffering from a nightmare', as 'a pain in the neck' – as someone who wanted to spoil what was now widely being called 'the party'. But Urquhart persisted, and on the afternoon of the day he had made his report from the aerial photographs he was dismissed from his duties. He was told he was suffering from nervous strain, that he needed to take some urgently needed leave and to rest. When asked what would happen if he refused to take leave he was told he would be court-martialled for disobeying orders.[7]

Despite the evidence of the last-minute aerial photographs, the parachute drop took place on 17 September. The 'Screaming Eagles' took the first bridge near Eindhoven but the Germans blew up the nearby canal bridge at Son before it could be captured. The 'All-Americans' finally captured the next bridge at Nijmegen after heavy fighting and a head-on assault across the river. But the battle at Arnhem, which came to be known as the 'bridge too far', was a disaster for the British paratroopers. A group led by Lieutenant-Colonel John Frost tried to hold the bridge and there were countless examples of heroism as this small force of lightly equipped paratroopers faced the well-armed German Panzer units. But the armoured relief column fighting its way up from Belgium was delayed by heavy

German resistance. The Red Devils were supposed to hold on for forty-eight hours. They fought bravely against the Panzer forces for nine days until being finally overcome. Only 2400 of 10,000 British paratroopers managed to escape. The rest were killed, wounded or taken prisoner. The defeat of Monty's plan not only set back the Allied cause but also gave a huge boost to the Germans as Allied soldiers approached the Fatherland. We have seen many examples of how the use of aerial photography helped win battles and improved understanding of what the enemy were up to. But in the case of Arnhem, ignoring the evidence of aerial photography led to disaster.[8]

After the failure of Market Garden, the 2nd Army Group APIS unit moved into the Dutch city of Eindhoven in October and was billeted in what had been a school. Geoffrey Stone found himself working there alongside another PI who was far from being a typical army officer. Captain Derek van den Bogaerde was charming, elegant and had the good looks of a matinee idol. Although Stone remembers him as something of a dilettante he could charm his way through any situation. Trained as a signaller and then transferred to photographic intelligence, he had briefly been a PI at Medmenham, where he had taken to the work with enthusiasm. 'I loved the detail, the intense concentration, the working out of problems, the searching for clues and above all the memorising,' Bogaerde later wrote.[9] As an Army officer he went on to join an APIS field unit with the 39 (Reconnaissance) Wing of the Royal Canadian Air Force. He arrived in Normandy a few weeks after D-Day. Living in a tent alongside his truck and caravan, he was strafed and shelled and saw men horribly wounded. He helped to identify enemy artillery positions, followed the movements of German armoured units and studied trench layouts and barbed wire entanglements. Richard Rohmer, one of the reconnaissance

pilots supplying Bogaerde and his team with photos to interpret, later wrote that he was part of a team that 'became the
eyes of the army watching and reporting the enemy's every
move in the area of the battlefield and the approaches to the
front line ... we were all-seeing hawks scouring the ground for
prey.'[10]

According to his own, probably rather embellished account,
Bogaerde entered Brussels the day after its liberation, was feted
by cheering crowds and given Krug champagne by a young
lady who was supposedly looking for her husband. He worked
on the planning for Market Garden and went forward with the
relief column to link up with the bridges that had been seized.
He saw plenty of 'action' and was shattered by what he called
'the catastrophe of Arnhem'. At Eindhoven, Bogaerde was
delighted to be based at last in a city rather than out in the field.
He could take a regular bath and go to the cinema. He went to
the ENSA performance of *The Merry Widow* every night for two
weeks, becoming word perfect in some of the scenes.[11] It was an
enjoyable break after months of grafting over a Stereo in his
truck just behind the front line.

In the last few months of the war, photo intelligence played
a role in the final campaigns in Europe and in Asia and the
APIS units continued to provide tactical intelligence for field
commanders advancing across France and Belgium, while the
work of strategic photo interpretation carried on at the Allied
Central Interpretation Unit at Medmenham. But the one serious
failure of photo intelligence nearly resulted in a catastrophe for
the Allies. In early December 1944 bad weather, low cloud and
thick morning fogs across northern Europe limited effective
aerial reconnaissance. Perhaps, too, the Allied generals were
over-confident that victory was within sight. But the Germans
had one powerful surprise move left to play. The overcast skies

coincided with the massing of the German army for a major counter-attack in the Ardennes forest. Hitler wanted to drive a wedge between the British and American forces and smash his way to Antwerp to recapture the supply base of their advancing armies. Three Panzer armies assembled along a forty-mile front in total radio silence, ensuring that no hint of their intentions was picked up by the code breakers listening in to Enigma communications.

Without any forewarning, and blinded by the lack of aerial reconnaissance, the German attack on 16 December came as a terrible surprise to the American units on that part of the front. Eisenhower responded quickly and sent in reinforcements, but in the first week many small American units were overwhelmed by the superior German forces. One rookie unit, newly arrived at the front, surrendered in huge numbers. Just before Christmas, snow began to fall on the battlefield as the German advance created a huge bulge into the Allied lines. Elite American paratroop regiments held on for dear life at a few critical points, like the area around St Vith and the crossroads at Bastogne. But it was only when the skies cleared just after Christmas that Allied air power could begin to relieve the besieged American troops.

Clearer skies also meant that photo recon flights could resume and the Allied armies began to restore control, although in England the weather remained atrocious – of thirty-five reconnaissance aircraft that took off from Benson at the end of December all but one were unable to return and were forced to land at another airfield. In the Ardennes, meanwhile, the overwhelming numbers of American reinforcements sent in, along with the German forces' lack of fuel, reversed the situation. By the end of January 1945, the Battle of the Bulge was over and Hitler's dreams of a breakthrough in the west had been shattered. His armies were now too weak to prevent the final assault on the Fatherland itself.

In mid January a group of six senior officers, British and American, set out to investigate what had gone wrong with the photo intelligence and to discover why it had failed to predict the German offensive. Douglas Kendall was one of the British investigating officers and Harvey Brown one of the Americans. One of the first visitors to Medmenham in the days before Pearl Harbor, Brown was now a leading figure in US aerial intelligence. During their investigation, Kendall and Brown found that despite the bad weather photographic reconnaissance flights had taken place on every day except one, 13 December, in the run-up to the German attack. The Tactical Reconnaissance Group supporting the First US Army had flown a total of 361 sorties. However, the photo interpreters had failed to spot the German armour assembling in the forests of the Ardennes, and what they *had* seen had been interpreted as routine movements of reserve units.[12] Kendall blamed the disaster on the failure of the many separate field units to link all the evidence that they had separately gathered. He believed that if it had been passed to a central interpretation unit like Medmenham then all the pieces of the jigsaw would have been put together and the imminence of a German counter-attack would have been predicted.[13] This no doubt was part of the problem. But the expectations of the Allied commanders were also a major factor. They had thought that the German armies were simply too weak to launch a major offensive, particularly across difficult terrain like that of the Ardennes. With this belief firmly in their minds, it would have taken extraordinarily powerful evidence to convince them otherwise.

In the early months of 1945, PR aircraft continued to photograph German railway marshalling yards and factories, some of which had now gone underground to take refuge from the Allied bombing offensive. Spotting underground factories was not difficult for the photo interpreters. Regardless of how deeply underground they were located, such sites left clear signs of what was going on around them. The scars from their construction, the quantities of earth or rocks that had been dug out, were usually visible on the landscape for months or years to come. Underground factories needed fans or air ducts, and these could clearly be seen from the air. Like all factories, they needed transport links like roads and railways. And it was possible to deduce from the power and water supplies how large their manufacturing capability was. Usually, the products of these factories were assembled in stockyards, which were rarely underground and showed up easily from the air. For instance, the V-2 rockets were transported in special railway wagons built in three sections. These were easily identifiable in the railway yards and so, even if the rockets themselves were not left in the open, it was possible to identify which factories were producing them. As Kendall wrote, 'it can be said with complete confidence that the existence of an underground factory is clearly visible on air photographs.'[14] Almost everything of industrial importance was visible to the spies in the sky.

In addition to this, British and American aircraft photographed the bridges across the Rhine, the final barrier to entering Germany. The models made assisted the crossings of the Rhine in late March. As Allied troops began to advance into the Fatherland itself, aerial reconnaissance supported every step of the way. Two PR squadrons were moved from Benson to a French airfield, Colommiers, to be nearer to the battle zone. But by the time they were ready to fly, the war was in its last days and the PR aircraft were left picking up odd jobs, like carrying documents and maps between Army headquarters. On

3 May, photographs were taken of German naval vessels trying to evacuate troops to Norway, and two days later all operational PR flying was cancelled. The final task of the Spitfires, Mosquitos and F-5s was to carry out reconnaissance flights over German units to ensure their surrender was being properly carried out.[15] The war in Europe had come to an end.

17

'80 per cent of All Intelligence'?

In 1938, General Werner Freiherr von Fritsch of the German army predicted that 'the military organisation which has the most efficient reconnaissance unit will win the next war'.[1] Von Fritsch was killed on the Eastern Front, so he did not survive to see his prediction come true. For, although the Germans began the war with an efficient photographic reconnaissance and photo interpretation system, they did not develop or improve it. The early years of triumphant victories made reconnaissance less of a priority and once the tide had turned the German war machine had other matters to worry about. Like so many military skills, once it had been lost it was difficult to re-create.

The British, on the other hand, who had learnt a lot about how to use aerial photography in the First World War, had forgotten all of it by 1939. They entered the war with a disastrous policy of sending slow flying, low level Blenheim light bombers on reconnaissance missions over enemy territory. Often their cameras froze up and the photos were unusable. With the wrong aircraft and the wrong techniques, these sorties became almost suicide missions for the poor pilots, who bravely carried on regardless.

It took a huge challenge to the established way of thinking to bring about a revolution in aerial photography at the RAF. This came slowly through 1939–40 with the introduction of the use of the fastest aircraft available, the Spitfire and later the Mosquito, for high speed, high altitude sorties across enemy airspace. One of the recurring themes of this book has been how it took unconventional and often eccentric figures, using unorthodox thinking, to challenge the conventional ways of getting things done. The Air Ministry and the RAF rarely look good in these internal battles. But in the end they did respond and adapt, and 'officialdom' accepted the advice of the mavericks. With the reconnaissance squadrons flying out of RAF Benson and a host of other stations in the Mediterranean and later in the Middle and Far East, the RAF developed a range of sophisticated techniques for aerial photography. And at Medmenham and its substations around the world, the RAF had created one of the most extraordinary establishments of the war. As inventive as Bletchley Park and as resourceful as a university research establishment, the men and women of Medmenham played a vital role in the intelligence war. It was said that 80 per cent of all intelligence in the Second World War came from aerial photography.[2]

In the early months of 1945, anticipating that the story of aerial photography and the new science of photo interpretation would soon be told to the public at large, the Air Ministry sent an official photographer to Medmenham. His images wonderfully captured the mood and the atmosphere of the work going on there. Men and women, British and American, posed for photographs in all parts of the grand house they had occupied for four years. The pictures recorded piles of prints and photographic boxes stacked up in every corner. The long lists of sorties and covers to be plotted and then interpreted were pinned up on wall charts. Dozens of interpreters, hunched over Stereos, examined hundreds of aerial photos. An album of photographic montages and typed captions was lovingly put together, called *The Chalk House with the Tudor Chimneys* – Churchill's nickname for Danesfield House. Maybe some of the photo interpreters would soon become famous, their names as well known as those of the more obvious battlefield heroes.

One photo interpreter did indeed become something of a star. Constance Babington Smith was known for her success in spotting the V-1. On a visit, Winston Churchill once glowingly referred to her as 'Miss Babington Smith of Peenemünde'.[3] At the end of the war she was sent to Washington to work on a special assignment at the Pentagon. Her lively personality, good looks and photogenic style in her smart WAAF uniform made her something of a natural for publicity. The Americans, realising it was she who had first spotted the V-1, wanted to get some mileage out of her presence and introduced her to a few press men. Had the German secret weapon programme continued uninterrupted, they might have developed a missile that could be launched not just across the Channel but even against the cities along the eastern seaboard of the United States. It was certainly something the German scientists were working on. Before long a headline appeared in one of the American tabloids, 'Connie Saves New York!'[4] The PIs had their heroine, Stateside at least.

However, as the end of the Second World War morphed slowly into the beginning of a new Cold War, the authorities quickly decided that the work that had gone on at

Medmenham was far too secret to be revealed to the general public. The skills developed for spying on Nazi-occupied Europe might soon be needed to take a look at what was happening in Soviet-occupied Eastern Europe. The photographs of the men and women at Medmenham were never released and all copies of *The Chalk House with the Tudor Chimneys* were withdrawn. We are lucky today that a few copies survived the cull.[5]

Over the years some stories did start to leak out, and in the mid 1950s Constance Babington Smith began to interview her wartime colleagues with the intention of writing about their work at Medmenham. When she finished her book it was serialised in the *Sunday Times* and Babington Smith asked Churchill to write the foreword. He refused. He had no doubts about the importance of the work carried out at Medmenham; he had heard many stories about the interpretation unit from his daughter, Sarah. But by now he was in his eighties and he had retired from a second, not very successful spell as Prime Minister. If he agreed to write the foreword to this book, how could he refuse to write many others? The floodgates would open and he no longer had the energy for that sort of thing.[6] Babington Smith's book, named after the wartime magazine produced at Medmenham, *Evidence in Camera*, came out in 1957. But it appeared without the formal endorsement of the man who had encouraged and supported the work of photo interpretation from the beginning of the war.

The story of Bletchley Park, too, was kept under wraps at the end of the war. For similar reasons, the government quickly realised that the techniques developed there could be of immense value in listening in to Soviet or Red Army communications after the war. It shocked contemporaries how quickly our wartime friend and ally became a potential foe. By March 1946, Churchill was talking of an 'Iron Curtain' that had descended across Europe, dividing East from West. The secret sciences of the Second World War had therefore to remain totally secret. If some of the details of photo interpretation were allowed out in the late 1950s, it was not until the mid 1970s that the story of code breaking and the work of the geniuses who struggled day and night at Bletchley Park was told. By that time the modern computer industry was established in embryo form. Alan Turing, an exceptional talent even among the code breakers who had done so much to lay the foundations of computing, had been hounded for being gay, and committed suicide by biting on a poisoned apple.

So, what role did photo reconnaissance and photo interpretation play in winning the war? There was no doubt that occasionally an individual photograph, often taken by a courageous pilot at great risk, revealed something remarkable. Michael Suckling's picture of the *Bismarck* sheltering in a Norwegian fjord near Bergen began the hunt that led to the sinking of the giant German warship and no doubt helped to save thousands of lives in the Battle of the Atlantic. His photo was called 'the picture that sank a battleship'.[7] But the photographs themselves always needed interpreting. Was this the *Bismarck* near Bergen, or some other large ship? Tony Hill's low level oblique of the Wurzburg radar on the clifftop at Bruneval led to the paratroop raid that became a turning point in the radar war. But someone still had to decide if this piece of apparatus was indeed a new form of radar or simply a radio transmitter. John Merrifield's reconnaissance photograph, which caught a V-1 at the moment of its test launch in November 1943, completed an extraordinary period of aerial surveillance that helped to put together the story of the flying bomb programme. Without doubt, the ability of the interpreters to deduce the workings of the flying bomb from a series of tiny specks on photographs taken from thirty thousand feet, is one of the greatest contributions made by photo interpretation to the Allied war effort. Working out how the V-1s were launched and finding all ninety-six Bois Carré launch sites not only led to the destruction of these sites but also to the delay of the entire Nazi secret weapons programme by several months at a critical moment of the war.

Other interpretations are more controversial. Did the photographs of the barges being assembled in the northern French and Belgian ports in September 1940 show that the Germans *were* intending to invade Britain? Or are they the crucial evidence that, by showing how minimal the preparations were, reveals that the Germans did *not* have the capability to mount a full scale invasion? At the time the interpreters were in no doubt that this was evidence of an army preparing to invade. Today, in retrospect, and particularly in the light of what we know was needed to mount the Allied invasion of France, we can 'read' the photographs quite differently and conclude that they are clear evidence of a lack of capability to invade.

One of the great strengths of the system of photo interpretation developed at Wembley and Medmenham was that the same photo could be used to reveal different types of information. What or where was that tank, aircraft or ship? This was the first question to answer in the quick-turnaround First Phase interpretation. How had the numbers of tanks changed? Was that airfield now serviceable? Was that ship ready to sail? These were the sorts of questions answered by Second Phase interpretation. Often this phase involved some sort of measuring. Could a tank cross this bridge? What was the storage capacity of that group of buildings? How many aircraft were ready to fly on this airfield? Then came the more complex questions. Was this aircraft a new variant or an improved model of a previous one? What was the annual output of this factory? How had the bombing affected the factory's output and when would it return to its previous capacity? These were the sorts of questions that Third Phase could answer, usually by making comparisons with earlier cover of the same site. Most of the photo interpreters at Medmenham who grappled with these questions were bright young people who had never seen an aerial photo before. But they all learnt the rigour and the processes involved in this extraordinary new science.[8]

By late 1942 military leaders accepted that no significant operation could take place without detailed aerial intelligence. The original scepticism about aerial photography had been banished and army commanders on the ground had to be 'air minded'. The photo interpreters could tell the location of enemy trenches, artillery and armour. They could assess the weight of armour a beach could support or find the railway hub that was the essential link in the enemy's supply chain. Every aspect of the enemy's defences could be analysed and reported on. On an operation as important as Overlord, photo intelligence helped to identify the beaches that were suitable for the landings. Then, by spotting the different types of defences and beach obstacles, it helped to find ways of defusing their impact. And, in the months leading up to the invasion, it monitored enemy movements and provided target material for attack aircraft. The Commander of the Allied Air Forces on D-Day, Air Chief Marshal Sir Trafford Leigh Mallory, wrote in his despatch on the invasion that 'Photographic Reconnaissance prior to D-Day was always very accurate and was throughout of vital importance.'[9] Almost any field commander could have written these words after any major offensive action in the last three years of the war. And he could have added that photo intelligence had helped to reduce the number of casualties considerably by providing clear information as to the enemy defences.

From the beginning of the war naval commanders had been keen to use aerial photographs to see what the German navy was doing, where it was harbouring and what its strength was. When the Italian navy surrendered in 1944, the admiral in command was asked why his ships had made such a poor showing in the war, bearing in mind his superiority in vessels and firepower over the Allies in the Mediterranean. He answered that 'no one could play chess blindfolded'. Although the Allies seemed to know where every one of his ships were at all times because they were being photographed daily, he never knew where the Allied warships were or how many there were.[10] If he is to be believed, photo intelligence (and the lack of it) had helped to reduce the impact of a potentially fatal rival in the Mediterranean.

When it came to the bombing of Germany, the surveys and reports issued by Medmenham were indispensable in identifying targets, planning raids and then in revealing the damage caused, even though those reports proved unpopular in the early stages of the offensive. The reports, of which thousands were produced, on the scope and output of German war factories were used by those engaged in producing the surveys that decided the priorities for targeting. 'Aerial photographs ... [played] an important part in these surveys as it was often the only means of detecting the increases in plant capacity', wrote the official in charge of the Enemy Resources Department at the Ministry of Economic Warfare.[11] Aerial photos were used to assess the damage to the Ruhr dams or to calculate the optimum moment to return to bomb a damaged chemical factory or steel works for a second or third time.

However, photo interpretation was a new science and still

subject to criticism. The official history of bombing is critical of
some of the damage assessment reports, claiming that the PIs
tended to exaggerate the scale of the damage. Aerial photographs provide an excellent picture of the damage to the
exterior of a building but not that caused to the building's con-
tents. The official history concluded: 'They gave a really
accurate picture of the effect of bombing on housing but they
were less useful in estimating the effects on industrial production for in many, indeed a majority, of cases, the machinery
might receive little or no injury when the roof of a factory was
destroyed by fire by incendiaries or shattered by the explosion
of a high explosive bomb of moderate weight.'[12] Aerial photographs did not always provide the complete answer to
questions about damage assessment.

As has been made clear, photo intelligence was only one part
of the intelligence war. On most occasions it succeeded because
it worked *alongside* other forms of human or signals intelligence
(HUMINT and SIGINT). Suckling did a brilliant job in spotting
and photographing the *Bismarck* but his success stemmed from
a tipoff from Sweden. Claude Wavell's ingenuity and instinct
led him to identify the strange paraboloid tower at Bruneval,
but it was only in discussion with R.V. Jones, who had already
picked up unusual short wave signals that he couldn't explain,
that both men were able to imagine that this strange object
could be a new form of radar. And as we have seen, the extraordinary work in interpreting what was happening in
Peenemünde went on within a framework of intelligence gathering that included listening in to POWs talking together,
reports from Resistance and underground operatives, and the
picking up and decoding of enemy messages. Rarely did photo
intelligence operate in a vacuum. It could confirm other reports,
provide the missing link or answer questions that otherwise

would remain a mystery. It could verify what a location looked like, and from this a great deal could be interpreted and understood. But it couldn't explain how the enemy were thinking or what they were planning, which SIGINT could occasionally do. And it couldn't tell you how the enemy or his supporters were feeling or how their morale was faring, which sometimes HUMINT could do.

So, in conclusion, it's impossible to quantify the achievement of photo intelligence other than to say that it made a supremely important contribution to wartime intelligence. The claim that '80 per cent of vital wartime intelligence came from aerial photos', made by General Lee Chennault,[13] has been often repeated. But Chennault led a very particular operation in the Second World War, in command of the Flying Tigers and then in supplying China by air. The alternative forms of intelligence on this remote front were, in truth, limited. However, the greatest strength of photo intelligence was that it was active. Other forms of intelligence were passive, in that they depended upon the chance fact of the enemy revealing something that you wanted to know. SIGINT relied upon the sending of signals that could be decrypted. HUMINT relied upon agents and resistance fighters telling you something they knew, or POWs knowing a piece of information that was of interest. Aerial photos could verify and often confirm or deny what you wanted to know. They were precise. But even then, if a commander did not want to hear what the evidence of aerial imagery showed up, for example that there were enemy troops sheltering in the nearby woods, or that a counter-attack was being prepared, the intelligence officer could do no more than repeat his unpopular report.

The biggest single limitation upon photo reconnaissance was undoubtedly the weather. The reconnaissance pilots had developed the skills to outperform most enemy interceptors, even jet fighters, but if they reached their target and it was covered with cloud there was almost nothing they could do. When the winter weather was bad and limited reconnaissance, as in the days before the Battle of the Bulge, the Allies were almost blind to the enemy's activities. This was far and away the biggest weakness in wartime reconnaissance. But even so photo intelligence was clearly a very major source of intelligence. Without the spies in the sky, the war would have gone on longer and Allied casualties at home, as well as at the front, would have been much worse. That in itself is a very fine achievement.

We have seen how aerial reconnaissance had many critics. Early in the war it was little understood and in the fierce competition for limited resources, rival commanders challenged the lavish claims made by supporters of PR and PI. Later in the war most of the comments were complimentary and many were enormously enthusiastic. But there were still disputes and one of these was between Scientific Intelligence and the PIs at Medmenham. The brilliant young scientist R.V. Jones repeatedly said it was *he* who spotted things and that the PIs were missing them. But then he had a better sense of what he was looking for. He wrote that he regarded himself as the equivalent of a 'fourth phase interpreter to supplement the first three phases of interpretation at Medmenham'. This was a good description. He had access to much more specialised scientific information than the PIs and so his interpretations were likely to be more advanced. Douglas Kendall, on the other hand, accused him of being an 'amateur interpreter'. Their falling out in July and August 1944 was doubtless a sign of the intense strain both men were under in trying to work out how the V-2 functioned. Fortunately, their dispute was quickly resolved.[14]

If the British and then the Americans had proved so ingenious in developing the secret science of photo intelligence, why were the Germans not equally good at photo reconnaissance and interpretation? The Luftwaffe certainly started the war with many advantages. It had good, fast aircraft. The cameras the Germans used for aerial photography were excellent and German optical lenses made by Zeiss were first rate. Just as Sidney Cotton had fooled the Germans by posing as a businessman and taking photos over German military installations in the months before the war, so the Germans had secretly photographed large parts of Britain from a variety of peaceable aircraft during 1938, and even from a Zeppelin that had been invited to tour the east coast in the summer of 1939. And just as the RAF eventually requisitioned a private aerial survey company, the Aircraft Operating Company, so did the Luftwaffe take over a civilian specialist air photography company. The Dornier 17 was the principal aircraft initially used for German long range reconnaissance. A two-engined light bomber designed in the mid 1930s, it could fly at higher altitude than the RAF's Blenheims and, with the quality lenses available to the Luftwaffe, carried out most German reconnaissance at about twenty thousand feet.[15] Short range photo reconnaissance was carried out by the Me 109.

But the Luftwaffe never removed the guns or armour from these aircraft. As a consequence they could never carry more than a single camera or fly at especially high altitude. Only when the Germans captured a Spitfire PR aircraft intact in France in 1940 did they see that British short range aircraft could carry up to three cameras. But they still did not change their system.

Because, in the first part of the war, German military activity had been offensive, the principal need had been for tactical military information, not for the strategic interpretation of their enemy's war economy. German photo intelligence never really moved on from this. There was never any central interpretation unit, as at Medmenham. PR was decentralised to air groups, Luftflotte, answering only to local requests for cover. And PI was carried out by corporals and non-commissioned officers who were not allowed to acquire specialist knowledge. Nothing is more symptomatic of the German disregard for photo interpretation than this. The Luftwaffe interpreters only ever looked for the military details they had been specifically asked to find and not for any additional information that a photograph might offer up.

As the war progressed so German losses mounted. The Luftwaffe had started the war with a substantial fleet of reconnaissance aircraft, way beyond the dreams of the Allies for many years. But by mid 1942, about half had been shot down, and the reconnaissance squadrons were never properly renewed. By this point of the war, priorities in Berlin were changing. There was a growing emphasis on defence. Reconnaissance still carried on, mostly performed by Ju 88s that were faster and could fly higher than the Dorniers. Much of the Eastern Front was still being photographed extensively. But in the Mediterranean and in the West it was a losing battle. Allied air forces were winning mastery of the skies. Many regions became no-go areas for German PR aircraft. Nowhere was this more apparent than over England. Not a single Luftwaffe PR mission was flown over London from late January 1941 until September 1944. The Germans entirely missed the huge military build-up in southern England that preceded D-Day – except for the dummy tanks and landing aircraft they were allowed to photograph along the south-east coast as part of the Allied deception campaign. And when the

Luftwaffe did overfly London again it was in Me 262 jet reconnaissance aircraft that were used to spot V-2 impacts in order to correct their flight paths. But without recent comparative cover the German photo interpreters could not tell which sites had suffered V-2 strikes and which were older scenes of bomb damage, and so they drew completely wrong conclusions about the V-2's destructiveness. German photo interpretation had fallen way behind, it was not integrated with other intelligence gathering, and in the second half of the war it simply stagnated – fortunately for the Allies.[16]

Aerial photography can be used to check stories, gather facts and correct myths. Over recent decades, aerial photographs have become more readily available. Millions of Allied wartime photographs, along with captured Luftwaffe aerial photos, are now accessible in the US National Archives at College Park, Maryland.[17] In the UK, more than ten million aerial photographs were declassified and classed as public records in the 1960s, and were passed on to Keele University. This entire collection forms the Aerial Reconnaissance Archives (TARA) and is now available in the archives of the Historic Monuments of Scotland in Edinburgh, as part of the National Collection of Aerial Photography.[18] Experts regularly use this material to search for unexploded wartime bombs in Britain, Germany and elsewhere in Europe, or to analyse changing land usage across the last seventy years.[19]

Historians and photo analysis experts have started to use this imagery to revise the standard accounts of wartime events. A historian has recently studied a set of aerial photos taken during Operation Goodwood in July 1944 while the battle was raging below to correct some of the stories that have entered the mythology of that battle.[20] It was a team of professional analysts at the National Photographic Interpretation Centre in Washington, led by Dino Brugioni, who found the photographs of Auschwitz (see Chapter 14). As the Germans destroyed much of the camp, including parts of the incriminating gas chambers and crematoria, before the Russians liberated Auschwitz in January 1945, these photographs provide a detailed aerial record of its layout and organisation. They can now be used to verify first-hand accounts from those who survived and from the fragmentary documents that remain. The photographs, in some of which smoke can be seen belching from the crematoria chimneys, are proof for anyone who needs it that the Holocaust really did take place.

Polish historians have used photographs taken over the Katyn Forest to provide evidence of the site of the mass murder and burial of thousands of Polish officers by the Soviets in 1940. These photographs were taken by Luftwaffe reconnaissance pilots who, like the pilots over Auschwitz, were photographing something else, in this case the railway and road junctions at Smolensk, when they strayed a few miles west over Katyn. Photographs dating from mid 1941 show ground disturbances that appear to be a series of mass graves. It was here that about fifteen thousand Polish offices had been murdered and thrown into trenches by the Soviet secret police, the NKVD. The Poles call them 'trenches of death'. After occupying the area, the Germans made much propaganda out of accusing the Russians of perpetrating the atrocity. The Soviets denied they had been responsible and instead claimed that the Germans had carried out the massacre after conquering Smolensk in 1941. But later photographs, taken after the Soviets reoccupied the region in September 1943, show signs of the further moving of bodies.

The truth was obscured by the denials and claims of the Soviets, who moved some of the bodies after the war to create an entirely new cemetery, turning it into a monument to German barbarity. It was only in 1992, after the end of the Cold War and the demise of the Soviet Union, that the Russian government produced the document signed by Stalin and other members of the Politburo, authorising the murder of up to twenty-two thousand Polish officers and other prisoners. The truth of who ordered the massacre and who carried it out is now clear. The photographs have helped to establish precisely where the atrocity took place and where the bodies of so many Poles now lie.[21]

No doubt aerial photographs will be used to clear up many more historical controversies, whether they concern appalling crimes or simple matters of misidentification. The American photoanalysts who found the Auschwitz photographs expressed their firm belief that 'aerial photography, interpreted with modern intelligence techniques and equipment, is a research source which could be profitably mined by the professional historian'.[22]

After the war ended, a secret history of aerial photography was written so that the lessons learnt in the Second World War would not be forgotten as those of the First World War had been. It noted that 'just as the reconnaissance pilots were triumphantly demonstrating an entirely new method of securing photos over enemy territory ... so did the photographic interpreters ... experience the stimulus of extracting information of vital interest from photos'. There was a powerful sense of excitement at the pioneering of new techniques and the invention of devices to develop a new secret science. The history concluded that at Medmenham the photo interpreters displayed those qualities of 'adaptability, successful improvisation, teamwork and intolerance of official apathy or antagonism' that helped so powerfully to win the war.[23] These are fine qualities that have come to the fore at times of need on several occasions in the nation's history. In the Second World War they were a vital ingredient in helping to bring victory to the Allied cause.

Epilogue

After the end of the war in the Pacific, Medmenham began to wind down quickly. The Americans went home in August 1945. There was a rapid exodus of many of the experienced PIs, who returned to civilian life and often to distinguished careers. In December 1945, Wing Commander Glyn Daniel was demobilised and returned to Cambridge as an archaeology don. He married the WAAF he had met in India and became a prolific author of scholarly as well as very readable and popular books, including a set of detective novels. In the mid 1950s, as chair of the immensely popular quiz show *Animal, Vegetable, Mineral?*, he became one of the first television celebrities. In 1974, he succeeded Grahame Clark (who had also been at Medmenham) as Professor of Archaeology at Cambridge.

At the end of the war in Europe, Captain Derek van den Bogaerde was sent to the Far East and when demobbed he had no idea what he would do next. He got a job as a teacher but before term began he thought he would try a bit of acting. Changing his name to Dirk Bogarde, he started to look for work. Within a few years he had become a cinema legend and one of the most famous and successful movie stars of his generation.

Section Officer Sarah Churchill also went back into show business after being demobbed. She married a photographer, Anthony Beauchamp, and started a career in the movies, playing opposite Fred Astaire in *Royal Wedding*. In later years she suffered from a drink problem. After being widowed she married again, to Baron Audley. Hazel Scott left the WAAF in early 1946, did a variety of odd jobs and a few years after the war married an army officer and started a family. Like many others of her generation, she always looked back on her wartime experiences as one of the most intense and exciting times of her life.

RAF photo intelligence moved out of Medmenham to nearby Nuneham Park, which was smaller but big enough for the peacetime needs of a team of about 350 men and women. Under the terms by which Danesfield House had been requisitioned, the RAF had to pay to restore the property to its condition in 1940. It was thought that this would be so expensive that, instead, the Air Ministry finally bought the house in 1948 and it became the headquarters for 90 Group (Signals). Several senior officers lived there and the old Banqueting Hall became what was known as the most luxurious officers' mess in the country. The Air Ministry finally sold Danesfield House in 1977 and the long association between the RAF and Medmenham came to an end. Carnation Foods took the property over but in 1991 Danesfield became a luxury country house hotel and conference centre, which it still is at the time of writing. Walking through the grand wood-panelled rooms and corridors today gives just a hint of the extraordinary atmosphere that prevailed there seventy years ago.

As the Cold War escalated, the government realised that the skills of photo reconnaissance and interpretation were still going to be needed, so an entirely new organisation was established in 1947. Its mission was to monitor troop movements in

Eastern Europe, to spy on the industrial capacity of the Soviet Union and to prepare target materials for any forthcoming nuclear assault. Reconnaissance flying began again at Benson and American squadrons returned there in 1948, the year in which NATO was formed. The twin-engined Canberra jet was first used for photo reconnaissance in March 1950 and British aerial photography entered the jet age. In 1953 there was another move and a change of title. Photo intelligence was now reorganised as the Joint Air Reconnaissance Intelligence Centre, and JARIC has remained the name for British reconnaissance and imagery intelligence since. JARIC moved to RAF Brampton near Huntingdon and much of the PR flying was transferred from Benson to RAF Wyton. JARIC has assisted in every conflict in which Britain has been involved since 1945, from the Korean War, through the Malayan Emergency and the Suez Crisis, to Northern Ireland, the Falklands, the Gulf War, the Balkans, the invasion of Iraq, the war in Afghanistan and the bombing of Libya. In addition, PR and PI skills have been devoted to a wide variety of more peaceable pursuits, ranging from the study of oil pollution at sea to surveying the spread of Dutch elm disease, and from the analysis of shipping movements in the English Channel to looking for the Loch Ness monster![1] Decades of defence cuts have left JARIC as a small but immensely professional digital analysis operation. In 2012 it will be re-formed into a new, broader-based aerial analysis unit.[2]

As the Cold War intensified, the US took the lead in developing the next stages of reconnaissance technology. Lockheed, who had supplied Sidney Cotton with his 12A airliner in 1938 and had built the F-5 reconnaissance aircraft, became the major player in the game. In the first half of the 1950s, at the top secret experimental Skunk Works outside Los Angeles, Lockheed designed and built the U-2 reconnaissance plane. This could fly at seventy-five thousand feet, well out of range of Soviet fighters and anti-aircraft missiles, and had a range of 2600 miles. Then, in July 1955, ten years after the end of the war, the first post-war summit took place at Geneva. Dwight D. Eisenhower, the general who had commanded the Normandy invasion of Europe, was by now a highly popular US President. He had much experience of photo reconnaissance and had been a great admirer of the work of the photo interpreters at Medmenham. At Geneva, Eisenhower made a speech proposing that both superpowers should be free to overfly each other's territory in order to be able to verify the armaments and weapons held by the other side. This, he argued, would be an essential element of mutual deterrence – knowing what armaments and specifically what nuclear capability the other side had would deter either side from launching an attack. There was little likelihood that Nikita Khrushchev, the new Soviet leader, would agree to such a proposal. And indeed he rejected Eisenhower's idea of 'Open Skies' as an American espionage plot.

So, early the following year, Eisenhower gave the go-ahead for the U-2 to begin secret flights over the Soviet Union. Packed with cameras and other electronic instruments for the monitoring of radio and radar signals, the U-2s began to photograph huge areas of Soviet Russia. The missions were controlled not by the US Air Force but by the CIA and each flight had specific Presidential approval.[3] Soon U-2 missions were crossing Soviet airspace from bases in Pakistan and Turkey. They also flew out of the UK. For four years these new spies in the sky looked down on Soviet Russia recording everything they wanted to see. The Soviets knew they were up there and tracked each flight with radar, but they could do nothing to intercept them. Premier Khrushchev, frustrated and annoyed by the provocation, told his

Kremlin colleagues that each spying flight 'spat in the face' of the Soviet people.[4]

Then, in May 1960, a new type of long-range Soviet missile succeeded in shooting down a U-2. The Americans put out a planned cover story that the plane had got lost on a high altitude weather mission. The Soviets revealed they had captured the pilot, Francis Gary Powers, and many of the cameras and other listening devices packed into the U-2. Eisenhower accepted responsibility and a planned summit in Paris collapsed. The temperature of the Cold War dropped a few degrees.

Two years later, a new crisis erupted when Khrushchev decided to install Soviet missiles on the island of Cuba in retaliation for the presence of American missiles in Turkey, not far from the Soviet Union's southern border. By late September 1962, the building of the missile launch sites had begun in complete secrecy. From these sites nuclear warheads could be fired at most cities within the United States. On the morning of Sunday 14 October a U-2 reconnaissance aircraft flew over Cuba and photographed the missile sites under construction on the west of the island. A team of CIA analysts led by Dino Brugioni interpreted the photographs and as soon as they had identified the missile sites, they informed President Kennedy. There then began the intense two week stand-off known as the Cuban Missile Crisis.

The story of those two weeks has been told many times,[5] but it probably marks the last hurrah of photographic intelligence. The photos of the missile sites were proof of what the Soviets were up to. They were even displayed at a specially convened meeting of the UN Security Council. Fortunately, after one of the tensest moments in the Cold War, a way out of the confrontation was eventually found. The Soviet missiles were withdrawn from Cuba. And quietly, without fanfare, the American missiles were withdrawn from Turkey.

Soon after the U-2 had started operational flying, the designers at Lockheed's Skunk Works had gone back to the drawing board to create the next generation of reconnaissance aircraft. Kelly Johnson had helped to design the P38 Lightning, the forerunner of the F-5 reconnaissance aircraft of the Second World War, and had led the U-2 development programme. He now began the long process of designing a totally new kind of aircraft that would be invisible to radar and would fly at higher altitudes and faster speeds than any other aeroplane. The challenges were immense. They had to use new materials like titanium in order to stop the craft from burning up at the speeds it would travel. To prevent the aircraft from sending off radar reflections its body had to be designed in an entirely new way, with the wings blended in to the body and the forward fuselage designed to deflect radar waves. The plane was covered with a black ferrite composite material that helped further absorb radar signals. With the loss of the U-2 in 1960 the development of this new craft became doubly important. When the plane finally entered operational service in 1966 it introduced the new science of 'stealth' to the world. It could fly at eighty thousand feet on the very edge of the earth's atmosphere. And it could travel at three times the speed of sound. It was called the SR-71 'Blackbird'.

The two-man crew who flew the Blackbird were more like astronauts wearing space suits and science fiction-like helmets than conventional pilots. The plane itself looked like an elegant, aerodynamic spear and it cut through the stratosphere like a knife through butter. Its six cameras could photograph a hundred thousand square miles of territory in an hour with sufficiently high resolution to read a car registration number on the ground. It carried devices to jam anti-aircraft missiles that might be sent up against it. The Blackbird brought back a wealth of information about Soviet nuclear capability, the location of its intercontinental ballistic missiles, its fighter bases and its bomber threat. In the October war in the Middle East in 1973, the Blackbird flew over the Arab countries assessing their military capabilities. The intelligence it gathered helped America in its negotiations for a ceasefire. During this war, in a single flight from the United States and back, with six midair refuellings, the Blackbird carried out a reconnaissance mission lasting 11 hours 20 minutes. Flying from Mildenhall in England, in April 1986, a Blackbird reconnaissance plane flew over Tripoli in Libya on a damage assessment flight following the American air raid on Colonel Gaddafi's headquarters. The Blackbird was the end of the line of fast, high altitude reconnaissance aircraft that had begun with the Spitfire and the Mosquito in 1940. It broke every record and still holds the official air speed record of 2194 mph, well above Mach 3. On one of its flights, in 1974, it flew from New York to London in an incredible 1 hour 54 minutes. Despite increasingly sophisticated radar controlled anti-aircraft missiles, not a single Blackbird was ever shot down.

However, by the time of the Blackbird's arrival, aerial photography taken by aircraft was already being superseded by photography from outer space. Satellites provided the new generation of spies in the sky. The first American military reconnaissance satellite, named Corona, entered service in 1960. It took film photographs of the earth through long lens telescopic cameras. The resolution did not at that time compare with aerial photographs taken from aircraft but thanks to a series of developments in what was called the Key Hole series, the quality and detail improved dramatically. At first, these early satellites ejected the exposed film in a capsule which then parachuted towards earth and was snatched by a transport aircraft fitted with a net, a precarious-sounding system which nevertheless seemed to work well most of the time. In the mid 1960s, the satellites started using parallel cameras to photograph the same land area twice during a pass, thus acquiring stereo imagery. They had reinvented what the PIs at Medmenham had known to be an essential part of photo interpretation – working in 3D.

During the 1970s, technicians gave up using film in satellites, transferring instead to electro optical scanners, the forerunners of the digital camera. The images recorded were encrypted and sent to the earth by radio signal. By the 1980s satellites were also recording information via thermal infrared and radar imaging techniques, which had the advantage of being able to see through clouds and to photograph at night. This was a breakthrough that would have been much envied at Benson and Medmenham, freeing aerial imagery from the vagaries of cloud cover. The Soviets of course developed their own reconnaissance satellites, in what they called the Cosmos series. Just as in the First World War, when the use of reconnaissance aircraft prompted the development of other fighter aircraft to shoot them down, so each side developed anti-satellite weapons to destroy the other side's reconnaissance satellites. But the 1967 Outer Space Treaty accepted the freedom of all nations to navigate space. Both superpowers took advantage of this and spent years busily looking into each other's backyard, and at the rest of the world as well. They built huge computers and high speed data processors to analyse the vast numbers of images and to do the work that the photo interpreters had once so painstakingly done with Stereos, slide rules and measuring devices they had built themselves.

During the Cold War most of this technology and the intelligence imagery recorded (known as IMINT) were kept top secret. But after the end of the Cold War, Russia began to sell the images recorded by its satellites on the open market. Countries that could not afford their own spy satellites began to buy the images they needed. That prompted the next revolution in aerial reconnaissance and surveillance, when in 1995 the Clinton administration declassified more than eight hundred thousand images taken by the American Corona spy satellites. Following this, private operators like IKONOS and Quickbird began to gather and sell satellite imagery. Commercial satellites were already being used extensively for weather forecasting and for communications. And in the last few years the distinction between military surveillance and commercial usage has become blurred. Some of the images of Iraq prior to the 2003 invasion and, more recently, of possible ballistic missile sites in North Korea have been taken not by the military but by these private operators.

The most recent stage of military reconnaissance and observation has come through the use of Unmanned Aerial Vehicles (UAVs), more colloquially known as 'drones'. One class of UAV is known as Predator. These aircraft can circle a site and stay in position almost endlessly, reporting back on the progress of a mission or simply carrying out continuous surveillance of something or someone regarded as suspicious. This has become known as the 'unblinking eye'. At the Joint Operations Centre in Iraq, by 2005, three huge plasma screens at one end of the room continuously relayed live pictures from different operations. Different teams from Intelligence, Operations, Medical and even a lawyer could constantly watch what was happening and call up aerial images from orbiting drones. Officers working at the centre called it the 'Death Star', because at any moment 'you could just reach out with a finger, as it were, and eliminate somebody.' Others watching incoming missiles or bombs impact their target live on the plasma screens referred to it as 'Kill TV'.

Up to three Predator drones could be in use in any one operation to ensure there was backup in the case of technical failures, and the imagery was continuous. According to one US intelligence chief, 'intelligence, surveillance and reconnaissance are most effective ... [when applied] 24/7 to achieve a greater understanding of how the enemy's network operates by building a pattern of life analysis.'[6] Although no one would have used these words at the time, in a sense building a 'pattern of life analysis' of the 'enemy's network' was precisely what they had been doing at Medmenham. But by the twenty-first century this was happening 'live' in real time, and the battle zone had become a digital battlefield.

Seventy years ago a remarkable group of talented men and women pioneered a secret science using aerial imagery. Today, battles are watched and controlled from anywhere around the world as commanders and politicians follow real-time aerial imagery from the battle zone. And anyone on their computer screen at home can look at aerial images of almost any street anywhere in the world. The rest is ... Google Earth.

Author's Note

I have my own modest story of using an aerial photograph to correct a small detail of history. In August 2003, I interviewed Captain Dick Winters, the leader of Easy Company in the 506th Parachute Regiment of the US 101st Airborne Division, for a television documentary.[1] Winters wrote a detailed memoir of the role of Easy Company from its early formation, through D-Day, Eindhoven and Bastogne, to the capture of the Eagle's Nest in Berchtesgaden in May 1945. His account became the basis for Stephen Ambrose's best-selling book *Band of Brothers*, and Ambrose's book was developed into the hugely successful, award-winning television series of the same name.[2] In both these versions Dick Winters (played by Damian Lewis in the TV series) is the central character as the commander of Easy Company. He had been a remarkable leader of men more than sixty years ago. And, even aged in his late eighties, he was a deeply impressive man to meet.

One incident that Winters relates is the capture of a 105 mm gun battery at Brécourt Manor, behind Utah beach, on the morning of D-Day, 6 June, to prevent it from firing down on to the beach and causing a massacre. Winters' account of this heroic episode, in which a small force of only twelve para-troopers under his command overwhelmed a well-defended position held by about fifty German paratroopers, was written up just a few days after the action when he was in hospital suffering from a minor injury. The incident was still fresh in his mind and he had no doubts about the accuracy of his memory. His account of capturing the guns is still used at the military academy at West Point as an example of how a small, well-led assault force can overcome and rout a much larger force in a well-defended position.

After the interview, in which he retold this story, I showed Winters an aerial photograph I had with me, taken over Brécourt Manor at about 11 a.m. on 6 June, just after Easy Company had taken control of the battery. The photo was blown up to poster size. Winters studied it with fascination and then puzzlement. He looked at it from several different angles. He asked me again when it was taken and I confirmed it had been taken on the very morning he captured the battery. Then, a little confused, he admitted that the layout of the guns in the picture was different to how he remembered it. There were four guns, sure enough, but they were in a different alignment. He showed me from his personal memoir the actual drawing he had made. They were not the way he had drawn them just a few days after the attack. Dick Winters had got it wrong. Stephen Ambrose had got it wrong. The film makers had got it wrong. West Point had it wrong.

In the end, this was a small thing. Winters had still captured the battery of four heavy guns. A small, lightly equipped attacking force had still overcome a much stronger group of defenders. But once again, an aerial photograph had been able to correct the record, in this case an old veteran's memory. He was glad of the correction and delighted to see his old battlefield, as it were

frozen in time on a black and white aerial photograph. He grace-
fully admitted that the camera can never lie. It is a fine epitaph
to the remarkable story of aerial photography in the Second
World War.

Acknowledgements

One hot day in the summer of 2003, Chris Going paid a visit to an independent television production company to talk about his work with historic aerial photographs. Going is an archaeologist who has gone on to work with computer programs to interpret aerial photography. My own fascination with photo intelligence and the story both of how aerial photographs were taken and how they were interpreted began on that day. Out of our meeting came the idea of a format for a television documentary that would create computerised graphic imagery of battlefields from aerial photographs actually taken during the course of the battle.

I was lucky enough to produce for Flashback Television a series of twenty-five programmes using this technique called *The Lost Evidence*. Commissioned by the History Channel in the US, the programmes proved a great success and have since been shown all around the world. So, in addition to thanking Chris Going, who aroused my own interest in the subject of aerial photography, I'd like to thank all the people who worked at Flashback on *The Lost Evidence*, with whom discussion and debate suggested some of the ideas covered in this book. They include David Edgar, Jobim Sampson, Paul Nelson, Tim Ball, Rachel Naughton, Una Shinners, Jacqui Edwards, Paul Bell, Stuart Heaney, Steve Baker, Gareth Johnson, Ashley Gething, Owen Parker, David Caldwell-Evans, Oliver Baker, Alex Leithead, Colin Barratt, Claire Titley, Miriam Honeyball, James Barker, Laureen Walker, Gerhard Elfers, Cherry Brewer, Stuart Rose, Ben Taylor, Chris Roots and Lucy Carter. Thank you all for your ideas and inspiration.

When studying the history of aerial photography and photo intelligence during the Second World War you cannot go far before coming across the Medmenham Club. This organisation is run by a team who have all had distinguished careers as photo interpreters in the post-war era. The help I have received from Mike Mockford, a leading figure in the organisation, has gone beyond all normal bounds. He has been generous with his own time, supremely efficient in all dealings across a couple of years and could not have been more helpful in opening the collection's archive at RAF Brampton to me. Chris and Christine Halsall, who work with Mike and are also prominent figures in the Club, have been equally helpful in passing on suggestions, ideas and recommendations. I owe an immense debt of gratitude to Mike and Shirley, Chris and Christine. The world of photo intelligence is supremely lucky in having them as the keepers of its flame.

I was delighted to be able to interview, in February and March 2010, several veterans who worked at Medmenham and its outstations during the war. It was a pleasure and a privilege to meet them and I thank them all for their time and their insights. Their contributions are individually acknowledged in the text and the notes.

I would like to thank the archivists and librarians at many institutions for their help and generous support. These include

Allen Packwood and the very helpful staff of the Churchill Archives Centre at Churchill College, Cambridge; the staffs of the RAF Museum at Hendon, of the Liddell Hart Centre at Kings College, London, of the Institute of Historical Research, London, and of the London Library; and, of course, the equally helpful and hard-working staff at the National Archives in Kew. I would also like to thank Suzanne Bardgett, Steve Woolford and Sean Rehling of the Imperial War Museum for arranging to show me the magnificent set of models made at Medmenham that survive in their collection at Duxford. The models are a remarkable tribute to the dedication and obsession with detail shown by the model makers.

Extracts from documents held by the Medmenham Collection Archive and photographs from the Collection are reproduced by courtesy of the Trustees of the Medmenham Collection.

At Little, Brown I want to thank Tim Whiting for his encouragement and support from the beginning, and Claudia Dyer and Iain Hunt for their wise recommendations and enthusiastic oversight of the project. Many thanks also to Steve Gove for his work on the manuscript.

Finally, as always, my thanks go to Anne for her patience and support.

Taylor Downing
April 2011

Glossary

Photo intelligence units

ACIU – Allied Central Interpretation Unit, formerly the CIU (see below), renamed from May 1944 to reflect the fact that RAF Medmenham had become a full Allied operation staffed mostly by British and American officers, but also consisting of Poles, French, Norwegians, Canadians, and others

CIU – Central Interpretation Unit, the central unit at which all photographic interpretation was organised, located at Danesfield House and called RAF Medmenham from April 1941 to the end of the war

Heston Flight – the unit set up by Sidney Cotton in the early months of the Second World War outside the formal structure of the RAF to experiment with new techniques of using fast Spitfires for photo reconnaissance, based in secret at the civilian airfield of Heston to the west of London. The men in this unit called themselves 'Sid Cotton's Air Force'

Paduoc House – the offices of the PIU

PI – photographic interpretation *and* photo interpreter

PIU – Photographic Interpretation Unit, the photo interpretation unit led by Peter Riddell at Wembley after the Aircraft Operating Company was requisitioned by the RAF in June 1940

PR – photographic reconnaissance

PRU – Photographic Reconnaissance Unit, the reconnaissance team flying out of Heston after Geoffrey Tuttle took over from Sidney Cotton in June 1940

Photo interpretation terms

Photogrammetry – the process of measuring the size of objects from aerial photographs, reliant upon knowing the scale of the photograph. The large Swiss-built Wild (pronounced *vilt*) A5 Stereo Plotter was designed to do this but it could also be done by any small scale measuring device

Scale – the ratio of the size of a photograph to the size of the area it covers. At the beginning of the war the RAF believed aerial photos had to be of a scale of 1:10,000 for useful information to be extracted. Improvements in interpreting techniques meant that military intelligence could be interpreted from scales of 1:25,000 or even smaller. The scale of an aerial photo is determined by the height above ground of the reconnaissance aircraft and the focal length of the camera lenses being used

Slide Rule – mechanical device for carrying out mathematical calculations; like a ruler with a slidable strip graduated with logarithmic scales of numbers. Used by photo interpreters to calculate the scale of an aerial photograph

Stereo – a small device like a pair of glasses on a mount, used for viewing two stereo photographs in order to get a 3D effect

Stereo pair – the two matching aerial photos that create a 3D effect when viewed on a Stereo

Third Phase PI Sections at Medmenham

A Section – naval and shipping

B Section – army, officially known as the Army Photographic Intelligence Section (APIS)

C Section – enemy airfields, led for some time by Ursula Powys-Lybbe

D Section – industry in occupied Europe

E Section – enemy camouflage

F Section – railways and transport

G Section – radio, radar and wireless, led by Claude Wavell

K Section – damage assessment

L Section – aircraft section, led by Constance Babington Smith

N Section – night photography during bombing raids, led by Bernard Babington Smith

Q Section – hunting for decoys, led by Geoffrey Dimbleby

V Section – model making

W Section – photogrammetric or detailed measuring of objects on aerial photographs

T Section – preparing of Target folders for bomber crews, led by Bertram Rota

Z Section – Second Phase unit including some specialist groups like the 'Topographical' Special Forces team

Other terms

Flak – anti-aircraft fire often consisting of shells exploding at high altitude around an aircraft. Actually derived from the German word for 'aircraft defence canon', **Fliegerabwehrkanone**, but universally used

Gee – navigational aid used from March 1942 by RAF Bomber Command to create a lattice-type grid of signals across northern Europe. By picking these up an aircraft could identify its own location to an accuracy of about 2 miles

H2 S – form of radar mapping used from 1943 by RAF Bomber Command. An aircraft carried its own short range radar and the navigator could identify key features of the landscape below on a circular screen

Hedgehog – steel stakes planted along beaches that the enemy imagined might be used for Allied landings, intended to destroy landing craft

HUMINT – intelligence from human resources, e.g. agents or resistance groups

Oboe – navigational aid used from 1943 by RAF Bomber Command, using two sets of radar signals transmitted from southern England to guide pathfinder aircraft to a target within an accuracy of about a hundred yards. Its limitation was that it was only effective up to about 250 miles from the English coast

Rommel's Asparagus – iron and steel rods planted in fields that the enemy imagined might be used for Allied landing or drop zones, intended to destroy gliders

SIGINT – intelligence from intercepting enemy signals, e.g. the code breaking of Enigma messages

Ultra – generic term for all the signals intelligence derived from decoding the German Enigma messages

Window – tiny strips of metal foil, dropped by the thousand to blind enemy radar, as in the bombing of Hamburg, July 1943

Notes

Abbreviations:
MED – Medmenham Collection, RAF Brampton
NA – National Archives, Kew
CHURCHILL – Churchill Archives Centre, Churchill College, Cambridge
RAFM – RAF Museum, Hendon

Prologue

1 This description of flying a reconnaissance mission is taken from several interviews with pilots and from many written accounts, including MED: DFG 5778, an undated account by John Saffrey written during the war, and MED: DFG 5693, Constance Babington Smith [CBS] Papers, interview notes with Gordon Hughes, 26 April 1956.
2 Col. Roy Stanley, *World War II Photo Intelligence*, p. 3.

Introduction

1 The word *boffin*, although not widely used today, in the 1940s was armed forces slang for a technician or research scientist who worked often anonymously and in secret. It was usually used affectionately, unlike modern equivalents such as *geek* or *nerd*. Its origins are obscure but it might have derived from a late 1930s abbreviation

of 'back office intelligence'. See Ronald Clark, *The Rise of the Boffins*, pp. 1ff.

2 For instance, Robert Harris, *Enigma* (1995) and the film of the book, with a script by Tom Stoppard (dir. Michael Apted, Manhattan Pictures International, 2001, starring Dougray Scott and Kate Winslet); *Station X*, the TV series (Darlow Smithson for Channel 4, 1998) and book by Michael Smith. The most recent histories include Asa Briggs, *Secret Days: Codebreaking in Bletchley Park* (2011); Ralph Erskine and Michael Smith, *The Bletchley Park Codebreakers* (2011); Sinclair McKay, *The Secret Life of Bletchley Park* (2010); B. Jack Copeland (and others), *Colossus: The Secret of Bletchley Park's Code Breaking Computers* (2010) and many others. Amazon.co.uk (accessed in April 2011) lists 122 titles.

3 The only two books that tell the story of Medmenham in any detail were written by former photo interpreters who had worked there during the war. Constance Babington Smith's *Evidence in Camera* was published in 1957 and Ursula Powys-Lybbe's *The Eye of Intelligence* in 1983.

4 Peter Mead, *The Eye in the Air*, pp. 11–15. For the Romantic poets like Shelley, Coleridge and Wordsworth, ballooning represented a symbol of hope and liberation, a means of escape from earthly concerns. See Richard Holmes, *The Age of Wonder*, pp. 161–2.

5 National Army Museum: *Manual of Military Ballooning*, School of Ballooning, Aldershot, 1896, p. 14.

6 Percy Walker, *Early Aviation at Farnborough*, Vol 1 p. 33.

7 Peter Reese, *The Flying Cowboy*, pp. 9–12.

8 Peter Mead, *The Eye in the Air*, p. 35.

9 H.G. Wells, 'Of a cross-channel passage', *Daily Mail*, 27 July 1909.

10 Taylor Downing, *Churchill's War Lab*, pp. 29–31.

11 Mead, *The Eye in the Air*, p. 46.

12 Walter Raleigh, *The War in the Air*, Vol. I, p. 9.

13 Roy Conyers Nesbit, *Eyes of the RAF*, p. 37.

14 Col. Roy Stanley, *World War II Photo Intelligence*, p. 26.

15 Douglas Haig, *War Diaries and Letters 1914–1918*, ed. Gary Sheffield and John Bourne, p. 403.

16 Nesbit, *Eyes of the RAF*, pp. 43–4.

17 H.A. Jones, *The War in the Air*, Vol. V, p. 228.

18 *Biographical Memoirs of Fellows of the Royal Society*, Vol. 9, November 1963, pp. 292–7.

19 The War Manual of 1928 ruled that 'the air force is responsible for taking and developing air-photographs while the army is responsible for their interpretation and distribution', *War Manual*, July 1928, ch. XII, para 27.

20 *Axis*, Vol. 8, 1937; Alexandra Harris, *Romantic Moderns*, pp. 25–9.

21 Nesbit, *Eyes of the RAF*, p. 63.

Chapter 1 – Secret Missions

1 Ralph Barker and Sidney Cotton, *Aviator Extraordinary*, p. 37.

2 Keith Jeffery, *MI6: The History of the Secret Intelligence Service 1909–1949*, pp. 295–9; F.W. Winterbotham, *The Nazi Connection*, pp. 50ff.

3 Barker and Cotton, *Aviator Extraordinary*, p. 113.

4 Winterbotham, *The Nazi Connection*, p. 194.

5 Bob Niven's log book records a total of at least twenty spying flights between February 1939 and the outbreak of war; see NA: AIR 41/6, Appendix V.

6 Fred Winterbotham says these photographs of Wilhelmshaven were not taken by Cotton at all but by Bob Niven on a separate sortie after war had been declared; Winterbotham, *The Nazi Connection*, p. 200. The only two first-hand accounts of these events from Fred Winterbotham and Sidney Cotton differ significantly on many aspects of the story and reflect the fact that the two men, allies at first in establishing how to carry out successful photo reconnaissance, later fell out.

7 Barker and Cotton, *Aviator Extraordinary*, p. 139.

8 NA: AIR 41/6, pp. 67, 84. See also MED: MHP 16, Douglas Kendall, *A War of Intelligence*, unpublished memoir, p. 64.

9 Barker and Cotton, *Aviator Extraordinary*, pp. 152–3.

10 Ibid., pp. 153–4.

Chapter 2 – Sid Cotton's Air Force

1 NA: AIR 41/6, Appendix XII. Longbottom's eight-page Memorandum is one of the key documents in the development of aerial photography.

Correctly predicting many of the features that came to characterise photo reconnaissance flying, it argues that the best method of avoiding anti-aircraft fire and enemy fighters 'appears to be the use of a small machine, relying solely on its speed, climb, and ceiling to avoid destruction . . . It would have no use for its armament or radio, and these could be removed, to provide extra available weight for more fuel, in order to get the necessary range, which a fighter does not normally have . . . In clear weather the aircraft would fly at a great height all the time it was over enemy territory . . . and with its great speed and advantage of height it could almost certainly elude fighters coming up to intercept it.' Longbottom calls for reconnaissance flights at thirty thousand feet with Leica 250 cameras, which would produce photos of a scale of 1:22,500. He recommends using fine-grain film, which gives extra detail, with standard RAF red filters known as Type 5 filter. For camouflage he suggests painting the underside of aircraft 'a pale blue with a dull surface to avoid reflections'. He also stresses the need for the pilot to be a qualified navigator, as in a small machine 'the facilities for accurate navigation are few'. And he predicts that 'Accurate forecasts of the upper winds would be a most important factor.' There are hardly any key factors in the development of aerial photography that are not addressed in Longbottom's historic Memorandum of August 1939.

2 Ralph Barker and Sidney Cotton, *Aviator Extraordinary*, p. 158.

3 NA: AIR 41/6, p. 78.

4 According to Jack Eggleston, a member of the Heston Flight, in Roy Conyers Nesbit, *Eyes of the RAF*, p. 90. See also MED: MHP 16, Douglas Kendall, *A War of Intelligence*, unpublished memoir, pp. 64–5.

5 NA: AIR 41/6, p. 113 – Bomber Command PIS Final Interpretation Report Nos. 129 and 131, 15 May 1940.

6 MED: MDM 1106, Lemnos Hemming, *Early World War II Aerial Reconnaissance*, unpublished paper, March 1946.

7 MED: DFG 161, Early Papers of the Aircraft Operation Company, pp. 2–3.

8 Barker and Cotton, *Aviator Extraordinary*, p. 168.

9 Ibid., p. 169; Nesbit, *Eyes of the RAF*, p. 93.

10 NA: AIR 41/6, p. 114.

11 Barker and Cotton, *Aviator Extraordinary*, pp. 173–7.

12 NA: AIR 41/6, pp. 115–16.

13 Barker and Cotton, *Aviator Extraordinary*, p. 183.

14 NA: AIR 41/6, p. 93.

15 Barker and Cotton, *Aviator Extraordinary*, p. 194.

16 Ursula Powys-Lybbe, *The Eye of Intelligence*, pp. 30–1.

17 F.W. Winterbotham, *The Nazi Connection*, p. 201.

18 Barker and Cotton, *Aviator Extraordinary*, pp. 199–200.

Chapter 3 – Crisis

1 NA: AIR 41/6, p. 189; F.H. Hinsley, *British Intelligence in the Second World War*, Vol. 1, pp. 170–1.

2 NA: AIR 41/6, p. 196.

3 For the general context of the dramatic events in the summer of 1940 see Taylor Downing, *Churchill's War Lab*, pp. 114–48.

4 Winston Churchill, *The Second World War*, Vol. II, pp. 295–6.

5 Denis Richards, *Royal Air Force 1939–1945*, Vol. I, *The Fight at Odds*, p. 161.

6 NA: CAB 66/9/24.

7 NA: AIR 41/6, p. 219: PIU Report 181, 21 July 1940.

8 Ibid., p. 222: Combined Intelligence Committee Report no. 85 Annexe A, 23 August 1940.

9 Ibid., p. 227: CIC Report no. 99 Annexe A, 6 September 1940.

10 Ibid., p. 229.

11 Charles Eade (compiler), *Secret Session Speeches by the Right Hon. Winston Churchill*, pp. 22–3.

12 Constance Babington Smith, *Evidence in Camera*, p. 62; Ursula Powys-Lybbe, *The Eye of Intelligence*, pp. 22–4.

13 NA: AIR 41/6, p. 230 – PIU Report no. 477, 19 September 1940.

14 Ibid., p. 224 – CIC Report no. 93 Annexe A, 31 August 1940.

15 Ibid., p. 235.

16 Babington Smith, *Evidence in Camera*, p. 29.

17 The RAF were good at recruiting scientists or specialists with urgently required skills straight into active service. The Army always insisted that everyone had to go through months of basic training but this did not apply in the RAF. This author's father, Peter Downing, was recruited into the top secret world of RAF operational research in October 1942 and had the same experience as Glyn Daniel of being

put straight into an officer's uniform. On being saluted in the street he had to rely on vague memories from the school cadet corps of how to salute back!

18　Glyn Daniel, *Some Small Harvest*, pp. 107–9.

19　MED: MHP 16, Douglas Kendall, *A War of Intelligence*, unpublished memoir, p. 74.

20　MED: PRJ 304, 'History of the Plotting Section at ACIU', written 1945, pp. 1–10. Here it is noted that the initial choice of women as plotters was due to the shortage of manpower but 'experience has proved that they are probably more suitable than men for this type of work'. The report, however, still concludes that there is far better 'execution of orders' if the plotters are put under the command of a (male) RAF officer.

21　Babington Smith, *Evidence in Camera*, p. 51.

22　Women were also trained by the RAF to do equal work with men as radar operators.

23　MED: DFG 6301, Memo from Works Section Officer re damage to AOC premises by bomb blast, 2 November 1940.

24　NA: AIR 41/6, p. 249.

25　Ibid., p. 258, minute dated 25 February 1941.

Chapter 4 – Medmenham

1　Glyn Daniel, *Some Small Harvest*, p. 131.

2　NA: AIR 41/7, p. 1.

3　Brian Urquhart, *A Life in Peace and War*, p. 52.

4　NA: AIR 41/6, p. 105.

5　MED: MDM 544, 'Biographical Notes on Alfred "Steve" Stephenson OBE', compiled by Christine Halsall for the Medmenham Collection, 2004.

6　Ursula Powys-Lybbe, *The Eye of Intelligence*, p. 48.

7　MED: MDM 241, Robert Idris Jones, *Royal Air Force Days 1939–1945*, unpublished memoir, p. 6.

8　Powys-Lybbe, *The Eye of Intelligence*, p. 48.

9　Constance Babington Smith, *Evidence in Camera*, p. 68.

10　Interview with Hazel Scott, who was on the same course as Sarah Churchill, 23 February 2010.

11 Interview with Elizabeth Hick (née Johnston-Smith), 11 March 2010.

12 MED: MHP 16, Douglas Kendall, *A War of Intelligence*, unpublished memoir, pp. 62, 73.

13 Powys-Lybbe, *The Eye of Intelligence*, p. 187.

14 MED: PRJ 296, 'History of G Section', written in 1945; Powys-Lybbe, *The Eye of Intelligence*, pp. 185–7; Babington Smith, *Evidence in Camera*, p. 147; Roy Conyers Nesbit, *Eyes of the RAF*, p. 107.

15 NA: AIR 41/7, p. 25.

16 There was considerable exaggeration after the war as to the numbers of photographs arriving at Medmenham for interpretation. The figures here are based on detailed analyses made during the war; see MED: PRJ 315, 'Historical Record of ACIU' and MED: PRJ 316, 'History of Central Print Library', both written in 1945, and MED: MDM 16, *The Chalk House with the Tudor Chimneys*, an unofficial but accurate photo album of the work at Medmenham made in 1945. For the total numbers working at Medmenham, see MED: MHP 16, Kendall, *A War of Intelligence*, p. 71. For the variation between numbers of exactly how many prints were stored and duplicates made, see for instance Powys-Lybbe, *The Eye of Intelligence*, pp. 42–4.

17 Bletchley Park is now accessible as a museum containing many details of the code-breaking story and is also the location of the National Museum of Computing; see http://www.bletchleypark.org.uk/

Chapter 5 – The Mad Men of Ham

1 Interview with Elizabeth Hick (née Johnston-Smith), 11 March 2010.

2 Interview with Geoffrey Stone, 10 March 2010.

3 Interview with Elizabeth Hick (the widow of Ernest 'Toby' Hick), 11 March 2010.

4 Glyn Daniel, *Some Small Harvest*, pp. 98–9; MED: MHP 16, Douglas Kendall, *A War of Intelligence*, unpublished memoir, p. 74; MED: KHG 206, 'Biographical Note on Prof Dorothy Garrod CBE' by Christine Halsall, 2005.

5 Daniel, *Some Small Harvest*, p. 132.

6 Sarah Churchill, *Keep on Dancing*, p. 63; interviews with Hazel Scott, 23 February 2010, and Suzie Morgan, 11 March 2010.

7 Churchill, *Keep on Dancing*, passim.

8 CHURCHILL: CHAR 1/369, 68–70.

9 Interview with Len Chance, 23 February 2010.

10 MED: MHP 16, Kendall, *A War of Intelligence*, p. 83.

11 Churchill, *Keep on Dancing*, pp. 63–4.

12 Interview with Howard Pickard, 17 February 2010.

13 Interviews with Hazel Scott, 23 February 2010, and Suzie Morgan, 11 March 2010.

14 Churchill, *Keep on Dancing*, p. 66; MED: MHP 16, Kendall, *A War of Intelligence*, pp. 76–7.

15 Daniel, *Some Small Harvest*, p. 132.

16 MED: MDM 242, Francis Cator, unpublished memoir, p. 65.

17 Ibid., pp. 70–2.

18 Interview with Len Chance, 23 February 2010.

19 MED: MHP 16, Kendall, *A War of Intelligence*, p. 78; interview with Gordon Stone, 10 March 2010.

Chapter 6 – Boffins at War

1 Ursula Powys-Lybbe, *The Eye of Intelligence*, pp. 93–5.

2 Winston Churchill, *The Second World War*, Vol. II, p. 529.

3 See Taylor Downing, *Churchill's War Lab*, pp. 214ff for a summary of the campaign to defeat the U-boat peril.

4 Powys-Lybbe, *The Eye of Intelligence*, pp. 116–21.

5 MED: PRJ 308, 'History of the Model Making Section', written 1945. The scale of the models vary from 1:6000 for those covering a large area to 1:500 for those depicting a much smaller area. Some of these models are still viewable in displays, for instance in the Airborne Assault Museum at Duxford; see http://www.airborneassault.org.uk/home/html/index.html. Many other models are held in store by the Imperial War Museum at Duxford and are used occasionally in exhibitions; see: http://duxford.iwm.org.uk

6 Powys-Lybbe, *The Eye of Intelligence*, pp. 60–6. The creation of 3D computer terrain models of the landscape from a mosaic of aerial photographs was at the heart of the series *The Lost Evidence* (producer: Taylor Downing; Flashback Television, 25 programmes between 2004 and 2007 for the US History Channel and shown

around the world). The computer-generated model was, of course, virtual rather than real but it was possible to fly around the CGI model and, for instance, up and down the D-Day beaches, or over the monastery at Monte Cassino, or around the island of Iwo Jima, and to look at any battle from both sides of the front line as it was raging, captured on the aerial photos.

7   Powys-Lybbe, *The Eye of Intelligence*, pp. 146–7.

8   Constance Babington Smith, *Evidence in Camera*, pp. 69–70.

9   MED: PRJ 300, 'History of L Section', written 1945.

10   Powys-Lybbe, *The Eye of Intelligence*, p. 84–6.

11   MED: MHP 16, Douglas Kendall, *A War of Intelligence*, unpublished memoir, p. 55.

12   MED: PRJ 298, memo from Group Captain Stewart dated 8 September 1942. A handwritten note from Kendall at the bottom of the memo shows that he was in full support of establishing *Evidence in Camera*.

13   MED: DFG 5785, CBS Papers, interview with Peter Stewart, 26 July 1956.

14   Sets of *Evidence in Camera* are available in many specialist libraries and the March 1945 edition has been republished in facsimile; see http://www.geoinformationgroup.co.uk/products/historic-aerial-photography

15   Col. Roy Stanley, *World War Two Photo Intelligence*, pp. 71–2.

Chapter 7 – A Rare Form of Bravery

1   MED: DFG 5791, CBS Papers, interview with Geoffrey Tuttle, 9 and 10 May 1956.

2   NA: AIR 41/6, p. 131.

3   Constance Babington Smith, *Evidence in Camera*, p. 54.

4   NA: AIR 41/6, p. 89.

5   Ibid., p. 90.

6   Nigel Smith, *Tirpitz: The Halifax Raids*, p. 60.

7   MED: DFG 5692, CBS Papers, interview with Gordon Hughes, 26 April 1956.

8   Roy Conyers Nesbit, *Eyes of the RAF*, p. 108.

9   Michael Bowyer, *Action Stations Revisited*, pp. 36ff.

10 Details of an 'average' reconnaissance flight come from a variety of sources and interviews including RAFM: *Coastal Command Review*, passim; MED: DFG 5692, CBS Papers, interview with Gordon Hughes, 26 April 1956; and also the interview with Richard Cussons in Smith, *Tirpitz: The Halifax Raids*, pp. 303–4.

11 Martin Francis, *The Flyer*, pp. 35–6.

12 Denis Richards, *Royal Air Force 1939–45*, Vol. 1, p. 225.

13 MED: DFG 5690, CBS Papers, interview with Eve Holiday, 30 May 1956.

14 Edward Leaf, *Above All Unseen*, pp. 63–4; MED: DFG 5691, CBS Papers, interview with Eve Holiday, 9 August 1956.

15 Flight Lieutenant Alfred Fane Peers Fane's diary is quoted in Ursula Powys-Lybbe, *The Eye of Intelligence*, pp. 109–10.

16 Winston Churchill, *The Second World War*, Vol. IV, p. 98. The quote is from a minute sent by Churchill dated 25 January 1942.

17 Smith, *Tirpitz: The Halifax Raids*, pp. 22, 94–5. Nigel Smith interviewed Squadron Leader Richard Cussons in the writing of his book. Cussons died in 2008.

18 NA: AIR 34/86; Leaf, *Above All Unseen*, pp. 73–4; Nesbit, *Eyes of the RAF*, pp. 122–6; Powys-Lybbe, *The Eye of Intelligence*, pp. 111–12.

19 RAFM: *Coastal Command Review*, November 1944, Vol. III No. 11.

20 MED: DFG 5690 & 5691, CBS Papers, interviews with Eve Holiday, 30 May and 9 August 1956.

21 RAFM: *Coastal Command Review*, October 1944, Vol. I No. 6.

Chapter 8 – The 'Warby' Legend

1 Tony Spooner, *Warburton's War*, p. 59.

2 Originally quoted in an article by Roy Nash on Warburton in *The Star* in 1958, and repeated in Spooner, *Warburton's War*, p. 67.

3 Denis Richards and Hilary St George Saunders, *Royal Air Force 1939–1945*, Vol. II, p. 181.

4 Spooner, *Warburton's War*, p. 93.

5 As well as the news coverage, a BBC *Timewatch*, 'The Mystery of the Missing Ace', was made on the Warburton story (producer: Lawrence Rees; transmitted 14 November 2003).

Chapter 9 – Finding the Targets

1 A.J.P. Taylor, *English History 1939–1945*, p. 459.
2 MED: DFG 5788, CBS Papers, interview with Hugh Hamshaw Thomas, 11 August 1956.
3 For the different accounts of who locked the PIs inside their office and refused to let them out, see MED: DFG 5772, CBS Papers, interview with Peter Riddell, 17 August 1957; MED: MDM 241, Robert Idris Jones, *Royal Air Force Days 1939–1945*, unpublished memoir, p. 4. See also Constance Babington Smith, *Evidence in Camera*, pp. 71–6; Sir Charles Webster and Noble Frankland, *The Strategic Air Offensive Against Germany 1939–1945*, Vol. 1, p. 141.
4 Ministry of Information, *Bomber Command*, p. 30.
5 Webster and Frankland, *The Strategic Air Offensive against Germany 1939–1945*, Vol. 1, p. 125.
6 See for instance Taylor Downing, *Churchill's War Lab*, pp. 237–48; Max Hastings, *Bomber Command*, pp. 106–22.
7 NA: 41/7, pp. 25–30; MED: PRJ 301, 'Historical Report on N Section', written 1945; Babington Smith, *Evidence in Camera*, pp. 78–89; Ursula Powys-Lybbe, *The Eye of Intelligence*, pp. 162–7.
8 MED: DFG 5655, CBS Papers, interview with Bernard Babington Smith, 19 April 1956.
9 Glyn Daniel, *Some Small Harvest*, pp. 133–4.
10 Webster and Frankland, *The Strategic Air Offensive Against Germany 1939–1945*, Vol. 1, pp. 178–9; the full report appears as Appendix 13 in Webster and Frankland, *The Strategic Air Offensive Against Germany 1939–1945*, Vol. IV, pp. 205–13.
11 Winston Churchill, *The Second World War*, Vol. IV, p. 250.
12 Powys-Lybbe, *The Eye of Intelligence*, pp. 67–70.
13 MED: PRJ 301, 'Historical report of N Section'.
14 NA: AIR 41/7, pp. 8–9.
15 *Target for Tonight*, photographed by Jonah Jones; edited by Stewart McAllister; written and directed by Harry Watt; Crown Film Unit, 1941, approx 45 mins. The film is preserved in the film collection of the Imperial War Museum. It is distributed on DVD by DD Home Entertainment and the Imperial War Museum.
16 Harry Watt's previous films include documentary classics like *Night Mail* (with Basil Wright) for the General Post Office Film Unit in 1936

and *London Can Take It* (with American reporter Quentin Reynolds reporting from London during the Blitz) for the Ministry of Information in 1940.

17 Daniel, *Some Small Harvest*, p. 135.

18 *The Dam Busters*, producer: Robert Clark; director: Michael Anderson; script by R.C. Sherriff based on the book by Paul Brickhill; Associated British Picture Corporation, 1955, starring Michael Redgrave as Barnes Wallis and Richard Todd as Guy Gibson. In the making of the film great effort was put into getting details right and many of those involved in the raid, including Barnes Wallis and surviving aircrew, were regularly consulted. RAF Scampton, the real base for 617 Squadron at the time of the raid, was used as the principal location.

19 The actual Medmenham 3D model of the Möhne Dam was used in filming *The Dam Busters*, and can be seen in the sequence in which Richard Todd gives the final briefing to the crews. Elements from the original model survive and are in store at the Imperial War Museum at Duxford.

20 NA: AIR 41/7, p. 118.

Chapter 10 – Assessing the Damage

1 RAFM: *Coastal Command Quarterly Review*, May 1943, p. 17.

2 Ibid., contains reports quoting both Fray and Gillanders; MED: DFG 5681, CBS Papers, interview with Ronald Gillanders, 19 March 1957.

3 Jonathan Falconer, *The Dam Busters*, p. 158.

4 Ursula Powys-Lybbe, *The Eye of Intelligence*, p. 152.

5 MED: PRJ 299, 'The Damometer', a five-page report on the working of the apparatus, written 1945; MED: DFG 5681, CBS Papers, interview with Ronald Gillanders, 19 March 1957.

6 RAFM: *Coastal Command Quarterly Review*, September 1942, Vol. I No. 5, p. 13.

7 Edward Leaf, *Above All Unseen*, pp. 87–9; Roy Conyers Nesbit, *Eyes of the RAF*, pp. 146–9.

8 NA: AIR 41/7, p. 120.

9 MED: PRJ 299: 'Assessment of Damage from Aerial Photographs', a history written in 1945.

10 Joseph Goebbels, diary entry, 29 July 1943 (there are many English-

language editions of his diaries); Albert Speer, *Inside the Third Reich*, pp. 283–4.

11 For instance, in Taylor Downing, *Churchill's War Lab*, pp. 270–3, 353–5; Max Hastings, *Bomber Command*, pp. 346–52.

12 British Gaumont Newsreel, 9 June 1942

13 MED: DFG 5681, CBS Papers, interview with Ronald Gillanders, 19 March 1957.

Chapter 11 – To the Mediterranean and India

1 This account is not a history of all the many photo intelligence units that operated around the world. That would require a large volume and has yet to be written. This chapter is, rather, an account of how the units that were set up from West Africa to Sri Lanka grew out of the experience gained at Medmenham.

2 MED: DFG 5770, CBS Papers, interview with Peter Riddell, 18 March 1957.

3 MED: DFG 5688, CBS Papers, interview with Ray Herschel, 6 March 1957.

4 MED: DFG 5677, CBS Papers, interview with Teddy Espenhahn, 8 December 1956.

5 NA: AIR 41/7, pp. 59–62; Captain Hamish Eaton, *APIS: Soldiers with Stereo*, p. 28.

6 Glyn Daniel, *Some Small Harvest*, pp. 136–50.

7 NA: AIR 41/7, p. 73.

8 Interview with Howard Pickard, 17 February 2010.

9 Daniel, *Some Small Harvest*, pp. 150–77; MED: DFG 5672, a short unpublished memoir by Glyn Daniel dated 6 May 1956.

10 NA: AIR 41/7, pp. 62–4.

11 Hazel Scott, *Peace and War*, pp. 54ff; interview with Hazel Scott, 23 February 2010.

12 NA: AIR 41/7, p. 122; Solly Zuckerman, *From Apes to Warlords*. pp. 181-196.

13 NA: AIR 41/7, p. 123.

14 Interview with Suzie Morgan, 11 March 2010.

15 Scott, *Peace and War*, pp. 59–62.

16 Interview with Hazel Scott, 23 February 2010.

17 MED: DFG 5688, CBS Papers, interview with Ray Herschel, 6 March 1957.
18 NA: AIR 41/7, p. 67.
19 Hazel Scott, *Peace and War*, pp. 67–93; interview with Hazel Scott, 23 February 2010.

Chapter 12 – Arguments with Allies

1 Elliott Roosevelt, *As He Saw It*, pp. 52–5.
2 Constance Babington Smith, *Evidence in Camera*, pp. 126–31.
3 Dino Brugioni, *Eyes in the Sky*, p. 5.
4 Col. Roy Stanley, *World War II Photo Intelligence*, p. 60.
5 Ibid., pp. 83–9.
6 Babington Smith, *Evidence in Camera*, pp. 138–9.
7 NA: AIR 41/7, p. 78.
8 Interviews with Suzie Morgan and Elizabeth Hick, both on 11 March 2010.
9 Stanley, *World War II Photo Intelligence*, p. 247.
10 NA: AIR 41/7, p. 81.
11 This was a view noted by others; see for instance Brian Urquhart, *A Life in Peace and War*, p. 61.
12 Roosevelt, *As He Saw It*, pp. 121–2.
13 MED: MHP 16, Douglas Kendall, *A War of Intelligence*, unpublished memoir, p. 65; NA: AIR 41/7, pp. 12–15.
14 NA: AIR 41/7, p. 13.
15 Ursula Powys-Lybbe, *The Eye of Intelligence*, pp. 156–7.
16 MED: MHP 16, Kendall, *A War of Intelligence*, p. 65.
17 Roosevelt, *As He Saw It*, p. 215.

Chapter 13 – Planning for Overlord

1 See Taylor Downing, *Churchill's War Lab*, pp. 274ff.
2 MED: PRJ 290, 'Historical report of B-Section at Medmenham', written June 1945; NA: AIR 41/6, pp. 203–4.
3 Captain Hamish Eaton, *APIS: Soldiers with Stereo*, p. 19.
4 Ursula Powys-Lybbe, *The Eye of Intelligence*, pp. 130–2; Col. Roy Stanley, *World War II Photo Intelligence*, pp. 303–9.

5 MED: PRJ 290, comments by Norman Falcon on the 'Historical report of B-Section at Medmenham', dated 11 June 1970.

6 Interview with Geoffrey Stone, 10 March 2010.

7 Eaton, *APIS: Soldiers with Stereo*, p. 33.

8 Ibid., p. 36.

9 Ibid., p. 43.

10 Interview with Geoffrey Stone, 10 March 2010.

11 NA: AIR 41/7, p. 52.

12 Interview with Geoffrey Stone, 10 March 2010.

13 NA: AIR 41/7, p. 143.

14 MED: PRJ 296, 'History of G Section at Medmenham', written July 1945.

15 These photos were used in a ninety-minute documentary, *D-Day – The Lost Evidence* (producers: Taylor Downing and David Edgar; director: Jobim Sampson; Flashback Television for the History Channel, June 2004). See also Chris Going and Alun Jones, *Above the Battle: D-Day – the Lost Evidence*.

16 RAFM: X001-0788, p. 30.

Chapter 14 – Special Operations

1 There is a difference of opinion as to who first discovered that the masts at Auderville were rotating. Claude Wavell sometimes takes the credit – see Constance Babington Smith, *Evidence in Camera*, p. 148 – but in his account R.V. Jones says it was his assistant, Charles Frank, who spotted that they were rotating; see R.V. Jones, *Most Secret War*, p. 190.

2 MED: DFG 5794, CBS Papers, interview with Claude Wavell, 24 May 1956.

3 The model is on display at the Airborne Assault Museum at the Imperial War Museum, Duxford.

4 NA: AIR 41/7, p. 96; Jones, *Most Secret War*, pp. 223–49.

5 MED: DFG 5794, CBS Papers, interview with Claude Wavell, 24 May 1956. Again, R.V. Jones has a slightly different account of this story, saying it was he who linked the frames of the radar with the Zeppelin works and personally suggested the site should be bombed. See Jones, *Most Secret War*, p. 230.

6   NA: AIR 41/7, p. 99.

7   MED: MHP 16, Douglas Kendall, *A War of Intelligence*, unpublished memoir, p. 49.

8   MED: DFG 5701, CBS Papers, interview with Douglas Kendall, 14 November 1956; MED: MHP 16, Kendall *A War of Intelligence*, pp. 124–6.

9   Jones, *Most Secret War*, p. 478.

10   MED: PRJ 312, 'Historical Account of the Handling of Topographical Reports', written July 1945.

11   MED: MDM 167, *The Chalk House with Tudor Chimneys*, 1945 photographic album, includes pictures of these devices but not an account of how they worked.

12   MED: PRJ 312, 'Historical Account of the Handling of Topographical Reports', p. 7 calls the airfield Kempsford. In fact most of the Special Duty squadrons flew from RAF Tempsford in Bedfordshire.

13   Martin Gilbert, *Winston S. Churchill*, Vol. VI, *Their Finest Hour*, p. 667; Taylor Downing, *Churchill's War Lab*, pp. 183–4.

14   *Carve Her Name with Pride*, based on the book by R.J. Minney (director: Lewis Gilbert; producer: Daniel Angel for the Rank Organisation, 1958). Virginia McKenna plays Violette Szabo. There is also a drama documentary, *Now It Can Be Told*, made after the end of the war by the RAF Film Unit about the Special Operations Executive, which interestingly features two agents themselves re-enacting parts of their training and a mission behind enemy lines.

15   Freddie Clark, *Agents by Moonlight*, pp. 333–6.

16   NA: AIR 41/7, p. 139.

17   Ian Kershaw, *Hitler: 1936–1945 Nemesis*, p. 494.

18   Martin Gilbert, *Auschwitz and the Allies*, pp. 285, 303.

19   NA: AIR 19/218.

20   Gilbert, *Auschwitz and the Allies*, p. 282.

21   Interview with Hazel Scott, 23 February 2010; Dirk Bogarde, *Cleared for Take Off*, p. 18.

22   For instance in interviews with Fred Knoller, Leon Greenman and Trude Levi, all inmates of Auschwitz, for Flashback Television, 28 and 29 July 2004; Gilbert, *Auschwitz and the Allies*, p. 308.

23   Dino A. Brugioni and Robert G. Poirier, *The Holocaust Revisited: A Retrospective Analysis of the Auschwitz-Birkenau Extermination Complex*.

24   See for instance Michael J. Neufeld and Michael Berenbaum, *The*

Bombing of Auschwitz, William D. Rubinstein, *The Myth of Rescue*, and the documentary *Auschwitz: The Forgotten Evidence* (producer: Taylor Downing; director: Lucy Carter; Flashback Television for Channel 4 and FR2 France, 2005), which uses the aerial photos to explore the question of why the Allies did not bomb Auschwitz.

Chapter 15 – Hunting the Vengeance Weapons

1 Constance Babington Smith, *Evidence in Camera*, pp. 177–8.
2 Interview with Ruth Kraft, a mathematician at Peenemünde, for Flashback Television, April 2001.
3 R.V. Jones, *Most Secret War*, pp. 67–71; Taylor Downing, *Churchill's War Lab*, pp. 149ff.
4 F.H. Hinsley, *British Intelligence in the Second World War*, Vol. 3 Part 1, pp. 362–3.
5 Both documents quoted in MED: MHP 16, Douglas Kendall, *A War of Intelligence*, unpublished memoir, pp. 84–5.
6 Ursula Powys-Lybbe, *The Eye of Intelligence*, p. 189.
7 Col. Roy Stanley, *V Weapons Hunt*, p. 49.
8 NA: CAB 121/211, COS (43) 259, 17 May 1943; MED: MHP 16, Kendall, *A War of Intelligence*, p. 87.
9 MED: MHP 16, Kendall, *A War of Intelligence*, p. 86.
10 Jones, *Most Secret War*, pp. 339–41.
11 Powys-Lybbe, *The Eye of Intelligence*, p. 191.
12 The latest reinterpretation of these photos concludes that probably these two objects were not actual A4 rockets but dummies being used for training purposes. But if this is the case, then they were of the same size and dimensions and they still gave the PIs an excellent idea of what they were looking for. See Stanley, *V Weapons Hunt*, p. 64.
13 Babington Smith, *Evidence in Camera*, pp. 182–3.
14 MED: MHP 16, Kendall, *A War of Intelligence*, p. 88.
15 General Dornberger said after the war that it put work back by two months. See F.H. Hinsley, *British Intelligence in the Second World War*, Vol. 3 Part 1, p. 385.
16 Babington Smith, *Evidence in Camera*, p. 184.
17 Ian Kershaw, *Hitler: 1936–1945 Nemesis*, pp. 601, 606.
18 MED: MHP 16, Kendall, *A War of Intelligence*, p. 95.

19 Stanley, *V Weapons Hunt*, p. 79; Constance Babington Smith's own description of finding the flying bomb is in *Evidence in Camera*, pp. 193–4.

20 Constance Babington Smith said some years later that it was Ursula Kay who spotted the P-20; see Stanley, *V Weapons Hunt*, p. 84. Flight Lieutenant George Reynolds is another possibility as there is a copy of the photo attributing it to him held by the Medmenham Collection. The likelihood is that whoever first spotted something, the whole of the team were then called in to take a look and to help identify it.

21 The two first-hand accounts of this, MED: MHP 16, Kendall, *A War of Intelligence*, pp. 100–4, and Babington Smith, *Evidence in Camera*, pp. 193–9, describe a slightly different order of events. The difference is almost certainly explained by the speed at which events happened in late November/early December 1943 and the years that had passed before the two accounts were written.

22 NA: AIR 41/7, pp. 129–30.

23 MED: MHP 16, Kendall, *A War of Intelligence*, p. 114.

24 According to Douglas Kendall, the Germans thought all the information about where the launch sites were located was coming from agents rather than photographic reconnaissance; see MED: MHP 16, Kendall, *A War of Intelligence*, p. 111. This however seems unlikely bearing in mind the elaborate attempts to disguise the Belhamelin sites.

25 F.H. Hinsley, *British Intelligence in the Second World War*, Vol. 3 Part 1, p. 430.

26 Dwight D. Eisenhower, *Crusade in Europe*, p. 260.

27 NA: AIR 41/7, p. 140.

28 R.V. Jones, *Most Secret War*, pp. 436–7.

29 MED: MHP 16, Kendall, *A War of Intelligence*, pp. 120–1. In his interviews with Constance Babington Smith, Kendall was even more critical of André Kenny for not realising there was no launch site for the A-4; see MED: DFG 5701, CBS Papers, interview with Douglas Kendall, 14 November 1956.

30 Interview with Cyril Demarne, Divisional Fire Officer, West Ham Brigade, for Flashback Television, 2 April 2001.

31 MED: MHP 16, Kendall, *A War of Intelligence*, p. 122.

Chapter 16 – Towards Victory

1 RAFM: *Coastal Command Review*, July 1944, Vol. III No. 7.
2 Ibid., September 1944, Vol. III No. 9.
3 NA: AIR 41/7, p. 156.
4 RAFM: *Coastal Command Review*, March 1945, Vol. IV No. 3; NA: AIR 41/7, p. 157.
5 Interview with Geoffrey Stone, 10 March 2010.
6 F.H. Hinsley, *British Intelligence in the Second World War*, Vol. 3 Part II, pp. 382–5.
7 Brian Urquhart, *A Life in Peace and War*, pp. 71–6.
8 The Air Ministry's post-war narrative of the incident denies that any photographic reconnaissance took place on 15 September but admits there was other information from Ultra of various German units refitting near Arnhem; see NA: AIR 41/67, p. 147. But it is clear that PR did provide clear evidence that enemy troops were in the vicinity; see Hinsley, *British Intelligence in the Second World War*, Vol. 3 Part II, p. 385.
9 Dirk Bogarde, *Snakes and Ladders*, p. 60.
10 John Coldstream, *Dirk Bogarde*, p. 110.
11 Dirk Bogarde, *Cleared For Take Off*, pp. 1–42; John Coldstream, *Dirk Bogarde*, pp. 106–32.
12 NA: AIR 41/68, p. 66; Hinsley, *British Intelligence in the Second World War*, Vol. 3 Part II, p. 419.
13 Constance Babington Smith, *Evidence in Camera*, pp. 222–3.
14 MED: MHP 16, Douglas Kendall, *A War of Intelligence*, unpublished memoir, p. 142.
15 NA: 41/7, pp. 165–9.

Chapter 17 – '80 per cent of All Intelligence'?

1 NA: AIR 41/7, p. 83.
2 Col. Roy Stanley, *World War Two Photo Intelligence*, p. 3. Dino Brugioni quotes a leading US reconnaissance officer who said 80 per cent of all military intelligence in the Second World War came from aerial photography: see Dino Brugioni, *Eyes in the Sky*, p. 31.
3 CHURCHILL: CHUR 4/460 A.

4   MED: MHP 16, Douglas Kendall, *A War of Intelligence*, unpublished memoir, p. 104. Kendall notes that the praise for Babington Smith in America was 'a little exaggerated, [but] the credit was well deserved'.

5   There is a copy in the Medmenham Collection, ref: MDM 167.

6   CHURCHILL: CHUR 4/459 B, 16 April 1957.

7   RAFM: *Coastal Command Review*, Mar 1943, Vol. I No. 11.

8   Stanley, *World War Two Photo Intelligence*, pp. 241–3.

9   NA: AIR 41/7, p. 146.

10 MED: MHP 16, Kendall, *A War of Intelligence*, p. 160.

11 Sir Charles Webster and Noble Frankland, *The Strategic Air Offensive Against Germany 1939–1945*, Vol. 1, p. 268.

12 Ibid., p. 269.

13 Stanley, *World War Two Photo Intelligence*, p. 3.

14 R.V. Jones, *Most Secret War*, pp. 451–2. The spat was resolved when Jones sent Kendall a cartoon drawn by one of his staff gently mocking the latest PI report. Kendall was much amused and hung the cartoon on his office wall. The joke cleared the air between the two men.

15 MED: MHP 16, Kendall, *A War of Intelligence*, p. 65.

16 NA: AIR 41/6, pp. 83–8.

17 http://www.archives.gov

18 http://aerial.rcahms.gov.uk

19 http://www.geoinformationgroup.co.uk/products/historic-aerial-photography

20 Ian Daglish, *Over the Battlefield: Operation Goodwood*, pp. 264–8 and passim. See for instance the story of the four 88mm Luftwaffe anti-aircraft guns at Cagny that were supposedly persuaded at gunpoint by Major von Luck to change role and fire on the advancing British tanks. Daglish (pp. 255–63) can find no evidence in the aerial photographs of this incident or as to the firing position of such a battery.

21 Waclaw Godziemba-Maliszewski, *Katyn: An Interpretation of Aerial Photographs Considered with Facts and Documents*.

22 Dino A. Brugioni and Robert G. Poirier, *The Holocaust Revisited: A Retrospective Analysis of the Auschwitz-Birkenau Extermination Complex*, p. 25.

23 NA: AIR 41/6, pp. 123–4.

Epilogue

1 MED: MDM 283, Group Capt. S.J. Lloyd, *A History of JARIC*, 2000, pp. 31–45.
2 In 2012 JARIC is moving to RAF Wyton and being reformed as the Defence Geospatial-Intelligence Fusion Centre, DGIFC, working with other groups of aerial analysts like those at GCHQ.
3 Dino Brugioni, *Eyes in the Sky*, pp. 146ff.
4 Jeremy Isaacs and Taylor Downing, *Cold War*, p. 179.
5 See for instance Isaacs and Downing, *Cold War,* pp. 212–30; Robert Smith Thompson, *The Missiles of October*; Aleksandr Fursenko and Timothy Naftali, *One Hell of a Gamble: Khrushchev, Castro and Kennedy 1958–1964*; Michael Dobbs, *One Minute to Midnight: Kennedy, Khrushchev, and Castro on the Brink of Nuclear War*; and the movie *Thirteen Days* (director: Roger Donaldson, 2000).
6 Mark Urban, *Task Force Black,* pp. 82–84.

Author's Note

1 The interview was carried out on 20 August 2003 near Harrisburg, Pennsylvania for a documentary, *D-Day – The Lost Evidence* (producers: Taylor Downing and David Edgar; director: Jobim Sampson; Flashback Television for The History Channel US, 2004).
2 Stephen Ambrose, *Band of Brothers*; *Band of Brothers*, producers: Steven Spielberg and Tom Hanks; DreamWorks Television for Home Box Office, 2001.

Bibliography

Primary Sources – Unpublished

The Medmenham Collection
The archives of the Medmenham Club known as the Medmenham Collection are a treasure trove for students of photo intelligence. Some of the core material I have used from here, with Archive reference numbers, include:

Constance Babington Smith [CBS] Papers, notes of interviews 1956–7, DFG 5651–5800

Francis Cator, unpublished memoir, MDM 242

Lemnos Hemming, *Early World War II Aerial Reconnaissance*, unpublished paper, March 1946, MDM 1106

Robert Idris Jones, *Royal Air Force Days 1939–1945*, unpublished memoir, MDM 241

Wing Commander Douglas Kendall, *A War of Intelligence*, unpublished memoir, MHP 16

Historical reports of each section at Medmenham, written in 1945, PRJ 290–312

All other documents from the Medmenham Collection are listed in the notes.

National Archives, Kew
Photographic Reconnaissance, Vol. 1, to April 1941, Air Historical
    Branch (1), Air Ministry, 1945, AIR 41/6
Photographic Reconnaissance, Vol. 2, May 1941–August 1945, Air
    Historical Branch (1), Air Ministry, 1948, AIR 41/7

In addition to the various narratives produced at the end of the war and held in AIR 41, the National Archives contain a vast mass of material produced by the Central Interpretation Unit at Medmenham, including in AIR 29 and AIR 34 the daily reports and all the bomb damage assessment reports. The War Cabinet papers and those of the Joint Intelligence Committee and the Combined Intelligence Committee are held in various CAB series.

Miscellaneous
Captain Hamish Eaton, *APIS: Soldiers with Stereo – An Account
    of Army Air Photographic Interpretation*, The Intelligence Corps
    Museum, 1978
Manual of Military Ballooning, School of Ballooning, Aldershot,
    1896, National Army Museum

All other documents are referred to in the notes.

Primary Sources – Published

Constance Babington Smith, *Evidence in Camera*, Chatto & Windus,
    London, 1957; new edition, Sutton Publishing, Stroud, 2004

Ralph Barker and Sidney Cotton, *Aviator Extraordinary*, Chatto & Windus, London, 1969

Dirk Bogarde, *Snakes and Ladders*, Chatto & Windus, London, 1978

Dirk Bogarde, *Cleared for Take Off*, Viking Press, London, 1995

Sarah Churchill, *Keep on Dancing: An Autobiography*, Weidenfeld & Nicolson, London, 1981

Winston Churchill, *The Second World War*, 6 vols, Cassell & Co, London, 1948–1954

Glyn Daniel, *Some Small Harvest*, Thames & Hudson, London, 1986

Dwight D. Eisenhower, *Crusade in Europe*, Doubleday, New York, 1948; republished by John Hopkins University Press, Baltimore, 1997

Douglas Haig, *War Diaries and Letters 1914–1918*, ed. Gary Sheffield and John Bourne, Weidenfeld & Nicolson, London, 2005

R.V. Jones, *Most Secret War*, Hamish Hamilton, London, 1978; republished by Penguin Press, London, 2010

R.V. Jones, *Reflections on Intelligence*, Heinemann, London, 1989

Ministry of Information, *Bomber Command*, HMSO, London, 1941

Ursula Powys-Lybbe, *The Eye of Intelligence*, William Kimber & Co., London, 1983

Elliott Roosevelt, *As He Saw It*, Duell, Sloan and Pearce, New York, 1946

Hazel Scott, *Peace and War*, Beacon Books, privately published, 2006

Albert Speer, *Inside the Third Reich*, Weidenfeld & Nicolson, London, 1970

Brian Urquhart, *A Life in Peace and War*, Weidenfeld & Nicolson, London, 1987

F.W. Winterbotham, *The Nazi Connection*, Weidenfeld & Nicolson, London, 1978

Solly Zuckerman, *From Apes to Warlords*, Hamish Hamilton, London, 1978

Secondary Sources

Stephen Ambrose, *Band of Brothers*, Simon & Schuster, New York, 1992

Michael Bowyer, *Action Stations Revisited: The Complete History of Britain's Military Airfields*, Crecy, Manchester, 2004

Dino A. Brugioni, *Eyes in the Sky: Eisenhower, the CIA and Cold War Aerial Espionage*, Naval Institute Press, Annapolis, Maryland, 2010

Dino A. Brugioni and Robert G. Poirier, *The Holocaust Revisited: A Retrospective Analysis of the Auschwitz-Birkenau Extermination Complex*, National Archives and Records Administration, College Park, Maryland, 1979; reprinted in *Studies in Intelligence*, CIA Center for the Study of Intelligence, Washington DC, 2000

Freddie Clark, *Agents by Moonlight: The Secret History of RAF Tempsford during World War II*, Tempus Publishing, Stroud, 1999

Ronald W. Clark, *The Rise of the Boffins*, Phoenix House, London, 1962

John Coldstream, *Dirk Bogarde: The Authorised Biography*, Weidenfeld & Nicolson, London, 2004

Ian Daglish, *Over the Battlefield: Operation Goodwood*, Pen and Sword, Barnsley, 2005

Taylor Downing, *Churchill's War Lab: Code-Breakers, Boffins and Innovators: The Mavericks Churchill Led to Victory*, Little, Brown, London, 2010

Charles Eade (compiler), *Secret Session Speeches of the Right Hon. Winston Churchill*, Cassell & Co., London, 1946

Jonathan Falconer, *The Dam Busters: Breaking the Dams of Western Germany 16–17 May 1943*, Sutton, Stroud, 2003

Martin Francis, *The Flyer: British Culture and the Royal Air Force 1939–1945*, Oxford University Press, Oxford, 2008

Martin Gilbert, *Auschwitz and the Allies*, Michael Joseph, London, 1981

Martin Gilbert, *Finest Hour: Winston Churchill 1939–1941*, Heinemann, London, 1983

Martin Gilbert, *Road to Victory: Winston Churchill 1941–1945*, Heinemann, London, 1986

Waclaw Godziemba-Maliszewski, *Katyn: An Interpretation of Aerial Photographs Considered with Facts and Documents*, Warsaw, 1995 (published in Polish and English)

Chris Going and Alun Jones, *Above the Battle: D-Day – The Lost Evidence*, Crecy, Manchester, 2004

Alexandra Harris, *Romantic Moderns: English Writers, Artists and the Imagination from Virginia Woolf to John Piper*, Thames & Hudson, London, 2010

Max Hastings, *Bomber Command*, Michael Joseph, London, 1979; republished by Pan Books, London, 1999

F.H. Hinsley, *British Intelligence in the Second World War*, 6 vols, HMSO, London, 1979–1990

Richard Holmes, *The Age of Wonder*, HarperCollins, London, 2008

Jeremy Isaacs and Taylor Downing, *Cold War: For Forty Five Years the World Held Its Breath*, Transworld, London, 1998; republished by Abacus, London, 2008

Keith Jeffery, *MI6: The History of the Secret Intelligence Service 1909–1949*, Bloomsbury, London, 2010

Ian Kershaw, *Hitler: 1936–1945 Nemesis*, Allen Lane, London, 2000

Edward Leaf, *Above All Unseen: The Royal Air Force's Photographic Reconnaissance Units 1939–1945*, Patrick Stephens, Sparkford, Somerset, 1997

Peter W. Mead, *The Eye in the Air: A History of Air Observation and Reconnaissance in the Army 1785–1945*, HMSO, London, 1983

Roy Conyers Nesbit, *Eyes of the RAF: A History of Photo-Reconnaissance*, revised edition, Sutton Publishing, Stroud, 2003

Alfred Price, *Targeting The Reich: Allied Photographic Reconnaissance over Europe, 1939–1945*, Greenhill Books, Barnsley, 2003

Walter Raleigh and H.A. Jones, *The War in the Air*, 6 vols, The Clarendon Press, Oxford, 1922–1937

Peter Reese, *The Flying Cowboy: Samuel Cody, Britain's First Airman*, Tempus, Stroud, 2006

Denis Richards and Hilary St. George Saunders, *Royal Air Force 1939–1945*, 3 vols, HMSO, London, 1953–1954

Nigel Smith, *Tirpitz: The Halifax Raids*, Air Research Publications, Walton-on-Thames, 2003

C.F. Snowden Gamble, *The Air Weapon*, Oxford University Press, Oxford, 1931

Tony Spooner, *Warburton's War: The Life of Maverick Ace Adrian Warburton*, Crecy, Manchester, 1994

Col. Roy M. Stanley, *World War II Photo Intelligence*, Sidgwick & Jackson, London, 1981

Col. Roy M. Stanley, *V Weapons Hunt: Defeating German Secret Weapons*, Pen and Sword, Barnsley, 2010

A.J.P. Taylor, *English History 1914–1945*, Oxford University Press, 1965

Mark Urban, *Task Force Black: The Explosive True Story of the SAS and the Secret War in Iraq*, Little, Brown, London, 2010

Percy B. Walker, *Early Aviation at Farnborough*, 2 vols, Macdonald, London, 1971 and 1974

Sir Charles Webster and Noble Frankland, *The Strategic Air Offensive Against Germany 1939–1945*, 4 vols, HMSO, London, 1961

Index

1 Photographic Reconnaissance
    Unit 136
1st Airborne ('Red Devils') 318,
    319–20
3rd Photo Group 226, 227
7th Photo Group 230
82nd Airborne ('All-American')
    318, 319
90 Group (Signals) 344
101st Airborne ('Screaming Eagles')
    318, 319, 353–4
336 Wing 221
506th Parachute Regiment 353–4
A Section (shipping) 112–16, 203–4
A-type cameras 15–16
A3 rockets 278–9
A4 (V-2) rockets 279, 283, 284,
    304–9, 339

Abbeville sites (flying bombs) 291
academics 5, 90, 99
Admiralty
    Aircraft Operating Company 46,
        50
    and Cotton 35, 36, 48–50, 56
    photographic reconnaissance 60
    Third Phase interpretation 113,
        116
aerial combat, start of 16–17

aerial photographs
    availability 339
    demand for 44
    lessons from World War II: 341
    object identification 88–9
    oblique 16, 30, 220, 258–9
    production capability 92–3
    requests for 100
    scale 43, 87–8
    stereoscopic viewing 86–7
    tracing 92
    use of 339–41
    see also aerial photography;
        photographic interpretation;
        reconnaissance missions
aerial photography
    artists 22–3
    developments 30
    night 179–81
    private companies 44
    reconnaissance missions 139–40
    scale 43
    World War I: 15–16, 17–20
aerial reconnaissance see
    photographic reconnaissance
Aerial Reconnaissance Archives
    (TARA) 339
Africa see North Africa
agents, undercover 94, 264

Air Ministry
  Aircraft Operating Company 45,
    50, 51
  bombing raids 177, 196
  and Cotton 36, 37, 50–1, 55, 56, 59
  Danesfield House 344
  Evidence in Camera 127
  intelligence 264, 304, 306, 336
  Longbottom's paper 40
  new aircraft 26
  photographic interpretation 51
  photographic reconnaissance 43,
    47, 59–61, 77–9
  Third Phase interpretation 121
  Tirpitz 48
  see also Jones, R.V.
Airborne Corps 318
aircraft
  bombers 22, 23, 184, 191
  identification 100, 121
  jets 120, 122, 311, 312–13, 316, 345
  L Section 121–2
  World War I: 21–2
  see also fighter aircraft;
    reconnaissance aircraft
Aircraft Operating Company 43,
  44–6, 50, 51
  see also Photographic
    Interpretation Unit
aircrew 166
airfields 63
  C Section 120–1
Alamein, El, Egypt 212–13
Algiers, Algeria 217, 227
Allenby, General 20
Allied Central Interpretation Unit
  (previously Central
  Interpretation Unit) 235
Allied co-operation 232–5
Allied offensive, Europe 316–21
Altazimeter 91–2
Ambrose, Stephen 353
America see United States
anti-aircraft batteries 142, 239–40
Antwerp, Belgium 308, 309
APIS see Army Photographic

Intelligence Section
appeasement 26
archaeologists 99
Ardennes 52, 322, 323
Army 12, 22, 79, 237, 238, 249
Army Intelligence Corps 238
Army Photographic Intelligence
    Section (APIS)
  field units 243–4, 317, 320
  Medmenham (B Section) 126,
    238–40, 247
  Norfolk House 236, 240, 245
Army School of Military
    Intelligence 242
Arnhem bridge 318, 319–20
artillery 239
artists 5, 22–3
Ashton, Frederick 103
Atlantic, Battle of 115
atomic bomb 262–3
Auchinleck, General 215
Auschwitz-Birkenau extermination
    camp 269–74, 340

B-17: 226
B-25 Mitchell 215
B Section (APIS; Medmenham) 126,
    238–40, 247
  see also Army Photographic
    Intelligence Section
Babington Smith, Bernard 100,
    180–1
Babington Smith, Constance
  aircraft identification 100, 121,
    122
  and Brown 225
  career 75, 328
  Evidence in Camera 329
  secret weapons 277, 286, 290,
    294–5, 296
  Target for Tonight 189
Baldwin, Stanley 26
ballooning 11, 12
Band of Brothers (Ambrose) 353
barbed wire 239, 260
barges 64–6

Barratt, Sir Arthur 53
Bastard, Frank 162
Battle of the Atlantic 115
Battle of Britain 63, 65, 257
Battle of the Bulge 322, 323
BE2c biplane 16
beaches 245
Beard, Albert Edgar 128, 239
Belgium 43, 46, 308, 309
Belhamelin sites (flying bombs)
    298–9, 301
Benson (RAF) 78, 129, 136, 234,
    345
Berlin 202
Bismarck 143, 144, 146, 147
Blackbird (SR-71) 348–9
Blenheim 34, 35, 40–1, 47, 57, 175,
    326–7
Blériot, Louis 13
Bletchley Park (SIS Code and
    Cypher School) 9–10, 95, 96
    post-war 329, 330
    shipping 211
    women 75–6
Blitz, British cities 76
Blizna 303
Blyth, Dickie 157
Bodyline, Operation 281, 290, 293
Bogarde, Dirk (Bogaerde, Derek van
    den) 104, 320–1, 343
Bois Carré sites (flying bombs) 293,
    294, 295, 297, 301
Bomber Command
    bombing problems 174–8, 181–4
    damage assessment 202
    photographic reconnaissance 60,
        79, 188
    planning 199
    PRU 175, 179–81
    railway raids 249
    target identification 184–6
    target selection 190
Bomber Harris *see* Harris, Sir
    Arthur
bombers 22, 23, 184, 191
bombing 17, 205, 316

see also atomic bomb; Bomber
    Command; Eighth Army Air
    Force; flying bombs; rockets
Bonham Carter, Lady Charlotte
    101–2, 104, 105, 109
Bottomley, Norman 176
Bowhill, Air Chief Marshal 134
Brachi, David 113, 114–15, 203
Brampton (RAF) 345
Braun, Werner von 278, 279, 303,
    306, 309
Brécourt Manor 353–4
Brew, Flight Lieutenant 202
Britain
    Battle of 63, 65, 257
    invasion threat 62–9
    and United States (US) 231–5
British-Canadian 21st Army Group
    247
British Intelligence *see* Secret
    Intelligence Service
Brooke, Alan 237
Brown, Harvey C., Jr. 225, 226, 323
Browning, General 318
Brugioni, Dino 340, 347
Bruneval 258, 259
    raid 256, 259–60
Bulge, Battle of the 322, 323
Burma 216
Butt, David 182–3
Butt Report 183
buzz-bombs *see* flying bombs

C Section (airfields) 120–1
C-type cameras 16
cameras
    1920s: 22
    American 227
    Cotton's innovations 30–1, 33, 36
    Heston Flight 42
    movie 187
    pre-1914: 12
    satellite 349–51
    World War I: 15–16, 19, 21
    World War II 3, 147–8
camouflage (E Section) 123–4

Campbell, Kenneth 142
camps *see* concentration camps;
    extermination camps
Canberra jet 345
Carter, Group Captain 84, 107
Casablanca Conference 231
Cator, Francis 107–10
Central Interpretation Unit (CIU)
    Allied co-operation 232–5
    formation 78–9
    overseas 209, 215, 216–18
    renamed Allied Central
        Interpretation Unit 235
    reviewed 188, 228
    see also Medmenham (RAF)
Chalk House with the Tudor
    Chimneys, The 328
Chamberlain, Neville 26, 176
Chance, Len 103, 109
Channel ports 64–5, 66, 67, 68
Chapman, Carl 171
Chennault, Lee 335
Cherwell, Lord *see* Lindemann
Churchill, Sarah (Sarah Oliver) 90,
    102–3, 104, 105–6, 344
Churchill, Tom 238, 243
Churchill, Winston
    Aircraft Operating Company 50
    Allied co-operation 233
    atomic bomb 262
    aviation 14
    Battle of the Atlantic 115
    Bomber Command 182, 183, 184
    and Cotton 49
    extermination camps 270
    Hitler, threat of 25
    invasion of Europe 237, 245
    invasion threat 62, 63, 66
    Medmenham visit 260
    photographic reconnaissance 37,
        100–1
    post-World War II: 329
    and Sarah Churchill 102, 106
    secret weapons 281, 287
    Tirpitz 152
    Ultra 96

CIU *see* Central Interpretation Unit
Clark, Grahame 99, 343
Coastal Command 60, 78, 134, 146,
    188
code-breaking 10, 95, 211, 330
    see also Bletchley Park
Cody, Samuel F. 13
Cold War 344–7
Colet Court School 80
Colommiers 324
colour film 186
Colvin, Howard 210
Combined Forces 261
Combined Intelligence Committee
    64, 65, 68
concentration camps 269
concert shows, Medmenham 103–4
condensation, cameras 19, 31, 36
convoys 150, 153–4, 211
Cook, William 282
Corona (satellite) 349
Cotton, Sidney
    Admiralty 35–7, 48–50, 56
    Air Ministry 36, 37, 50–1, 55, 56,
        59
    aircraft modifications 40–2
    early career 26–8
    French operation 46, 53, 54
    and Hemming 43, 45
    Heston Flight 38, 39, 47
    and Longbottom 32
    personality 39, 57
    photographic reconnaissance
        29–34, 56–7, 133
    SIS 29, 32
    women's suitability for PI 75
Cripps, Sir Stafford 292, 293
Crossbow, Operation 294–7
Cruewell, General 280
Cuban Missile Crisis 347
Cunningham, Admiral 162, 163
Cussons, Richard 135, 153

D-Day 245, 252–3, 353–4
    see also Overlord, Operation
D Section (industry) 126, 187–8,

198–9, 262–3, 333
Dakeyne, Peter 136
Dam Busters, The 191
Dam Busters raid 190–7
damage assessment
    K Section 126, 196–200, 206–7,
        234, 334
    Pantellaria 219
Damometer 199–200
Danesfield House 80, 344
    see also Medmenham
Daniel, Glyn 72–3
    billets 82–3
    discipline 107
    and Hopkin 182
    overseas 214–15, 217
    post-war 343
    recruiting 99, 101
    Target for Tonight 189
David, Villiers 101
De Havilland 148
    see also Mosquito
de Havilland, Geoffrey, Jr. 149
Dearden, Flight Sergeant 203
decoys
    Overlord 251–2
    Q Section 125–6
Deeley, Geoffrey 117
Delhi, India 215
Delhi Central Photographic
    Interpretation Section 215,
    216–17
Demarne, Cyril 307
Denmark 52
Denning, Ned 48
Deuxième Bureau 29, 30
dicing missions see low level
    missions
Dieppe raid 241–2
Dimbleby, Geoffrey 124, 125
Directorate of Intelligence (RAF) 79
dogfights 17
Doolittle, James 232
Dornberger, Walter 278
Dornier 17: 337
Dowding, Sir Hugh 41

drones (Unmanned Aerial Vehicles)
    351–2
Durbin, Leslie 117

E Section (camouflage) 123–4
E-type camera 19
Eadon, Shirley 127
Easy Company 353–4
Eder Dam and valley 192, 195, 196,
    197
Egypt 20, 208, 211–12
Eighth Army 221
Eighth Army Air Force 202, 207,
    228, 234
Eileen ('Betty of the Bush';
    Warburton's wife) 160, 172
Eindhoven bridges 318, 319
Eisenhower, Dwight E.
    Battle of the Bulge 322
    Geneva summit 346
    invasion of Europe commander
        232
    model makers 119, 253
    secret weapons 302
    and Tedder 248
electro optical scanners 350
Elizabeth, Queen Consort 87
Enigma 95, 258, 262
Evidence in Camera (Babington
    Smith, C.) 329
Evidence in Camera (magazine)
    127–8
exams, photographic interpretation
    89–90
experimental photographic unit 38
experimental weapons see flying
    bombs; rockets
extermination camps 269–74

F-5 Lightning aircraft 171, 226–7,
    228, 251, 345
F-24 camera 22
F-52 camera 147
F Section (railways) 116–17, 248
factories see industry
Fairchild K17 (camera) 227

Fairhurst, Tim 154
Falcon, Norman 247, 282, 291
Fane, Alfred Fane Peers 151–2
Far East 215–17
Farben (I.G.) factory, Monowitz 271
fighter aircraft
  inter-war years 26, 30
  World War I: 16–17, 19
  World War II: 2, 17, 34–5, 56, 200, 227
  see also Battle of Britain
Fighter Command 39, 41, 59, 63
film, colour 186
film library, Medmenham 92
fire damage 198
firestorms 204–5
First Phase interpretation 69, 112, 249, 331
flak see anti-aircraft batteries
Fleming, Ian 35
flying
  first reconnaissance aircraft 14
  high altitudes 1–2, 42, 138–40
  night 178
  World War I: 15
  see also reconnaissance missions
flying bombs (V-1) 290, 294–303
  London, attacks on 299–302
  Peenemünde 290
  photographic interpretation 295, 296, 300, 303
  raids on sites 298, 301
  sites 291, 293, 294, 295, 297, 298–9, 301
  working of 296–7
flying suits 27
Focke Wolf, FW 190: 200, 201, 313
fog see weather
Fokker E2 monoplane 16–17
France 11, 29, 30
  see also D-Day
Fray, Jerry 194
freight movements 117
French school of photographic interpretation 46
Freya radar stations 72, 258, 259

Freyburg, General 212
Fritsch, Werner Freiherr von 326
Frost, John 256, 259
FW 190: 200, 201, 313

G Section (radio, radar and wireless) 252, 258, 260
Garrod, Dorothy 99
'Gee' navigational aid 184, 185
Geneva summit 346
George VI, King 87
German scientists 309
Germany
  invasion preparations 52, 62
  photo intelligence 128–9, 326, 337–9
  radar 72, 257–8, 259
  rearmament 25–6
  Ruhr 190–3, 196, 197
Gibraltar 209
Gibson, Guy 191, 192
Gillanders, Ronald 188, 192, 195–6, 206
gliders 122
Gneisenau 142
Goebbels, Joseph 205, 292, 299
Goodwood, Operation 339
Göring, Herman 62, 65, 289
Great Britain see Britain
Greece 161
Greenhill, Flying Officer 143
Grierson, James 15
Growse, Pauline 103

H2S navigational aid 185–6
Haagsche Bosch, The Hague 307–8
Hadden, Ron 167
Hague, The 307–8
Haig, Sir Douglas 19, 20
Hall, Bill 244
Hall, James G. 230
Hamburg, Germany 204–5
Hammerton, Flight Officer 121
Hamshaw Thomas, Hugh 20, 21, 73–4, 175, 187, 281
Harris, Sir Arthur ('Bomber Harris')

175, 184, 188, 193, 205, 233
Hays, Pilot Officer 315
Heath, Walter 63–4
hedgerows, Normandy 254
Heisenberg, Werner 263
Hemming, Lemnos 43, 45, 51, 71,
    83
Heron, Alec 199, 200, 204
Herschel, Ray 210, 211, 222
Heston 29, 38, 61, 76–7
Heston Flight 38, 39–43, 46, 47, 51
    see also Photographic
        Development Unit
Hick, Toby 99
high altitude flight 1–2, 42, 138–40
Hill, Tony 137, 141, 157–8, 258, 259,
    330
Himmler, Heinrich 306
Hitler, Adolf
    1930s 25
    invasion threat 62
    Jews 268
    Peenmünde raid 289
    secret weapons 278, 284, 292, 306
Holiday, Eve 143, 145, 152
Holocaust 274
    see also Jews
Home Forces Army Intelligence
    (Norfolk House) 236, 245
Hood, HMS 147
Hopkin, Bryan 182
Horsfall, Sidney 149
Hughes, Gordon 134, 135, 138, 157,
    170, 221, 258
Human Intelligence (HUMINT)
    93–5, 334, 335
Hurricane 26, 164, 215

identification of objects 88–9
I.G. Farben factory, Monowitz 271
IMINT (imagery intelligence) 350
India 213–15, 216
industry
    D Section 126, 187–8, 198–9,
        262–3, 333
    Industry Section, PIU 74

underground 324
intelligence
    aerial photography 10, 96–7
    Air Ministry 264, 304, 306, 336
    Army 236, 238, 242, 245
    Combined Intelligence
        Committee 64, 65, 68
    Human (HUMINT) 93–5, 334,
        335
    imagery (IMINT) 350
    intelligence officers 214
    Joint Intelligence Committee 59,
        100–1, 148, 281
    MI5 94
    military 70
    RAF 79
    Signals (SIGINT) 95, 334, 335
    Ultra 96, 166, 262, 291
    War Office 280
    wartime 93–7
    see also photo intelligence; Secret
        Intelligence Service
invasion of Britain threat 62–9
invasion of Europe see Overlord,
    Operation
Iraq 351
Italy 220–2, 244

Japan 214, 216
JARIC (Joint Air Reconnaissance
    Intelligence Centre) 345
Jericho, Operation 267–8
Jeschonnek, General 289
jet aircraft 120, 122, 311, 312–13,
    316, 345
Jews 268, 269–70
    see also Holocaust
Johnson, Kelly 348
Johnston-Smith, Elizabeth 90, 98
Joint Air Reconnaissance
    Intelligence Centre (JARIC)
    345
Joint Intelligence Committee 59,
    100–1, 148, 281
Joint Photographic Reconnaissance
    Committee (JPRC) 100–1, 234

Jones, Idris 87
Jones, R.V.
  atomic bomb 262
  Oslo Report 279
  photographic interpretation 306, 336
  radar 257, 258, 259, 260, 334
  rockets 282, 285, 305, 306
JPRC (Joint Photographic Reconnaissance Committee) 100–1, 234
Ju 88: 132, 338

K Section (damage assessment) 126, 196–200, 206–7, 234, 334
Katyn Forest 340–1
Kelson (Cotton's valet) 53
Kendall, Douglas
  Allied co-operation 233, 235
  atomic bomb 263
  Battle of the Bulge 323
  bombing problems 182
  character 71
  decoys 124
  France 46, 52, 53, 54
  good photo interpreters 90
  and Jones, R.V. 306, 336
  multi-service operation 240
  operational command 100, 101, 290
  secret weapons 290, 293, 296, 297, 299, 305–6
  training 73, 84
  Ultra 262, 291
  underground factories 324
Kenny, André 281, 283, 293
Kent, Peter 99
Khrushchev, Nikita 346, 347
Kiel, Germany 52
Kluge, Field Marshal von 316
Kola peninsula 154
Komet (Me 163): 286, 313, 315
Korean War 316

L Section (aircraft) 121–2
L-type camera 19

La Marsa, Italy 220
Lancaster 191, 192
landing areas, occupied Europe 263–5
landscape models see terrain models
Langhorne, Ruth 217
Laws, Victor 18, 23
Laycock, Brigadier 243
Liège, Belgium 308
Lightning 215, 348
  F-5: 171, 226–7, 228, 251, 345
Lindemann, Sir Frederick (Lord Cherwell) 181, 182, 282, 287
Linton, David 143, 145–6
Lloyd, Hugh Pughe 165, 166, 210
Lobban, Flying Officer 311
Lockhart, Wing Commander 264
Lockheed 345–6
  12A: 29, 30, 31, 33
  U-2: 346–7, 348
  see also Lightning
London 301–2, 303, 306–7
Longbottom, Maurice 'Shorty' 32, 39, 40, 42, 48, 52, 133
low level (dicing) missions 131–2, 162, 251, 259, 300
Ludlow-Hewitt, Sir Edgar 176
Luftwaffe 26, 63–4, 337–9
Luqa, Malta 160–1
Lysander 34–5

'Mad Men of Ham' 101
Malta 160–1, 163, 210–11, 220
mapping 44
Market Garden operation 318–20
Maryland 160, 163, 209, 210
masts, heights of 91
McAlpine, Sir Malcolm 289
McLoy, John 271
Me 109: 337
Me 163 (Komet): 286, 313, 315
Me 262: 311–12, 313, 314, 315, 339
Mediterranean 162–3, 167, 208, 211, 217–20, 333
Mediterranean Photographic

Intelligence Centre 221
Medmenham (RAF; Central
    Interpretation Unit) 5–7
  academics 5, 90, 99
  Allied Central Interpretation Unit
    235
  Americans 5, 93, 229, 343
  artists 5
  atmosphere 5, 98, 107
  and Bletchley Park 9–10
  Churchill's visit 260
  Combined Forces secret unit 261
  commanders 84, 107, 127
  communications 93
  discipline 107, 108–11
  established 82–5, 179
  inter-Allied operation 228, 235
  life at 104–11
  magazine 127–8
  mini-Medmenhams 209, 215,
    217–18
  multi-service operation 5, 240
  personnel 83, 93, 226, 229
  photographs of 327–8, 329
  PI aids 91–2
  post-war 343, 344
  reports 93
  role of 327
  Second Phase interpretation 112,
    124, 230, 264–5, 331–2
  security 105–6
  social life 103–4
  Technical Control Officer 100,
    101
  women 5, 83
  work of 6–7, 92–3, 104, 108, 112
  see also Central Interpretation
    Unit; Third Phase
    interpretation
Menzies, Sir Stewart 94
merchant ships 113–14
Merrifield, John 295, 330
Messerschmitt
  Me 109: 337
  Me 163 (Komet): 286, 313, 315
  Me 262: 311–12, 313, 314, 315, 339

MI5 (British home intelligence) 94
MI6 see Secret Intelligence Service
Middle East 31–2
Middle East Command 211–12
Milch, Erhard 290
military intelligence 70
Millen, Samuel 136
Miller, Allister 222
minefields 239
mineral prospecting 44
mini-Medmenhams 209, 215,
    217–18
Ministry of Economic Warfare 187,
    190
Miranda, A.J. 28
Mitchell, Reginald 23
Model Making Section (V Section)
    78, 117–20, 213, 219, 229, 253
models 118–19
  Bruneval 259–60
  Dam Busters 192
  Italy 244
  Overlord 119, 250, 253
  Pantellaria 219
  Peenemünde 287
  Rhine 324
  Torch 213
Möhne Dam 192, 194, 197
Moiseiwitsch, Benno 104
Montgomery, General 212, 247, 316,
    318
Moody, Ron 116
Moore-Brabazon, John 17–18, 19, 21
Moren, Paddy 162
Morgan, Suzie 220
Mosquito
  designed 148–9
  Egypt 211
  enemy encounters 200–1
  Far East 215, 216
  flying bombs 300
  and Me 163: 315
  and Me 262: 311–12, 313, 314, 315
  as reconnaissance aircraft 201,
    227, 313, 327
  XVI: 249

Mount Farm 230, 234
Mountbatten, Lord 215
movie cameras 187

N Section (night bombing) 181
navigation 2, 3, 140
    aids 184, 185–6
navigators 149
Nearne, Eileen 266
negatives, photographs 92
Newall, Sir Cyril 37–8
Nicholas, Lothian 221, 222
night flying 178
night photography 179–81, 186–7
    N Section 181
Nijmegen bridges 318, 319
Niven, Bob 29–30, 31, 36, 39, 133, 134
No. 1 Photographic Reconnaissance
    Unit 136
Norfolk House 236, 240, 245
North Africa 161, 213, 217–19, 226–8
North African Central
    Interpretation Unit 218, 219, 227
North America see United States
Norway 52
Nuneham Park 85, 344

Oakington (RAF) 179
object identification 88–9
oblique photographs 16, 30, 220, 258–9, 300
'Oboe' navigational aid 184, 185
observers
Ogilvie, Pat 180
Ohain, Pabst von 313
oil prospecting 44
Oliver, Sarah see Churchill, Sarah
Oliver, Vic 102
Operations
    Bodyline 281, 290, 293
    Crossbow 294–7
    Goodwood 339
    Jericho 267–8

Market Garden 318–20
    see also Overlord
Orr, Robin 103
Oslo Report 279
Outer Space Treaty 350
Overlord, Operation 245–54, 302
    D-Day 245, 252–3, 353–4
    invasion armada 68
    models 119, 250, 253
    photographic reconnaissance 236, 332
    United States 231–2
oxygen 2, 138

P-38 Lightning see Lightning
Paduoc House (Photographic
    Interpretation Unit) 61, 73, 76
Palestine 20
Pantellaria, Italy 219
pathfinders 186
Patton, George S. 220
Peck, Richard 36, 37, 41, 51
Peek, E. 285
Peenemünde research
    establishment 277–9, 286, 287, 290
    raid 287–9
Peirse, Sir Richard 47, 49–50, 184
Phipps, Julian 128
photo intelligence (Britain)
    importance of 6–7, 10, 96–7, 206, 332–3, 335
    operating structure 59–60, 62, 130
    role in intelligence 334–5
    wide ranging 274
    see also aerial photographs; Army
        Photographic Intelligence
        Section; Central
        Interpretation Unit;
        photographic interpretation;
        photographic reconnaissance
photo intelligence (Germany)
    128–9, 326, 337–9
photo intelligence (United States)
    222, 225–7, 231, 232, 235
photo interpretation see

photographic interpretation
photo interpreters (PIs)
    aids developed 90–2
    good 90
    nature of work 130
    officers 70
    publicity 189–90
    recruitment 84, 99, 109
    support staff 70, 93
    see also photographic
        interpretation; training PIs
photogrammetry 44
Photographic Development
    Interpretation Unit 51
Photographic Development Unit
    (previously Heston Flight) 51,
    52, 53, 54–5
    see also Photographic
        Reconnaissance Unit
photographic interpretation (PI)
    aids developed 90–2
    Air Ministry 51
    Aircraft Operating Company
        45–6, 51
    detractors 126–7
    development of 6–7
    First Phase interpretation 69, 112,
        249, 331
    RAF abandons 22, 34
    repeated covers 52
    Second Phase interpretation
        69–70, 112, 124, 230, 264–5,
        331–2
    as specialist intelligence work 70
    three-phase system 4–5, 69–70,
        71, 112, 331–2
    women 74–6, 83
    work of largely unknown 10
    World War I: 18, 21
    see also Central Interpretation
        Unit; Medmenham; photo
        intelligence; photo
        interpreters; Third Phase
        interpretation
Photographic Interpretation Unit
    (PIU; previously Aircraft

Operating Company) 61, 70,
    71, 74, 76, 78
    see also Central Interpretation
        Unit
Photographic Library, Medmenham
    92, 93
photographic reconnaissance (PR)
    Butt Report 183
    Cotton 29–34, 56–7
    German 128–9
    JPRC 100–1
    Longbottom's paper 40
    pre-1914: 11–15
    principles 56–7
    restructured 59–61, 77–9
    weather 335–6
    World War I: 15–21, 21
    see also aerial photographs; photo
        intelligence; photographic
        interpretation;
        reconnaissance aircraft;
        reconnaissance missions
'Photographic Reconnaissance of
    Enemy Territory in War'
    (Longbottom) 40
Photographic Reconnaissance Unit
    (PRU; previously Photographic
    Development Unit; later No 1.
    PRU) 61, 133, 136
Photographic Section, Medmenham
    93
photographs see aerial photographs
photography, advent of 12
PI see photo interpreters;
    photographic interpretation
Pickard, Charles 190
Pickard, Howard 104–5, 216
Piggott, Stuart 239
pilots
    availability 77
    crash landings 135
    elite reputation 157
    importance of 10
    missing 135
    nature of work 130, 132, 134–5
    qualities for PR 3–4, 133–4

pilots – *continued*
  social life 141
  training 134
  see also reconnaissance missions
Piper, John 22, 23
Portal, Sir Charles 127, 183
ports 64–5, 66, 67, 68, 114, 210
Pound, Sir Dudley 48–9, 50
Powers, Francis Gary 347
Pownhall, Maurice 128
Powys-Lybbe, Ursula 121
PR *see* photographic reconnaissance
PR XI: 201
Predator (UAV) 351–2
Prinz Eugen 123–4, 143, 146, 153
prisoners 93–4, 267–8
PRU *see* Photographic
  Reconnaissance Unit

Q Section (decoys) 125–6

radar 257, 295, 334
  Germany 72, 257–8, 259
radar stations 72, 91
  G Section 252, 258, 260
radio installations 72, 91, 295
radio, radar and wireless (G
  Section) 252, 258, 260
radios 16
RAF *see* Royal Air Force
RAF Medmenham *see* Medmenham
railways 99, 203, 216, 249, 270
  F Section 116–17, 248
Ratcliffe, Christina 165
rearmament, Germany 25–6
recognition models 118
reconnaissance aircraft
  B-17: 226
  B-25 Mitchell 215
  BE2c biplane 16
  Blenheim 34, 35, 40–1, 47, 57, 175,
    326–7
  Canberra 345
  Dornier 17: 337
  Hurricane 164, 215
  Ju 88: 132, 338

Lockheed 12A: 29, 30, 31, 33
Lysander 34–5
Maryland 160, 163, 209, 210
Me 109: 337
Me 262: 339
Reconnaissance Experimental 1
  (RE-1) 14
Spitfire *see* Spitfire
SR-71 Blackbird 348–9
U-2: 346–7, 348
weapons 163
see also Lightning; Mosquito;
  Spitfire
Reconnaissance Experimental 1
  (RE-1) 14
reconnaissance missions
  aerial photography 139–40, 258–9
  clear days 92
  damage assessment 200, 202
  flying routine 1–4, 137–40
  low level 131–2, 162, 251, 259,
    300
  nature of 132, 134–5, 158
  see also pilots
reconnaissance pilots *see* pilots
Renault factory, Billancourt 187–8
revenge weapons *see* vengeance
  weapons
RFC (Royal Flying Corps) 14, 15,
  17, 18
Rhine, Germany 33, 324
Riddell, Peter
  Bomber Command PRU 175, 176
  and Daniel 73
  overseas 209, 210, 211, 213–14
  PIU command 62, 83, 84
  three-phase system 69, 71, 121
  training 89
roads 117, 164
Robinson, Jack 244
Robson, Dr 138
rockets 277–90, 303–9
  A3: 278–9
  Blizna 303
  intelligence reports 279–80
  London, attacks on 303, 306

Peenemünde 277–9, 286, 287
photographic interpretation 2,
    280–2, 283–4, 285, 304
scientific debate over 282
test remains acquired 304–5
V-2 (A4): 279, 283, 284, 304–9, 339
workings of 305
roll film 21
Rommel, Erwin 161, 208, 219, 246
Roosevelt, Elliott 169, 171, 224–5
3rd Photo Group 227
Allied co-operation 230–2, 234,
    235
Roosevelt, Franklin D. 224, 231,
    233, 237, 245
Rota, Bertram 100, 185
Rowell, Robert 282, 291
Royal Air Force (RAF) 19, 22, 23,
    26, 109, 238
see also photographic
    reconnaissance
Royal Flying Corps (RFC) 14, 15,
    17, 18
Royal Naval Air Service 19
Royal Navy 79, 211
Ruhr, Germany 190–3, 196, 197
Runsted, General von 252
Russia see Soviet Union
Russian convoys 150, 153–4

San Severo, Italy 221–2, 304
Sandys, Duncan 281, 284, 292
satellites 349–51
scale, photographs 43, 87–8
scanners, electro optical 350
Scharnhorst 142
Schneider Trophy 23
School of Photography 18
Scientific Intelligence 304, 306,
    336
see also Jones, R.V.
Scott, Hazel 218–19, 220, 221,
    222–3, 344
Searle, Humphrey 103
Second Phase interpretation 69–70,
    112, 124, 230, 264–5, 331–2

Secret Intelligence Service (SIS;
    MI6)
agents 94, 266
Code and Cypher School
    (Bletchley Park) 9–10, 95, 96
Cotton 29, 32
Germany 26
Winterbotham 28
secret weapons see flying bombs;
    rockets
shadows 88–9
shipping 64–6
1940-41: 141–7
1942-43: 150–7
A Section 112–16, 203–4
camouflage 123–4
Mediterranean 162–3, 164, 167,
    210–11
Sicily 169, 219–20, 243
'Sid Cotton's Air Force' 42
see also Heston Flight
Sidcot flying suits 27
Siegfried Line 33, 45–6
Signals Intelligence (SIGINT) 95,
    334, 335
Simon, Neil 291, 293
SIS see Secret Intelligence Service
Slessor, Sir John 202
slide rules 88
Smalley, James 135–6
smoke screens 126
Smuts, Field Marshal 74, 205–6
SOE (Special Operations Executive)
    94, 266
Sorpe Dam 192, 196
south-east Asia 215
South East Asia Command 215,
    216
Soviet Union 346–7, 350–1
Spaatz, Carl 233
Special Operations Executive (SOE)
    94, 266
Speer, Albert 205
Spender, Humphrey 44
Spender, Michael 44–5, 51, 65, 66,
    72, 89

Spitfire
  availability 77
  cameras 3
  commissioned 26
  Far East 215
  first photographic sortie 42
  Heston Flight 41–2, 47, 51–2
  Middle East 211–12
  modifications 41–2
  PR ID: 136
  PR IV: 137
  as reconnaissance aircraft 1, 40,
    47, 202, 313, 314, 327
  XI: 217, 249
  XIX: 314, 316
spying from the sky see aerial
  reconnaissance; photo
  intelligence
squadrons, photographic units 18
SR-71 Blackbird 348–9
St Eval 61
St Nazaire raid 261–2
Stephenson, Alfred 'Steve' 84–5,
  238
Stereo pair (photographs) 87, 200
Stereo (viewing frame) 86–7
stereoscopic viewing 86–7
Steventon, Donald 276, 277
Stewart, Peter 107, 127
Stone, Geoffrey 98–9, 242–3, 247–8,
  249, 317, 320
Street, Sir Arthur 233
Suckling, Michael 144–6, 330, 334
Supermarine 23
  see also Spitfire
surveying 44, 225
Swinemünde 276
Sylt raid 174–8
Syria 20
Szabo, Violette 266

T Section (targeting) 126, 184, 185,
  333
TARA (Aerial Reconnaissance
  Archives) 339
Taranto, Italy 162–3, 210

target identification 184–6
target selection 190, 333
Target for Tonight 189–90
targeting (T Section) 126, 184, 185,
  333
Taylor, Alistair 132, 149, 149–50, 157
Tedder, Sir Arthur 211, 217, 219,
  234, 248
teleprinters 93
Theil, Walter 288
Third Phase interpretation 70,
  112–26, 332
  aircraft (L Section) 121–2
  airfields (C Section) 120–1
  Allied co-operation 230
  Army Photographic Intelligence
    Section (B Section) 126,
    238–40, 243–4, 245, 247
  camouflage (E Section) 123–4
  damage assessment (K Section)
    126, 196–200, 206–7, 234, 334
  decoys (Q Section) 125–6
  flying bombs 295, 296, 300, 303
  industry (D Section) 126, 187–8,
    198–9, 262–3, 333
  Model Making (V Section) 78,
    117–20, 213, 219, 229, 253
  night bombing (N Section) 181
  radio, radar and wireless (G
    Section) 252, 258, 260
  railways (F Section) 116–17, 248
  rockets 2, 280–2, 283–4, 285, 304
  shipping (A Section) 112–16,
    203–4
  targeting (T Section) 126, 184,
    185, 333
  uniqueness of 128
  see also terrain models
Thoma, General von 280
Thompson, Molly 124
three-phase system (photographic
  interpretation) 69–70, 71, 112
  First Phase 69, 112, 249, 331
  Second Phase 69–70, 112, 124,
    230, 264–5, 331–2
  see also Third Phase interpretation

Tirpitz 48, 113, 150–1, 152, 153, 155, 156–7, 262
topographical team (Z section) 264–5
Torch landings 213, 243
Tournachon, Gaspard Félix 12
towers, heights of 91
tracing 92
training PIs
  Americans 226
  Army 238, 242
  CIU 84, 85–9, 118
  models 118
  need for 47
  RFC 18
trains *see* railways
trench warfare 15–16
Trenchard, Hugh 17, 19
trenches 239
troop/supplies movements 99
Turing, Alan 330
Tuttle, Geoffrey
  Blitz 77
  briefings 131–2, 137
  Heston Flight 39–40
  letters to 135, 136
  Photographic Development Unit 55, 59
  Photographic Reconnaissance Unit command 61
  pilot selection 133
  systems 71

U-2: 346–7, 348
U-boats 114–15, 141, 203–4
Ultra intelligence 96, 166, 262, 291
undercover agents 94, 264
underground factories 324
United States (US)
  bombing 206
  and Britain 231–5
  Eighth Army 221
  Eighth Army Air Force 202, 207, 228, 234
  Italy 221
  Medmenham, personnel at 83, 93, 226, 229
  photo intelligence 222, 225–7, 231, 232, 235
Unmanned Aerial Vehicles (UAVs) 351–2
Urquhart, Brian 318
US *see* United States
Usedom 276
USSR *see* Soviet Union

V-1 *see* flying bombs
V-2 (A4) rockets 279, 283, 284, 304–9, 339
V Section (model making) 78, 117–20, 213, 219, 229, 253
Vaenga, Russia 154–6
vengeance (revenge) weapons 292, 299
  see also flying bombs; rockets
Venice, Italy 222–3

WAAF *see* Women's Auxiliary Air Force
Walker, 'Sleepy' 155
Wall, Flight Lieutenant 311–12
Wallis, Barnes 191
Walton, 'Wally' 39, 53
War Office 100, 238, 280
Warburton, Adrian 'Warby' 159–60, 161–71, 210, 220, 221, 227
warships 113
wartime intelligence 93–7
'watermarks' (water features) 185
waterways 117
Watt, Harry 189
Watt, Robert Watson 257
Watten site 284–5
  raid 289
Wavell, Claude 71–2, 73, 91–2, 252, 257, 258, 334
weapons, aircraft 16–17, 163
weather 19, 335–6
Westwood, Bryan 115–16
Whalley, Flying Officer 295
White Hart, Benson 141
Whiteley, Tich 162

Whittle, Frank 21, 313
Wick (RAF) 61, 143
Wild A5 Stereo Plotter 44, 48
Wilhelmshaven, Germany 33, 48
Winant, James 233
Winterbotham, Fred 28–9, 35
Winters, Dick 353–4
women, photographic
    interpretation 70, 74–6, 83
Women's Auxiliary Air Force
    (WAAF) 73, 74, 75, 83
  overseas 217, 218–19, 220
  photographic interpretation 70
  tracing 92
Wood, Sir Kingsley 174
World War I 15–21

Wright, Orville and Wilbur 13
Wurzburg radar stations 258, 259
Wyton (RAF) 345

'X' missions 43, 46

Yool, George 236

Z Section (topographical) 264–5
Zuckerman, Solly 219, 248

About the Author

Taylor Downing is a television producer and writer. He was educated at Latymer Upper and Christ's College, Cambridge, where he took a Double First in History. He worked at the Imperial War Museum and for several years has run Flashback Television, an independent production company, where he has produced more than two hundred documentaries, including many award-winning historical films. His most recent books include *Churchill's War Lab* and *Cold War* (with Sir Jeremy Isaacs). Taylor Downing is married and lives in London and East Devon.